The
Reader's
Handbook

The
Reader's
Handbook

Reading Strategies for College and Everyday Life

THIRD EDITION

Brenda D. Smith

Emerita, Georgia State University

PEARSON

Longman

New York   Boston   San Francisco
London   Toronto   Sydney   Tokyo   Singapore   Madrid
Mexico City   Munich   Paris   Cape Town   Hong Kong   Montreal

Acquisitions Editor: Melanie Craig
Development Editor: Janice Wiggins-Clarke
Senior Supplements Editor: Donna Campion
Media Supplements Editor: Jenna Egan
Marketing Manager: Thomas DeMarco
Production Manager: Bob Ginsberg
Project Coordination, Text Design, and Electronic Page Makeup: Nesbitt Graphics, Inc.
Senior Design Manager/Cover Designer: Nancy Danahy
Cover Image: © Harry Sieplinga/HMS Images/Getty Images, Inc.
Photo Researcher: Clare Maxwell
Senior Manufacturing Buyer: Dennis J. Para
Printer and Binder: Edwards Brothers Malloy
Cover Printer: The Lehigh Press, Inc.

For permission to use copyrighted material, grateful acknowledgment is made to the copyright holders on pp. C-1–C-6, which are hereby made part of this copyright page.

Library of Congress Cataloging-in-Publication Data

Smith, Brenda D., [date]–
   The reader's handbook : reading strategies for college and everyday life/Brenda D. Smith—3rd ed.
      p. cm.
   Includes bibliographical references and index.
   ISBN 0-321-36511-9 (student edition)—ISBN 0-321-42352-6 (annotated instructor's edition)
   1. Reading (Higher education)—Handbooks, manuals, etc.   2. Study skills—Handbooks, manuals, etc.   I. Title
LB2395.3.S65 2007
42B.4071'1—dc22

                                          2006008949

Visit us at www.ablongman.com

ISBN 0-321-36511-9 (Student Edition)
ISBN 0-321-42352-6 (Annotated Instructor's Edition)

   12—V069—13

To my husband, Dick, and to my daughter, Julie

Brief CONTENTS

Preface

The Reader's Handbook, Third Edition, is now a comprehensive reading textbook designed to fit the curriculum needs of college students. A new Part 5 features ten longer reading selections for the application and practice that are essential for college success. Many short exercises have been added throughout the text to strengthen students' understanding of core reading skills such as main idea, details, inference, and vocabulary. This exciting new third edition is divided into five parts for greater flexibility in meeting the needs of entering college students.

The materials in this textbook are appropriate for several reading levels. The chapters move up the curriculum from introductory reading skills to textbook application. Explanations, instructions, and exercises on reading skill development are presented first. Next, those skills, along with other study techniques for learning, are applied in the various disciplines in the core curriculum such as psychology, history, and business. Finally, techniques and strategies are presented for everyday personal and business reading such as print and electronic media, advertisements, and workplace reading. This third edition is a stand-alone textbook with the additional application selections in Part 5. It can also be used with a variety of print materials such as magazines, newspapers, and novels. For reading courses paired or linked with a specific core curriculum course such as history or psychology, *The Reader's Handbook* offers the needed instruction, models, and practice for reading success.

Ample practice exercises are provided so that students can test their skills, particularly for such essential tasks as determining the main idea and recognizing inferences. Each explanation in the *Handbook* is followed by a model and practice exercises, when appropriate. Suggestions are made for additional practice using a variety of print media and Internet materials.

The Reader's Handbook, Third Edition, remains a unique reference manual to use both as a textbook and as a continuing resource for reading skills, techniques, and strategies. This book is a "keeper"—a guide for students as lifelong readers and learners.

What's New in the Third Edition?

The third edition of *The Reader's Handbook: Reading Strategies for College and Everyday Life* retains the features that made the first and second editions so effective. To them we have added several new features:

Part 5. This new part contains ten longer reading selections from a variety of disciplines: health, history, psychology, business, literature (short stories and essays) and a Web site. The selections give students opportunities to apply skills presented earlier in the book and offers additional comprehension and vocabulary questions.

Student Success chapter. Part 1 begins with a new chapter on Student Success, intended to motivate and encourage a realistic assessment of new challenges. Internal and external distractions are identified, and academic behaviors that lead to success are described.

Additional practice exercises in core reading skills. In response to requests for more exercises in the important core reading skills, we have added activities to help students improve their skills in finding the main idea; identifying major and minor details; recognizing patterns of organization; making inferences; using figurative language; drawing conclusions; identifying the author's point of view, purpose, and tone; distinguishing between fact and opinion; and thinking critically.

Why a *Reading* Handbook?

The Reader's Handbook is a flexible and informative teaching tool to support group and individualized classroom instruction. The easy-to-follow format offers many choices in meeting students needs. This new edition, with its ten reading selections in Part 5 provides a comprehensive reading textbook for the skills needed for college success. The *Handbook* also meets the needs of other trends in reading instruction:

1. Some reading instructors prefer to use a variety of print materials such as magazines, newspapers, and novels in lieu of a set group of exercises and reading selections from a single text. *The Reader's Handbook* works perfectly with this instructional approach. Rather than rely on handouts for classroom presentations, instructors can use the *Handbook* as a common source for introducing, explaining, and modeling reading skills and study strategies. Instructional time with the students can then be followed by the instructor's choice of practice materials, which may also be individualized for specific student needs.

2. Although some students take one college reading course before exiting into regular coursework, others take several such courses. Still others take developmental courses at the same time they take college-level courses. Because the range of topics and reading levels included in *The Reader's Handbook* is so broad, it permits flexibility of use across several different courses.

3. Some reading courses are linked or paired with a specific core curriculum course, such as history or psychology. Students study reading skills and apply them directly to studying and learning in the content course. *The Reader's Handbook* offers the flexibility and explanations of skills, models, and practice necessary to make such courses successful.

4. Some colleges now either encourage or require students to have laptop computers in the classroom, and most are increasing the emphasis on integrating electronic technology. With its Net Search activities, dedicated Companion Website coverage of reading electronic media, and the optional *MyReadingLab* multimedia software, *The Reader's Handbook* offers a complete electronic reading package.

Because the *Handbook* contains more than enough material for a semester of college reading, instructors can select and emphasize chapters that reflect the expectations, demands, and interests of their particular student populations and institutions. For example, the chapter on reading in the humanities might be of greater importance at a liberal arts institution, while the chapter on reading in the life and natural sciences might take precedence for students entering an allied health sciences program.

By including personal and business reading, instructors can integrate the academic with the recreational and immediate. Instructors may want to begin the semester with the chapters in Part 4 to demonstrate the impact reading has on daily life. Students can bring in a handful of their most recent solicitations for credit cards and music clubs, as well as examples of memos and newsletters from their jobs.

The *Handbook* is also a long-term reference book. Students can return to material later in their academic or professional careers as the information is needed in a history course, a biology course, or an office management position.

Organization

This third edition has five parts:

Part 1: Reading Strategies offers an explanation of methods for mastering reading skills, beginning with a motivating chapter on student success and then a chapter exploring the reading process, levels of reading, and strategies for active involvement in the stages of reading. The following chapters include instruction on vocabulary development, main idea and supporting details, patterns of organization, inference, point of view, and graphic illustrations. The goal of Part 1 is to give students the necessary skills for reading that can then be applied to the many challenges of academic and everyday reading.

Part 2: Study Strategies begins with a chapter on critical thinking that stresses a purposeful and organized approach to assessing information. The chapter on reading rate and flexibility explains efficient methods for processing information, and the final chapter focuses on techniques for remembering textbook information. These techniques include annotating, summary writing, notetaking, outlining, mapping, and mnemonics.

Part 3: Reading in the Disciplines focuses on the types of reading that students will encounter in the various academic areas. The chapters address reading in specific disciplines, such as the humanities, literature, social sciences, natural and life sciences, mathematics and computer science, business, and vocational and technical fields. Each chapter begins with an explanation of the overall thrust of the discipline, including the intellectual frameworks of interpretation that affect student learning. Predictable patterns of organization in the textbooks are explained, followed by suggestions for successful studying, strategies for learning new vocabulary, and a discussion of discipline-specific terminology. Questions to guide reading are offered, along with study tips. Internet activities at the end of the chapter reinforce learning. Students are further prepared for academic work with a chapter on reading scholarly and reference works. The goal of Part 3 is to provide an enduring resource for students throughout their college experience by providing meaningful insights into reading and learning in each discipline.

Part 4: Reading in Everyday Life shifts to reading in the "real" world. Chapter topics include print media, electronic media, and workplace and personal reading. Each chapter contains explanations of format and purpose, suggestions for efficient and effective comprehension, and short practice exercises. Because students are already engaged in most of these reading activities, the applications in this section have both immediate and future relevance and are geared toward helping students become enlightened consumers and critical thinkers.

Part 5: Reading Selections includes ten interesting selections for application and practice. In this part, students are given an opportunity to apply the skills they have learned in earlier parts of the book. In addition, comprehension and vocabulary questions give students feedback so that they can monitor their progress.

Special Features and Benefits

- To guide the reader, each chapter and section is referenced with **colored tabs** printed on the sides of the pages. The format is compact and portable, and comb binding adds to ease of use.

- Both **academic readings from actual freshman college texts** and **popular readings from magazines and newspapers** are included as models and as the basis for practice exercises.

- **Net search** activities encourage students to amplify textbook study through Internet research. Detailed instructions on how to use the Internet are presented in Chapter 20. A book-specific Longman Web site is also available: www.ablongman.com/smith.

- Tips are offered on **reading electronic material critically.**

- **Reader's Tip** boxes give easy-to-access advice for readers, condensing strategies for improving reading into practical hints for quick reference. (A complete list of Reader's Tips appears on the last page of the book and the inside back cover.)

■ **Small-Group Exploration** activities at the end of each chapter provide collaborative application and critical thinking opportunities.

■ **Vocabulary development strategies** and corresponding exercises are presented in a separate chapter early in the book and include instruction in using context clues, prefixes, suffixes, and roots.

■ For reading in the various college disciplines, tips are given to help students **think like historians or scientists. Different perspectives for interpretation** are explained in appropriate areas.

■ **Newspaper organization** is explained and **magazines are differentiated** according to purpose, with tips for consumer purchasing decisions.

■ The types of **contemporary fiction and nonfiction books** are described, with tips on selecting books for pleasurable reading.

■ **Charts, diagrams, and graphs** are explained, and examples of each are provided in full color.

■ Tips for managing **workplace and personal mail** include suggestions for reading letters, memos, newsletters, bills, and advertisements.

■ The most common **library reference works** are described, with tips on how to find relevant research references.

The Text-Specific Ancillary Package

The Annotated Instructor's Edition (0-321-42352-6) is an exact replica of the student edition with all answers printed directly on the fill-in lines provided in the text.

The Instructor's Manual (0-321-41378-4) contains supplemental teaching suggestions, overhead transparency masters, and additional vocabulary exercises.

The Test Bank (0-321-41381-4) offers tests for each chapter in *The Reader's Handbook*. Each test is printed on 8 1/2 x 11 paper and can be easily duplicated.

The Reader's Handbook Web site. For those who have already integrated an electronic component into the reading curriculum and equally for those who plan to do so, the book's Web site **(www.ablongman.com/smith)** offers a wealth of exercises, readings, Internet resources, and links to activities in *The Reader's Handbook*.

In addition to these book-specific supplements, many other skills-based supplements and testing packages are available for both instructors and students. All these supplements are available either at no additional cost or at greatly reduced prices.

The Longman Developmental English Package

Longman is pleased to offer a variety of support materials to help make teaching reading easier on teachers and to help students excel in their coursework. Many of our student supplements are available at no additional cost or at a greatly reduced price when packaged with *The Reader's Handbook*, Third Edition. Contact your local Longman sales representative for more information on pricing and how to create a package.

Support Materials for Reading and Study Skills Instructors:

The Printed Test Bank for Developmental Reading (0-321-08596-5) offers more than 3,000 questions in all areas of reading, including vocabulary, main idea, supporting details, patterns of organization, critical thinking, analytical reasoning, inference, point of view, visual aides, and textbook reading.

The Electronic Test Bank for Developmental Reading (0-321-08179-X) offers more than 3,000 questions in all areas of reading, including vocabulary, main idea, supporting details, patterns of organization, critical thinking, analytical reasoning, inference, point of view, visual aides, and textbook reading. Instructors simply choose questions, then print out the completed test for distribution OR offer the test online.

The Longman Guide to Classroom Management (0-321-09246-5). This guide is designed as a helpful resource for instructors who have classroom management problems. It includes helpful strategies for dealing with disruptive students in the classroom and the "do's and don'ts" of discipline.

The Longman Guide to Community Service-Learning in the English Classroom and Beyond (0-321-12749-8). Written by Elizabeth Rodriguez Kessler of California State University—Northridge, this monograph provides a definition and history of service-learning, as well as an overview of how service-learning can be integrated effectively into the college classroom.

The Longman Instructor's Planner (0-321-09247-3). This planner includes weekly and monthly calendars, student attendance and grading rosters, space for contact information, Web references, an almanac, and blank pages for notes.

For Students

Vocabulary Skills Study Cards (0-321-31802-1). Colorful, affordable, and packed with useful information, Longman's Vocabulary Study Card is a concise, 8 page reference guide to developing key vocabulary skills, such as learning to recognize context clues, reading a dictionary entry, and recognizing key root words, suffixes, and prefixes. Laminated for durability, students can keep this Study Card for years to come and pull it out whenever they need a quick review.

Reading Skills Study Card (0-321-33833-2). Colorful, affordable, and packed with useful information, Longman's Reading Skills Study Card is a concise, 8 page reference guide to help students develop basic reading skills, such as concept skills, structural skills, language skills, and reasoning skills. Laminated for durability, students can keep this Study Card for years to come and pull it out whenever they need a quick review.

The Longman Textbook Reader, Revised Edition (with answers 0-321-11895-2; without answers 0-321-12223-2) offers five complete chapters from our textbooks: computer science, biology, psychology, communications, and business. Each chapter includes additional comprehension quizzes, critical thinking questions, and group activities.

The Longman Reader's Portfolio and Student Planner (0-321-29610-9). This unique supplement provides students with a space to plan, think about, and present their work. The portfolio includes a diagnostic area (including a learning style questionnaire), a working area (including calendars, vocabulary logs, reading response sheets, book club tips, and other valuable materials), and a display area (including a progress chart, a final table of contents, and a final assessment), as well as a daily planner for students including daily, weekly, and monthly calendars.

The Longman Reader's Journal (0-321-08843-3). The first journal for readers, The Longman Reader's Journal, written by Kathleen McWhorter, offers a place for students to record their reactions to and questions about any reading.

The Longman Planner (0-321-04573-4). Ideal for organizing a busy college life! Included are hour-by-hour schedules, monthly and weekly calendars, an address book, and an almanac of tips and useful information.

10 Practices of Highly Effective Students (0-205-30769-8). This study skills supplement includes topics such as time management, test taking, reading critically, stress, and motivation.

***Newsweek* Discount Subscription Coupon (12 weeks)** (0-321-08895-6). *Newsweek* gets students reading, writing, and thinking about what's going on in the world around them. The price of the subscription is added to the cost of the book. Instructors receive weekly lesson plans, quizzes, and curriculum guides as well as a complimentary *Newsweek* subscription. The price of the subscription is 59 cents per issue (a total of $7.08 for the subscription). *Package item only.*

Interactive Guide to *Newsweek* (0-321-05528-4). Available with the 12-week subscription to *Newsweek*, this guide serves as a workbook for students who are using the magazine.

Research Navigator Guide for English (0-321-20277-5). Written by H. Eric Branscomb and Doug Gotthoffer, this is designed to teach students how to conduct high-quality online research and to document it properly. Research Navigator guides provide discipline-specific academic resources in addition to helpful tips on the writing process, online research, and finding and citing valid sources. Research Navigator guides include an access code to Research Navigator™, providing access to thousands of academic journals and periodicals, the NY Times Search by Subject Archive, Link Library, Library Guides, and more.

Penguin Discount Novel Program. In cooperation with Penguin Putnam, Inc., Longman is proud to offer a variety of Penguin paperbacks at a significant discount when packaged with any Longman title. Excellent additions to any developmental reading course, Penguin titles give students the opportunity to explore contemporary and classical fiction and drama. The available titles include works by authors as diverse as Toni Morrison, Julia Alvarez, Mary Shelley, and Shakespeare. To review the complete list of titles available, visit the Longman-Penguin Putnam Web site: www.ablongman.com/penguin.

Oxford American College Dictionary (0-399-14415-3). Drawing on Oxford's unparalleled language resources, including a 200-million-word database, this college dictionary contains more than 175,000 entries and more than 1000 illustrations, including line drawings, photographs and maps. *Available at a significant discount when packaged with a Longman textbook—only $15.*

The New American Webster Handy College Dictionary (0-451-18166-2). A paperback reference text with more than 100,000 entries.

Multimedia Offerings

Interested in incorporating online materials into your course? Longman is happy to help. Our regional technology specialists provide training on all of our multimedia offerings.

MyReadingLab (www.myreadinglab.com). This exciting new Web site houses all the media tools any developmental English student will need to improve their reading and study skills, and all in one easy to use place. Resources for reading and study skills include:

- **Reading Roadtrip 5.0 Website.** The best selling reading software available, Reading Roadtrip takes students on a tour of 16 cities and landmarks throughout the United States, with each of the 16 modules corresponding to a reading or study skill. The topics include main idea, vocabulary, understanding patterns of organization, thinking critically, reading rate, notetaking and highlighting, graphics and visual aids, and more. Students can begin their trip by taking a brand new diagnostics test that provides immediate feedback, guiding them to specific modules for additional help with reading skills. New version 5.0 includes a brand new design, a new Pioneer Level (4th–6th grade level), and new readings.

- **Longman Vocabulary Website.** The Longman Vocabulary Website component of MySkillsLab features hundreds of exercises in ten topic areas to strengthen vocabulary skills. Students will also benefit from "100 Words That All High School Graduates Should Know," a useful resource that provides definitions for each of the words on this list, vocabulary flashcards and audio clips to help facilitate pronunciation skills.

- **Longman Study Skills Website.** This site offers hundreds of review strategies for college success, time and stress management skills, study strategies, and more. Students can take a variety of assessment tests to learn about their organizational skills and learning styles, with follow-up quizzes to reinforce the strategies they have learned.

- **Research Navigator.** In addition to providing valuable help to any college student on how to conduct high-quality online research and to document it properly, Research Navigator provides access to thousands of academic journals and periodicals (including the NY Times Archive), allowing reading students to practice with authentic readings from college level primary sources.

State-Specific Supplements

For Florida Adopters

Thinking Through the Test: A Study Guide for the Florida College Basic Skills Exit Test. This workbook, by D. J. Henry, helps students strengthen their reading skills in preparation for the Florida College Basic Skills Exit Test. It features both diagnostic tests to help assess areas that may need improvement and exit tests to help test skill mastery. Detailed explanatory answers have been provided for almost all of the questions. *Package item only—not available for sale.* Available Versions:

- ■ **Thinking Through the Test: A Study Guide for the Florida College Basic Skills Exit Tests: Reading and Writing,** Second Edition (0-321-27660-4)

- ■ **Thinking Through the Test: A Study Guide for the Florida College Basic Skills Exit Tests: Reading and Writing, with Answers,** Second Edition (0-321-27756-2)

- ■ **Thinking Through the Test: A Study Guide for the Florida College Basic Skills Exit Tests: Reading** (0-321-27746-5)

- ■ **Thinking Through the Test: A Study Guide for the Florida College Basic Skills Exit Tests: Reading, with Answers** (0-321-27751-1)

Reading Skills Summary for the Florida State Exit Exam (Student/0-321-08478-0). Written by D. J. Henry, this is an excellent study tool for students preparing to take Florida College Basic Skills Exit Test for Reading. This laminated reading grid summarizes all the skills tested on the Exit Exam. *Package item only—not available for sale.*

CLAST Test Package, Fourth Edition (Instructor/Print ISBN 0-321-01950-4). These two, 40-item objective tests evaluate students' readiness for the Florida CLAST exams. Strategies for teaching CLAST preparedness are included.

For Texas Adopters

The Longman THEA Study Guide (Student/0-321-27240-0). Created by Jeannette Harris specifically for students in Texas, this study guide includes straightforward explanations and numerous practice exercises to help students prepare for the reading and writing sections of THEA Test. *Package item only—not available for sale.*

TASP Test Package, Third Edition (Instructor/Print ISBN 0-321-01959-8). These 12 practice pre-tests and post-tests assess the same reading and writing skills covered in the Texas TASP examination.

For New York/CUNY Adopters

Preparing for the CUNY-ACT Reading and Writing Test (Student/0-321-19608-2). This booklet, prepared by reading and writing faculty from across the CUNY system and edited by Patricia Licklider, is designed to help students prepare for the CUNY-ACT exit test. It includes test-taking tips, reading passages, typical exam questions, and sample writing prompts to help students become familiar with each portion of the test.

Acknowledgments

I appreciate the initial guidance of Susan Kunchandy in revising the third edition and the continued support of Melanie Craig. Janice Wiggins-Clarke, my developmental editor, has been invaluable in this process, working diligently at each stage of the process to produce a book that will deliver what students and teachers need. I very much appreciate her focus, interest, enthusiasm, and hard work.

I also appreciate the insightful and constructive comments from my colleagues in the college reading profession who reviewed the first, second, and third editions of the *Handbook*. Their suggestions reflect their creativity, ability, and devotion to student achievement. Their students are fortunate to have such knowledgeable, conscientious, and concerned instructors.

Sheila Allen
Harford Community College

Shirley Hart Berry
Cape Fear Community College

Linda Black
St. John's River Community College

Kathleen S. Britton
Florence-Darlington Technical College

Jessica Carroll
Miami-Dade Community College

Carol S. Chadwick
Wayne County Community College

Denise Davis
St. Louis Community College at Florissant Valley

Linda Edwards
Chattanooga State Technical Community College

Tami Ficca
Arapahoe Community College

Danette Walls Foster
Central Carolina Community College

Elizabeth A. Frye
Lane Community College

Barbara Grossman
Essex County College

Carol Helton
Tennessee State University

Debra Hoppman
Kirkwood Community College

Linda Houston
The Ohio State University Agricultural Technical Institute

Emily Johnson
Georgia Perimeter College

Bill Keniston
Normandale Community College

Audrey Kirkwood
Bass State University

Jill A. Lahnstein
Cape Fear Community College

Eric Nefferdorf
Delaware Technical and Community College

Beth Parks
Kishwaukee College

Melinda Schomaker
Georgia Perimeter College

Sharon Snyders
Ivy Technical Community College

Carol Spanklin
Delaware Technical and Community College

Catherine Stephens
Manatee Community College

Durelle Tuggle
Georgia Southern University

Loraine Woods
Jackson State University

Sylvia Ybarra
San Antonio College

BRENDA D. SMITH

Part 1

Reading Strategies

Chapter

1

Student Success

1a What Makes a Successful College Student?

Are you ambitious? Are you motivated to be the best that you can be? If you answered yes to these questions, you are on your way to becoming a successful college student.

Yet ambition and motivation aren't all you'll need to be successful. You need to have good concentration and good academic behaviors, and this chapter will help you in both areas.

1b What Is Concentration, and How Can It Be Improved?

Concentration is essential for student success. **Concentration** can be defined as the process of *paying attention*—that is, focusing your full attention on the task at hand. Concentration is a skill that is developed through self-discipline and practice. It is a habit that requires time and effort to develop. Athletes have it, surgeons have it, and successful college students must have it.

Someone once said that the mark of a genius is the ability to concentrate completely on one thing at a time. This is easy to do when the task is fun and exciting, but it becomes more difficult when you are required to read something that is not very interesting to you. In such cases you may find yourself looking from word to word and spacing out.

Poor Concentration: Causes and Cures

Students often say, *My mind wanders when I read. How can I keep my mind on what I'm doing?* Or they may say, *I finished the assignment, but I don't understand what I just read.* If these are your feelings, you have poor concentration skills. The solution to poor concentration involves a series of practical short-range and long-range planning strategies for reducing both external and internal distractions.

External Distractions

External distractions are the temptations of the physical world that draw your attention away from your work. They are the other people in the room, the noise in the area, the time of day, and your place for studying. To control these external distractions, you must create an environment that says, *Now this is the place and the time for me to get my work done.*

Create a Place for Studying.   Start by making your own private study space. This may be in the library or in your bedroom; wherever it is, choose a straight chair and face a wall. Get rid of gadgets, magazines, and other temptations that may trigger the mind to think of *play.* Stay away from the bed because it triggers *sleep.* Spread out your papers, books, and other study materials and create an atmosphere that signals *work.* Try to study regularly, in the same place at the same times.

Use a Pocket Calendar, Assignment Book, or Personal Digital Assistant.   At the beginning of your courses, record the dates for tests, term papers, and special projects on a calendar or personal digital assistant (Palm Pilot). Use this planner to organize all course assignments. A look at the calendar will remind you of the need for both short-term and long-term planning. Assigned tests, papers, and projects will be due whether you are ready or not; your job is to devise a plan for getting ready.

Schedule Weekly Activities.   Successful people do not let their time slip away; they manage time rather than let time manage them. Plan realistically, and then follow your plan.

Use the weekly time chart shown on the facing page. First, write in your fixed activities—class hours, work time, mealtimes, bedtime. Next, estimate how much time you plan to spend on studying and how much

Weekly Time Chart

Time	Sun.	Mon.	Tues.	Wed.	Thurs.	Fri.	Sat.
8 – 9							
9 – 10							
10 – 11							
11 – 12							
12 – 1							
1 – 2							
2 – 3							
3 – 4							
4 – 5							
5 – 6							
6 – 7							
7 – 8							
8 – 9							
9 – 10							
10 – 11							
11 – 12							

on recreation. Plug those estimates into the chart. For studying, indicate the specific subject and the exact place involved.

Practice 1 Weekly Time Chart

Make a new chart at the beginning of each week because your responsibilities and assignments will vary. Learn to estimate the amount of time you will need for typical assignments. Always include time for a regular review of lecture notes.

Examinations require special planning. Many students do not realize how much time it takes to study for a major exam. Spread your studying out over several days and avoid last-minute cramming sessions. Allow additional time for special projects and term papers to avoid deadline crises.

Take Short Breaks. Although it is not necessary to write this on the time chart, remember that you need short breaks. Lengthy study sessions will tire you and affect your concentration. Try the *50:10 ratio*: study hard for fifty minutes, take a ten-minute break, then go right back to the books for another fifty minutes.

Internal Distractions

Internal distractions are those personal concerns that come repeatedly to your mind as you try to keep your attention focused on an assignment. Students have to run errands, pick up laundry, make telephone calls, and pay bills. How do you stop worrying about getting an inspection sticker for the car or picking up tickets for Saturday's game when you need to be concentrating fully on an assignment?

Make a List. To gain control over these disruptions, make a list of everything that's on your mind and affecting your concentration. Jot down on paper your concerns and weigh each one to see if immediate action is necessary. If it is, take action. Make that phone call, write that e-mail, or finish that chore. Maybe it will take a few minutes, maybe half an hour, but it will have been time well spent if the quality of your study time—your concentration power—has improved. Taking action is the first step in getting something off your mind.

For a big problem that you can't tackle immediately, ask yourself, *Is it worth the amount of brain time I'm dedicating to it?* Take a few minutes to make notes on possible solutions. Notes and an action plan will help relieve the worry and clear your mind for studying.

Now list five things that are on your mind that you need to remember to do. Alan Lakein, a pioneer specialist in time management, calls this a

to-do list. In his book *How to Get Control of Your Time and Your Life,*[1] Lakein claims that successful business executives start each day with such a list. Rank the activities on your list in order of priority and then do the most important things first.

Practice 2 To-Do List

Make a list of five things that you need to remember to do. Renumber the items in order of importance.

1. _____

2. _____

3. _____

4. _____

5. _____

Increase Your Self-Confidence. Negative thoughts (*I'll never pass this course; I can't get in the mood to study*) can be powerful internal distractions. To counter such thoughts, you need to have faith in yourself and your ability to be what you want to be. How many people do you know who have passed the particular course? Are they smarter than you? Probably not. Can you do as well or better than they did? Of course!

Spark an Interest. When you are interested in something, your concentration will not waiver. Make a conscious effort to stimulate your curiosity before reading. Make yourself want to learn something. Ask, *What do I already know about this?* and *What do I want to learn about this?*

Set a Time Goal. An additional trick to spark your enthusiasm and increase concentration is to set a time goal. Short-term goals will create a self-imposed pressure to pay attention, speed up, and get the job done. After looking over the material, project the amount of time you will need to finish it. Estimate a reasonable completion time and push yourself to meet the goal. The purpose of a time goal is not to "speed read" the assignment but rather to be realistic about the amount of time you'll need to spend on a task and to learn how to estimate future study time.

---

[1] Alan Lakein, *How to Get Control of Your Time and Your Life* (New York: Signet, 1974).

1c What Are Successful Academic Behaviors?

Along with good concentration skills, you must have good academic behavior to be successful in college. Evaluate and eliminate behaviors that waste your time and interfere with your goals. Direct your energy toward activities that will improve your chances for success. Adopt the following behaviors of successful students.

Attend Class. College professors usually distribute an outline of what they plan to cover during each class period. Although they may not always check class attendance, the organization of the daily course work assumes perfect attendance. College professors *expect* students to attend class, and they do not usually repeat lecture notes or give makeup lessons for those who are absent, although some professors will post lecture notes on a course Web site. Be responsible and set yourself up for success by going to class regularly. You paid for it!

Be on Time. At the beginning of a class, professors usually present an overview of the day's work, answer questions, and clarify assignments. Arriving late puts you at an immediate disadvantage: You are likely to miss important "class business." In addition, tardy students distract both the professor and other students. Wear a watch and get yourself moving.

Be Aware of Essential Class Sessions. Every class session is important, but the last class before a major test is critical. Students will ask questions about the exam, and those questions will stimulate your thinking. In reviewing, answering questions, and rushing to finish uncovered material, the professor often drops important clues to exam items. Unless you are seriously ill, take your tests as scheduled; make-up tests are usually more difficult. In addition, be in class when the exams are returned to hear the professor's description of an excellent answer.

Read Assignments Before Class. Activate your knowledge on the subject before class by reading homework assignments. At the very least, look at the pictures and read the captions. Jot down related questions.

Review Lecture Notes Before Class. Always, always, always review your lecture notes before the next class period and preferably within twenty-four hours after the class. Review with a classmate during a break or on the phone. Fill in gaps and make notations to ask questions to resolve confusion.

Consider Using a Tape Recorder. If you are having difficulty concentrating or you are a strong audio learner, ask the professor's permission to tape-record the lecture. Take notes as you record, and later you can review your notes with the recording to fill in gaps.

Pass the First Test. Stress interferes with concentration. Do yourself a favor and over-study for the first exam. Doing well on that exam will help you avoid tension while studying for the second one.

Predict the Exam Questions. Never go to an exam without first predicting test items. Turn chapter titles, subheadings, and boldface print into questions, then brainstorm the answers. For example, change the subheading "Creating a New National Government" into the essay question "How did the colonists create a new national government?" and outline possible answers on paper. This kind of preparation will boost self-confidence.

Network with Other Students. You are not in this alone; you have lots of potential study buddies who can offer support. Collect the names, phone numbers, and e-mail addresses of at least two classmates who are willing to help you if you do not understand the homework, you miss a day of class, or you need help on an assignment. And be prepared to help your classmates in return; that will strengthen your own grasp of a subject.

Form a Study Group. Studying with others is not cheating; it is making wise use of available resources. Collaborate to divide study tasks. Many professors assist networking efforts by posting the class roll with e-mail addresses. Use the Internet to create an academic support group to lighten your workload and boost your grades.

Learn from Other Student Papers. Talking about an excellent paper is one thing, but actually reading one is another. In each discipline we need models of excellence. Find an "A" paper to read. Don't be shy; ask the "A" students (who should be proud and flattered to share) or ask the professor. Don't miss this important step in becoming a successful student.

Practice 3 Campus Facts

Form a collaborative study group in class or on the Internet to answer the following questions. Divide responsibilities among group members to seek information that will provide answers.

1. Where are the academic advisors located? _____

_____

2. Where is the learning lab, and what kind of help is offered? _____

_____

3. When does the college offer free study skills workshops? _____

_____

4. Where can you use a computer and check your e-mail? _____

_____

5. Where do you get an identification number for the Internet? _____

6. Where is your professor's office, and what are his or her phone number

and e-mail address? _____

7. What kind of financial aid is available, and where can you find this

information? _____

_____

8. What services does the dean's office offer to students? _____

_____

9. How late is the library open on weekends? _____

_____

10. What free services does the counseling center offer? _____

_____

Use the Syllabus.   The syllabus is a general outline of the goals, objectives, and assignments for the entire course. It includes examination dates, course requirements, and an explanation of the grading system. Most professors distribute and explain the syllabus on the first day of class.

Ask questions to help you understand the "rules and regulations" in the syllabus. Keep it handy as a ready reference and use it as a plan for learning. Hole punch or staple it to your lecture notes. Devise your own daily calendar for completing weekly reading and writing assignments.

Practice 4 Review Your Own Course Syllabus

Examine your syllabus for this college reading course and answer the following questions.

1. How many weeks are in your quarter or semester? _____

2. When is your next test and how much does it count? _____

_____

3. Will your next major exam have a multiple-choice or essay format?

_____

4. What is your professor's policy on absences? _____

_____

5. Which test or assignment constitutes the largest portion of your final

grade? Explain. _____

_____

6. Do you have questions that are not answered in your syllabus? Name

two issues that you would like the professor to clarify. _____

_____

_____

Small-Group EXPLORATION

Form a five-member group and select one of the following questions. Brainstorm and then outline your major points on a transparency. Choose a group member to present the group's findings to the class. Individual assignments can also be made.

- What are the top ten time-wasters for college students?
- What are the top ten worst places that students choose to study?
- What are your top ten expectations for this college reading course?
- What do you assume are your professor's top ten expectations for you as a student in the course?

Net SEARCH

The two Web sites listed here offer tips on becoming a successful student. After reviewing the Web sites, create a list of ten student success tips that are not mentioned in this chapter and share it with classmates.

www.how-to-study.com
www.academictips.org

Chapter

2

Strategic Reading

2a What Is Strategic Reading?

Strategic readers, first and foremost, are good thinkers. They use specific techniques for understanding, studying, and learning. They understand that reading is a process with many different stages, not just a single, solitary act.

In the beginning, young readers decode alphabetical symbols to pronounce short words. Then they link the words into meaningful sentences that eventually connect to tell entertaining stories. Thus reading starts with word recognition, understanding meaning, and a reader's appreciation or connection. However, as the purposes for reading move from enjoying stories to learning from textbooks, the demands on the reader become more rigorous and the reader's understanding and mastery of the skills becomes more important. Throughout this textbook you will find discussion and practice exercises on the strategies that experts have determined help students achieve success in college reading. Your challenge is to understand these strategies and know when, why, and how to use them.

Understand the Levels of Reading Comprehension

What is expected of a good reader? Reading comprehension is frequently defined by literal, interpretive, and applied levels of understanding.

1. **Literal Level: What did the author say?** At the literal level you understand the facts that are clearly stated in the material. This is the basic, least sophisticated level of reading. At this level you may not understand the overall purpose of the passage, but you can answer detail questions such as *who, what, when,* and *where: What was the Gold Rush? When was the first strike? Where in California did it begin?*

2. **Interpretive Level: What did the author mean by what was said?** At the interpretive level you make guesses and draw conclusions from the stated facts, the suggested meaning, and the author's attitude toward the subject. You can answer *why* and *how* questions to figure out the connections between ideas and events: *How did the discovery of minerals shape the growth of towns in the West? Why were so many western miners penniless with lost dreams?*

3. **Applied Level: How does the author's message apply to other situations?** The applied level calls for reaction, reflection, and critical thinking. This highest, most sophisticated level involves analyzing the parts, synthesizing to find relationships, and evaluating the message. You will combine what is said with what is suggested and apply it to new situations and experiences, thereby making wider use of what you have just learned. You are aware of the author's style and technique and of your own level of appreciation. You judge the value of the information and the quality of the writing. You will ask questions like *How was the gold rush of the late 1840s like the Internet explosion of the 1980s? Why does the author emphasize the violence of the gold rush rather than the enthusiasm?*

2
Strat.
Rdg.

| EXAMPLE | Mark the comprehension level of the following questions as literal (L), interpretive (I), or applied (A).

_____ 1. Why did John Rolfe's marriage to Pocahontas, the daughter of Chief Powhatan, suggest a favorable political union for the colonists?

_____ 2. How do the actions and results of the Japanese attack on Pearl Harbor in 1941 compare with the September 11, 2001, terrorist attack on the World Trade Center?

_____ 3. What percentage of the world's population depends on firewood for cooking and heat?

EXPLANATION The first is *interpretive* (I) because you must comprehend a sequence of complex relationships; the second is *applied* (A) because you are taking knowledge from one situation and applying it to another; the third asks for a *literal* (L) comprehension of a detail or fact.

Practice 1

Mark the comprehension level of the following questions as literal (L), interpretive (I), or applied (A).

_____ 1. How did the lessons of the Great Depression in the United States affect economic policy making in India, Egypt, and South Africa?

_____ 2. Why were the economic causes of *La Matanza*, the Slaughter of 1932 in El Salvador, not understood worldwide?

_____ 3. How can the results of Pavlov's experiments with dogs be used to teach behavior modification techniques for children?

_____ 4. In what country was Julio Iglesias born?

_____ 5. Why did Cassandra Medley title her award-winning play *A . . . My Name Is Alice?*

_____ 6. How does the author connect the American and French revolutions?

_____ 7. Whom did Condoleezza Rice replace as Secretary of State?

_____ 8. Why did the Russians believe they would be successful in invading Afghanistan in 1979?

Engage in Three Stages of Reading

Experts divide good reading into three stages of thinking that occur before, during, and after the actual reading of the words. First, good readers *preview* to predict and plan. Next, they *build meaning* by anticipating, visualizing, and relating ideas while reading. Last, good readers *recall and react* to what they have learned. This is true for magazine articles, letters, novels, and textbooks.

2b What Is Previewing?

Previewing, the first stage of reading, is a method of assessing the material, your knowledge of the subject, and your goals for reading.

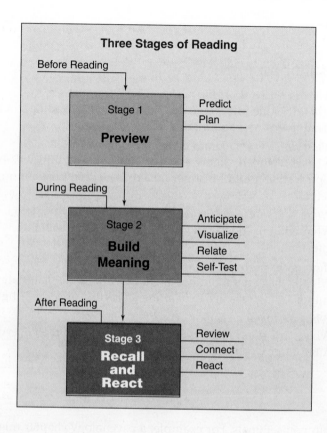

When you preview, you look over the material to predict what it is probably about. Then you ask yourself what you already know about the topic, you decide what you will probably know after you read, and you make a plan for reading.

Use Signposts for Answering Preview Questions

Previewing can be a hit-or-miss activity because there may or may not be an introductory paragraph, concluding statements, or subheadings. Novels do not have these organizational guideposts, but most textbooks and many magazine articles do. Because there are differences in writing styles, no one set of rules will work for all materials. The following are typical features to consider when you preview.

Learning Questions. Many articles and textbook chapters start with questions intended to heighten your interest and stimulate your thinking. Such questions signal what the material will cover and thus

✓ Reader's TIP

Questions for Previewing

- ■ *What is the topic of the material?*
  What does the title suggest? What do the subheadings, boldfaced print, italics, and summaries suggest?

- ■ *What do I already know about the subject?*
  What do I already know about this or a related topic? Is this new topic a small part of a larger idea or issue that I have thought about before?

- ■ *What is my purpose for reading?*
  What will I need to know when I finish? What will I do with the information?

- ■ *How is the material organized?*
  What is the general outline or framework of the material? Is the author listing reasons, explaining a process, or comparing a trend?

- ■ *What will be my plan of attack?*
  What parts seem most important? Do I need to read everything with equal care? Can I skip some parts?

help you set goals. For example, a psychology chapter might begin, *How accurate is your memory?*

Title. The title of a book, chapter, or article gives the first clue to its content. Some titles are designed to be clever to attract attention, but most try to communicate the important thought in the text. Use the five-W technique and ask *who, what, when, where,* and *why* of the title. For example, *What does Judy Brady's title "I Want a Wife" suggest?*

Introductory Material. For an overview of an entire book, read the table of contents for organization and the preface for the author's perspective on the subject. Many textbooks provide an outline at the beginning of each chapter. Others begin with an introductory paragraph that summarizes the content.

Subheadings. Subheadings are the titles of sections within chapters, and they describe their section's content. Usually subheadings appear in boldface or italic type and outline the author's message. To heighten your interest, turn the subheadings into questions to anticipate what you will need to know from the reading. For example, change the subheadings in a marketing text, "Buying Decision Behaviors" and "Measuring Current Market Demand," to *What are the different types of buying decision behaviors?* and *How and why do you measure current market demand?*

Italics, Boldface, and Numbers. Italic and boldface type highlight words that deserve special emphasis, usually terms that you will need to define and remember. Numbers are used to list important details that you may need to learn.

Visual Aids or Marginal Notations. A biology professor at a major university tells his students to at least look at the illustrations and read the captions in the assigned material before coming to class, even if they don't read the entire assignment. He wants his students to have a visual overview. Authors use photos, diagrams, charts, and graphs to convey meaning and heighten interest. Additional notations and definitions may be included in the margins to further simplify the material.

Concluding Summary or Review. Articles and textbook chapters usually end with a summary of the most important points. This may be several paragraphs or a bulleted list of the important ideas. Regardless of its form, the summary can help you recall the material and reflect on its importance.

Practice 2

Preview to answer these questions on the following selection, "Mardi Gras."

1. Using the subheadings, what does the material seem to communicate about Mardi Gras?

   _____

   _____

2. What do you already know about the subject?

   _____

3. How is the material organized?

   _____

Now read the passage to answer the following questions.

4. In what European country did the New Orleans Mardi Gras originate?

   _____

5. Who sponsors the Mardi Gras balls? _____

6. What is your reward if you find the baby in your piece of the king cake?

_____

Mardi Gras

Why do thousands of people from all over the world gather at the curve of the Mississippi River, in the Crescent City, each year? Moreover, why do these people throw colorful plastic beads, eat purple, green, and gold king cake, and watch glittering krewes parade through the streets?

5   Even after the devastation of hurricane Katrina, people still gather in New Orleans, Louisiana, from January 6 through Ash Wednesday to participate in these colorful traditions in celebration of Mardi Gras, a carnival that represents a period of fun before a period of sacrifice. Although the crowds are much smaller post-Katrina, the Mardi Gras tradition continues. To fully appreciate Mardi Gras's unique traditions, you should first know its history.

10   **Origins**

Mardi Gras was introduced to America in 1699 by the French-Canadian explorer Sieur d'Iberville. On March 3, 1699, the explorer set up camp about 60 miles south of New Orleans, the day Mardi Gras was being celebrated in France. Before long, the people of New Orleans, which was under French rule 15 at the time, embraced the holiday. They began a **cultural tradition** which had been celebrated in the Christian countries of Europe since the ancient Romans embraced Christianity.

Revelers catch beads thrown from the King Cotton float in the New Orleans Mardi Gras parade.

The first documented Mardi Gras parade occurred in 1837. Today, about 60 different parades occur between January 6 and Ash Wednesday, each having a theme and mock royalty. Local papers publish parade routes and provide lists of the krewes participating in each parade.

Krewes

Krewes are social clubs whose members wear distinctive masks, sponsor balls, and plan parades for the Mardi Gras celebration. The oldest krewe, originally called The Mystick Krewe of Comus, was formed in 1856 by six men from Mobile, Alabama. Comus was the first organization to use the term *krewe* to describe itself. Comus also started the custom of having a secret Carnival society. Other krewes include Babylon, Carrollton, Iris—a women's krewe formed in 1917—and the Original Illinois Club, a black krewe created in 1894.

Customs

In addition to the krewes and parades, there are several other Mardi Gras traditions: (1) Parade riders usually throw beads, doubloons (coins), small toys, or candy to the crowds as they pass. These items are called *throws*. (2) *King cakes* are baked and frosted with the Mardi Gras colors of purple, green, and gold, and a plastic baby, representing the Christ child, is hidden inside. Whoever gets the piece of cake with the baby must, by tradition, provide the next king cake or host the next king cake party. (3) Each krewe traditionally hosts a *ball,* which may be a secret event or open to interested visitors.

Summary

From its beginning and through the centuries, Mardi Gras has been a period of noisy merrymaking. People gather to party and share traditions, from throwing beads to looking for plastic baby toys. These traditions, created and upheld by the krewes of New Orleans, have been shared for hundreds of years and continue to bring people together in the Crescent City.

Practice 3

Read the table of contents of this text and glance through the chapters. Notice the format of the chapters and selectively scan the subheadings. Use your previewing to answer the following questions.

1. What is the purpose of each of the five major sections of this book?

_____

_____

_____

2. What chapter covers vocabulary? _____.

3. In which chapter would you find tips on remembering textbook information? _____

4. What chapter contains tips for reading and studying biology textbooks? _____.

5. In which chapter would you find instructions for reading graphs and charts? _____

6. What is the purpose of Part 5 of this text? _____

Preview to Activate Schemata

What do you bring to the printed page? As a reader, you already know a lot, and when you preview you should activate your schema for what you think the topic will be.

A **schema** (plural, *schemata*) is like a computer chip in your brain that holds all you know about a subject. Each time you learn something new, you pull out the computer chip on that subject, add the new information, and return the chip to storage. The amount of information on the chip varies according to previous experience. For example, a biologist would have a more detailed schema for DNA than would a freshman biology student. However, if you know that DNA is used in solving crimes, you have the beginning of a new schema.

Use Prior Knowledge

Most experts agree that the single best predictor of your reading comprehension is what you already know. That is, once you have struggled to learn about a subject, the next time you encounter the subject it will be easier to learn more. Be comforted to know that during your difficult initial encounter with new subjects, you are building schemata you will reuse later. Tell yourself, *The smart get smarter, and I'm getting smart!*

|EXAMPLE| Read the following sentences—which may include unfamiliar words—and activate your schema to answer the questions.

> In the last century, more Americans have been killed by tsunamis than by earthquakes and volcanoes. To detect such a danger, at least fifty years ago the government set up tsunami warning centers in Hawaii and Alaska. Japan and Chile also have tsunami warning systems. Unfortunately, such systems were not set up on the Indian Ocean.

1. What do you already know about the subject? _____

_____

2. How can you connect with this information? _____

_____

⎿EXPLANATION⏌ You will recall the tragic tsunami that hit the countries bordering the Indian Ocean in December 2004. Over 200,000 were killed by the huge waves of water. You may not know how the warning systems work, but you know that, if properly warned, the residents of the Southeast Asian beaches could have moved to higher ground and many lives would have been saved.

Practice 4

Read the following sentences and activate your schema to answer the questions.

Passage 1

   Sleep patterns vary with the species. Although you many think the opposite, large mammals need less sleep than small ones do. Elephants, for example, snooze for only about four hours a day and usually while standing up. Male lions are top predators with no threatening enemies, and they can sleep for 12 hours a day. Tiny bats hibernate all winter and hang motionless for weeks. How do these sleep patterns fit the particular needs of each species? Are these creatures engaging in REM or non-REM sleep, and how do their sleep needs compare to humans?

1. What do you already know about the subject?

_____

_____

2. How can you connect with this information?

_____

_____

Passage 2

   Plants offer limitless possibilities for medicine. The heart medication digitalis comes from flowering foxglove, and scientists are hoping to produce antitumor drugs from the polyacetylene poisons in marigolds.

3. What do you already know about the subject?

_____

_____

4. How can you connect with this information?

_____

Passage 3
    Molecular biologists have given investigators a convincing crime detector, the DNA fingerprint. Because of the differences in genes among individuals, a pattern of markedly different RFLPs can be produced from blotting.

1. What do you already know about the subject?

_____

2. How can you connect with this information?

_____

_____

2c How Do You Build Meaning While Reading?

If you watch two students reading silently, can you tell which student comprehends better? Probably not. The behaviors of good silent readers are thinking behaviors that cannot be observed by a watchful eye. These behaviors, however, can be described by experts. To find out what good readers do, Beth Davey studied the research on good and poor readers. She discovered that, both deliberately and unknowingly, good readers **build meaning** by using five thinking strategies.[1]

The first three thinking strategies are perhaps the easiest to understand and the quickest to develop. The last two strategies reflect a deeper understanding of the process of getting meaning and suggest a reader who both knows and controls. We call this ability to know and control _metacognition._

Seek Metacognitive Awareness

The term _metacognition_ combines the Greek _meta_, suggesting an abstract level of understanding as if viewed from the outside, and _cognition_, referring to knowledge or skills that you possess. If you know how to read, you are operating on the cognitive level when you read. To operate on a metacognitive level, you must know the processes involved in reading and be able to regulate them.

_____

[1]Beth Davey, "Think Aloud—Modeling for Cognitive Processes of Reading Comprehension," _Journal of Reading_ 27 (October 1983), pp. 44–47.

✔️ Reader's TIP

Thinking Strategies for Reading

- *Make predictions. (Develop hypotheses.)*
  From the passage title, I predict that this section will describe the use of acupuncture for pets.

- *Describe the mental picture you're forming from the information. (Develop images during reading.)*
  I have a picture of this scene in my mind: My cat is lying on the table with acupuncture needles sticking out of her fur.

- *Share an analogy. (Link prior knowledge with new information in the text; we call this the "like-a" step.)*
  This is like the Chinese using acupuncture to relieve pain.

- *Verbalize a confusing point. (Monitor your ongoing comprehension.)*
  This part just doesn't make sense.
  This conclusion is different from what I had expected.

- *Demonstrate correction strategies. (Correct your lagging comprehension.)*
  I'd better reread.
  Maybe I'll read ahead to see if it gets clearer.
  I'd better change my mental picture of the story.
  This is a new word to me—I'd better check the context to figure it out.

For example, if you are reading a chemistry assignment and failing to understand it, you must first recognize that you are not comprehending. Next, you must identify what and why you don't understand. You may then attempt a correction strategy such as clarifying a definition. If that does not work, you try another strategy. The point is to know when you don't have it, and to know what to do about getting it. One researcher calls this "knowing about knowing."[2]

Many poor readers do not know that they don't know. They seem unaware that gaps of knowledge exist, and they continue to read. Not only do they fail to monitor and recognize, but they probably do not know enough about the reading process to be able to attempt a correction strategy to

---

[2]A. L. Brown, "The Development of Memory: Knowing, Knowing About Knowing, and Knowing How to Know," in H. W. Reese, ed., *Advances in Child Development and Behavior*, vol. 10 (New York: Academic Press, 1975), pp. 104–146.

```
┌──────────────────────────────────────────┐
│                      ┌─ Cognition         │
│                      │  ┌──────────────┐  │
│                      │  │ 1. Predict   │  │
│                      │  │ 2. Picture   │  │
│  Metacognition  ────┤  │ 3. Relate    │  │
│                      │  └──────────────┘  │
│                      │                    │
│                      │  4. Monitor and Self-Test │
│                      └─ 5. Correct        │
└──────────────────────────────────────────┘
```

✓ Reader's TIP

Develop a Metacognitive Sense for Reading

■ *Know about reading.*
Be aware of the many strategies you use to comprehend. They include knowledge about words, main ideas and supporting details, and implied ideas. Consider the purpose and organization of the material.

■ *Know how to monitor.*
Monitoring is an ongoing process throughout your reading. Use predicting and questioning to confirm or discard ideas. Continually clarify and self-test to check learning and pinpoint gaps in comprehension.

■ *Know how to correct failures.*
Reread to reprocess a complex idea. Unravel a confusing writing style at the sentence level. Read ahead for ideas that unfold slowly. Consult a dictionary or other sources to fill in background knowledge you lack. Pause to summarize and connect ideas.

counteract faulty comprehension. Good readers, on the other hand, see failure only as a need to reanalyze the task. They know they will eventually correct their problems and succeed.

EXAMPLE Apply both your cognitive and metacognitive knowledge to the reading of the following practice exercise. Interact with the material, monitor it, and predict the concluding phrase before reading the options. The reader's thoughts are highlighted in handwriting.

1. Porpoises are attributed human feelings because they have helped endangered
swimmers to safety. Scientists question whether they like humans
or whether they like to push things and cite support for the latter
with a study in which a porpoise voluntarily pushes

Ocean, Sea World,
Help people

Movies and TV shows
on amazing rescues

  a. a young boy.
  b. a weighted air mattress.
  c. a drowning swimmer.
  d. one of the scientists.

Meaning of push things?

Guess something not human

EXPLANATION   As you read, visualize what you already know
about porpoises. The study cited seeks to prove that porpoises like to
push anything, so the answer would need to show them pushing something that is not human. Thus the answer is *b*.

Practice 5

Read the following fairly complicated passage, and as you read make a
conscious effort to use the five strategies to unravel the meaning and answer the questions. Be aware of how you predict, picture, relate, monitor,
and correct.

Bottleneck Effect

Natural disasters caused by floods and fire can produce a genetic bottleneck in which a genetic population is drastically reduced. Thus the following
generations are not representative of the original population but are representative only of the survivors. Because of their remarkable similarity within the
species, cheetahs are believed to be examples of a bottleneck effect from a past
disaster.

1. How did you predict the definition of the bottleneck effect?

2. What other disasters might produce the bottleneck effect?

3. How could you prove a remarkable similarity among cheetahs?

4. Why would the original population result in greater variation?

5. Reread or underline any part of the passage that you found confusing.

2d Why Recall After Reading?

Recalling is telling yourself what you have learned, relating it to what you already know, and reacting to it to form your own opinion. All of this occurs while you are reading, but making a deliberate stop when you finish an article, a section, or a chapter can help you fill gaps and pull together the many parts into an organized and meaningful whole. Have a conversation with yourself to update your computer chip; good readers take the time to make connections. Recalling solidifies learning.

While sorting through ideas, you also accept and reject information based on your own opinions, and you answer the questions *Did I enjoy the reading? Was the selection well written? Do I agree or disagree with the author? How many of the ideas am I going to accept?*

Recall by Writing

Good readers also benefit from taking the time to write about what they have read. Writing is a powerful learning tool that helps you translate and discover your own thinking. Experts define writing as a mode of learning, which means that writing is a process that helps students blend, reconcile, and gain personal ownership of new knowledge. When you write about a subject, you not only discover how much you know and do not know, but you also begin to make meaningful personal connections.

A humorous comment on the power of writing asks, How do I know what I think until I see what I say? Writing can be hard work, but it helps you clarify what you have learned. Answering multiple-choice questions after reading requires one type of mental processing, and writing about the reading requires another. Writing is a valuable resource in the learning process; use its power to take your recall to a higher level.

EXAMPLE Read the following passage, then reflect on and react to it by answering the recall questions that follow.

Creating Music

Despite what people may think, rarely is a hit song written late at night by a musician who is suddenly struck by a flash of creative inspiration. More likely the hit is created by two songwriters who sit in a room for hours bouncing ideas off each other until one of those ideas strikes a mutual emotional chord. Such teamwork in songwriting provides several advantages. First, each writer acts as a built-in audience and critic for the other as the song develops. Second, each writer's mind is opened by the other to new views that would not have been generated by working alone. Third, when finding a band and a singer to demonstrate the song, each writer has a network of potential artists, so the possibilities are doubled. Lastly, creating music with a cowriter is much more fun than working alone.

1. Recall: Why would you choose to write a song with a cowriter?

_____

2. Relate: How would you go about finding someone who is compatible?

_____

3. React: Why would you not want to collaborate as a songwriter?

_____

[EXPLANATION] In answering the three questions, you need to recall what you read, relate it to your own experience, and form an opinion based on the information.

Reader's TIP

Recalling After Reading

■ *Pinpoint the topic.*
Focus on the subject. Use the title and the subheadings to help you recognize and narrow down the topic of the material.

■ *Select the most important points.*
Poor readers want to remember everything, thinking that all facts have equal importance. Good readers pull out the important issues, set priorities, and identify significant supporting information.

■ *Relate the information.*
Facts are difficult to learn in isolation. For example, historical events may appear to be isolated happenings rather than the result of previous occurrences. Network your new knowledge to enhance memory.

■ *React.*
Evaluate and form opinions about the material and the author. Decide what you wish to accept and what you will reject. Blend old and new knowledge, and write about what you have read.

Practice 6

Read the following passage, then reflect on and react to it by answering the recall questions that follow.

Recognizing and Creating Your Markets

When the Late John H. Johnson, the founder of *Jet* and *Ebony*, saw a need, he filled it. In 1942 he noticed that the *Chicago Defender*, a black newspaper, became well worn by being passed from hand to hand. That told Johnson there was a need for news in black communities. Using a mailing list from his insurance company boss and $500 from his mother's pawned furniture, Johnson sent out solicitation letters for potential subscribers. Over 3,000 respondents wanted his new magazine, *Negro Digest,* even though it was not yet printed. As the magazine's popularity grew, he had to convince newsstands to carry the magazine. He sent friends to request copies and thus convinced merchants to place orders. When the magazines arrived at the newsstands, he gave friends money to quickly purchase them. Johnson's second magazine, *Ebony,* evolved in 1945 when he looked at *Life* magazine and realized that African Americans needed to see glossy photographs of themselves. To gain advertisers for his magazines, Johnson used economic logic to convince companies to employ African-American models to sell products. Later, when told that black models had a hard time finding cosmetics for their skin tones, Johnson founded Fashion Fair Cosmetics in 1973. Johnson was an expert at recognizing and creating markets, and his personal fortune is now estimated at $350 million.

1. Recall: What steps did Johnson take to help ensure the success of

   Negro Digest? _____

   _____

   _____

2. Relate: What needs have you recognized in the market for business

   ideas that might bring similar success? _____

   _____

3. React: How do Johnson's experiences seem both ordinary or

   extraordinary? _____

Small-Group EXPLORATION

Form a five-member group and select one of the following questions. Brainstorm and then outline your major points on a transparency. Choose a group member to present the group's findings to the class. (Individual assignments can also be made.)

- How do you know when you are really reading—as opposed to when you are holding the book and watching the words go by?
- Why do the rich get richer and the smart get smarter?
- What does the phrase "knowing about knowing" mean?
- By your junior year in college, what schemata should you have developed for academic success?

Net SEARCH

Locate a site on the Internet that provides information about metacognition and do one of the following exercises.

■ Describe the difference between cognition and metacognition.

■ List two researchers on the topic of metacognition and summarize their findings.

An Overview of Metacognition
www.gse.buffalo.edu/fas/shuell/cep564/metacog.htm

North Central Regional Education Library
www.ncrel.org/sdrs/areas/issues/students/learning/lr1thth.htm

Chapter

3

Vocabulary

3a	How Do You Learn New Words?
3b	What Clues Help You Understand the Meanings of New Words?
3c	What Resources Can Help You with Words?
3d	What Are Analogies?

3a   How Do You Learn New Words?

Whether you know it or not, you are already successful at vocabulary building. On the average, you learned 3,000 to 5,000 words each year from kindergarten through twelfth grade, with only 300 of those new words being taught by teachers. In each of those years you encountered 15,000 to 30,000 unknown words, and you survived.

Yet the English language contains about one million words, so greater challenges await you. If you stumble over many unknown words when you read, you lose concentration and start focusing on the words rather than the message. Thus, recognizing the meanings of words is essential to your comprehension and your rate of reading. Not only do you need to know general words, but as a college student you face a new subject-area vocabulary each time you listen and read in a new course. The following techniques can help you remember new words.

Use Associations

Certain new words, especially at the college level, are hard to remember because we don't hear them every day and can't easily work them

FAST FACT

The combination *ough* can be pronounced in nine different ways. The following sentence contains them all: "A rough-coated, dough-faced, thoughtful ploughman strode through the streets of Scarborough; after falling into a slough, he coughed and hic-coughed."

into a conversation. To learn a new word, first try to remember the word in the context in which it was used, then visualize the word in a situation that is meaningful to you. Create a scenario for associating your new word. Recall your new word in a meaningful phrase or scene rather than in isolation.

EXAMPLE   Do you know the word *wail?* Perhaps you have heard of the Wailing Wall in the Old City of Jerusalem, where worshipers go to mourn losses. To remember the word *wail*, think of the phrase *wailing wall* and visualize that sacred spot, the only remaining wall of an ancient temple. To link another and less serious connection, associate a rhyming word such as *tail* in a scenario such as *Cats wail if you rock on their tails.* Associations of this kind can leave an unforgettable picture in your mind.

WAIL
(wail)
to cry out loudly

Sounds like:
TAIL

Cats **WAIL** if you rock on their **TAILS**

Use Concept Cards

Concept means "idea." Use an index card to expand the definition of a single word into a fully developed idea. With such a concept card, you create a story or scenario for the new word by providing a sentence, a picture, and a source reference. See the sample concept card on page 32.

On the front of the card, write the word within a meaningful phrase or sentence and note where you encountered it. On the back of the card, write the definition and draw a picture that illustrates how you are using the word in your phrase, sentence, or scenario. Try to use humor to strengthen memory links, as demonstrated by the various cartoons in this chapter.

Practice Using Your New Words

Review your concept cards regularly. Look at the word on the front of each card and quiz yourself on its definition. When appropriate, use your new word in conversation. In addition, notice unfamiliar words you hear and see. You will probably encounter your new words more than you would have imagined.

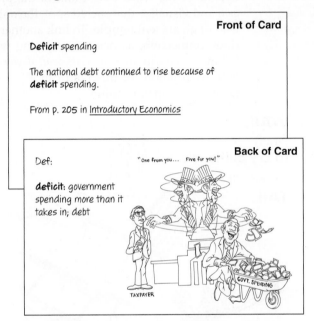

Front of Card

Deficit spending

The national debt continued to rise because of **deficit** spending.

From p. 205 in Introductory Economics

Back of Card

Def:

deficit: government spending more than it takes in; debt

"One from you... Five for you!"

TAXPAYER

GOVT. SPENDING

3b What Clues Help You Understand the Meanings of New Words?

To unlock the meaning of a new word, first try to figure out the definition from the context of the sentence and paragraph in which it is used. Next, look for a familiar root, prefix, or suffix in the structure of the word itself. The following suggestions can help you unlock the meanings of new words.

Use Context Clues

In some cases, words are defined directly in the sentences in which they appear; in other instances, the sentences offer clues or hints that enable you to arrive indirectly at the meaning. Examples of how different types of **context clues** can help you figure out word meanings follow.

Definition.   The unknown word is defined within the sentence or paragraph.

EXAMPLE With a week of adventures behind them, the hungry campers quickly started to *devour* the pizzas that had been ordered for them, eagerly eating every crumb.

EXPLANATION The definition, set off by a comma, follows the phrase in which the word appears. *Devour* means "to eat greedily."

Practice 1

For each of the context clue exercises in this section, mark *a, b, c,* or *d* for the meaning closest to that of the boldfaced word. Do not use your dictionary. If a word is unfamiliar, you must rely on the context clue strategy.

_____   **1.** Illegal identification cards were **confiscated** by the police at the door of the nightclub and not given back to the owners.
  a. reviewed
  b. seized
  c. returned
  d. accepted

_____   **2.** After complaining about his new job for two long months and being generally unhappy, the **disgruntled** employee was finally fired by his manager.
  a. overworked
  b. tired
  c. selfish
  d. discontented

_____   **3.** The **destitute** man who lost his job and home now has to live on the charity of the shelter.
  a. unskilled
  b. dangerous
  c. nervous
  d. homeless

_____   **4.** Derrick seems to be a **malcontent** person since he has never been pleased with his parents, his job, or his school and is now joining a protest march against the government.
  a. reconciled
  b. dissatisfied
  c. grateful
  d. indifferent

_____ 5. The king praised the **valiant** deeds of the knight who coura-
geously saved others while putting his own life at risk.
   a. selfish
   b. interesting
   c. brave
   d. religious

_____ 6. Promise that you will not **divulge** the secret because I do not
want our plans revealed to anyone.
   a. tell
   b. hide
   c. keep
   d. hint at

_____ 7. If the rental video equipment is **defaced** or ruined in any
way, you will have to pay for its repair.
   a. used
   b. damaged
   c. adjusted
   d. lost

_____ 8. Although some people enjoy it, others find sewing to be a
tedious job that requires long, fatiguing hours and close attention to detail.
   a. rewarding
   b. tiring
   c. creative
   d. fascinating

_____ 9. Because my membership in the fitness club had **expired,** the
desk clerk would not let me enter until I signed up for another year.
   a. run out
   b. been lost
   c. been abused
   d. been denied

_____ 10. We begged and pleaded, but the guard remained **adamantly**
against allowing anyone else into the club because of the fire
code, and he refused to change his mind.
   a. uncertainly
   b. politely
   c. stubbornly
   d. unreasonably

Descriptive Details. Descriptive details suggest the meaning of the
unknown word.

EXAMPLE Even though the NHL player for the United States team lost his *momentum* when he was tripped by his opponent, he quickly regained his energy and moved the puck toward the goal.

EXPLANATION As the last part of the sentence describes, *momentum* means forward motion.

Martin Hanzal (*right*) from the Czech Republic trips Philip Kessel (*left*) from the U.S. during the Ice Hockey World U18 Championship match played in Pilsen, Czech Republic, in April 2005.

3
Vocab.

Practice 2

_____ 1. Since the punishment was **mandatory,** the honor council gave the prescribed number of detentions without further discussion.
   a. simple
   b. required
   c. questionable
   d. excessive

_____ 2. The rumor of an alien invasion was only a **hoax** circulated by playful college students, yet it scared some imaginative believers who thought it might be real.
   a. misprint
   b. joke
   c. dream
   d. mistake

3
Vocab.

_____ 3. Single walkers should **shun** dark streets at night because they may be dangerous.
a. avoid
b. cross
c. stroll
d. follow

_____ 4. The **inept** lawyer handling the murder case forgot to ask the key witness important questions that proved the crime had been planned for months. The lawyer was a total failure.
a. famous
b. powerful
c. skillful
d. incompetent

_____ 5. The **novelty** of watching elephants roam the plains wore off after two weeks on safari. We became accustomed to seeing hundreds of wild elephants from our Land Rover.
a. beauty
b. newness
c. fear
d. power

_____ 6. Maria's **exorbitant** spending on expensive clothing she can't afford has caused her to come up short with her half of the rent money.
a. inadequate
b. sane
c. excessive
d. miserly

_____ 7. John's **concise** summary notes of the meeting eliminated unnecessary details yet covered all the topics discussed.
a. wordy
b. brief but comprehensive
c. illegible
d. incomprehensible

_____ 8. Deon didn't feel that he could follow the landlord's **stringent** rules forbidding parties and music after 10 p.m., so he looked elsewhere for a place to live.
a. strict
b. unfair
c. lenient
d. limited

_____ **9.** Each year of sun exposure added another layer of sun damage deep within Rena's skin until the **cumulative** effects finally reached her skin's surface in the form of brown spots.
a. shrinking over time
b. increasing by repeated additions
c. stretching
d. harmful

_____ **10.** Sophie's collection of jazz, classical, country, and rock CDs reflect her **eclectic** taste in music.
a. varied
b. similar
c. expensive
d. limited

Examples. An example before or after the word suggests the word's meaning.

EXAMPLE After three days at sea, the fisherman was *famished*. He said he could eat an entire whale if catching one were still allowed.

EXPLANATION Because the fisherman said he could eat an entire whale, *famished* means "extremely hungry."

Practice 3

_____ **1.** In an effort to **pacify** the angry customer, the sales clerk immediately agreed to a full refund.
a. satisfy
b. arouse
c. intimidate
d. provoke

_____ **2.** Although she did not think her adornments were **detrimental,** many potential employers suggested that her tattoo and nose ring were not in keeping with their company's image.
a. noticeable
b. silly
c. damaging
d. attractive

_____ 3. Jorge's positive attitude was **infectious.** Soon after he joined our team, everyone became optimistic and showed renewed interest and enthusiasm for our project.
a. humorous
b. pleasant
c. tending to spread to others
d. hopeful

_____ 4. The brothers had an **antagonistic** relationship. They were on opposite sides of every issue and always seemed ready to engage the other in a fight.
a. harmonious
b. fraternal
c. familiar
d. argumentative

_____ 5. Cleaning out the stockroom seemed **interminable.** After working for three hours I still couldn't see the back wall because there were so many boxes of inventory to open and organize.
a. unending
b. limited
c. unnecessary
d. easy

_____ 6. We waited in the mall for the storm to **abate.** Once the lightning had stopped, we felt it was safe to go outside even though it was still raining and windy.
a. unfold
b. decrease in intensity
c. continue
d. commence

_____ 7. The Army Corps of Engineers often leases lands to private citizens for a **nominal** fee. Some families have 99-year leases on lakefront properties at $1.00 per year.
a. extravagant
b. very small
c. costly
d. reasonable

_____ 8. Controversial topics have a **polarizing** effect on people. After our last meeting ended with members taking sides in a heated discussion, we banned all talk about politics, religion, and changing the school mascot.
a. dividing
b. contributing
c. uniting
d. confusing

———— 9. The hurricane had put many lives in **peril.** High winds carried flying debris, and we feared for our safety, vowing never to stay in the path of another hurricane.
  a. safekeeping
  b. hysterics
  c. confusion
  d. danger

———— 10. Paul **surmised** that his ex-girlfriend wanted to resume their relationship when he heard that she had been asking about him. He didn't realize that she already had another boyfriend.
  a. knew
  b. proved
  c. guessed
  d. verified

3
Vocab.

Comparison. A similar situation suggests the meaning of the unknown word.

EXAMPLE Before being offered a generous five-year contract, the quarterback underwent more *scrutiny* than a fugitive being investigated by the FBI.

EXPLANATION Since the FBI thoroughly examines the records of fugitives, the comparison suggests that the quarterback's talent was investigated in detail to make sure he was worth the money. *Scrutiny* means "inspection."

SCRUTINIZE
(SKROOT uh nyze)
to look very carefully; to examine
Link: SCREW EYES

"U.S. Customs officials have SCREW EYES when they SCRUTINIZE baggage."

Practice 4

_____ 1. Performing in Europe at age 24, she was a **consummate** pianist, far better than the top performers who were twice her age.
   a. extremely skilled
   b. enthusiastic
   c. intelligent
   d. thoughtful

_____ 2. The golfer studied the roll of the green and remained as **intent** on sinking the putt as a baseball batter is on hitting a home run.
   a. calm
   b. focused
   c. carefree
   d. distracted

_____ 3. Emily was so nervous before her speech that her **tenacious** hold on her note cards was as tight as a bank robber's grip on a hundred thousand in cash.
   a. firm
   b. hesitant
   c. useless
   d. lifeless

_____ 4. Marcus is self-taught but so **adept** at fixing computer software problems that he always finds the technical difficulty. Having him fix your system is as good as having a professional from Microsoft working for you.
   a. technically unskilled
   b. eager
   c. expert
   d. unfamiliar

_____ 5. For Charles to invite the good-looking new girl over on the **pretext** of helping him with his homework is like the wolf inviting Little Red Riding Hood to walk to Grandma's house so they can eat cookies.
   a. benefit
   b. invitation
   c. obligation
   d. reason

_____ 6. Before the dentist performed the needed root canal, the sudden throbbing **twinges** in the patient's jaw felt like forks jabbing away at the nerve below the tooth.
a. dull toothaches
b. sudden, sharp pains
c. numb spots
d. exposed nerves

_____ 7. When Tameika questioned her boyfriend about giving her a surprise birthday party, he was as **evasive** as a corporate CEO who changes the subject when asked about excessive bonus payments.
a. vague in answering
b. frank in answering
c. direct with the truth
d. honest

_____ 8. Sharon sensed **impending** trouble when she opened the mail from the lawyer, much like the danger one anticipates when a violent thunderstorm is approaching.
a. immediate
b. unnecessary
c. upcoming
d. avoidable

_____ 9. When news of the company's financial scandal broke, its stock price **plummeted** faster than a bag of bricks dropped from the roof of their high-rise headquarters.
a. held
b. increased
c. evened out
d. dropped

_____ 10. An IRS audit can **intimidate** some people almost as much as jumping from an airplane with a parachute.
a. puzzle
b. frighten
c. relieve
d. satisfy

Contrast. An opposite situation suggests the meaning of the unknown word.

EXAMPLE Even though her dog was _docile_ most of the time, he became a fierce tiger difficult to control when a stranger entered the house.

EXPLANATION *Even though* are signal words indicating that an opposite is coming. Thus *docile* means the opposite of *difficult to control*; it means "easily controlled or obedient."

DOCILE
(DAHS ul)
easily taught or controlled;
obedient, easy to handle
Link: **FOSSIL**

"A DOCILE FOSSIL."

Practice 5

_____ **1.** Unlike **remiss** students, others double-check their assignments and supplies before leaving for class so as to arrive prepared.
a. cautious
b. considerate
c. reliable
d. careless

_____ **2.** Although some professors can explain complicated theories in **succinct** terms, others ramble at length, making the subject more complicated than necessary.
a. wordy
b. brief
c. harsh
d. fascinating

_____ **3.** The 2-year-old twins' **exemplary** behavior at the Christmas party was far different from their usual rude and noisy conduct.
   a. model
   b. loud
   c. imperfect
   d. disobedient

_____ **4.** Though **pandemonium** ruled before the lecture began, once Professor Walters walked through the door you could hear the clock on the wall ticking to the quiet anticipation of the audience.
   a. whispering
   b. calm
   c. fear
   d. noisy disorder

_____ **5.** Although she had auditioned for a minor supporting role, Aisha won the part of the **pivotal** character in the college play.
   a. substitute
   b. supporting
   c. most important
   d. secondary

_____ **6.** One juror seemed **perplexed** by the defendant's alibi even though the rest of the jury felt absolutely certain that his story was true.
   a. horrified
   b. puzzled
   c. amazed
   d. assured

_____ **7.** Harrison will never have a change of mind on this subject; he's as **obstinate** as they come once he makes a decision.
   a. uncertain
   b. stubborn
   c. flexible
   d. easily influenced

_____ **8.** Even though the automobile driver using the cell phone was **oblivious** to the traffic problems he was causing, the drivers around him were ever mindful of what he was doing.
   a. unaware
   b. attentive
   c. mindful
   d. joyous

_____ 9. You need only a **rudimentary** knowledge to plug in a new TV, but it takes a highly complicated understanding to hook up and program the VCR.
   a. skilled
   b. technical
   c. electronic
   d. beginning

_____ 10. John sensed that the warning about his inferior work was an **ultimatum** and not the beginning of a series of suggestions for improvement.
   a. polite gesture
   b. continuation
   c. final notice
   d. first notice

Practice 6

Use a variety of context clues to write the meanings of the following words.

1. After kicking his brother and biting his sister, the **recalcitrant** child was punished by his parents. **(example)**

   _____

2. The movements of the swimmers were **synchronized,** with each raised arm twisting in the same graceful pattern. **(definition)**

   _____

3. Alongside the roads in the South, kudzu can be as **pervasive** as fire ants in covering a mound of earth. **(comparison)**

   _____

4. Her **nonchalant** attitude seemed out of place because everyone else was enthusiastic and really cared about working on the house for Habitat for Humanity. **(contrast)**

   _____

5. When the plane responded to air **turbulence** with rapid rolls and dips, the passengers felt as though they were on a roller coaster ride. **(comparison)**

   _____

6. She refused to **quibble,** to argue about trivial matters, when they had much more important decisions to make than whose turn it was to pick the restaurant. **(definition)**

_____

7. The **fallacy** that you can't go swimming for an hour after eating because you'll get cramps is simply a mistaken belief. **(definition)**

_____

8. In a fair system of **retribution,** where the punishment fits the crime, if you saved someone from drowning in a flood you might earn a monetary award from the mayor in a public ceremony, but if you stole a car, someone could steal something from you. **(examples)**

_____

9. Eva was **ruthless** and unkind when she fired lazy workers. Juan, however, tried to be a little more gentle when dismissing an undesirable employee. **(contrast)**

_____

10. Laura tends to **digress** when she tells a long story. She is very easily distracted from the point and adds details that are boring and unrelated. **(descriptive details)**

_____

Use Word Parts

Many new words are made up of parts of familiar words. One expert claims that knowing approximately 30 key word parts will help you unlock the meaning of 14,000 words. Whether or not this claim is exaggerated, it emphasizes the importance of knowing and understanding word parts: **roots, prefixes,** and **suffixes.**

Roots.   The **root** is the stem or basic part of the word. The roots that we use are derived primarily from Latin and Greek. For example, _port_ is a root derived from Latin meaning "to carry," as in the word _porter._ Insert other words using the root _port_ in the following blanks. Use the words in the box below to fill in the blanks.

airport	import	portable	transport

To carry something across the country _____

The facility from which flights leave _____

To bring goods into the country for sale _____

Can be carried from one place to another _____

The answers are *transport, airport, import,* and *portable.* Letters may change slightly when creating new words with a root. For example, *thermo* is a root meaning "heat," but the *o* drops for the word *thermal* as in *thermal blanket.* Think creatively to connect and expand your vocabulary through word parts.

EXAMPLE   The root forms *miss* and *mit* mean "to send" or "to let go." This root branches out into a large word family. Write a word that includes the root *miss* or *mit* for each of the following three sentences. Use the words in the box below to fill in the blanks.

admissions	permission	submitted

1. Because the club officers were late in completing the application, the

   college would not okay or grant written _____ for the banners to be displayed on campus.

2. The _____ office on campus that accepts all students reported increased applications for fall semester as well as higher test scores for applicants.

3. Your final research paper must be turned in or _____ no later than the last class session.

EXPLANATION   The correct answers are *permission, admissions,* and *submitted.*

Practice 7

The following exercises include frequently used roots. Use the indicated root to form an appropriate word to complete each sentence.

vinc, vict: conquer

1. Lafayette and his troops fought with George Washington in his

   _____ over the British at Yorktown.

fer: bring, bear, or yield

2. The _____ student who was switching enrollment from the community college requested that a transcript be sent to the state university so her application could be processed promptly.

tact, tang: to touch

3. The fishing line became ＿＿＿＿＿ and had to be cut because no one could straighten it.

manu: hand

4. Sports cars usually have a straight gear shift, which means that grears must be changed ＿＿＿＿＿ rather than automatically.

vis, vid: to see

5. Alyssa always wears a ＿＿＿＿＿ when playing tennis in order to shade her eyes from the sun.

clud, clus: shut

6. At the ＿＿＿＿＿ of the interview, Shaundra thanked the interviewer for his time and restated that she would really like to have the job.

gest: carry, bear

7. After eating a heavy meal, take a while to ＿＿＿＿＿ your food before starting vigorous exercise.

tui, tuit, tut: guard, teach

8. Ramone was having trouble with chemistry, so he signed up for the free ＿＿＿＿＿ sessions offered each week in the learning lab to help with chemistry homework.

put: think

9. Sergio wanted to buy a laptop ＿＿＿＿＿ for college so he could take it to the library.

ver, veri: true, genuine

10. The autographed baseball came with a certificate of authenticity to ＿＿＿＿＿ that the famous player actually signed it.

Prefixes. A **prefix** is a group of letters with a special meaning that is added at the beginning of a word. For example, *in* or *im* means "not," as in "impossible." Insert other words using the prefix *im* or *in* to fit the following definitions. Use the words in the box below to fill in the blanks.

imbalance	immature	imperfect	invisible

Not full grown or mature ＿＿＿＿＿＿＿＿＿

To have flaws or not be perfect ＿＿＿＿＿＿＿＿＿

Cannot be seen _____

Not having equal weight on both sides _____

The answers are *immature, imperfect, invisible,* and *imbalance.* Knowing prefixes can help you identify meaning.

EXAMPLE The prefix *dia* means "through." Form a word beginning with *dia* for each of the following sentences. Use the words in the box below to fill in the blanks.

diagnose	diagram	diameter

1. If you cannot understand the directions for assembling the tent or

   the DVD player, refer to the directional _____ for
   visual assistance.

2. Even after the patient had described her symptoms, the doctor was

   still unable to _____ the exact problem without
   ordering more medical tests.

3. In geometry, a straight line drawn through the center of a circle is

   called the _____ of the circle.

   EXPLANATION The answers are *diagram, diagnose,* and *diameter.*

Practice 8

The following sentences include words with frequently used prefixes. Use the prefix given to supply an appropriate word for each sentence.

post: after

1. Because of the rain, the baseball game will be _____
   for two hours or rescheduled if the rain does not stop.

bene: well, good

2. Vitamins can be very helpful, and some experts suggest that taking

   vitamin C may be _____ to the healing process.

extra: beyond, outside

3. Because the movie was expected to be a blockbuster, the studio went

   to _____ expense to film the stampede scenes with
   hundreds of live buffalo.

hypo: under

4. Those who fear the pain will be glad to hear that medical inhalers may

replace _____ needles for giving flu shots and other vaccines.

para: beside, alongside, position

5. The auto accident left Stephen _____ in both legs, but doctors urged that with therapy he would walk again.

super, supr: over, above, beyond, of greater quality

6. Deirdre was sure she could be a good manager and

_____ for the sorority rush-week activities because she had directed a staff of six in organizing a summer charity event.

pre: before

7. Since break-ins had occurred in the area, residents took the extra

_____ of double-checking the locks on all doors and windows before going to bed.

bi, bin, bis: two, twice

8. To get a better view and to see the entertainers close up, carry your

opera glasses or _____ with you to the circus.

circ, circum: around

9. If you wear shoes that are too tight, you can cut off the blood

_____ in your feet and cause them to ache.

pro: forward, forth

10. Russell had taken on extra duties at work in hopes of moving up

and being _____ from sales associate to floor manager, which would mean a raise in pay.

FAST FACT

Only four words in the English language end in *dous:* tremendous, horrendous, stupendous, and *hazardous.*

Suffixes. A **suffix** is a group of letters with a special meaning that is added at the end of a word. A suffix alters the meaning of a word and changes the way the word can be used in the sentence. For example, the *er* in *porter* means "the person who" and makes the word name a person. On the other hand, adding *able,* which means "capable of," to *port* creates the word *portable,* which means that an object is "capable of being carried." Thus the meaning is only slightly altered, but the suffix changes the way the word can be used. Insert other words using the suffix *er* to fit the following definitions. Use the words in the box below to fill in the blanks.

carpenter	buyer	gardener	painter

One who builds a house _____

One who paints a house _____

One who buys a house _____

One who maintains the flowers at a house _____

The answers are *carpenter, painter, buyer,* and *gardener.* Some suffixes have more meaning than others, but all alter the way the word can be used in a sentence.

EXAMPLE The suffix *ist* means "one who" or "that which." Form a word ending with *ist* for each of the following three sentences. Use the words in the box below to fill in the blanks.

artist	dentist	pianist

1. If you have a toothache, go to your _____ immediately.

2. The _____ played the piano with such force that the audience stood to applaud.

3. The picture was painted by a well-known American

   _____.

EXPLANATION The answers are *dentist, pianist,* and *artist.*

Practice 9

The following sentences include words with frequently used suffixes. Use the suffix given to supply an appropriate word for each sentence.

ion, sion, tion: act of, state of, result of

1. Although she did not seek the _____ as club president, her name was put on the list by a classmate and she was elected.

ful: full of

2. The recipients were _____ for the hard work and support of the student volunteers and thanked each one accordingly.

osis, esis, asis: a course of action, a process, or a condition

3. In a state of _____ a willing subject reaches an unconscious level of thinking and may be able to remember events that are not available to her or his conscious mind.

arium, orium: place for

4. Visitors can walk through a glass tunnel with fish swimming over and around them in one section of the new _____.

ence, ency: action, quality

5. The new puppy definitely needed to attend _____ school because his owners were not able to change his undesirable behaviors.

able, ible: able, can do

6. Dean didn't feel at all _____ after his breakup with Brooke, so he avoided parties in favor of being alone and away from inquiring friends.

al: relating to

7. Professor Dukes usually had an _____ section on his tests that you could choose to answer or not, depending on whether you needed the extra credit.

en: made of, make

8. Katrina dropped her most difficult course this semester in order to _____ her academic load because of a new part-time job.

ary, ery, ory: relating to, quality, place where

9. Tara's primary needs for privacy and quiet were not being met in the overcrowded college _____, so she began to look for off-campus housing.

ous: full of, having

10. The unexpected and _____ letter had no signature but contained haunting details of an unsolved murder that had occurred the previous year.

Reader's TIP

Frequently Used Roots

Root	Meaning	Example
alter, hap	to change	*alteration, mishap*
ama, philo	to love	*amiable, philosophy*
anima	breath, spirit	*animate*
aqua	water	*aquarium*
aster, astro	star	*disaster, astronomy*
aud	to hear	*audible, auditory*
bio	life	*biology*
cap	head	*caption, capitulate*
cap, capt	to take	*capture*
card, cor, cord	heart	*cardiac, core, cordial*
cosmo	order, universe	*cosmonaut*
cresc	to grow, increase	*crescendo*
cryp	secret, hidden	*cryptogram*
dent	teeth	*dental*
derma	skin	*dermatologist*
duc, duct	to lead	*reduce, conduct*
ego	self	*egotist*
equ, iso	equal	*equivocal, isometric*
err, errat	to wander	*erratic*
ethno	race, tribe	*ethnic*
fac, fact	to do, make	*manufacture*
fract	to break	*fracture, infraction*
frater	brother	*fraternity*
gene	race, kind, sex	*genetics, gender*
grad, gres	to go, take steps	*graduation, digress*
gyn	woman	*gynecology*
hab, habi	to have, hold	*inhabit, habitual*
helio, photo	sun, light	*heliotrope, photograph*
homo	man	*Homo sapiens*
lic, list, liqu	to leave behind	*derelict, relinquish*
lith	stone	*monolith*
loc	place	*location, local*
log	speech, science	*logic, dialogue*
loquor	to speak	*loquacious, colloquial*
lum	light	*illuminate*
macro	large	*macrocosm*
manu	hand	*manual, manuscript*

(continued)

Root	Meaning	Example
mater	mother	*maternity*
med	middle	*mediate*
meter	to measure	*barometer*
micro	small	*microscope*
miss, mit	to send, let go	*admit, permission*
morph	form	*morphology*
mort	to die	*immortalize*
mut, muta	to change	*mutation*
nat	to be born	*natal, native*
neg, negat	to say no, deny	*negative, renege*
nym, nomen	name	*synonym, nomenclature*
ocul	eye	*oculist, monocle*
ortho	right, straight	*orthodox, orthodontist*
osteo	bone	*osteopath*
pater	father	*paternal*
path	disease, feeling	*pathology, antipathy*
phag	to eat	*esophagus, phagocyte*
phobia	fear	*claustrophobia*
phon, phono	sound	*symphony, phonics*
plic	to fold	*duplicate, implicate*
pneuma	wind, air	*pneumatic*
pod, ped	foot	*tripod, pedestrian*
pon, pos	to place	*depose, position*
port	to carry	*porter, portable*
pseudo	false	*pseudonym*
psych	mind	*psychology*
pyr	fire	*pyromaniac*
quir	to ask	*inquire, acquire*
rog	to question	*interrogate*
scrib, graph	to write	*prescribe, autograph*
sect, seg	to cut	*dissect, segment*
sol	alone	*solitude*
soma	body	*somatology, psychosomatic*
somnia	sleep	*insomnia*
soph	wise	*sophomore, philosophy*
soror	sister	*sorority*
spect	to look at	*inspect, spectacle*
spir	to breathe	*inspiration, conspire*
tact, tang	to touch	*tactile, tangible*
tele	distant	*telephone*
ten, tent	to hold	*tenant, intent*

3
Vocab.

(continued)

Root	Meaning	Example
tend, tens	to stretch	*extend, extension*
the, theo	God	*atheism, theology*
therma	heat	*thermometer*
tort	twist	*torture, extort*
ven, vent	to go, arrive	*convention, advent*
verbum	word	*verbosity, verbal*

✔ Reader's TIP

Frequently Used Prefixes

Prefix	Meaning	Example
a, an	without, not	*atypical, anarchy*
ab	away, from	*absent, abnormal*
ad	toward	*advance, administer*
ambi, amphi	both, around	*ambiguous, amphibious*
anno	year	*annual*
anti, contra, ob	against	*antisocial, contradict*
auto	self	*autograph, automobile*
bene, eu	well, good	*benefactor, eulogy*
bi, du, di	two, twice	*bicycle, duet, dichotomy*
cata, cath	down, downward	*catacombs, cathode*
cent, hecto	hundred	*centipede, hectare*
con, com, syn	with, together	*congregate, synthesis*
de	down, from	*depose, detract*
dec, deca	ten	*decade*
demi, hemi, semi	half	*hemisphere, semicircle*
dia	through	*diameter, diagram*
dis, un	not, opposite of	*dislike, unnatural*
dys	ill, hard	*dystrophy*
ex	out, from	*exhale, expel*
extra	beyond, outside	*extralegal*
hyper	above, excessive	*hyperactive*
hypo	under	*hypodermic*
il, im, in	not	*illogical, impossible*
im, in	in, into	*inside, insert, import*
infra	lower	*infrared*
inter	between	*intercede, interrupt*
intra	within	*intramural*
juxta	next to	*juxtaposition*

(continued)

Prefix	Meaning	Example
mal, mis	wrong, ill	malformed, mislead
mill	thousand	milligram
nove, non	nine	novena, nonagon
oct, octo	eight	octopus
omni, pan	all	omnipotent, pantheist
per	through	perennial, pervade
peri, circum	around	perimeter, circumvent
poly, multi	many	polygamy, multiply
post	after	postscript
pre, ante	before	prepared, antebellum
pro	before, for	promoter
proto	first	prototype
quad, quatra, tetra	four	quadrilateral, tetrad
quint, penta	five	quintuplet, pentagon
re	back, again	review, reply
retro	backward	retrogress, retrospect
sequ	follow	sequence
sex, hexa	six	sextet, hexagon
sub	under	submarine, subway
super	above, over	supervise
temp, tempo, chrono	time	tempo, chronological
trans	across	translate, transcontinental
tri	three	triangle
uni, mono	one	unicorn, monocle
vice	in place of	viceroy

3
Vocab.

✓ Reader's TIP

Frequently Used Suffixes

Suffix	Meaning	Example
able, ible	capable of	durable, visible
acy, ance, ency, ity	quality or state of	privacy, competency, acidity
age	act of, state of	breakage
al	pertaining to	rental
ana	saying, writing	Americana
ant	quality of, one who	reliant, servant
ard, art	person who	wizard, braggart
arium, orium	place for	auditorium

(continued)

Suffix	Meaning	Example
ate	cause to be	*activate*
ation	action, state of	*creation, condition*
chrome	color	*verichrome*
cide	killing	*homicide*
er, or	person who, thing which	*generator*
esque	like in manner	*picturesque*
fic	making, causing	*scientific*
form	in the shape of	*cuneiform*
ful, ose, ous	full of	*careful, verbose*
fy, ify, ize	to make, cause to be	*fortify, magnify, modify*
hood, osis	condition, state of	*childhood, hypnosis*
ics	art, science	*mathematics*
ism	quality, doctrine of	*conservatism*
itis	inflammation of	*appendicitis*
ive	quality of, that which	*creative*
latry	worship of	*idolatry*
less	without	*homeless*
oid	in the form of	*tabloid*
tude	quality, degree of	*solitude*
wards	in a direction	*backwards*
wise	way, position	*clockwise*

3
Vocab.

3c What Resources Can Help You with Words?

In addition to using word parts and context clues to understand new words, several different resources can also help. Dictionaries, depending on the size and edition, contain a wealth of information far beyond word definitions, and textbook glossaries provide definitions for discipline-specific words. A thesaurus does not define words, but it is a handy tool for looking for synonyms—words that have the same meaning.

RHYMES WITH ORANGE

Use a Dictionary

Unless an unknown word is crucial to your understanding, use the dictionary as a last resort for finding the definition of a word while you are reading. Remember, stopping in the middle of a paragraph breaks your concentration and causes you to forget what you were reading. Mark unknown words by putting a dot in the margin, and then, when you have finished reading, look them up in the dictionary.

Dictionaries contain more than just the definition of a word. They contain its pronunciation, spelling, derivation or history, and parts of speech, along with its many different meanings. An entry may also include an illustration or give examples of the use of the word in context. Consider the following entry:

3
Vocab.

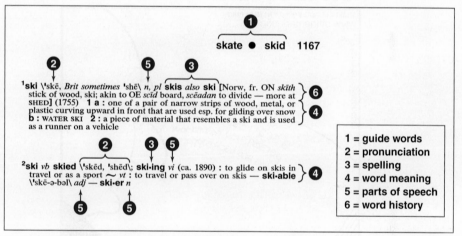

By permission. From *Merriam-Webster's Collegiate® Dictionary*, 11th Edition © 2004 by Merriam-Webster, Incorporated (www.Merriam-Webster.com).

FAST FACT

Underground is the only word in the English language that begins and ends with the letters *und*.

Guide Words. The two words at the top of each dictionary page are guide words. They represent the first and last words on the page. Because words in a dictionary are in alphabetical order, you can use the guide words to determine quickly if the word you are looking for is on that particular page. The guide words for the sample entry are *skate* and *skid*.

Pronunciation. Each word is divided into sounds (or syllables) after the boldfaced main entry. Letters and symbols are used to indicate special sounds. A key to understanding the special sounds appears at the bottom of one of the two pages open to you.

Spelling.   Spellings are given for the plural form of the word (if the spelling changes) and for any special endings. This is particularly helpful when letters are dropped or added to form the new word. In the sample entry, the plural of *ski* can be spelled correctly in two ways: It can be either *skis* or *ski.*

Word Meaning.   Frequently a word has many meanings. For example, *car* means "automobile" as well as "the cargo part of an airship." In such a case, the dictionary uses a number to indicate each new meaning. In the sample entry, notice that a ski can be a narrow strip of wood or a piece of material that resembles a ski.

Parts of Speech.   For each meaning of a word, the part of speech is given in abbreviation. For example, *n* means *noun,* *adj* means *adjective,* *adv* means *adverb,* and *vb, vi,* or *vt* means *verb.* Other abbreviations are listed in a section in the front of your dictionary. In the example, *ski* is both a noun and a verb.

3
Vocab.

Word History. The language in which the word originally appeared is listed after the pronunciation or at the end of the entry. For example, *L* stands for Latin and *Gk* stands for Greek. Usually the original meaning is also listed. *Ski* is derived from the Norwegian (*Nor*) word *skīth*, which means "stick of wood."

Practice 10

Use this dictionary excerpt to label the statements that follows either *T* (true) or *F* (false).

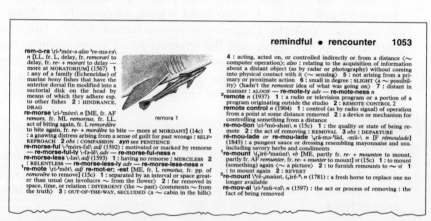

remindful ● rencounter   1053

rem·o·ra \ri-'mȯr-ə *also* 're-mə-rə\ *n* [LL, fr. L, delay, fr. *remorari* to delay, fr. *re-* + *morari* to delay — more at MORATORIUM] (1567) **1** : any of a family (Echeneidae) of marine bony fishes that have the anterior dorsal fin modified into a suctorial disk on the head by means of which they adhere esp. to other fishes **2** : HINDRANCE, DRAG

re·morse \ri-'mȯrs\ *n* [ME, fr. AF *remors*, fr. ML *remorsus*, fr. LL, act of biting again, fr. L *remordēre* to bite again, fr. *re-* + *mordēre* to bite — more at MORDANT] (14c) **1** : a gnawing distress arising from a sense of guilt for past wrongs : SELF-REPROACH **2** *obs* : COMPASSION **syn** see PENITENCE

re·morse·ful \-'mȯrs-fəl\ *adj* (1592) : motivated or marked by remorse — re·morse·ful·ly \-fə-lē\ *adv* — re·morse·ful·ness *n*

re·morse·less \-ləs\ *adj* (1593) **1** : having no remorse : MERCILESS **2** : RELENTLESS — re·morse·less·ly *adv* — re·morse·less·ness *n*

¹re·mote \ri-'mōt\ *adj* re·mot·er; -est [ME, fr. L *remotus*, fr. pp. of *removēre* to remove] (15c) **1** : separated by an interval or space greater than usual ⟨an involucre ~ from the flower⟩ **2** : far removed in space, time, or relation : DIVERGENT ⟨the ~ past⟩ ⟨comments ~ from the truth⟩ **3** : OUT-OF-THE-WAY, SECLUDED ⟨a ~ cabin in the hills⟩

remora 1

4 : acting, acted on, or controlled indirectly or from a distance ⟨~ computer operation⟩; *also* : relating to the acquisition of information about a distant object (as by radar or photography) without coming into physical contact with it ⟨~ sensing⟩ **5** : not arising from a primary or proximate action **6** : small in degree : SLIGHT ⟨a ~ possibility⟩ ⟨hadn't the *remotest* idea of what was going on⟩ **7** : distant in manner : ALOOF — re·mote·ly *adv* — re·mote·ness *n*

²remote *n* (1937) **1** : a radio or television program or a portion of a program originating outside the studio **2** : REMOTE CONTROL 2

remote control *n* (1904) **1** : control (as by radio signal) of operation from a point at some distance removed **2** : a device or mechanism for controlling something from a distance

re·mo·tion \ri-'mō-shən\ *n* (15c) **1** : the quality or state of being remote **2** : the act of removing : REMOVAL **3** *obs* : DEPARTURE

ré·mou·lade *or* re·mou·lade \₁rā-mə-'läd, -mü-\ *n* [F *rémoulade*] (1845) : a pungent sauce or dressing resembling mayonnaise and usu. including savory herbs and condiments

¹re·mount \(₁)rē-'maúnt\ *vb* [ME, partly fr. *re-* + *mounten* to mount, partly fr. AF *remunter*, fr. *re-* + *munter* to mount] *vt* (15c) **1** : to mount (something) again ⟨~ a picture⟩ **2** : to furnish remounts to ~ *vi* **1** : to mount again **2** : REVERT

²re·mount \'rē-₁maúnt, (₁)rē-'\ *n* (1781) : a fresh horse to replace one no longer available

re·mov·al \ri-'mü-vəl\ *n* (1597) : the act or process of removing : the fact of being removed

_____   **1.** *Remoulade* is a spicy sauce that is similar to mayonnaise.

_____   **2.** *Remoras* attach to other fish.

_____   **3.** To call someone a *remora* suggests that the person is a hindrance or a drag.

_____   **4.** The words *remora* and *remorse* were derived from the same Latin root.

_____   **5.** *Remorseless* means the opposite of *remorseful*.

_____   **6.** When meaning "slight," the word *remote* can be used correctly in the phrase *only a remote possibility*.

_____   **7.** The word *remote* was first used to indicate a radio program originating outside the studio in 1957.

_____   **8.** The word *remount* can be used correctly as a verb or a noun.

Study Word Origins

The study of word origins is called **etymology.** Not only is it fascinating to trace a word back to its earliest recorded appearance, but your knowledge of the word's origin can strengthen your memory of the word. For example, the word *narcissistic* means "egotistically in love with yourself." Its origin is a Greek myth in which a beautiful youth named Narcissus falls in love with his own reflection and, owing to his vanity, is turned into a flower. Thus the myth creates an intriguing image that can enhance your memory link for the word.

The amount of information on word origins varies with the type of dictionary. Because of its size, a small paperback dictionary usually contains very little information on word origins, whereas the textbook-size *Webster's New Collegiate Dictionary* offers much more. For the fulest information on word origins, visit the reference room in your college library and use an unabridged dictionary such as *Webster's Third New International Dictionary, Random House Dictionary of the English Language,* or *American Heritage Dictionary of the English Language.*

3
Vocab.

Practice 11

Many English words have their roots in mythology, religion, or literature. Read the dictionary entries that follow to discover the following origins and meanings. In some cases you will cross-reference and read two entries to research an origin.

> **nem•e•sis** \'ne-mə-səs\ *n* [L, fr. Gk] **1** *cap* : the Greek goddess of retributive justice **2** *pl* **-e•ses** \-ˌsēz\ **a** : one that inflicts retribution or vengeance **b** : a formidable and usu. victorious rival or opponent **3** *pl* **-eses a** : an act or effect of retribution **b** : BANE 2

By permission. From *Merriam-Webster's Collegiate*®
Dictionary, 11th Edition. © 2004 by Merriam-Webster,
Incorporated (www.Merriam-Webster.com).

1. The meaning of *nemesis* is _____

2. It originates from _____

> **Pan•de•mo•ni•um** \ˌpan-də-'mō-nē-əm\ *n* [NL, fr. Gk *pan-* + *daimónion* evil spirit   more at DEMON] **1** : the capital of Hell in Milton's *Paradise Lost* **2** : the infernal regions : HELL **3** *not cap* : a wild uproar : TUMULT

By permission. From *Merriam-Webster's Collegiate*®
Dictionary, 11th Edition. © 2004 by Merriam-Webster,
Incorporated (www.Merriam-Webster.com).

3. The meaning of *pandemonium* is _____

4. It originates from _____

_____

> **tan·ta·lize** \'tan-tə-ˌlīz\ *vb* **-lized; -liz·ing** [*Tantalus*] *vt* (1597) : to tease or torment by or as if by presenting something desirable to the view but continually keeping it out of reach ∼ *vi* : to cause one to be tantalized — **tan·ta·liz·er** *n*

> **Tan·ta·lus** \'tan-tə-ləs\ *n* [L, fr. Gk *Tantalos*] (14c)   **1** : a legendary king of Lydia condemned to stand up to the chin in a pool of water in Hades and beneath fruit-laden boughs only to have the water or fruit recede at each attempt to drink or eat   **2** *not cap* : a locked cellarette with contents visible but not obtainable without a key

By permission. From *Merriam-Webster's Collegiate®
Dictionary*, 11th Edition. © 2004 by Merriam-Webster,
Incorporated (www.Merriam-Webster.com).

5. The meaning of *tantalize* is _____

_____

6. It originates from _____

_____

> **Her·cu·le·an** \ˌhər-kyə-'lē-ən, ˌhər-'kyü-lē-\ *adj* (1513)   **1** : of, relating to, or characteristic of Hercules   **2** *often not cap* : of extraordinary power, extent, intensity, or difficulty ⟨∼ tasks⟩ ⟨∼ proportions⟩

> **Her·cu·les** \'hər-kyə-ˌlēz\ *n* [L, fr. Gk *Hēraklēs*] (13c)   **1** : a mythical Greek hero renowned for his great strength and esp. for performing 12 labors imposed on him by Hera   **2** [L (gen. *Herculis*)] : a northern constellation between Corona Borealis and Lyra

By permission. From *Merriam-Webster's Collegiate®
Dictionary*, 11th Edition. © 2004 by Merriam-Webster,
Incorporated (www.Merriam-Webster.com).

7. The meaning of *Herculean* is _____

8. It originates from a _____

_____

Notice Words with Multiple Meanings

Some words are confusing because they have several different meanings. For example, the dictionary lists more than 30 meanings for the word *run*. To determine the proper meaning of a word, you must use the context of the sentence and paragraph in which the word occurs. Many **multiple-meaning** words are simple words that are used frequently. When you are puzzled by an unusual use of a common word, study the context for its meaning.

EXAMPLE Write the meaning of each boldfaced word between the parentheses that follow, and then write a sentence using a different meaning of the word.

1. Craig wanted to **loaf** around the apartment on Sunday because he had worked late all weekend. (_be lazy or idle time_) Go to the grocery and buy a loaf of bread.

2. Do you **part** your hair in the middle or on the side? (___divide___) Gloria tried out for the part of Josephine in the college play.

Practice 12

The boldfaced words in the following sentences have multiple meanings. Write the meaning of the boldfaced words between the parentheses. Then write a sentence that uses a different meaning of the word.

1. The father could no longer **bear** the sounds of his son's drum practice.
   (   )

2. Frequent long-distance calls quickly **run** up your phone bill.
   (   )

3. Stockbrokers cannot always **bank** on market increases. (   )

4. The receptionist was hesitant to miss another day for fear of being **canned.** (   )

5. The umpire **sided** with the home team. (   )

6. The new roommate had moving boxes so heavy they felt as if they were full of **lead.** (   )

7. The DVD-of-the-Month-Club's offer of four DVDs for $1.00 each seemed too good to be true; was there a **catch** of some kind?
   (   )

8. Do you **mind** if I interrupt your reading to ask you a question?
   (   )

Notice Easily Confused Words

Many pairs of words cause confusion because they sound exactly alike or almost alike but are spelled and used differently. *Principal* and *principle* are examples. A common error is to write, "The new school principle is Mrs. Thompson." (The wrong word has been used.) Remember, the *al* word refers to a person, or "pal," and the *le* word refers to a ru*le*. To keep most of these words straight, you must memorize and associate.

✔ Reader's TIP

Easily Confused Words

Study the following list of easily confused words and learn their differences.

1. **capital:** city
   capitol: building
2. **cereal:** breakfast food
   serial: sequential episodes
3. **cite:** quote
   sight: vision
   site: place
4. **aisle:** row
   isle: island
5. **accept:** receive
   except: all but
6. **angle:** in math
   angel: in heaven
7. **birth:** have a baby
   berth: bed
8. **stationary:** fixed position
   stationery: writing paper
9. **vain:** conceited
   vein: blood vessel
10. **your:** ownership
    you're: contraction of "you are"
11. **confident:** sure
    confidant: one you tell secrets to

12. **lien:** legal claim on another's property
    lean: bend or tilt
13. **personnel:** employees
    personal: private
14. **loose:** not firmly attached
    lose: be defeated
15. **differ:** to disagree in opinion
    defer: to postpone
16. **coarse:** rough textured
    course: route to be taken
17. **moral:** ethical
    morale: confidence or spirits
18. **lesson:** wisdom gained from experience
    lessen: to decrease
19. **emit:** put out or give off, discharge
    omit: to leave out
20. **expense:** cost
    expanse: uninterrupted space or area

Practice 13

Circle the boldfaced word that correctly fits the context of each sentence.

1. Books and articles must be properly _____**cited, sighted, sited**_____ when referenced in _____**your, you're**_____ reports.

2. The _____**cereal, serial**_____ numbers on the computers in the State _____**Capital, Capitol**_____ were difficult to locate.

3. She was _____**accepted, excepted**_____ by all of the colleges to which she applied _____**accept, except**_____ one.

4. The grass on this golf _____**coarse, course**_____ requires the greenskeeping _____**personnel, personal**_____ to work every day to keep it in top condition.

5. It was no surprise that the highly ranked team's _____**moral, morale**_____ was low. After all, no one expected them to _____**loose, lose**_____ to the team ranked in last place.

6. He was _____**confident, confidant**_____ his sister would be hired after he made such a glowing recommendation.

7. The homeowners learned their _____**lesson, lessen**_____ about checking references after the subcontractors, who were never paid by the home improvement company, placed a _____**lien, lean**_____ on their home.

8. She wanted to _____**emit, omit**_____ the costume requirement from the party invitation because not everyone could afford the _____**expense, expanse**_____ of a Mardi Gras outfit.

9. When booking a flight, he tries to get an _____**aisle, isle**_____ seat so that he can stand up easily to stretch his legs.

10. Even though she did not agree with her mom's caution of unnecessary credit card use, she decided to _____**differ, defer**_____ the purchase of a new stereo system until she could buy it for cash.

Use Your Textbook Glossary

Textbooks contain words and phrases that may not be found in your dictionary. This may sound strange, but it is true. For example, what does *loss leader* mean? Each word is listed separately in a dictionary, but the two words are not listed together as a term and defined in all dictionaries. Looking up *loss* and then looking up *leader* will not give you a correct definition of the phrase as it is used in the field of marketing. However, the glossary at the back of a marketing textbook will define *loss leader* as "a product whose price has been cut below cost to attract customers to a store." A textbook's glossary defines words and phrases as they apply to that particular field of study. Consult it before using the dictionary for words that seem to be part of the terminology of the discipline.

Practice 14

The following exercise will give you an idea of the types of words and the amount of information presented in a glossary. Notice that many of the words take on a special meaning within the particular field of study.
Use the following excerpt from a psychology textbook glossary to label the statements below either *T* (true) or *F* (false).

3
Vocab.

> **contingency contracting** establishing an agreement (contract) with one to reinforce appropriate behaviors; often involving token economies (p. 483)
> **contingency management** bringing about changes in one s behaviors by controlling rewards and punishments (p. 483)
> **continuity** the Gestalt principle of organization claiming that a stimulus or a movement will be perceived as continuing in the same smooth direction as first established (p. 104)
> **continuous reinforcement (CRF) schedule** a reinforcement schedule in which every response is followed by a reinforcer (p. 171)
> **contrast** the extent to which a stimulus is in some physical way different from surrounding stimuli (p. 99)
> **control group** participants in an experiment who do not receive a treatment or manipulation (p. 29)

_____ 1. A system whereby you pay your child a dollar each day that all homework is completed is called **contingency contracting.**

_____ 2. In a pharmaceutical research study, members of the **control group** receive the new medication.

_____ 3. Giving a dog a biscuit after every single jump represents a **continuous reinforcement schedule.**

Use a Thesaurus

Dr. Peter Mark Roget, an English physician, collected lists of related words as a hobby. In 1852 his lists were published in a book called *Roget's Thesaurus,* which has been frequently revised over the years by the addition of new words and the deletion of obsolete ones.

Roget's Thesaurus is not a dictionary and is not generally used while reading. Instead, it is a valuable source for writers who don't want to use the same word over and over. Suppose, in writing a history term paper, you notice that you have already used the word *cause* twice in one paragraph and you hesitate to use it again. To find a substitute, consult *Roget's Thesaurus*. You will find noun alternatives such as *origin, basis, foundation, genesis,* and *root.* If you need a verb substitute for *cause,* you will find the synonyms *originate, give rise to, bring about, produce, create, evoke,* and many others. Probably more than a hundred words are listed as relating to *cause,* but not all of them are synonymous. Selecting the one that fits your need in the sentence, adds variety to your writing, and maintains the same shade of meaning that you desire.

Words in a thesaurus are indexed in alphabetical order, and familiar dictionary abbreviations are used for parts of speech. The following example from *Roget's Thesaurus* shows the entry for the word *immediate.*

---

immediate *[adj1]* *instantaneous; without delay*
actual, at once, at present time, at this moment, critical, current, existing, extant, first, hair-trigger*, instant, live, next, now, on hand*, paramount, present, pressing, prompt, up-to-date*, urgent; SEE CONCEPTS *567, 585, 812, 820*
immediate *[adj2]* *near; next*

In this thesaurus, asterisks (*) indicate slang and SEE CONCEPTS indicates that related words can be found in the back of the book under the numbers given.

Your word-processing program probably has a thesaurus. In *Word,* the thesaurus is found in *Tools/Language.* (In *WordPerfect,* it is found in *Tools,* directly under *Spell Check.*) To use it, select the word for which you need a synonym and then click on the thesaurus. An array of words will appear, from which you can choose an option that fits the context of your sentence.

Practice 15

Use the following entry for *reconsider* from *Roget's Thesaurus* to select an alternative word that fits the meaning of *reconsider* in the sentences below.

---

reconsider *[v]* *think about again*
amend, change one's mind, consider again, correct, emend, go over, have second thoughts*, polish, rearrange, reassess, recheck, reevaluate, reexamine, rehash, replan, rethink, retrace, review, revise, reweigh, rework, run through, see in a new light*, sleep on, take another look, think better of*, think over, think twice*, work over; SEE CONCEPT *17*

---

1. Legislators decided to *reconsider* the Constitution to grant the right of free speech. _____

2. Most members were able to *reconsider* their schedule and meet on Monday afternoon rather than Monday morning. _____

3. Although many options have been discussed, perhaps you would like to *reconsider* the first two. _____

3d   What Are Analogies?

Analogies are comparisons that measure not only your word knowledge, but also your ability to see relationships. They can be challenging, difficult, and fun. Use logical thinking and problem-solving skills first to pinpoint the initial relationship and then to establish a similar relationship between two other words. Select a word to complete the analogy in the following example.

EXAMPLE   *Cow* is to *herd* as *seagull* is to _____.

EXPLANATION   The first step in solving an analogy is to pinpoint the initial relationship. What is the relationship between *cow* and *herd*? Because a cow is a member of a herd, you might say that it is one part of a larger whole. To complete the analogy, you must establish a similar relationship for *seagull*. In what larger group does a seagull belong? You've guessed it! *Flock* is the answer.

Analogies are indeed challenging. They test logical thinking as well as vocabulary. Working through analogies is an experience in problem solving.

Reader's TIP

Categories of Analogy Relationships

Synonyms: similar in meaning
Find is to *locate* as *hope* is to *wish*.

Antonyms: opposite in meaning
Accept is to *reject* as *rude* is to *polite*.

(continued)

Function, use, or purpose: identifies what something does; watch for the object (noun) and then the action (verb)
Car is to *transport* as *blanket* is to *warm.*

Classification: identifies the larger group association
Sandal is to *shoe* as *sourdough* is to *bread.*

Characteristics and description: shows qualities or traits
Nocturnal is to *raccoon* as *humid* is to *rain forest.*

Degree: shows variations of intensity
Fear is to *terror* as *dislike* is to *hate.*

Part to whole: shows the larger group
Page is to *book* as *caboose* is to *train.*

Cause and effect: shows the reason (cause) and result (effect)
Study is to *graduation* as *caffeine* is to *insomnia.*

Practice 16

Study the following analogies to establish the relationship of the first two words. Identify that relationship, using the categories outlined above. Then choose *a, b, c,* or *d* for the word that duplicates that relationship to finish the analogy.

1. *Present* is to *gift* as *cassette* is to _____.

Relationship: _____
a. VCR
b. tape
c. music
d. record

2. *V-neck* is to *sweater* as *nonfiction* is to _____.

Relationship: _____
a. a book
b. fiction
c. art
d. music

3. *Scissors* is to *cut* as *pencil* is to _____.

Relationship: _____
a. lead
b. point
c. write
d. answer

4. *Winter* is to *summer* as *night* is to _____.

Relationship: _____
a. evening
b. day
c. bedtime
d. spring

5. *Happy* is to *joyous* as *tired* is to _____.

Relationship: _____
a. exhausted
b. rested
c. amused
d. excited

3
Vocab.

Small-Group EXPLORATION

Form a five-member group and select one of the following questions. Brainstorm and then outline your major points on a transparency. Choose a group member to present the group's findings to the class. Individual assignments can also be made.

■   How do you use context clues when listening to a professor lecture?

■   What dictionaries would you recommend for college students to own?

■   For what professions would a study of Latin be most beneficial?

■   How would you recommend that students remember new words?

Net SEARCH

Use the Internet to do one of the following activities.

■   Find a Web site on vocabulary expansion that will e-mail you a new word every day.

■   Find a Web site in which you can investigate the origin of first names. Look up the origin of your own name and the names of four friends or family members.

Chapter

4

Main Idea

4a What Is a Main Idea?

4b What Is a Topic?

4c What Is a Detail?

4d What Are the Strategies for Stating Main Ideas?

4a What Is a Main Idea?

The **main idea** of a passage is the central message that the author is trying to communicate to the reader. It can be stated in one sentence that condenses specific ideas in the passage into a general, all-inclusive statement of the author's message. Other terms frequently used to indicate the main idea are main point, central focus, and controlling idea.

Understanding the main idea is crucial to your comprehension of any text. Without grasping the main idea, you miss the focal point or heart of the message around which supporting ideas are organized. In fact, if all reading comprehension techniques were reduced to one basic question, that question might be *What main idea is the author trying to get across?* Whether you read a single paragraph, a chapter, or an entire book, your most important single task is to understand the main idea of what you read.

4b What Is a Topic?

One of the first steps in finding the main idea of a passage is to determine the **topic** being discussed. A topic is the general subject that the passage explains. Suppose that a friend mentions an interesting article. Your first question might be *What was it about?* Your next question would be, *What point was the author trying to make?* In this example, the first answer is the topic and the second is a statement of the main idea. In written material, the topic of a passage is usually suggested by the title or a bold-faced heading of the selection or subsection. For instance, a news article on the increasing of state spending by $250 million might be titled "Increased Government Spending Bill Passed" which certainly suggests the topic. A sports article explaining that major league baseball players and owners have agreed on a new steroid policy with more testing and greater penalties might be titled "Baseball's New Steroid Policy Takes Effect in 2006." Thus, like a newspaper headline, the topic labels the subject but does not reveal the focus of the message.

Distinguish General and Specific Ideas

Paragraphs, articles, chapters, and books contain many specific ideas that support one general concept. Sometimes the concept is simple; at other times it is complicated. However, before tackling paragraphs, let's begin with single words. Pretend that the sentence ideas in a passage have been reduced to a short list of keywords. Pretend also that within the list is a general term that expresses an overall subject for the keywords. For example, if *Buick, Honda, Mercedes,* and *cars* were listed as the keywords in a paragraph, the general term would be *cars.* Similarly, if in another passage the key ideas were *trucks, vans, motor vehicles,* and *cars,* the general term would be *motor vehicles.* The general term encompasses or categorizes the key ideas and is considered the topic for the list. What general term would pull together and unify the following specific terms?

Items: *broccoli, spinach, lettuce, cabbage*

Vegetables—or, to be more specific, *green vegetables*—is the general topic for the list. Categorizing ideas and recognizing relationships are the basic steps for determining the main idea of a passage.

EXAMPLE   The following list contains a phrase that describes a general topic and three specific phrases related to the topic. Circle the general topic for the group.

Scramble the eggs

Grill the sausage

Pour the juice

(Fix a big breakfast)

EXPLANATION   The first three specific activities are involved in fixing a big breakfast. The last phrase is the general subject or topic.

4
Main
Idea

This ad is meant to encourage people to drink milk. The main idea is stated directly for the reader in the phrase, "Got Milk?" or, in other words, "Drink milk."

Practice 1

Circle the phrase that could be the topic for each group below.

1. make a touchdown   play football
   kick a field goal   block and tackle

2. wear a bathing suit   dive into the water
   swim in a pool   complete 20 laps

3. flatten dough   sprinkle cheese on top
   make a pizza   spread tomato sauce

4. log on   read, delete, and reply
   write to friends   check e-mail messages

5. collect kindling   build a fire
   strike a match   add logs

6. adjust water temperature   rinse off soap

    take a shower   lather soap on body

7. purchase ticket   go to the movies

    buy popcorn   find seat in theater

Recognize the General Topic for Sentence Groups

Now let's move from single words and short phrases to categorizing the related thought in sentences. By definition, a **paragraph** is a group of sentences that develop a single general topic. The next practice exercises contain groups in which the sentences of a paragraph are listed numerically. Decide what general topic best encompasses each group of sentences.

EXAMPLE Read the following list of sentences and circle the phrase that best expresses the topic of the sentences.

1. The backers of the new Ford Motor Company wanted to build a car for the rich so as to maximize profits.

2. Henry Ford disagreed and insisted on producing a car that the guys who built it could afford to buy.

3. Ford's dream was realized, and the first Model T was hailed as America's Everyman car, a product for mass consumption.

    The first American cars

    (Ford's affordable car)

    Fords for the rich

EXPLANATION The sentences describe Ford's determination to build an affordable car, so the second phrase most accurately describes the topic of the sentences. The first phrase is too broad, and the third is a somewhat inaccurate detail.

Practice 2

Circle the phrase that best describes the topic or subject for each group of sentences.

Group I

1. The American game of baseball has become a favorite sport in Japan.

2. In America, a baseball player can exercise unique talents and stand out as an individual.

3. For Japanese fans, "team spirit" is essential, which means subordinating individual needs for the benefit of the group.

    Enthusiastic Japanese fans

    Cultural differences in baseball

    Unique talents for baseball

Group 2

1. Club members wanted to show support for President Martin Van Buren, a native of Old Kinderhook, New York, so the *OK* was borrowed from his hometown and became their watchword.

2. According to the writer Allen Walker Read, the expression began at the OK Club in New York in 1840.

3. Many have guessed and joked about the derivation of that popular American expression, "OK."

Martin Van Buren seeks second term

Origin of "OK"

Allen Walker Read discovers original club

Group 3

1. The poinsettia, the popular and colorful December plant, was brought to the United States from Mexico.

2. While working in Mexico almost 200 years ago, Joel Poinsett of South Carolina was impressed by the shrub with the brilliant red "flowers."

3. On his return home, Poinsett carried and later propagated cuttings or pieces of the plant that the Mexicans called "star flower."

Poinsett works in Mexico

Mexican flowers

Mexican transplant brings holiday cheer

Group 4

1. Margaret Mitchell's prize-winning novel *Gone with the Wind* is the world's top selling book after the Bible.

2. According to reports from the museum dedicated to Mitchell, the book presently sells at the rate of one copy every 2.5 minutes.

3. To add to the book's popularity, Mitchell was awarded a Pulitzer prize for her story of Scarlett and Rett at Tara.

Pulitzer awarded to Mitchell

Gone with the Wind remains popular

The Margaret Mitchell Museum

Read the following groups of three sentences, then write a phrase that best states the subject or general topic for each group.

Group 5

1. Researchers do not know the effects of television violence on viewers.

2. Many experts believe that explicit violence in the mass media contributes to violence and aggression in society.

3. The issue is important because in the typical American home the television set is turned on an average of seven hours per day.

General Topic? _____

_____

Group 6

1. Orphaned at age 14, Calamity Jane worked the mining towns to support her brothers and sisters and then enlisted in the Army as a scout for the Indian campaigns.

2. A skilled sharpshooter and a fearless rider, Calamity Jane was one of the adventurers who helped tame the American West.

3. Calamity Jane rode for the Pony Express and carried the U.S. mail over 50 miles of the rough Black Hills between Deadwood and Custer.

General Topic? _____

_____

4

Main

Idea

Group 7

1. The official language of the Universal Postal Union (UPU) is French.

2. Even in the United States, postal workers stamp mail with the French words *Par Avion*, rather than with the English *Air Mail*.

3. The phrase *Par Avion* was chosen for UPU before World War II.

General Topic? _____

_____

Group 8

1. In the 1820s and 1830s, life was harsh for the fur trappers who blazed the western trails that settlers in wagon trains would later follow.

2. In a single year as many of 80 percent of the trappers could die.

3. Death might come from a gunshot wound, a grizzly bear, or an Indian attack.

General Topic? _____

_____

Recognize the Topic and a General Sentence Within a Sentence Group

Often the main idea is clearly stated in a general sentence within a passage. The following list of sentences forms a paragraph. Two sentences express specific support and one sentence expresses the general idea about the subject. As you did in the previous exercises, circle the phrase that best describes the subject or topic of the sentences. Then circle the number of the sentence that best expresses the general subject.

EXAMPLE

1. Dwight Eisenhower created the interstate highway system.
2. Superhighways linked America, spurred trade, and turned America into an automotive society.
3. The $330 billion superhighway network increased jobs.

Eisenhower's contribution

Money for roads

(Superhighway success)

EXPLANATION The second sentence best expresses the general subject. The other two offer specific supporting ideas. The third phrase, "Superhighway Success," best describes the general subject or topic of the material. The first two phrases are details.

**4
Main
Idea**

Practice 3

Circle the number of the sentence that best expresses the general subject. Then circle the phrase that best describes the subject of the sentences.

Group 1

1. In 1950 businessman Frank McNamara was embarrassed that he did not have enough cash to pay the bill for a client dinner at a popular New York restaurant.
2. McNamara's wife drove to his rescue with cash.
3. Spurred by this incident, McNamara started the first plastic credit card for use in restaurants, which was called the Diner's Club card.

McNamara's error

Cash policy in restaurants

The birth of plastic money

Group 2

1. Sections are dipped in sodium hydroxide to remove any remaining acid.
2. Canning companies use chemicals to remove the whitish membranes of mandarin oranges without mutilating them.
3. After being subjected to steam, cold water, and peeling, the fruit is placed in hydrochloric acid for two hours to remove stringy fibers.

Dangerous chemicals in foods

Processing foods for safety

Chemicals in orange processing

Group 3

1. A 160-pound man will have a blood alcohol concentration (BAC) of about 0.04 percent one hour after drinking two 12-ounce beers on an empty stomach.

2. Certain driving skills can be impaired by blood alcohol concentrations as low as 0.02.

3. Even moderate drinking, much less than the legal limit, can have a negative impact on driving skills and contribute to accidents.

   The problems of alcohol

   Driving under the influence

   A standard drink

Group 4

1. There is a surprising connection between the development a child undergoes early in life and the level of success that the child will experience later in life.

2. Early childhood generally refers to the period from birth through age five.

3. A child's knowledge of the alphabet in early childhood is one of the most significant predictors of what that child's tenth-grade reading ability will be.

   The importance of an early learning start

   The elementary years

   Prenatal care

4
Main
Idea

The following sentence groups contain three specific supporting sentences. Write a phrase that briefly states the general topic of the sentences, and then write a general sentence that states the overall message for the group.

Group 5

1. The Suez Canal was a manmade assault on nature that dramatically shortened the voyage between the Mediterranean Sea and the Indian Ocean.

2. In 1914 engineers completed the Panama Canal, which united the Atlantic and Pacific oceans and cut the voyage from New York to California by 7,800 miles.

3. By 1994 cars were able to whiz through the Chunnel and thus travel under the English Channel without waiting for a ferryboat to go from France to England.

General topic? _____

General sentence stating the main idea? _____

_____

Group 6

1. Placing chocolates wrapped in brightly colored foil beside unwrapped ones in a gift box livens up the presentation.

2. Chocolates with highly flavored centers or strong-smelling nutmeats are wrapped to prevent the flavors from spreading to other pieces in the gift box.

3. Foil wraps can extend the shelf life of fragile chocolates by reducing the candy's exposure to oxygen.

General topic? _____

General sentence stating the main idea? _____

_____

4
Main
Idea

Group 7

1. Velvalee Dickinson owned and managed a doll shop in New York City during World War II, but she needed to make more money to pay her debts.

2. Soon Dickinson had additional income, but alert FBI code-breakers discovered that mysterious letters concealed in Dickinson's dolls contained sensitive military secrets.

3. For her involvement in using dolls to pass secrets about U.S. naval activity to the Japanese, Dickinson was tried for treason and sentenced to a West Virginia prison until 1951.

General topic? _____

General sentence stating the main idea? _____

_____

_____

Group 8

1. In 1990, an art dealer bought a painting by Marc Chagall for $312,000.

2. In 1993, the art dealer had the same Chagall painting copied by a forger and then sold the forgery for $514,000.

3. In 1998, the art dealer sold the authentic Chagall for $652,000, making a net profit of $854,000 (minus what he paid the forger).

General topic? _____

General sentence stating the main idea? _____

_____

_____

4c   What Is a Detail?

   Details develop, explain, and support the main idea. Specific details can include reasons, incidents, facts, examples, steps, and definitions. They add interest and vivid images, to the material, and they provide support to convince the reader of the author's position. On the topic of "Slam Spam E-Mail," for example, the main idea would be to get rid of spam, and the details might provide such supporting points as the inconvenience for receivers and the cost to service providers, as well as the fact that one spammer sent 825 million messages.

Differentiate Topic, Main Idea, and Supporting Details

   The following example gives a topic, a main idea, and a supporting detail for a paragraph. Remember that the topic is a word or phrase that describes the subject or general category for a group of specific ideas. Frequently the topic is stated as the title of a passage. The main idea, on the other hand, is a complete sentence that states the writer's position or focus on the topic. The supporting details are the specifics that develop the topic and main idea.

4
Main
Idea

| EXAMPLE |

Topic: The world's most popular brand

Main Idea: Coca-Cola is probably the world's best-known brand.

Detail: On any one day, Coke is drunk by 1 billion people in 200 countries.

Practice 4

Compare the items and indicate which is the topic (*T*), the main idea (*MI*), and the supporting detail (*D*).

Group 1

_____ **1.** Chinese officials hope to control floodwaters, generate electricity, and facilitate navigation by building a dam on China's longest river, the Yangtze.

_____ **2.** New dam for the Yangtze.

_____ **3.** The Three Gorges Dam, scheduled to be completed by 2009, is predicted to cost $24 billion.

Group 2

_____ 1. The original French recipe combined the mallow root with sugar, but now the mallow has been replaced with gum arabic and egg whites to save money.

_____ 2. The mallow plant, marsh vegetation eaten in ancient Egypt, is no longer used in the production of marshmallows.

_____ 3. No longer any mallow in the marshmallow.

Group 3

_____ 1. Ticks survive without a blood meal.

_____ 2. Ticks that feed on vertebrates can survive for several months without blood meals from birds, bats, deer, rabbits, dogs, horses, rodents, or humans.

_____ 3. Records show that brown dog ticks have survived as long as 200 days without a blood meal.

Group 4

_____ 1. As the pepper is tasted, piperine bites not only the tongue but also the delicate membranes of the nose, which stimulate the body to expel it.

_____ 2. The sneezing effects of pepper.

_____ 3. Piperine, a chemical found in black and white pepper, makes us sneeze.

Group 5

_____ 1. Global warming can cause severe weather extremes such as typhoons, drought, and rising sea levels.

_____ 2. In the specific areas affected, such severe weather causes loss of life, destruction of property, and damage to roads and crops.

_____ 3. The effects of global warming.

Group 6

_____ 1. A new trick in one state has police with radar guns disguised as construction workers or line workers who radio their back-ups about approaching speeding vehicles.

_____ 2. New tricks to catch speeders.

_____ 3. In some states the police are trying unusual ways to apprehend speeding motorists.

Find the Twist of the Main Idea

Topics are titles or general categories; they are not main ideas. In the example in Section 4b, if the words *broccoli, spinach, lettuce,* and *cabbage* were ideas in a paragraph, the general topic that unifies the items would be *vegetables,* but the main idea could not be expressed by simply saying "vegetables." The word *vegetables* answers the question *What is the passage about?* but not the question *What main idea is the author trying to convey?*

In fact, using the same four details as support, a writer could devise several very different paragraphs about vegetables:

1. Eating green vegetables provides vitamin, mineral, and antioxidant benefits. (Details would explain the special nutrients derived from the green vegetables.)

2. Green vegetables can be used creatively to add color and design to an autumn buffet table. (Details would describe how to use green vegetables in decorative food displays.)

Thus, the main idea is the twist, slant, or point that the author gives to the topic. Details are used to support that twist.

4d   What Are the Strategies for Stating Main Ideas?

Use this three-step method for asking questions to determine the main idea of a paragraph, an article, or a book:

Step 1: Establish the topic.

Question: Who or what is this about?

What general word or phrase names the subject? The topic should be broad enough to include all the ideas, yet narrow enough to focus on the direction of the details. For example, identifying the topic of an article as "politics," "federal politics," or "corruption and dishonesty in federal politics" might all be correct, but the last may be the most descriptive of the actual contents.

Step 2: Identify the key supporting terms.

Question: What are the major details or key terms?

Look at the details that seem to be significant to see if they point in a particular direction. What aspect of the subject do they address? What seems to be the common message? Details such as kickbacks to senators, overspending on congressional junkets, and lying to the voters could support the idea "corruption in federal politics."

Step 3: Focus on the message of the topic.

Question: What main idea is the author trying to convey about the topic?

This statement of the main idea should be:

- A complete sentence
- Broad enough to include the significant details
- Focused enough to reflect the author's slant

In the example about corruption in federal politics, the author's main idea might be that voters need to ask for an investigation of seemingly corrupt practices by federal politicians.

The order in which you use the three questions may vary depending on your prior knowledge of the material. When the material is familiar, main idea construction may be automatic, and the significant details would be obvious. When the material is unfamiliar, as frequently occurs in college reading, first identify the details through key terms and concepts and then form a main idea statement.

Find Stated Main Ideas

You can understand a passage better when the main idea is stated directly, particularly when it is stated at the beginning of the passage. Such an initial main idea offers a signpost that briefs you on what to expect and overviews the author's message. Unfortunately, writers do not always follow this pattern. You need to be skilled both in finding and, especially, in constructing main ideas.

EXAMPLE Read the following example and use the three-step method to determine the main idea.

Walt Disney's new cartoon technology and creative story lines were welcomed by the public when they first appeared on the screen. His Mickey Mouse, the animated and clever problem solver, became a national symbol for the strong American spirit that could not be trampled by the hardships of the Depression. Snow White and the Seven Dwarfs, Disney's first animated feature movie, was enjoyed for its courageous characters and love of life.

1. Who or what is the topic of this passage? _____
2. What are the key terms or major details? Underline them.
3. What main idea is the author trying to convey about the topic?

   Which sentence states it? _____

EXPLANATION The topic of the passage is "Disney's Acceptance by the Public." The details give specifics such as Mickey's becoming a national symbol and *Snow White* being well received. The author states the main idea in the first sentence.

4
Main
Idea

Practice 5

Apply the three-question technique to identify the topic, major details, and stated main idea of the following passages.

Passage 1

   Dalmatians, now firehouse mascots, were once an important part of fire-fighting. Having no fear of horses, the dogs sped in front of the horse-driven carts, barking a warning to allow firefighters to get to a fire quickly. Dalmatians have historically been used for serious work because they have speed, en-durance, intelligence, and excellent memories. These four-legged firestation he-roes have long been replaced by motorized trucks and blaring sirens.

1. Who or what is the topic of this passage?

_____

2. What are the key terms or major details? Underline them.
3. What main idea is the author trying to convey about the topic?

Which sentence states it? _____

Passage 2

   In 1945 airfares were fixed by a cartel, an association of businesses that make agreements to limit competition and fix prices. Juan Trippe at Pan American, however, disagreed with the practice and worked hard to change it. On his first attempt at cutting the cost of trans-Atlantic fares, the British re-fused to allow his Pan Am plane to land in London. Trippe tried another tactic. He found a route outside the cartel's control from New York to San Juan, Puerto Rico. He packed each flight with one-way fares of $75. The route was popular; and the airline flourished. This was just the beginning; Juan Trippe's vi-sion was for average people to be able to enjoy airline travel, and he continued to work against the cartel until his dream became a reality.

1. Who or what is the topic of this passage?

_____

2. What are the key terms or major details? Underline them.
3. What main idea is the author trying to convey about the topic?

Which sentence states it? _____

Passage 3

   Of your 140,000 genes, which ones contain errors that make you prone to disease? By 2025 your doctor and a computer will attempt to prevent or cure diseases by repairing defective genes with drugs. Your genetic profile will be recorded on a computer chip, which will be used to prescribe customized med-ications. Surgery will be considered a pharmaceutical failure.

1. Who or what is the topic of this passage?

_____

2. What are the key terms or major details? Underline them.

3. What main idea is the author trying to convey about the topic?

Which sentence states it? _____

Passage 4

Since President Harry Truman's appointment of Georgia Neese Clark in 1949, a woman has always been the appointed Treasurer of the United States. This has become a long-standing tradition, but it is not a rule. Thus, the practice could be changed with the next administration, and a man could be appointed. The Treasurer is heavily involved in marketing and the manufacturing process for currency.

1. Who or what is the topic of this passage?

_____

2. What are the key terms or major details? Underline them.

3. What main idea is the author trying to convey about the topic?

Which sentence states it? _____

Notice the Variety of Locations for Main Ideas

Main idea statements can be positioned at the beginning, in the middle, or at the end of a paragraph. The beginning and concluding sentences of a passage can be even combined for a main idea statement. The following diagrams demonstrate the different possible positions for stated main ideas within paragraphs. The examples illustrate how a paragraph changes with the position of the main idea, which is shown in boldfaced print.

1. An introductory statement of the main idea appears at the beginning of the paragraph.

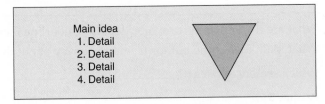

Main idea
1. Detail
2. Detail
3. Detail
4. Detail

EXAMPLE **Using a few simple mental strategies can improve memory performance.** A beginning step in improving memory is to pay attention and make an attempt to encode information. Next, link it to your long-term memory by adding ideas that are meaningful to you. Make up an interesting story with the information or create visual images. Finally, take the time to rehearse your learning and correct lagging faults.

2. **A concluding statement of the main idea appears at the end of the paragraph.**

   EXAMPLE   A beginning step in improving memory is to pay attention and make an attempt to encode information. Next, link it to your long-term memory by adding ideas that are meaningful to you. Make up an interesting story with the information or create visual images. Finally, take the time to rehearse your learning and correct lagging faults. **Using a few simple mental strategies can improve memory performance.**

3. **Details are placed at the beginning to arouse interest, followed by a statement of the main idea in the middle of the paragraph.**

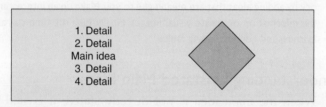

   EXAMPLE   A beginning step in improving memory is to pay attention and make an attempt to encode information. Next, link it to your long-term memory by adding ideas that are meaningful to you. **Using a few simple mental strategies can improve memory performance.** Make up an interesting story with the information or create visual images. Finally, take the time to rehearse your learning and correct lagging faults.

4. **Both the introductory and concluding sentences state the main idea.**

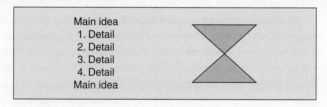

   EXAMPLE   **Using a few simple mental strategies can improve memory performance.** A beginning step in improving memory is to pay attention and make an attempt to encode information. Next, link it to your long-term memory by adding ideas that are meaningful to you. Make up an interesting

4
Main
Idea

story with the information or create visual images. Finally, take the time to rehearse your learning and correct lagging faults. **Try these simple memory hints to improve your performance.**

Unfortunately, readers cannot always rely on a stated main idea being provided. Fiction writers rarely, if ever, use stated main ideas. The following is an example of a paragraph with an unstated main idea.

5. **Details combine to make a point, but the main idea is not directly stated.**

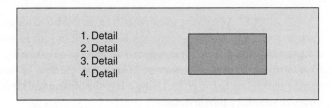

1. Detail
2. Detail
3. Detail
4. Detail

EXAMPLE   A beginning step in improving memory is to pay attention and make an attempt to encode information. Next, link it to your long-term memory by adding ideas that are meaningful to you. Make up an interesting story with the information or create visual images. Finally, take the time to rehearse your learning and correct lagging faults.

Understanding Unstated Main Ideas

When the main idea is not directly stated, it is said to be *implied*, which means that it is suggested from words in several different sentences. Usually for reasons of style and impact, the author has chosen not to express the main idea concisely in one sentence. It is your job as a reader to connect the details and focus the message. Systematically use your questioning steps to state the main idea in your own words. Formulating unstated main ideas can be challenging.

EXAMPLE   In the passage below the main idea is not stated, but it may be determined by answering the three questions that follow.

In Western cultures psychotherapists or counselors promote the idea that people should be happy. They believe that all change is possible, and that change is relatively easy. On the other hand, Eastern cultures are more tolerant of conditions regarded as outside human control. Thus they have a less optimistic view of change. Western therapists want to fix problems, whereas Eastern therapists teach clients to live with and accept troubling emotions.

1. Who or what is the topic of this passage?

_____

_____

2. What are the key terms or major details? Underline them.

3. What main idea is the author trying to convey about the topic?

EXPLANATION The first sentence describes psychotherapy in Western cultures, the second describes it in Eastern cultures, and the third sentence describes it in both. The topic is "Differences in Eastern and Western psychotherapy," and the main idea is that "Eastern and Western cultures differ in their approach to psychotherapy."

Practice 6

Read the passages below and answer the questions to formulate the unstated main idea.

Passage 1

Americans exchange around one billion colds per year, an average of two or three colds for every adult. Infectious cold germs can live for hours in the environment, so take precautions. To avoid contamination, wash your hands frequently to keep from transferring germs to your eyes, mouth, and nose. Drink more water. The winter air dries your nose and throat and allows viruses to attack. Relax and network with friends because a healthy mind strengthens the immune system.

1. Who or what is the topic of this passage?

_____

2. What are the key terms or major details? Underline them.

3. What main idea is the author trying to convey about the topic?

_____

_____

Passage 2

What is the true cost of eating meat? Producing one single pound of beef requires seven pounds of grain, which in turn needs 7,000 pounds of water to grow. Unfortunately, water is becoming scarce, with the United States now pumping out more water than rains can replenish. In a world where many people are hungry, livestock are consuming 70 percent of the wheat and corn. Implicated in pollution, contamination, and thus the outbreak of diseases, livestock waste production is 130 times greater than that of people. How much longer can you afford tenderloin or even a hamburger?

1. Who or what is the topic of this passage?

_____

2. What are the key terms or major details? Underline them.

3. What main idea is the author trying to convey about the topic?

_____

Passage 3

Researchers question why the average broken fingernail takes four to six months to grow back to its normal length, while the average toenail takes nine to twelve months. To answer this mystery, dermatologists first suggest that the trauma of physical contact makes nails grow faster. Fingernails are constantly hitting against objects, while toenails receive less stimulation. Second, sunlight may be a contributing factor in promoting growth since nails tend to grow faster in the summer. Fingernails are usually exposed to light, while toenails are typically covered by shoes. Lastly, circulation affects growth. Blood flows more sluggishly in the feet than in the hands.

1. Who or what is the topic of this passage?

_____

2. What are the key terms or major details? Underline them.

3. What main idea is the author trying to convey about the topic?

_____

Passage 4

Of the five varieties of corn, only one faithfully pops. In their soft starch centers, excellent popcorn kernels maintain a 13.5 percent level of water. This center is surrounded by a hard, enamel-like starch. Heating the corn causes the water inside the kernel to expand. The exterior starch enamel resists the pressure as long as possible. Finally the water bursts out and explodes into the delicious popcorn we buy at the movie theater. Both the water and the resistance are important. Other varieties of corn can store the water but cannot withstand the pressure long enough to explode.

1. Who or what is the topic of this passage?

_____

2. What are the key terms or major details? Underline them.

3. What main idea is the author trying to convey about the topic?

_____

_____

Passage 5

If the president of your college asked you to head a task force to study student and faculty parking options, how would you organize the committee to arrive at workable conclusions? Although this position would require you to be an understanding and diplomatic leader, which of the following basic leadership styles would you choose? The authoritarian leader is one who gives orders and expects others to follow. The democratic leader lets group members share ideas and tries to gain a majority decision. The laissez-faire leader allows the group to run the show with a great deal of freedom in making decisions.[1]

1. Who or what is the topic of this passage?

_____

2. What are the key terms or major details? Underline them.

3. What main idea is the author trying to convey about the topic?

_____

_____

Passage 6

Dating back 4,000 years, the Code of Hammurabi, one of the oldest records of laws, included some unusual forms of punishment. One such punishment was branding. This penalty served four functions. First, because the brand was a mark or letter corresponding to the offense committed, it identified the offender to the community. Next, this form of punishment acted as a general prevention to future crimes. Third, it was a method of identifying future offenders. Finally, it was often

---

[1]Adapted from Henslin, *Essentials of Sociology*, 5th ed., p. 127.

combined with other punishments, such as banishment. Although popular in the 1600s and 1700s, branding fell out of favor as a punishment in the 1800s. England officially abolished branding as a punishment in 1779.[2]

1. Who or what is the topic of this passage?

_____

2. What are the key terms or major details? Underline them.

3. What main idea is the author trying to convey about the topic?

_____

Finding the Main Idea in Longer Selections

Understanding the main idea of longer selections requires a little more thinking than finding the main idea of a single paragraph. Since longer selections such as articles or chapters include more material, the challenge of tying the ideas together can be complicated. Each paragraph of a longer selection usually represents a new supporting detail and the reader must fit the many pieces together under one central theme.

Thesis is a familiar word in English composition classes. You have probably had practice in stating a thesis sentence for English essays. Recall that a thesis sentence narrows a topic to a central idea and asserts your specific opinion about the topic. Think of the main idea of a longer selection as a thesis statement.

In asking questions to find the main idea of a longer selection, the reader still begins with *What is the topic?* The next question is *What are the key supporting details in each paragraph?* The last question is *What main idea is the author trying to convey?*

Use the following suggestions to determine the main idea of longer selections.

- Think about the significance of the title. What does the title suggest about the topic? Perhaps the title is *Rising Tuition Costs*.

- Read the first one or two paragraphs to see what the author asserts about the topic. Is the author expressing an opinion or position on the topic? For example, in the college newspaper a student may write an article opposing rising tuition costs, whereas a college administrator would more likely argue to justify the increases.

- As you read, decide what each paragraph contributes. What is the main idea of each individual paragraph, and how does it develop the overall message? A student article opposing tuition hikes might include paragraphs on other escalating expenses such as housing, books, and transportation. An administrator, on the other hand,

_____

[2]Adapted from James Fagin, *Criminal Justice*, p. 371.

might develop paragraphs on rising salaries, material costs, and state budget shortfalls.

■ Consider the main ideas of the individual paragraphs as supporting details, and determine how the thoughts combine to support a single focus for the selection. Rather than write a summary of all the paragraph details, focus on formulating a general sentence that captures the point of the reading and answers the question *What main idea is author trying to convey in this long selection?*

The main idea of the student article might be, "A 20% tuition hike would result in dropouts because students are already burdened with paying for increases in housing, books, and transportation." The administrator's dueling main idea might be stated, "Tuition must increase by 20% to meet rising salaries, material costs, and state budget shortfalls."

EXAMPLE Read the following longer selection to determine the overall main idea. Write a main idea for each paragraph, then use those details to state a general main idea or thesis statement for the entire selection.

Etiquette Lessons from History

Formal etiquette, accepted rules of conduct, began to appear long ago. Even though many of those accepted practices are centuries old, they still provide guidance for our actions today.

1st Main Idea: _____

When feudalism reached its highest point in the twelfth and thirteenth centuries, chivalry was the ideal of courteous knightly conduct, stressing loyalty by a knight to his God, his lord, and his lady. Originating in France and Spain, chivalry soon spread throughout the Continent and to England. It was a fusion of Christian and military ideals with piety, loyalty, bravery, and honor as virtues.

2nd Main Idea: _____

At meals, people always waited for those of higher rank to be served. This is where the phrase "seated above the salt" originated. Salt was a very expensive commodity at this time, and only those of high rank and fortune could afford it. To be seated above the salt meant that you were seated where you could use the salt provided by your host.

3rd Main Idea: _____

The knight and his lady shared a "trencher," that is, a stale piece of bread that was used as a plate during the meal. He used his knife to cut a large portion of meat to be placed on the trencher, and then cut the meat into smaller pieces for consumption. The knight always made sure that his lady received the choicest piece of meat from the trencher. He also used his knife to spear any vegetables that might accompany the meal. Once the meal was finished, the trenchers, which by then were softened by the absorbed juices from the meal, were eaten by the servants.[3]

4th Main Idea: _____

EXPLANATION Your main idea sentences should be similar to the following:

1. Old rules of conduct guide modern etiquette.
2. Chivalry was the ideal of courteous knightly conduct.
3. Seating and serving order at meals depended on rank.
4. The knight and his lady shared a trencher from which he gave the lady the choice piece of meat.

The topic of this longer selection was suggested by its title, "Etiquette Lessons from History." The first paragraph serves as an introduction and thus you might guess that the selection will explain how old rules of conduct guide modern etiquette. The second paragraph defines the concept of chivalry and the other two paragraphs give examples of the courteous behavior of knights in feudal times.

What main idea is the author trying to convey about etiquette and

history in these paragraphs? _____

Your main idea statement should be similar to this: "The chivalry of feudal times, which is the courteous conduct of a knight with his lord and lady, still guide the rules of etiquette that are observed today." The statement makes an assertion about the topic but does not summarize all specific details.

Practice 7

Read the following longer selection to determine the overall main idea. Write a main idea for each individual paragraph, then state a general main idea or thesis statement for the entire selection

Passage I

The Fork

The story of how the fork made its way to the table is a tale of romance and a journey across continents and civilizations. It began sometime around the year 1000 when a nobleman from Venice was traveling through the Middle East. He met a beautiful Turkish princess and fell in love. After a very brief courtship,

---

[3]Roy Cook, Gwen Cook, and Laura Yale, *Guide to Business Etiquette.*

they were married and returned to Venice. In her dowry was a box of eating utensils common to the Middle East since around 600 but oddities in Venice. These strange utensils were forks.

1st Main Idea: _____

_____

Needless to say, a foreign princess who practiced this strange way of eating with a fork instead of a knife and fingers caused quite a stir. However, as sensible as it may seem today, the fork's place at the table was short lived. Church leaders were appalled at the use of this utensil. After all, they said, it was an insult to God who had given people fingers for eating. When the princess became ill and died, they felt vindicated and said that her death was caused by the use of the fork. Thus, the fork fell into disfavor and became an object to be avoided.

2nd Main Idea: _____

_____

This strange pronged eating utensil did not reappear on the tables of Italians for over 300 years. But it was the Italians, specifically Catherine de Medici of Florence, who introduced it to the rest of Europe. In 1533, she brought several of these unique eating instruments with her as she moved to Paris after her marriage to King Henry II. By the mid-1600s, the practice of dipping one's hands into a common eating pot was no longer acceptable.[4]

3rd Main Idea: _____

_____

What main idea is the author trying to convey in this selection?

_____

_____

_____

Passage 2

Corn Feeds Urban Development

About two thousand years ago, when most North Americans were wandering and hunting, two urban civilizations flourished in the central Mexican highlands. The most urban of these were the Aztecs with their crowning city of Teotihuacán supporting a thriving population approaching 100,000. Teotihuacán even had paved streets and a pyramid as large as those in Egypt. The other urban group, the Incans, were located in the Andes Mountains of Peru. They also had impressive cities and beautiful pyramids. The difference between the simple

---

[4] Roy Cook, Gwen Cook, and Laura Yale, *Guide to Business Etiquette.*

life of the wandering peoples of the north and the developed urban culture of central Mexico can be explained in a single word: corn. The Aztecs and Incas had it. The peoples farther north did not.

1st Main Idea: _____

_____

_____

Originally, corn was unimpressive. Its cobs were only an inch long. The people of central Mexico, the Mesoamericans, domesticated corn by planting only the seeds of the largest and hardiest plants. The resulting improved corn made possible a Neolithic revolution, the transition from hunting-gathering to a predominantly farming way of life. By 2000 B.C.E. nearly every valley in central Mexico and every mountainside above the central and South American rainforests bristled with cornstalks.

2nd Main Idea: _____

_____

_____

The northward advance of corn was blocked by the great Mexican desert. Eventually, however, corn came to the attention of the people of the Southwest. The Hohokam and Mogollon of Arizona and New Mexico and the Anasazi of the Colorado Plateau planted it. Within several centuries, corn transformed the lives of these people. Communities abandoned hunting grounds and settled near rivers. They built trenches and canals to channel water to the crops. They dammed gullies to capture runoff from flash floods and constructed homes near the cornfields.

3rd Main Idea: _____

_____

The culture of the Southwest now changed from centering on hunting to revolving around corn. Sun and water became the focus of religious beliefs, as well as symbols of life and rebirth. Priests-astronomers carefully measured changes of the seasons. If corn were planted too early, it might shrivel before the late summer rains. If planted too late, it might be destroyed by frost. Corn was stored in villages near sacred ceremonial pits, and the control of the corn surplus became a key to political power.[5]

4th Main Idea: _____

_____

---

[5]Mark Carnes and John Garraty, *The American Nation*, 11th ed., pp. 8–9.

What main idea is the author trying to convey in this selection?

_____

_____

_____

Passage 3

Danger from Rollovers

Rollovers are complex crash incidents that are particularly violent in nature, with a higher fatality rate than other kinds of crashes. For instance, in 2002 rollovers accounted for nearly 33 percent of all deaths from passenger vehicle crashes, with more than 10,000 deaths. The majority of those fatalities were the result of not wearing seatbelts. Rollovers, more so than other types of crashes, reflect the interaction of driver, road, vehicle, and environmental. While all types of vehicles can roll over, taller and narrower vehicles such as SUVs, pickups, and vans have higher centers of gravity and thus are more susceptible to rolling over if involved in a single-vehicle accident.

1st Main Idea: _____

_____

_____

Rollovers occur in one of two ways: tripped or untripped. According to the National Highway Traffic Safety Administration (NHTSA), 95 percent of single-vehicle rollovers are tripped. This occurs when a vehicle leaves the roadway and slides sideways, digging its tires into soft soil or striking an object such as a curb or guardrail. The high tripping force applied to the tires in these situations can cause the vehicle to roll over. A second type of rollover is untripped. This is less common, occurring less than 5 percent of the time, and mostly to top-heavy vehicles. Instead of having an object serve as a tripping mechanism, untripped rollovers usually occur during high-speed collision-avoidance maneuvers.

2nd Main Idea: _____

_____

Several factors can cause a vehicle to roll over. One major factor is speed. Some 40 percent of fatal rollover crashes involved excessive speeding, and nearly three-fourths of them occurred in areas with a posted speed limit of 55 miles per hour or higher. Another reason is alcohol. Nearly half of all fatal rollover crashes involve alcohol, which can negatively affect your judgment, muscular coordination, and vision, making you more likely to lose control of your vehicle. Finally, the location of the accident can also be a cause. Rural roads, which tend to be undivided and without barriers, are more likely to be the scene of a fatal rollover. Almost three-fourths of fatal rollovers occur in rural areas where the posted speed limit is typically 55 miles per hour or higher.

3rd Main Idea: _____

What main idea is the author trying to convey in this selection?

_____

_____

Passage 4

Indian Skills

Because of their courage, determination, and fighting spirit, American Indians began serving as military scouts early in our country's history. George Washington recognized their abilities as valuable soldiers when he wrote in 1778, "I think they can be made of excellent use as scouts and light troops." By the War of 1812, many tribes had become involved in the military. During the Civil War, Indians fought for both sides as auxiliary troops. In 1866, the U.S. Army established the Indian Scouts, who were active in the American West in the late 1800s. In addition, Native Americans from Indian Territory who were recruited by Teddy Roosevelt's Rough Riders saw action in Cuba in the Spanish-American War in 1898.

1st Main Idea: _____

_____

American Indians continued to make a contribution to the American military in the early twentieth century. It is estimated that more than 12,000 American Indians served during World War I. Approximately 600 Oklahoma Indians, mostly Choctaw and Cherokee, were assigned to the 142nd Infantry of the 36th Texas-Oklahoma National Guard Division. The 142nd saw action in France, and its soldiers were widely recognized for their contributions in battle. Four men from this unit were awarded the Croix de Guerre, while others received the Church War Cross for gallantry.

2nd Main Idea: _____

_____

Native Americans continued to serve with distinction in several conflicts following World War I. More than 44,000 American Indians, out of a total Native American population of less than 350,000 served during World War II in both European and Pacific theaters of war. Later, battle-experienced American Indian troops from World War II were joined by newly recruited Native Americans to fight Communist aggression during the Korean conflict. Since then, thousands of Native Americans have volunteered to serve in Vietnam, Granada, Panama, Somalia, and the Persian Gulf.

4
Main
Idea

3rd Main Idea: _____

_____

What main idea is the author trying to convey in this selection?

_____

_____

_____

Small-Group EXPLORATION

Form a five-member group and select one of the following questions. Brainstorm and then outline your major points on a transparency. Choose a group member to present the group's findings to the class. Individual assignments can also be made.

- In your own writing for college classes, why is it usually easier to state the main idea or thesis at the beginning of your essay?
- Why are there usually no stated main ideas in fiction?
- Why does prior knowledge of the subject make it easier to get the main idea?
- Analyze the five locations for the main idea (see Section 4d), and explain the value or strength of each to a writer.

Net SEARCH

Journalists twist details into different main ideas to capture a reader's attention. Conduct a search to compare how a current news story is reported in three different online newspapers. How does the focus on the topic differ in each? Which source do you find most interesting and why?

4

Main

Idea

Chapter

5

Details

5a Can You Recognize Levels of Importance Among Details?

Details can be ranked by their level of importance in supporting a topic or main idea. Some details offer major support of the topic—as if to say, First, second, third, and finally. Other details expand on major details by providing more facts, visual images, and illustrations to help the reader understand. All details play a part in our enjoyment of reading, but it is necessary to recognize their various levels of importance. To illustrate these levels, reduce the ideas in the following passage to key words and then rank them in support of the topic.

> A relaxing face and head massage attacks several key areas to release tensions acquired in daily living. For tense eyebrows, gently squeeze the tissue around the eyebrows between the thumb and the forefinger. This area can become tense for people who squint. Also, computer work can create tension headaches in the brows. Moving to a second area, the ears are massaged with the thumb and index finger. The ears can be sensitive for people who endure the daily weight of glasses. Include the soft cartilage of the ear lobes. For overall satisfaction, mobilize the scalp and let the skin move freely. This action increases circulation. This also provides circulation to hair follicles that promotes healthy hair.[1]

---

[1]Patricia Benjamin and Frances Tappan, *Handbook of Healing Massage Techniques*, 4th ed.

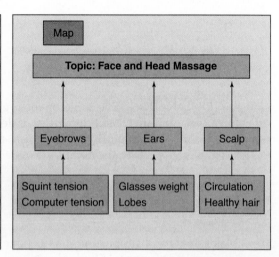

The topic is clearly *face and head massage*. Mark the key words and phrases that support the topic. Would you say that the key words are *eyebrows, ears,* and *scalp*? These are the three major areas for massage. If they are the major details, how would you show the relationship of minor details such as *squint tension, computer tension, glasses and weight, lobes, circulation,* and *healthy hair*?

The preceding outline and map will help you visualize the levels of importance and the relationship of the major and minor details in the passage.

Before considering paragraphs, understand the levels of importance by working the words and phrases. To organize related words or ideas into levels of importance, state the general topic first, then form subcategories of details—first the major details, then the minor details. Either an outline or a map diagram can be used to organize information into levels of importance.

| EXAMPLE | Arrange the following words into an outline to show their relationships and levels of importance:

Words: oyster, fish, bass, seafood, shellfish, shark, lobster

Topic: _____

   I. _____

      A. _____

      B. _____

II. _____

   A. _____

   B. _____

$\boxed{\text{EXPLANATION}}$ The topic or most general term is *seafood*. The next most general terms or subcategories of details are *fish* and *shellfish*, and either term could come first. Under *fish*, the specific details are *bass* and *shark*. Under *shellfish*, the details are *oyster* and *lobster*.

Practice 1

Major ideas and supporting details have been mixed together in the following lists of words. Think about how the ideas should be organized, and insert the missing items into the outline provided.

Group 1

Words: *Dateline,* Newspapers, *People, New York Times,* Magazines, Television, *Washington Post,* Media, *60 Minutes, Newsweek*

Topic: _____

   I. _____

     A. _____

     B. _____

   II. _____

     A. _____

     B. _____

   III. _____

     A. _____

     B. _____

Group 2

Words: Montezuma, European, Martin Luther King, Jr., Historical Figures, Napoleon, Latin American, Queen Elizabeth I, Castro, Abraham Lincoln, American

Topic: _____

   I. _____

     A. _____

     B. _____

5
Details

II. _____

   A. _____

   B. _____

III. _____

   A. _____

   B. _____

Group 3

Words: Van, Freight, Transportation, Jet, Subway, Automobile, Airplane, SUV, Prop plane, Train

Topic: _____

I. _____

   A. _____

   B. _____

II. _____

   A. _____

   B. _____

III. _____

   A. _____

   B. _____

Group 4

Words: Apples, Melon, Orange, Fruit, Cantaloupe, Red Delicious, Citrus, Granny Smith, Honeydew, Lime

Topic: _____

I. _____

   A. _____

   B. _____

II. _____

   A. _____

   B. _____

III. _____

   A. _____

   B. _____

5

Details

Group 5

Words: Lungs, Hamstring, Organs, Rib, Body, Muscles, Heart, Skeleton, Bicep, Skull

Topic: _____

   I. _____

      A. _____

      B. _____

   II. _____

      A. _____

      B. _____

  III. _____

      A. _____

      B. _____

Group 6

Words: Disney World, Opera, *The Aviator*, Music, Theme parks, Rock concert, Universal Studios, Movies, Entertainment, *Finding Nemo*

Topic: _____

   I. _____

      A. _____

      B. _____

   II. _____

      A. _____

      B. _____

  III. _____

      A. _____

      B. _____

5b   Can You Distinguish Between Major and Minor Details?

Details support, develop, and explain a main idea. Specific details can include reasons, incidents, facts, examples, steps, and definitions. Your task is to recognize the major details and to pull them together into a main idea.

Remember that all details are not of equal importance; some are major and some are minor. The importance of a particular detail, therefore, depends on (a) what point the author is making and (b) what information is essential to develop, explain, or prove that point. Major details tend to support, explain, and describe main ideas; minor details tend to support, explain, and describe the major details.

To determine which details are of major and minor significance, first identify the author's main point and then ask the following questions:

1. What details explain or prove the main idea? (They are the major details.)
2. What details support or explain other details? (They are the minor details.)

Minor details add interest and generally fill out a passage, but they are not essential to the logical development of the point. In other words, the point could be made without them. Major details, however, directly support the main idea and are vital to understanding the passage.

EXAMPLE   Read the following paragraph (the main idea is in bold-faced print) and decide which details are major and which are minor.

> **For better or worse, thousands of people all over the world are turning to e-therapy, a new idea that uses e-mails for an ongoing online conversation with a trained therapist.** To illustrate its growing popularity, after a well-known senator mentioned such a website on national television, the site received more than 400,000 e-mail inquires over the next few days. *There are several advantages of e-therapy.* For example, clients are less embarrassed to ask for help. Also, sessions are cheaper. In addition, client and therapist do not have to be at the same place at the same time, which can be especially helpful for clients who live in rural areas without access to mental health care or clients who are too shy or frightened to make a regular appointment. *E-therapy, however, does have its disadvantages.* Since it is on the Internet, imposters who are not qualified can easily pose as therapists. In addition, the therapist cannot see the client and observe important visual and auditory cues.[2]

1. What main idea is the author trying to convey? _____
2. Are the following details major or minor in their support of the author's main idea?

_____ a. After a prominent senator mentioned such a website on national television, the site received more than 400,000 e-mail inquires over the next few days.

[2]Adapted from Samuel Wood, Ellen Green Wood, and Denise Boyd, *The World of Psychology*, 5th ed.

_____ **b.** Several advantages of e-therapy are that clients are less embarrassed to ask for help, sessions are cheaper, and client and therapist do not have to be at the same place at the same time.

_____ **c.** Imposters can easily pose as therapists on the Internet.

EXPLANATION The main idea is that for better or worse people who need emotional help are turning to e-therapy, which is an ongoing online interaction with a trained therapist. The major supporting details are the advantages and disadvantages of e-therapy. Thus, both *b* with three advantages and *c* with an important disadvantage would be major details in support of the main idea. The fact that a senator's television conversation sparked almost a half million e-mails is a minor detail. The following concept map displays relationships within the passage.

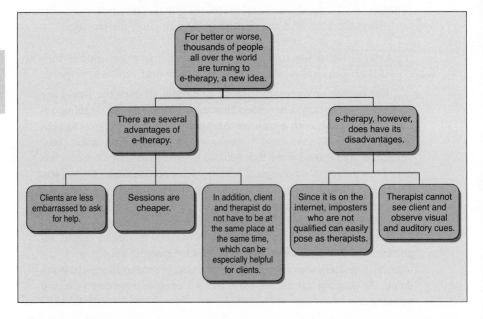

**Reader's** TIP

Key Words That Signal Details

■ Notice key words for major details:

| one | first | another | furthermore | also | finally |

■ Notice key words for minor details:

| for example | to illustrate | to be specific | that is | this means |

Practice 2

Read the following passages and identify the author's main point. Then determine which of the details listed are major and which are minor in supporting the main idea. Apply the skills that you use in reading this short passage to the longer units that you study in college textbooks.

Passage I

Estee Lauder's career fits the business advice to "act locally, think globally." She did both with success. Lauder began in New York City and eventually turned her cosmetics company into a huge global business. Lauder, the daughter of immigrants, grew up living above her father's hardware store in Queens, New York. Her uncle, a chemist, created skin cream that she liked and began to sell. Realizing the potential, she aggressively called on department store executives until Saks Fifth Avenue allowed her counter space to sell her products. She "acted locally" by personally showing up on Saturdays to teach the sales staff how to give personal attention to customers and to offer free gifts. As global opportunities arouse, Lauder opened new cosmetics counters in stores world/wide. She attended every new opening in cites from Paris to Moscow. She told her son that she wanted to "grow a nice little business." Now the company controls 45 percent of the American cosmetics market and sells in 118 countries. The Lauder family owns shares in the company worth more than $6 billion.

5
Details

1. What main idea is the author trying to convey?

_____

_____

2. Which details are major and which are minor in supporting the author's point?

_____ **a.** Lauder grew up living above her father's hardware store in Queens, New York.

_____ **b.** The company sells in 118 countries.

_____ **c.** Lauder personally showed up to teach the sales staff how to give personal attention to customers and to offer free gifts.

Passage 2

Try house-swapping to cut your vacation expenses on hotels. Several home-exchange networks, such as HomeLink and Intervac, list thousands of opportunities on the Web for an annual fee of less than $100. Once you discover an attractive option, you contact the family and make your own arrangements. In a few cases, a car may even be included in the deal. Perhaps this summer you could swap your apartment for one in Paris for a week or a month. Some locales are more popular than others; if you live in New York, Miami, or Los Angeles, you may be deluged with requests.

1. What main idea is the author trying to convey?

_____

2. Which details are major and which are minor in supporting the author's point?

_____   **a.** Home-exchange networks list the exchange opportunities on the Internet.

_____   **b.** A car may be included in the deal.

_____   **c.** New York and Miami are popular swap requests.

Passage 3

Most Americans are apparently heeding the message that smoking is the foremost cause of preventable disease and death in the United States. The percentage of American adults who smoke has been decreasing and is currently under 25%. Although breaking the habit is difficult, 90% of ex-smokers reported quitting on their own. Aids such as nicotine gum and the nicotine patch are helpful. In further proof that the message is being heard, smoking is more likely to be viewed as a socially unacceptable behavior now than in the past. Most restaurants and many buildings have become smoke-free zones. Lone smokers must now huddle outside office buildings for the pleasure of damaging their T cells and increasing their risk of heart disease, lung cancer, and emphysema.[3]

1. What main idea is the author trying to convey?

_____

_____

_____

2. Are the following details major or minor in their support of the author's main idea?

_____   **a.** Aids such as nicotine gum and the nicotine patch are helpful.

_____   **b.** The percentage of American adults who smoke has been decreasing and is currently under 25%.

_____   **c.** Smoking is more likely to be viewed as a socially unacceptable behavior now than in the past.

Passage 4

Car-rental bargains abound in Florida because the state is the biggest, most competitive car-rental market in the world. Companies complain that an oversupply of cars artificially lowers prices. Vacationers can benefit by booking low rates

---

[3]Adapted from Samuel Wood, Ellen Green Wood, and Denise Boyd, _The World of Psychology_, 5th ed.

for weekly leisure rentals. Business travelers, on the other hand, rent only for a few days and are forced to tap their expense accounts and pay higher daily rates.

1. What main idea is the author trying to convey?

_____

2. Are the following details major or minor in their support of the author's main idea?

_____ **a.** There is an oversupply of cars in Florida.

_____ **b.** Business travelers tap their expense accounts.

_____ **c.** The weekly leisure rentals are cheapest.

Passage 5

Chances are you spend time in natural sunlight. You could benefit from using sunscreens with sun protection factor (SPF) numbers of 15 or more. The SPF number gives you some idea of how long you can stay in the sun without burning. For example, if you normally burn in 10 minutes without sunscreen, you should be protected from burning for 150 minutes using SPF 15. Swimming and perspiration reduce the actual SPF value for many sunscreens, so be sure to reapply even if the product claims to be water-resistant.

1. What main idea is the author trying to convey?

_____

_____

2. Are the following details major or minor in their support of the author's main idea?

_____ **a.** The SPF number indicates how long you can stay in the sun without burning.

_____ **b.** If you normally burn in 10 minutes without sunscreen, you are protected for 150 minutes with SPF 15.

_____ **c.** Some sunscreens claim to be water-resistant.

Passage 6

Edward Teach, the infamous British pirate known as Blackbeard, was originally trained as a privateer, legally attacking and plundering his queen's enemies' ships. However, he became such an expert buccaneer that eventually he took command of his own sailors and ship. He began robbing defenseless vessels with rich cargoes that were sailing in the Atlantic and the Caribbean. From 1716 to 1718 Blackbeard developed a ruthless and colorful reputation as a fearsome pirate who grew his hair long and tied his braided beard with black ribbons. Eager to make the seas safe from the pirates, Alexander Spotswood, the governor of Virginia, sent two sloops to end the pirate's ambushes and plundering. Blackbeard was shot and beheaded near his favorite hideout on Ocracoke

Island in North Carolina. His head was suspended from the bow of Lt. Maynard's sloop as a warning to all would-be pirates. The location of Blackbeard's treasure, however, still remains a mystery.

1. What main idea is the author trying to convey?

_____

_____

2. Are the following details major or minor in their support of the author's main idea?

_____ a. Blackbeard robbed ships in the Atlantic Ocean and the Caribbean Sea.

_____ b. Blackbeard was eventually shot and beheaded.

_____ c. A privateer is hired to attack enemy ships on behalf of the crown.

Interpret Longer Reading Selections

5
Details

Apply your skills to longer reading selections. Each of the following passages has one overall main idea, and each paragraph develops a major supporting detail for that main idea. As you read, ask yourself *What is the topic? What main idea is the author trying to convey about the topic?* and *What are the major supporting details?*

Practice 3

Passage 1

Of all the cognitive skills humans possess, none is more important for clarity of thinking and academic success than vocabulary. How, then, can you build a more powerful vocabulary? You can greatly increase your vocabulary by realizing that almost all words belong to larger networks of meaning that your mind is already geared toward organizing. A few simple and logical techniques such as the following can help you unlock the meaning of unfamiliar words.

You can think analytically about words you already know and relate new words to them. What do the words *antiseptic* and *septic tank* have in common? You use an *antiseptic* to prevent bacterial infection of a wound; a *septic tank* is used for removing harmful bacteria from water containing human waste. A logical conclusion would be that septic has something to do with bacteria. Thus, if a doctor says a patient is suffering from *sepsis*, you can guess that the patient has a bacterial infection.

Another logical technique is to be aware of word connections that may be hidden by spelling differences. You may know that both *Caesar* and *Czar* refer to some kind of ruler or leader. But you may not know that they are exactly the same word, spoken and spelled somewhat differently in Ancient Rome (*Caesar*) and in Russia (*Czar*). Now, if you're taking a history class in which you learn about *Kaiser* Wilhelm, who led Germany during World War I, thinking analytically about his title may help you realize that it is exactly the same word as *Caesar* and *Czar*, with a German spelling.[4]

1. What main idea is the author trying to convey?

   _____

   _____

2. Are the following details major or minor in their support of the author's main idea?

   _____   **a.** A *septic tank* is used for removing harmful bacteria from water containing human waste.

   _____   **b.** Be aware of word connections that may be hidden by spelling differences.

   _____   **c.** *Kaiser* Wilhelm led Germany during World War I.

Passage 2

   One historian has called the Columbian exchange, a biological give-and-take, the most important consequence of the conquest of the New World. The phrase refers to the transatlantic exchange of plants, animals, and diseases that occurred after the first European contact with the Americas.

   The worse result of the exchange was the exposure of Native Americans to Old World diseases. Epidemics of smallpox, measles, typhus, and influenza struck Native Americans with great force, killing half, and sometimes as much as 90 percent, of the people in communities exposed to them. The only American disease to infect the Old World was syphilis, which then appeared in Spain just after Columbus returned from his first voyage.

   The Columbian exchange also introduced Old World livestock to the New World. Columbus brought horses, sheep, cattle, pigs, and goats with him on his second voyage in 1493. Native Americans had few domesticated animals and initially marveled at these large beasts. However, with few natural predators to limit their numbers, livestock populations boomed in the New World, competing with native mammals, such as bison, for good grazing. Eventually the Plains Indians became exceptionally skilled riders. They found it easier to hunt buffalo on horseback than on foot, and the women valued horses as beasts of burden.

   European ships carried unintentional passengers as well, including the black rat and honeybees, both previously unknown in the New World. Ships also brought weeds such as thistles and dandelions, whose seeds were often embedded in hay for animal fodder.

---

[4]Adapted from Samuel Wood, Ellen Green Wood, and Denise Boyd, *The World of Psychology*, 5th ed.

Europeans brought a variety of seeds and plants in order to grow familiar foods. Columbus's men planted wheat, chickpeas, melons, onions, and fruit trees on Caribbean islands. European plants did not always fare well, at least not everywhere in the New World, so Europeans learned to cultivate native foods, such as corn, tomatoes, squash, beans, and potatoes, as well as nonfood plants such as tobacco and cotton. They carried many of these plants back to Europe, enriching Old World diets with new foods.[5]

1. What main idea is the author trying to convey?

_____

_____

_____

2. Are the following details major or minor in their support of the author's main idea?

_____ **a.** Plains Indians found it easier to hunt buffalo on horseback than on foot, and the women valued horses as beasts of burden.

_____ **b.** The worse result of the exchange was the exposure of Native Americans to Old World diseases.

_____ **c.** The Columbian exchange also introduced Old World livestock to the New World.

_____ **d.** Europeans brought a variety of seeds and plants in order to grow familiar foods.

_____ **e.** Tobacco and cotton are nonfood items.

Passage 3

Cathy Hughes faced many challenges to become the successful chairwoman of Radio One, the largest African-American owned radio broadcaster in the United States. Today Hughes has a personal wealth of close to $300 million and is the first Black woman to head a publicly traded company.

Hughes's first big challenge in the industry was to turn around an ailing university radio station. While working as a lecturer at Howard University in 1973, she was asked to manage and head sales for the college's station. In one year, Hughes increased revenues from $250,000 to $3 million, and the station rose from No. 38 to No. 3 in the market. In addition, she invigorated programming by creating "Quiet Storm," a romantic evening radio format that is now copied in many markets.

In 1980 Hughes took a big jump and bought her first radio station. She and her husband put together a group of investors and borrowed $1 million. In order to get the loans she needed, Hughes contacted three different banks before she found a new female loan officer who agreed to lend her $600,000.

<hr>

[5]Adapted from David Goldfield et al., *The American Journey*, Brief 3rd ed.

5
Details

With the new radio station, her battle was just beginning. The monthly debt payments were crushing, and her marriage failed. Hughes lost her house, and her car was repossessed. She had to sleep on the floor of the radio station. In addition, she was a single mom raising a son. To make loan payments, she brought in $50,000 by selling a rare white-gold pocket watch made by slaves that had belonged to her great-grandmother. For 18 months she cooked on a hot plate and washed in a public bathroom at the station. Again, she was innovative with programming and changed the station from R&B music to 24-hour talk. Hughes took on an additional job as talk show host because she could not afford to hire talent. After six years of struggle, the station finally made a profit.

In the next ten years Hughes went on a bold but calculated buying spree. Today her empire includes 68 radio stations and a new cable station, all worth over $2 billion. Her son Alfred, who grew up at the station and is now 39, works with her as CEO of Radio One. He says, "My mother had a vision to do something with her life and her mantra is that if you can believe it and conceive it, you can achieve it."

1. What main idea is the author trying to convey?

_____

_____

2. Are the following details major or minor in their support of the author's main idea?

_____ a. Hughes's first big challenge in the industry was to turn around an ailing university radio station.

_____ b. One year, the revenues were $250,000 at the Howard University station.

_____ c. She invigorated programming by creating "Quiet Storm," a romantic evening radio format.

_____ d. In 1980 Hughes took a big jump and bought her first radio station.

_____ e. She found a new female loan officer who agreed to lend her $600,000.

_____ f. To get the loans she needed, Hughes contacted three different banks.

_____ g. With the new radio station, her battle was just beginning.

_____ h. For 18 months, she cooked on a hot plate and washed in a public bathroom at the station.

_____ i. Her son Alfred, who grew up at the station and is now 39, works with her as CEO of Radio One.

Passage 4

Lipids are hydrophobic (from the Greek *hydro*, water, and *phobos*, fearing), which means that they do not mix with water. You have probably observed this chemical behavior in an unshaken bottle of salad dressing: The oil, which is a type of lipid, separates from the vinegar, which is mostly water. If you shake the bottle, you can force a temporary mixture long enough to douse your salad with dressing, but what remains in the bottle will quickly separate again once you stop shaking it. Lipids are a diverse set of molecules; two examples are fats and steroids.

Fats, though often criticized, perform essential functions within the body. The major portion of a fatty acid is a long hydrocarbon, which like the hydrocarbons of gasoline, stores much energy. In fact, a pound of fat packs more than twice as much energy as a pound of carbohydrate such as starch. This compact energy storage enables a mobile animal such as a human to get around much better than if the animal had to lug its stored energy around in the bulkier form of carbohydrate. The downside to this energy efficiency is that it is very difficult for a person trying to lose weight to "burn off" excess body fat. It is important to understand that a reasonable amount of body fat is both normal and healthy as a fuel reserve.

Fats can be **saturated** or **unsaturated.** Most animal fats, such as lard and butter, have a relatively high proportion of saturated fatty acids. Diets rich in saturated fats may contribute to cardiovascular disease by promoting atherosclerosis. In this condition, lipid-containing deposits called plaques build up within the walls of blood vessels, reducing blood flow and increasing risk of heart attacks and strokes. In contrast, unsaturated fats, such as those found in vegetable oils (corn oil and canola oil) and fish oils (cod liver oil), are less likely to form solids and are usually liquid at room temperature. The exception is tropical plant oils such as cocoa butter, a main ingredient in chocolate.

Steroids, which are very different from fats in structure and function, are also classified as lipids because they are hydrophobic. Cholesterol, which gets a lot of bad press because of its association with cardiovascular disease, is a steroid and an essential molecule in your body. Cholesterol is also the "base steroid" from which your body produces other steroids, including estrogen and testosterone, the steroids that function as sex hormones.

The controversial drugs called synthetic anabolic steroids are variants of testosterone, the male sex hormone. Because anabolic steroids structurally resemble testosterone, they also mimic some of its effects. Some athletes use anabolic steroids to build up their muscles quickly and enhance their performance. Anabolic steroids, along with many other drugs, are banned by most athletic organizations because there is evidence that these substances can cause serious mental and physical problems, including violent mood swings, deep depression, liver damage, high cholesterol, a reduced sex drive, and infertility.[6]

5
Details

---

[6]Adapted from Neil Campbell, Lawrence Reece, and Eric Simon, *Essential Biology*, 2nd ed., pp. 42–43.

1. What main idea is the author trying to convey?

_____

2. Are the following details major or minor in their support of the author's main idea?

_____ **a.** Fats, though often criticized, perform essential functions within the body.

_____ **b.** You have probably observed this chemical behavior in an unshaken bottle of salad dressing: The oil, which is a type of lipid, separates from the vinegar, which is mostly water.

_____ **c.** The downside to this energy efficiency is that it is very difficult for a person trying to lose weight to "burn off" excess body fat.

_____ **d.** Vegetable oils and fish oils are less likely to form solids at room temperature.

_____ **e.** Steroids are also classified as lipids because they are hydrophobic.

_____ **f.** Cholesterol gets a lot of bad press because of its association with cardiovascular disease.

_____ **g.** Estrogen and testosterone are steroids that function as sex hormones.

_____ **h.** Anabolic steroids, along with many other drugs, are banned by most athletic organizations.

5
Details

Small-Group EXPLORATION

Form a five-member group and select one of the following questions. Brainstorm and then outline your major points on a transparency. Choose a group member to present the group's findings to the class. Individual assignments can also be made.

■ What type of career opportunities would be most appropriate for people who like to focus on main ideas? Why?

■ What type of career opportunities would be most appropriate for people who enjoy details? Why?

■ Using a sports topic, create an outline similar to those in the first practice exercise in this chapter. Include three major supporting details and eight minor details.

■ Write a paragraph that includes the following key words that signal details: _first, another, furthermore, finally, for example, to be specific._

Net SEARCH

Research a famous entertainer and create an outline similar to those in the first practice exercise in this chapter. Include four major supporting details and eight minor details.

5
Details

Chapter

6

Organizational Patterns

6a | What Are the Patterns for Organizing Ideas?

Details in support of a main idea are organized in patterns that can be recognized by the reader. In fact, the main idea can dictate the pattern of organization a writer will use to deliver the message. A **pattern of organization** is a vehicle or structure for presenting a message. Before beginning to write, an author must ask, *If this is what I want to say, what is the best way to organize my message?*

From a number of possible patterns, a writer chooses the organizational structure that seems most appropriate. For example, if you wanted to convey the message or main idea that freshmen receive more support at junior colleges than at large universities, you would probably organize the message through a pattern of comparison and contrast. Or if you wanted to explain that a college degree can lead to expanded opportunities, promotions within companies, salary increases, and ultimately greater job satisfaction, the idea might best be communicated through a pattern of cause and effect.

Suppose you were writing an orientation article describing the support services available at your own college. You could summarize those resources in a list pattern, or you could discuss them in the time order in which a freshman might need them. Within your article you might have a separate paragraph describing or defining a relatively unknown service on campus, with examples of how it has helped others. Thus, one long article might have an overall pattern of listing, yet it could contain individual paragraphs that follow other patterns. Therefore, your choice of organizational pattern will determine the way you structure your message.

Why is it important to identify organizational patterns? Because they signal how facts will be presented, they are blueprints for you to use while reading. The number of details in a textbook can be overwhelming; identifying the author's pattern can help you to master the complexities of the material by allowing you to predict the format of upcoming information.

✓ Reader's TIP

Patterns of Organization and Signal Words

■ **Addition** (providing additional information)	furthermore, again, also further, moreover, besides, likewise
■ **Cause and Effect** (showing one element as producing or causing a result or effect)	because, for this reason, consequently, hence, as a result, thus, due to, therefore
■ **Classification** (dividing items into groups or categories)	groups, categories, elements, classes, parts
■ **Comparison** (listing similarities among items)	in a similar way, similarly, parallels, likewise, in a like manner
■ **Contrast** (listing differences among items)	on the other hand, bigger than, but, however, conversely, on the contrary, although, nevertheless
■ **Definition** (initially defining a concept and expanding with examples and restatements)	can be defined, means, for example, like
■ **Description** (listing characteristics or details)	is, as, like, could be described

(continued)

- **Generalization and Example**
  (explaining with examples
  to illustrate)

  to restate, that is, for example,
  to illustrate, for instance

- **Location or Spatial Order**
  (identifying the
  whereabouts of objects)

  next to, near, below, above,
  close by, within, without,
  adjacent to, beside, around,
  to the right or left side,
  opposite

- **Simple Listing**
  (randomly listing items
  in a series)

  also, another, several,
  for example

- **Summary**
  (condensing major
  points)

  in conclusion, briefly,
  to sum up, in short,
  in a nutshell

- **Time Order, Sequence,
  or Narration**
  (listing events in
  order of occurrence)

  first, second, finally, after,
  before, next, later, now,
  at last, until, thereupon,
  while, during

Importance of Signal Words

Authors use signal words and phrases such as *furthermore, on the other hand*, and *to illustrate* to link thoughts together for the reader. These words help the reader logically connect and anticipate ideas. For example, if you want to continue your listing of services on campus, you would use *also, in addition*, and *furthermore*. If you wanted to indicate contrast or an opposite direction, you would use *on the other hand, but*, and *although*.

Signal words are also called **transitions,** a term that defines their purpose, to guide the reader from one thought to another smoothly. Because signal or transitional words point out the movement of ideas, they also alert the reader to the patterns of organization of paragraphs. If a passage is loaded with words such as *like, in a similar way*, and *likewise,* you would predict that a comparison is being made. On the other hand, the words *because, consequently, hence*, and *as a result* suggest a cause-and-effect pattern of thought.

Although key words can certainly signal a particular pattern, the most important clue to the pattern is the main idea itself. Several patterns may appear within a single selection. Your aim as a reader is to anticipate the overall pattern and place the supporting details into its broad perspective.

The following are examples of the patterns of organization found most frequently in textbooks. After reading each example paragraph, enter the key points into the blank outline display to show that you understand the pattern.

6
Org.
Patt.

Simple Listing

With a simple listing, items are randomly given as a series of supporting facts or details. These supporting elements are of equal value, and the order in which they are presented is of no importance. Changing the order of the items does not change the meaning of the paragraph. Signal words often used as transitional words to link ideas in a paragraph with a pattern of simple listing are *in addition, also, another, several, for example,* and *a number of.*

| EXAMPLE |

Interviewing for a Job

There are several things you should remember when interviewing for a job. Be sure to arrive on time—there is no excuse for being late. Attend to your appearance and dress to look like a successful company employee. Also, do not smoke, chew gum, or accept candy, even if it is offered.

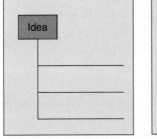
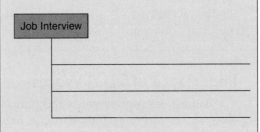

Classification

To simplify a complex topic, authors frequently begin introductory paragraphs by stating that the information that follows is divided into a certain number of groups or categories. The divisions are then named and the parts are explained. Signal words often used for classification include *two divisions, three groups, four elements,* and *five classes.*

| EXAMPLE |

Mammals

Mammals are classified according to class, order, and species. As one of the eight classes of vertebrates, mammals make up the class called *Mammalia.* The *Mammalia* class is further divided into orders, which are groupings of mammals according to their probable evolutionary development. Finally, within each of the orders, mammals are categorized into species. Members of a species can breed among themselves but not with members of another species.

 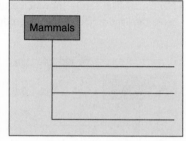

Definition

In textbooks, an entire paragraph is frequently devoted to defining a complex term or idea. The concept is defined initially and then expanded with examples and restatements.

EXAMPLE

Carpal Tunnel Syndrome

Carpal tunnel syndrome is a painful disorder that interferes with the use of the hand and can be caused by repetitious wrist movements such as computer typing. The condition creates pressure on the median nerve as it passes through a canal formed by the bones and ligaments in the wrist.

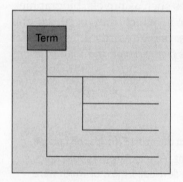 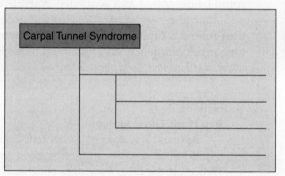

Description

Description is like listing; the characteristics that make up a description are no more than a definition or a simple list of details.

EXAMPLE

The Statue of Liberty

The Statue of Liberty was given to the United States by France in 1884 as an expression of friendship and a symbol of liberty. The 151-foot bronze statue stands on Liberty Island in Upper New York Bay, about 1.5 miles southwest of

Manhattan. The statue shows Liberty as a proud woman whose crown represents the light of liberty shining on the seven seas and seven continents.

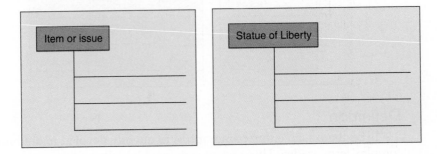

Time Order, Sequence, or Narration

The time order pattern of organization is usually expanded to include both sequence and narrative. A time order pattern lists events that must occur in a specific, planned order. Changing the order would disrupt the meaning. Thus, a listing of historical events with their dates would be developed in a time or chronological order. Being also sensitive to timing, instructions and directions are usually developed in a time order that could be described as a sequence. Narratives such as novels, biographies, and anecdotes are stories told in the order in which they occurred and thus follow a time or chronological pattern. Signal words often used for time order, sequence, and narration include *first, second, third, after, before, when, until, at last, next,* and *later.*

6
Org.
Patt.

| EXAMPLE |

Rap Music Development

Rap music first appeared in New York City in the mid-1970s. It soon became popular in other urban areas, especially among African-American teenagers. Throughout the 1980s many styles of rap music developed, most of which were unique to specific regions of the country. Collaborations between rhythm and blues, rock, and rap artists were common in the 1990s, and they served to increase the popularity of rap music.

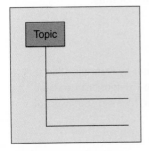
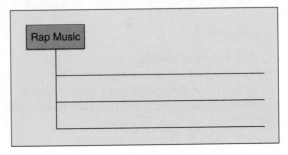

Comparison-Contrast

In the comparison-contrast pattern of organization, items are presented according to the similarities and differences among them. Signal words often used for comparison-contrast include *different, similar, on the other hand, but, however, bigger than, in the same way,* and *parallels.*

EXAMPLE

Introverts and Extroverts

Introverts tend to be shy people who focus on inner thoughts and creative ideas. By contrast, extroverts are sociable people who turn their mental interests toward events, people, and things of the outer world. The average person has a healthy balance of both qualities.

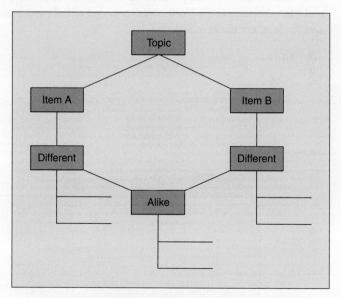

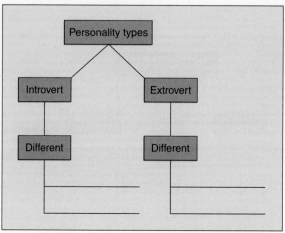

Cause and Effect

In a cause-and-effect pattern, one element is shown to produce another element: the happening or *cause* stimulates the particular result or *effect*. Signal words often used in a cause-and-effect pattern are *for this reason, consequently, on that account, hence,* and *because.*

EXAMPLE

Moving North

Between 1910 and 1970, 6.5 million African Americans migrated out of the South. Both the "push" of hardship in the rural South and the "pull" of opportunity in the urban North led people to move to Northern cities such as New York, Chicago, Cleveland, and Philadelphia. World War I and World War II created labor shortages in the North, which provided one of many financial incentives for Southern blacks to migrate.

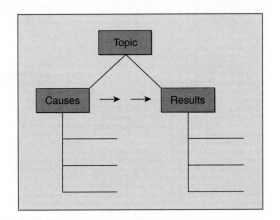

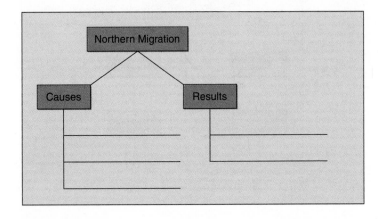

Mixed Patterns

The previous examples have illustrated single patterns of development, but frequently authors will mix patterns. For example, a paragraph might begin with a definition of *El Niño* and then move into a cause-and-effect pattern for discussing the resulting weather changes.

EXAMPLE

El Niño

El Niño is a warming of the eastern tropical Pacific Ocean that can cause unusual weather patterns worldwide. Some scientists explain that the warming is a buildup of excess heat in the western Pacific Ocean. This warming of normally cold waters occurs during the winter months and was first recorded in the early 1500s. (*El Niño* is Spanish for "the boy child," and the term is used to refer to the Christ child.)

What happens to oceans also affects the atmosphere. Thus, El Niño's warm ocean waters have affected weather conditions around the world. In 1982 and 1983, El Niño caused a severe drought in Australia and Indonesia while simultaneously creating an unusually large number of thunderstorms in California. Even as far away as South Africa, El Niño has caused decreased seasonal rains, which led to a severe drought in the late 1990s.

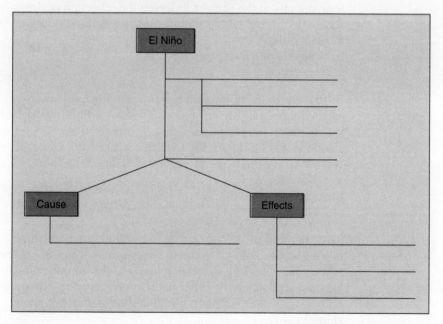

Practice 1

Read the following first sentences of paragraphs and select the letter of the organizational pattern that you predict the author will use.

_____ 1. Bad or fetid breath in the morning is caused by sulfur-bearing compounds. Because the salivary flow is lessened during sleep, microorganisms in the mouth convert food and plaque into amino acids and peptides that break down into compounds with a resulting unpleasant sulfur odor.
   a. classification
   b. cause and effect
   c. addition

_____ 2. Butterflies seek the natural protection of the undersides of leaves or stems during a rainstorm. Their delicate bodies could be damaged by the wind or raindrops. When resting, butterflies look like teardrops as their folded wings repel falling water.
   a. description
   b. definition
   c. summary

_____ 3. A few suggestions can help you avoid "red-eye" in your next photographs. Use an extender to move the flash at least three inches away from the camera lens. Ask your subjects not to look directly at the camera to lessen the reflection of the flash. Also, avoid taking pictures when it is dark.
   a. description
   b. simple listing
   c. time order

6
Org.
Patt.

_____ 4. In 1042 the game of football began when the English unearthed the skulls of vanquished Danish soldiers and kicked them around the field. Later, this "headball" was changed to a softer cow bladder. In the twelfth century King Henry II wanted to eliminate the violence and banned the sport.
   a. time order
   b. simple listing
   c. location

_____ 5. Saltwater and freshwater fish differ in their methods of obtaining water. The salt in ocean water draws water out of the fish through its skin, so the fish needs to drink continuously. Freshwater fish, on the other hand, do not need to drink water because water is drawn into their bodies through their skin.
   a. simple listing
   b. contrast
   c. classification

_____ 6. In summary, dolphins are always awake and alert to danger. As stated previously, sleep occurs in cycles. For eight hours a dolphin is totally awake, for eight hours the left hemisphere of the brain sleeps, and for the next eight hours the right hemisphere sleeps.
   a. summary
   b. addition
   c. spatial order

_____ 7. Furthermore, vaporization makes beeswax candles dripless and smokeless. Moreover, the high melting point makes them burn brighter and longer.
   a. definition
   b. generalization
   c. addition

_____ 8. With the emergence of coffee shops on every corner, café latte and cappuccino have grown in popularity. Both are made from dark roasted espresso beans in a similar brewing process. Likewise, both are enhanced by the addition of warm milk.
   a. summary
   b. comparison
   c. addition

_____ 9. "Flying the hump" meant flying supplies to China across the dangerous Himalayan Mountains. The United States lost more than 600 transport planes in the 3.5 years of flying this route during World War II.
   a. description
   b. time order
   c. definition

_____ 10. A single float in the Rose Parade uses an amazing number of flowers. This number ranges from 30,000 to 150,000. To illustrate the magnitude, that is more flowers than the average florist uses in five years.
   a. generalization and example
   b. comparison
   c. summary

6
Org.
Patt.

Practice 2

Read the following paragraphs and identify the dominant pattern of organization used by the author. Select from the following list:

simple listing	classification	definition	description
time order	comparison-contrast	cause and effect	

1. Cinco de Mayo is a holiday celebrated on May 5 each year by Mexicans and Mexican Americans. It commemorates the 1862 victory of Mexico over France at the Battle of Puebla. *Cinco de Mayo* is Spanish for "Fifth of May."

   Organizational pattern: _____

2. *Delicious* apples have a solid, dark-red color and an oval shape with five knobs on the bottom. On the other hand, the *Granny Smith* variety of apples is bright green. Like *Delicious* apples, *Granny Smith* apples are medium to large in size; however, they have a round shape as opposed to oval.

   Organizational pattern: _____

3. Fully developed jazz music originated in New Orleans at the beginning of the 1900s and has since taken on many sophisticated forms. Swing and the boogie-woogie styles of jazz emerged in the 1930s, followed by bebop and cool jazz in the 1940s. Next, hard bop, or funky jazz, became popular in the 1950s, followed by fusion in the 1970s. Finally, during the late 1900s, many young musicians returned to historical styles, including swing and bebop.

   Organizational pattern: _____

4. College basketball teams compete with one another based upon common associations, divisions, and conferences. Most colleges, including Duke and Georgetown, belong to the National Collegiate Athletic Association, while smaller colleges, such as Concordia and Houston Baptist, belong to the National Association of Intercollegiate Athletics. Schools with the largest enrollments compete in Division I, with smaller schools competing in Division II or III. Finally, teams compete within conferences based upon geographic location. There are more than 100 conferences, including the Big East, Big Sky, and Sun Belt conferences.

   Organizational pattern: _____

5. Embarrassing bad breath can have several different causes. A serious cause is that bad breath can be a symptom of diabetes, a kidney disorder, or a sinus infection. Another cause is foods such as onions and garlic that have oils that get into the blood and then the lungs, which exhale odors with each breath. Most commonly,

however, the cause is food molecules rotting in the mouth; they can be treated by brushing, flossing, and cleaning bacteria from the tongue. At night, salivation shuts down and does not flush away microscopic bits of food.

Organizational pattern: _____

6. Optimists tend to be better able to cope with stress than pessimists, an ability that may reduce their risk of illness. Optimistic people expect positive outcomes, and that helps them be more stress-resistant. Pessimists, on the other hand, often feel a sense of hope-lessness. A study of men from Finland revealed that those who reported moderate to high feelings of hopelessness died at two to three times the rates of those reporting low or no hopelessness.

Organizational pattern: _____

7. The craigslist Web site was started by Criag Newmark of San Francisco as a community service. Now more than 2 billion people view the Web site each day. On craigslist you can find apartments for rent, sell items, and even locate missing relatives. It is estimated that this privately held company has already cost California newspapers as much as $65 million per year in classified advertising revenue

Organizational pattern: _____

8. WD-40 was originally invented to prevent rust and corrosion on Atlas missiles. Surprisingly, WD-40 has many uses that were never envisioned by its inventors, who made forty attempts at creating the final product. Most of us know that WD-40 will protect tools from rust, quiet squeaky hinges, and free stuck doors, bolts, and zippers. (Try using the product to remove those sticky price labels from glass.) It will also loosen bubble gum from hair and carpets. In addi-tion, one teacher reports that she successfully used it to clean old chalk boards in the classroom and make them shine

Organizational pattern: _____

9. Consumer attitudes have sparked a new thrust in marketing called *green marketing*. This means that companies are trying to prevent pol-lution and operate in environmentally ways. These companies prac-tice the three R's of waste management, which are reducing, reusing, and recycling. For example, McDonald's napkins and carry-out drink trays are made from recycled paper; just making its drinking straws 20 percent lighter saves a million pounds of waste per year.

Organizational pattern: _____

10. Because of the advances in technology in the 1980s and 1990s, America has become an instant society. With news coverage on CNN or FOX for twenty-four hours a day, viewers no longer need to wait for the nightly news. Why worry while waiting for a friend when you can dial your friend's cell phone for a progress report? Who waits for the mail when you can send messages and documents by e-mail? As a consequence of this technology, people in the United States now become irritated at having to wait. We depend on instant information and expect instant results.

Organizational pattern: _____

6b How Do Transitional Words Signal Organizational Patterns?

Single words can signal levels of importance, connections, and the direction of thoughts. For example, when a friend begins a sentence with "I like you very much," would you prefer that the next word be *also* or *however?* The word *also* signals more of the same, hinting that you could anticipate another pleasant compliment. On the other hand, *however* signals a change of thought, so brace yourself for a negative remark. If instead the next word were *consequently* or *therefore,* you could anticipate a positive result or reward for the positive feelings.

Such words are **transitions** or signal words, that connect parts of sentences and lead readers to anticipate continuation or change in the writer's thoughts. They are the same signal words that suggest patterns of organization and they are categorized as follows:

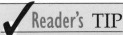 Reader's TIP

Condensed Signal Word Review for Transition

- Signal **Addition:** in addition, furthermore, moreover
- Signal **Examples:** for example, for instance, to illustrate, such as
- Signal **Time:** first, second, finally, last, afterward
- Signal **Comparison:** similarly, likewise, in the same manner
- Signal **Contrast:** however, but, nevertheless, whereas, on the contrary, conversely, in contrast
- Signal **Cause and Effect:** thus, consequently, therefore, as a result

Practice 3

Choose a signal word or phrase from the lists to complete the sentences that follow.

however	consequently	for example	likewise	furthermore

1. Betty Shabazz, the widow of Malcolm X, recognized the value of a college education; _____, she returned to college to earn a doctorate and become a college teacher and administrator.

2. Anthropologists must be persistent. _____, Louis and Mary Leakey initially found primitive tools in Olduvai Gorge, but it was 28 years later that Mary discovered the first skull.

3. His real name was Samuel Langhorne Clemens; _____, millions know him as Mark Twain.

4. Some of the brightest dogs to teach are German shepherds. _____, border collies, poodles, and golden retrievers are equally intelligent and can learn new tasks after five repetitions.

5. People enjoy eating rare steaks. _____, some people use raw steak to cover an open wound, as did the ancient Egyptians.

nevertheless	therefore	in this case	similarly	moreover

6. Some vitamins act as antioxidants, which means they neutralize free radicals and _____ reduce the risk of cancer.

7. Despite the benefits of antioxidants, new research _____ shows a danger in their use because some minerals in multivitamins cause vitamin C to be released as a free radical.

8. Additional research on vitamins should be done. _____, doctors should be cautious in recommending vitamins that may not be needed.

9. The death was attributed to botulism. _____, the poison was traced to a swollen can of food that should have been discarded.

10. Freshman composition is a required course; _____, a study skills seminar is also required.

on the contrary	for this reason	second
to illustrate	by the same token	

11. A cut in the skin breaks the protective covering around the body

    and _____ a cut can be dangerous.

12. To give CPR, first lift the neck and tilt the chin upward to open the

    airway. _____, check for breathing by holding your
    ear to the victim's mouth.

13. Dogs can be conditioned to respond with saliva to smell.

    _____, humans will sometimes salivate when
    smelling cookies baking.

14. An elephant's trunk has more than 40,000 muscles and is super-

    sensitive. _____ this sensitivity, an elephant can pick
    up a small coin with its trunk.

15. The invention of the pizza was not a frivolous one.

    _____, this first flat bread served as both a plate for
    food and a utensil to sop up gravies.

| for example | afterward | such as | as a result | however |

16. A new research study has found that insufficient sleep causes an
    increase in a hormone that tells your brain that you are hungry.

    _____ of this imbalance, overeating and weight gain
    are more likely to occur.

17. Brianna hastily refused a date with Robert when he asked her out

    but, _____, had second thoughts.

18. E-bay can be a resource for ridding yourself of unwanted goods.

    You must, _____, take precautions to safeguard
    against fraud whether you are buying or selling.

19. E-bay buyers, _____, need to be sure that what they
    are buying is authenic, and sellers need to be careful that stolen
    credit cards are not used to purchase their goods.

20. Since childhood obesity has become a major health concern in the
    United States, it has triggered concern for other health problems

    among children _____ diabetes and heart disease.

6
Org.
Patt.

Small-Group EXPLORATION

Form a five-member group and select one of the following questions. Brainstorm and then outline your major points on a transparency. Choose a group member to present the group's findings to the class. Individual assignments can also be made.

- Why are some people better than other at following complicated directions for assembling equipment such as an exercise machine or a bicycle?

- What type of career opportunities would be most appropriate for people who like to focus on main ideas and for those who enjoy details?

- Compare the strategies needed for successful learning in history and psychology.

- Contrast the strategies needed for successful learning in literature and mathematics.

- Create introductory sentences for five paragraphs in which the details would be organized in each of the following patterns: simple listing, definition, description, time order or sequence, and comparison-contrast.

- Create introductory sentences for four paragraphs in which the details would be organized in each of the following patterns: cause and effect, narration, argument, process.

Net SEARCH

Find information on the Internet so that you can compare or contrast the following topics. Write a brief summary, using transitional words to guide your reader.

Canon and Nikon Digital Cameras

Scientology and Christianity

Chapter 7

Inference

7a What Is an Inference?

An **inference** is a meaning that is suggested rather than directly stated. Inferences are implied through clues that lead you to make assumptions and draw conclusions. For example, instead of making the direct statement "These people are rich and influential," an author could imply that idea by describing an expansive mansion and well-connected friends. The phrase "reading between the lines" means understanding an inference because a *suggestion,* rather than a direct statement, conveys the meaning. For example, what is implied financially in "The shopper used plastic to continue her 'Party now, pay later' downward spiral"? The speaker is sarcastically implying that the shopper does not have the money to pay for purchases and is steadily accumulating credit card debt. To avoid confusing the terms, remember the following:

Infer: To conclude   **Inference:** A conclusion

Imply: To suggest   **Implication:** A suggestion

Recognize Inferences in Advertising

Inference can be a powerful advertising tool. In cigarette ads the public is enticed through suggestion, rather than fact, into spending millions of dollars on a product that is known and explicitly stated to be unhealthful. Depending on the brand, the act of smoking would offer the refreshment of a mountain stream, the independence of a cowboy, or the sophisticated elegance of the urban rich. In the ads, smoking is never directly praised nor is pleasure promised; instead, the positive aspects are *implied.* The emotionalism of the full-page advertisement is so seductive that consumers hardly notice the words peeking from the bottom of the page: "Warning: The Surgeon General Has Determined That Cigarette Smoking Is Dangerous to Your Health." A cigarette ad would appear here as an example, but tobacco companies no longer grant copyright permission for such use. Do you wonder why? What inference have the companies figured out?

Practice 1

Examine the following advertisement, note the implied meaning, and answer the questions.

1. What is directly stated about the product?

_____

2. What is the product and how is it usually viewed?

_____

_____

3. What two images are used in the advertisement to suggest lightness?

_____

4. What does the ad suggest about the product?

_____

_____

5. Who seems to be the potential customer for the product?

_____

_____

Recognize Inferences in Paragraphs

Authors and advertisers have not invented a new comprehension skill; they are merely capitalizing on an already highly developed skill of daily life. Suppose you have a part-time job off campus. When a coworker asks, "How do you like your boss?" you might answer, "I think she wears nice suits" rather than "I don't like my boss." You avoided making a direct negative statement, but you suggested disapproval by what was left unsaid. In everyday life, we make inferences about people by examining what people say, what they do not say, what they do, and what others say about them. The intuition of everyday life applied to the printed word is the *interpretive* level of reading.

7
Inf.

Practice 2

Read the following passage and mark each inference statement as *T* (true) or *F* (false).

On the morning of December 12, 1799, George Washington, our foremost Founding Father, rode his horse into a driving sleet storm to oversee the daily chores of his farms. Five hours later he arrived back home at Mount Vernon soaked. Rather than take the time to change clothes, Washington politely went straight to greet his waiting dinner guests in saturated clothes. The next day he went out again in bad weather to mark some trees for cutting. That night he had trouble breathing, and doctors were called. The eager but unknowing doctors bled him by slitting his wrists and draining a pint of blood every hour. They blistered his throat with scorching hot cloths to remove infection. Washington died on December 14 of what modern doctors now believe to have been an abscess on his tonsils or epiglottitis, an inflammation at the entrance of the larynx. Both would have responded well to antibiotics.

_____ **1.** The author implies that it was critical that Washington check his farms on December 12.

_____ **2.** Washington was a man who liked to stick to his established schedule.

_____ **3.** The author implies that the marked trees were to be cut on December 14.

_____ **4.** The author implies that Washington did not change clothes because he did not want to inconvenience his dinner guests.

_____ **5.** The bleeding and scorching by the doctors were most likely the foremost remedies of the day.

_____ **6.** The author implies that if Washington had the same illness today, he could be successfully treated with a few pills.

Recognize Inferences in Humor

Jokes and cartoons require you to "read between the lines" and make a connection. They are funny because of what is unstated rather than what is stated. When listeners catch on to a joke, that means they have made the connection and recognized the unstated inference.

EXAMPLE   What inference makes the following joke funny?
Question: How many politicians does it take to change a lightbulb?
Answer: None. They only promise change.

EXPLANATION   The inference is that politicians make lots of promises to voters that they do not keep.

7
Inf.

Practice 3

Explain the inferences that make the following jokes funny.

Joke 1
"I never eat food with additives or preservatives," boasted a health fanatic. "And I never touch anything that's been sprayed or fed chemical grain."
"Wow, that's wonderful," her friend marveled. "How do you feel?"
"Hungry," she moaned.

—S. Bader in *Laughter, the Best Medicine*

Inference: _____

_____

Joke 2

An excited woman called her husband at work. "I won the lottery!" she exclaimed. "Pack your clothes!"

"Great!" he replied. "Summer or winter clothes?"

"All of them—I want you out of the house by six!"

—Ashley Cooper in *Laughter, the Best Medicine*

Inference: _____

_____

Joke 3

There's a new garlic diet around. You don't lose weight, but you look thinner from a distance.

—Red Shea in *Laughter, the Best Medicine*

Inference: _____

_____

Practice 4

Explain the inferences that make the following cartoons funny.

Cartoon I

"Yes, Mrs. Winslow, I *know* you tried to keep him away from school!"

7
Inf.

Inference: _____

_____

_____

Cartoon 2

THE FAR SIDE®   By GARY LARSON

© 1981 FarWorks, Inc. All Rights Reserved/Dist. by Creators Syndicate

"Don't be alarmed, folks—he's completely harmless unless something startles him."

Inference: _____

_____

Connect with Prior Knowledge

Like cartoonists and stand-up comics, authors use inferences that require you to link prior knowledge to what you are currently reading or hearing. Suppose that you are telling a joke. If your listener does not share the background knowledge to which the joke refers, your attempt at comedy will fall flat because he or she will not understand the implied meaning. Listeners cannot connect with something they don't know about, so you must choose the right joke for the right audience. Similarly, authors give implied meaning clues that may draw on an assumed knowledge of history, current issues, or social concerns.

In college reading, **prior knowledge** is expected and specifics are frequently implied rather than directly stated. For example, if a sentence began, "Just as Ali held the torch over his head before lighting the Olympic flame," you would probably know that "Ali" refers to Muhammad Ali, the former world heavyweight boxing champion who carried the torch to light the flame in the opening ceremonies of the 1996 Olympic Games in Atlanta. The specifics are not directly stated, but you use prior knowledge to "add up" the details that are meaningful to you to infer time and place.

Practice 5

Read the passages and then indicate *a*, *b*, or *c* to answer the questions that follow.

Passage I

The President announced the preliminary Emancipation Proclamation five days after one of the bloodiest encounters of the war, the Battle of Antietam. The Proclamation, which allowed slavery to continue in the four Union border states, caused widely differing reactions. Democrats in Congress wanted to impeach the President, Republicans worried about losing upcoming elections, and abolitionists and female activists criticized the President for not completely ending slavery.

7
Inf.

_____ **1.** The name of the U.S. President who issued the Emancipation Proclamation is
    a. Washington
    b. Johnson
    c. Lincoln

_____ **2.** The war to which the passage refers is the
    a. American Revolution
    b. Civil War
    c. Spanish-American War

    3. Underline the clues to your answers.

Passage 2

In terms of social change and upheaval, it was one of the most turbulent decades of the century. Protests against the Vietnam War turned neighbor against neighbor. In a single year both Martin Luther King, Jr., and Robert Kennedy were killed by assassins' bullets. Even in the arts, audiences were polarized by the shock of nudity in the Broadway production of *Hair*, as well as the association of drugs, "free love," and rock music. At the end of the decade, however, time stood still for one brief moment as people united to listen to Neil Armstrong say, "That's one small step for man, one giant leap for mankind."

_____ 1. The decade referred to is the
  a. 1920s
  b. 1940s
  c. 1960s

_____ 2. Neil Armstrong spoke the words quoted in the passage when
  a. he first stepped onto the surface of the moon
  b. Martin Luther King, Jr., was buried
  c. the Vietnam War ended

3. Underline the clues to your answers.

Passage 3

During the cruel winter, half of the Pilgrims died. Squanto, who now spoke halting English, agreed to stay and help them. He showed the Pilgrims how to grow corn, catch fish, and store food for the next winter. In the fall they celebrated the abundance with a feast of Thanksgiving.

_____ 1. The time is the
  a. 1490s
  b. 1620s
  c. 1770s

_____ 2. The place is
  a. New York
  b. Virginia
  c. New England

3. Underline the clues to your answers.

Passage 4

A few months after the carpenter James W. Marshall found a bright yellow mineral near a sawmill on John Sutter's ranch, the story broke in the San Francisco newspaper. Word spread and the rush was on. Within a year the state's population grew from 14,000 to over 100,000.

_____ 1. The state is
  a. California
  b. Nevada
  c. Colorado

_____ 2. The mineral was
  a. copper
  b. gold
  c. silver

3. Underline the clues to your answers.

7
Inf.

Passage 5

In the 1975 Stephen Spielberg film *Jaws*, Captain Quint describes the reason for his great hatred of sharks. He tells the story of the real-life sinking of the USS *Indianapolis* during the war. The vessel was on a secret mission returning from Guam after delivering parts of the bomb that would be dropped on Hiroshima. Because of the nature of the mission, the ship was not in radio communication. When it was attacked, an estimated 800 to 850 sailors successfully abandoned ship. Their real nightmare began, however, when thousands of sharks circled and relentlessly attacked the floating sailors until only 316 were finally rescued on August 2, 1945.[1]

_____ 1. The war mentioned was
   a. World War I.
   b. World War II.
   c. Iraq War.

_____ 2. The enemy submarine that torpedoed the ship was commanded by the
   a. Vietnamese.
   b. Japanese.
   c. Chinese.

3. Underline the clues to your answers.

Passage 6

In the second round of the semifinals, Duke advanced by beating Mississippi State, 63 to 55. Earlier the same day, Utah won over Oklahoma, 67 to 58. If these two winning teams are victorious on the court again tonight, they will play each other on Friday to decide who goes to the NCAA Final Four.

_____ 1. The playoff games are in the sport of
   a. basketball.
   b. baseball.
   c. football.

_____ 2. This tournament is regularly played in
   a. September and October.
   b. May and June.
   c. March and April.

3. Underline the clues to your answers.

Your responses on these passages depend on your own knowledge of history and on your general knowledge. If you did not understand some of the references and inferences, you might ask *How can I expand my prior knowledge?* The answer is not an easy formula or a quick fix; it is a matter of broadening your horizons by reading more widely and participating actively in the world around you.

_____
[1]Adapted from *www.history.navy.mil/photos/sh-usn/usnsh-i/ca35.htm*

Recognize Slanted Language

Writers choose words to manipulate the reader and thus to control the reader's attitude toward a subject. Such words are referred to as having a particular *connotation,* or slant. The dictionary definition of a word is its **denotation,** and the feeling or emotion surrounding a word is its **connotation.** For example, a real estate agent showing a run-down house to a prospective buyer would refer to the house's condition as *neglected* rather than *deteriorated.* Although both words mean "run down," *neglected* sounds as if a few things have been ignored or forgotten, whereas *deteriorated* sounds as if the place is falling apart and rotting away.

In our society, some words seem automatically to have a positive or negative slant. The words *socialist, cult member,* and *welfare state* have a negative emotional effect on many people, while the words *the American worker, democracy,* and *everyday people* tend to have a positive effect. The overall result of using slanted language is to shift the reader's attitude toward the author's own positive or negative point of view.

Practice 6

Label the following phrases as either *P* (slanted positively) or *N* (slanted negatively).

_____ 1. a ruthless corporate manager

_____ 2. family folks of rural America

_____ 3. freedom of the press

_____ 4. honest and open dialogue

_____ 5. questionable contracting procedures

_____ 6. nationwide volunteerism

_____ 7. legitimate licensing requirements

_____ 8. the chatterbox next door

_____ 9. responsible recycling

_____ 10. safeguarding greenspace

7
Inf.

7b What Is Figurative Language?

Most of us are familiar with the phrase "raining cats and dogs." When you hear someone say this, do you imagine a heavy rain or animals falling from the sky? With **figurative language,** words are intentionally used out of their usual context so that they take on new meaning. When words are combined in this way, fresh images are created to make a concept come alive or to clarify meaning. The "cats and dogs" comparison creates an exaggerated humorous effect, but on a literal level it does not make sense. As you can imagine, new speakers of English can be confused by a literal translation of figurative language.

The purpose of using figurative language is to enrich the message with visual images and to spark the imagination. Among the types of figurative language that you will encounter in your reading are similes, metaphors, personification, idioms, and irony.

Simile

A **simile** is a comparison of two unlike things, using the word *like* or *as*. Similes usually add to the characteristics of a noun or verb. In the sentence "His words were like knives to my heart," the simile describes the words as cutting and hurtful. The image produced by the simile adds intensity, danger, and excitement to the message.

Practice 7

Write the meaning of the boldface similes in the following sentences.

1. The petals dropped **like softly falling snowflakes.**

   _____

2. Suddenly the market was **as still as the eye of a hurricane.**

   _____

3. Uncle Bob's spirit drooped **like a hound dog that couldn't hunt.**

   _____

4. For the first hour of the party she felt **like driftwood floating in mid-ocean.**

   _____

5. Aunt Mary was stretched out on the sofa **like a kitten in warm sunshine.**

   _____

7
Inf.

Metaphor

A **metaphor** is a direct comparison of two unlike things that does not use the word *like* or *as*. A metaphor and a simile can communicate the same idea; they are differentiated only by the presence or absence of *like* or *as*. For example, an earlier example of a simile could be converted to a metaphor by omitting *like*: "His words were knives to my heart." The message is the same, but here the comparison is directly stated. Shakespeare used a similar metaphor in *Hamlet* when he wrote, "I will speak daggers to her."

Both metaphors and similes tend toward **hyperbole,** which is an overstatement or exaggeration for greater dramatic effect. For example, comparing a swimming pool to Lake Michigan would be hyperbolic, but it could also be a simile or a metaphor.

Practice 8

Write the meaning of the boldface metaphors in the following sentences.

1. **My worries were weights** from which I could not escape.

   _____

2. **Monday was D Day** for the corporate proposal.

   _____

3. **Juan had become the heart and soul** of the team.

   _____

4. **Her faith was the blanket** that protected her mind.

   _____

5. At the sound of an error, the **music director became a predatory bird.**

   _____

Personification

Personification is attributing human characteristics to nonhuman things. Personification can create a mood.

Practice 9

Write the meaning, mood, or feeling that the boldface personification adds to the message in the following sentences.

1. The **living room ached for** a decorator's touch.

   _____

2. The **car screamed** down the straightaway at 125 miles per hour.

   _____

3. **Your heart will sing and dance** when you read the message.

   _____

4. The money cried to be spent on clothes.

_____

5. The bicycles nudged the pedestrians off the trail.

_____

Idiom

Idioms are expressions that have taken on a generally accepted meaning over many years of use but do not make sense on a literal level. Idioms can be similes and metaphors. For example, "sleep like a log" is both a simile and an idiom because it is an accepted and often-used expression that is not literally true. In fact, "sleep like a log" has been so overused in our language that it has become a **cliché,** an overworked phrase that should be avoided in formal writing. Idioms can be slang expressions that add zest to our conversations but should not be used in academic writing.

Practice 10

Explain the meaning of the idioms in the following sentences.

1. No man is an island.

_____

2. We can get in on the ground floor.

_____

3. Cross that bridge when you come to it.

_____

4. Keep your nose to the grindstone.

_____

5. Please keep that under your hat.

_____

Irony

Verbal irony is the use of words to express a meaning that is the opposite of what is said literally. In other words, it is saying one thing and suggesting another. If the intent is to ridicule, the irony can also be called _sarcasm._ Recognizing that a speaker does not literally mean what was said can be challenging, and the reader can sometimes be tricked.

In **situational irony,** events occur that are contrary to what was expected, as if in a cruel twist of fate. For example, Juliet awakens to find

7
Inf.

that Romeo has killed himself because he thought she was dead. The following verse, written before child labor laws, illustrates both verbal and situational irony:

> The golf links lie so near the mill
> That almost every day
> The laboring children can look out
> And see the men at play.
>
> —Sarah N. Cleghorn, "The Golf Links."

While the words *laboring* and *play* seem to apply to the wrong groups of people, the message of the poem is serious.

Practice 11

Complete the story in each of the following sentences by choosing the response that best shows irony.

_____ 1. He knew he had to take control and face the day. It was now or never, so he
   a. raised his hand to volunteer.
   b. hit the alarm's snooze button and went back to sleep.
   c. read the next chapter.
   d. closed his eyes and took one step forward.

_____ 2. While students were enjoying the International Club Party she had worked so hard to plan, Veronica
   a. talked to her friends.
   b. thought she deserved to be thanked for all her efforts.
   c. stayed home to study for a Spanish exam that was assigned at the last minute.
   d. thought it could not have turned out better.

_____ 3. As the river rose higher and higher,
   a. neighbors piled sandbags to protect the house.
   b. police evacuated the neighborhood.
   c. the Johnsons started to panic.
   d. Teddy wished he had never sold his houseboat and moved inland.

_____ 4. After adopting two children, the couple
   a. were satisfied with their family.
   b. had twins.
   c. supported international adoption groups.
   d. saved money for the children's education.

_____ **5.** After she had refused a job with Microsoft, her employer
   a. went on the New York Stock Exchange.
   b. was purchased by a foreign investor.
   c. posted higher annual earnings than IBM.
   d. was bought up by Microsoft.

Term	Definition	Example
Simile	A comparison of two unlike things using *like* or *as*	His words were *like* knives to my heart.
Metaphor	A comparison of two unlike things without using *like* or *as*	His words were knives to my heart.
Hyperbole	An exaggeration	A thousand knives pierced my heart when he told me he was leaving.
Personification	Giving human characteristics to nonhuman things	His words of farewell pounded a thousand nails in my heart.
Idiom	Expressions with accepted meanings but that do not make sense on a literal level	My nephew looks as if he grew a foot between Christmas and New Year's Day.
Cliché	An overworked phrase	I've been sleeping like a log.
Verbal Irony	The use of words to express the opposite of the literal meaning.	Mark Twain once remarked that he was embarrassed by the praise he received: "They never said enough."
Situational Irony	Events occurr that are contrary to what was expected	In "The Ransom of Red Chief," by O. Henry, the kidnappers finally offer money to the parents of the hyperactive child they abducted because they cannot handle him.

7
Inf.

7c How Do You Recognize Implied Meaning?

Reading would be rather dull if the author stated every idea, never giving you a chance to figure things out for yourself. In a mystery novel, for example, you take pleasure in carefully weighing each word, action, conversation, description, and fact in an effort to identify the villain and solve the crime before the revelation at the end.

Use your already highly developed inferential skills, those you have built up through everyday life, to interpret implied meaning.

✔ **Reader's** TIP

Recognizing Implied Meaning

■ Consider attitude in the choice of words.

■ Unravel actions.

■ Interpret motives.

■ Use suggested meaning and facts to make assumptions.

■ Draw on prior knowledge to make connections.

■ Base conclusions on stated ideas and unstated assumptions.

EXAMPLE Note the inferences and label the following statements *T* (true) or *F* (false).

> Immigrants to the United States from the Dominican Republic have sometimes been called the "invisible" Latinos because they have not established an identity as distinct as those of Mexican Americans, Puerto Ricans, or Cuban Americans. Their ancestry is a mixture of both African and Spanish heritage, and their cuisine is distinctive and delicious. Dominican restaurant operators in New York City, however, call their food Spanish-American so as not to drive away customers who are unfamiliar with Dominican recipes. The satisfied patrons leave these restaurants thinking they have enjoyed the dishes of a Cuban or Puerto Rican chef, and the Dominican-American talent remains unrecognized.

_____ 1. The author suggests that Dominican Americans suffer job discrimination.

_____ 2. Dominican restaurant operators feel that many New Yorkers would not choose to eat at a Dominican restaurant.

_____ 3. After restaurant patrons have enjoyed the food, they are told that it was Dominican.

EXPLANATION The first sentence is false because there is no indication that Dominican Americans suffer job discrimination; however, they have not yet created an identifiable cultural niche for themselves. The second sentence is true because Dominicans label their food as Spanish-American. The third sentence is false because patrons leave thinking the food was Cuban or Puerto Rican.

Practice 12

Read the following passages and identify the suggested inferences as *T* (true) or *F* (false).

7
Inf.

Passage 1

At about the same time that the Nineteenth Amendment to the Constitution was passed in 1920, a "sexual revolution" of sorts was happening, most often represented by the "flapper," who smoked and drank publicly, wore dresses above her knees, wore bright makeup, and danced the Charleston. Ironically, even with this increased social freedom and new political opportunity to vote, women's roles changed very little. Generally speaking, women did not become a powerful political force, job opportunities did not change, and women's working wages continued to be lower than those for men. Most women worked after they left their parents' homes, then quit when they got married. It was as if women had been given the tools to work toward equality, but they did not learn how to use them until many, many years later.

_____ 1. The Nineteenth Amendment gave women the right to vote.

_____ 2. The public behavior of flappers in the 1920s undermined the political power of women.

_____ 3. The author implies that prior to the 1920s women did not smoke publicly.

_____ 4. The author implies that economic change was slow in coming for women.

_____ 5. The author implies that men were responsible for the slow progress toward equality for women.

Passage 2

To view the exotic animals and birds of the Costa Rican tropical rain forest, sign up for a canopy tour. You will stand on 100-foot platforms built in the uppermost branching layers of the trees where two-thirds of the forest species live. On some tours you can stroll misty skywalks that connect forest paths, suspension bridges, and viewing platforms. For a more adventurous tour, you can be lifted to the first platform in a climbing harness and then comfortably glide along a wire propelled by pulleys to the next treetop platform. Begin your trip in the Monteverde Cloud Forest, sometimes called "crowd forest," by climbing to the first platform through the hollowed-out interior of a giant strangler fig tree.

_____ 1. The strangler fig tree in the Monteverde Cloud Forest is dead.

_____ 2. Older tourists select the climbing harness so they do not need to walk.

_____ 3. The author feels that the Monteverde Cloud Forest is overcrowded.

_____ 4. The weather on the canopy tours is likely to be damp.

_____ 5. The tours are named for the dense, canopy-like cover of the treetops.

7
Inf.

Passage 3

A year after 4 million New Yorkers cheered Charles Lindbergh's achievement, Amelia Earhart became the first woman to fly across the Atlantic Ocean alone. Rather than follow his route to Paris, Earhart departed from Newfoundland and landed in Wales in 1928. She enjoyed acclaim and continued to break records. In 1937 Earhart and navigator Fred Noonan left Miami to fly around the world along the Equator. After stops in Brazil, Africa, Asia, and New Guinea, Earhart began the 2,600-mile flight to a small Pacific island. Earhart's last radio message reported empty fuel tanks. No trace of the plane or crew has ever been discovered.

_____ 1. The author suggests that Earhart was honored by a large New York parade.

_____ 2. Charles Lindbergh was the first man to fly across the Atlantic alone.

_____ 3. In her attempt to fly around the world, Earhart flew from west to east.

_____ 4. The author suggests that Earhart most likely crashed into the Pacific island.

_____ 5. Lindbergh's historic solo flight was in 1927.

Passage 4

The Roman Empire needed soldiers to leave home and fight in the territories. To meet the demand for troops, the mad emperor Claudius II forbade marriage. Young lovers, however, would secretly go to the Christian bishop Valentine to be wed. When Claudius discovered this, he put Valentine in prison after the bishop would not convert to paganism. While awaiting his fate, Valentine and the blind daughter of the jailer fell in love. On the day of his execution, February 14, the bishop left his love a farewell note signed "Your Valentine."

_____ 1. The author suggests that the Christian bishop's story is the origin of Valentine's day.

_____ 2. Claudius felt that married men were more reluctant to leave home to fight.

_____ 3. Claudius was a popular emperor with the Roman people.

_____ 4. The author suggests that the young lovers wed by Valentine were also punished.

_____ 5. Claudius was a pagan.

Passage 5

Although you may not have read this in school, medieval warfare was not a male-only activity. The men in battle were aided by a group of captive laundresses who were an essential part of every campaign. Aside from the infidels, body parasites and infection were serious enemies in the holy wars for fighting men who wore thirty to sixty pounds of padded armor. Delousing was a necessity, and soap and water were in demand.

_____ 1. The contributions of the washerwomen in the Crusades are not usually mentioned in history books.

_____ 2. The women washed for the Crusaders of their own free will.

_____ 3. The Crusaders fought the infidels in the holy wars.

_____ 4. Clean clothing helped keep the soldiers healthy.

_____ 5. Bathing with soap and water prevented the spread of lice.

Passage 6

Finally, a million and a half years after the cave chefs used fire for cooking, an absolutely new method of preparing food was introduced. This new magic, microwave cooking, has now evolved from the unique and expensive to the commonplace and reasonable. In the process, electromagnetic energy agitates the water molecules in food, thereby producing sufficient heat for cooking. The magnetron, the essential tube for creating microwaves, was invented by two scientists who were working to improve Britain's radar defense system against the Nazis in World War II. Six years later an engineer who was testing the magnetron tube noticed that the chocolate candy bar in his pocket had melted. Following his hunch, he brought popcorn and raw eggs into the laboratory the next day. He placed them within range of the microwaves, and both exploded under the pressure, cooking from the inside out. More research and several years later, the Tappan Company sold the first microwave oven for $1,295.

_____ 1. Microwave cooking does not use any form of fire.

_____ 2. The ability of microwaves to cook was discovered by accident.

_____ 3. Cooking on microwave ovens in Britain jammed Nazi radar and allowed British planes to fly undetected.

_____ 4. The popcorn in the laboratory exploded before it was cooked.

_____ 5. The price of microwave ovens has fallen over the years.

7d   How Do You Draw Conclusions?

To arrive at a conclusion, you must make a logical deduction from both stated and unstated ideas. Using the hints as well as the facts, you rely on prior knowledge and experience to interpret motives, actions, and outcomes. Because conclusions are drawn on the basis of perceived evidence, and because perceptions differ, conclusions can vary from reader to reader. Generally, however, the author attempts to direct you to a preconceived conclusion.

EXAMPLE Read the following paragraph, write a conclusion, then describe the basis for the stated conclusion.

In 1962, César Chávez decided to do the impossible—to establish a migrant farmworkers' union with a guaranteed right to organize, to earn a minimum wage, and to have safe work standards. At the time, migrant farmworkers averaged incomes of only $2,000 per year, and existing state laws requiring toilets, rest periods, and drinking water were not enforced. The union was formed, but trouble occurred in 1965 when a grape pickers' strike became irreconcilable and violent. To oppose the violence, Chávez went on a hunger strike that lasted 21 days, losing 35 pounds and endangering his own health. Finally a national boycott of table grapes forced growers to settle the dispute, which resulted in increased wages, improved working conditions, health care benefits, disability insurance, and pension plans.

Conclusion: César Chávez provided leadership in obtaining

workplace rights for a group of people who had previously been

ignored and exploited.

What is the basis for this conclusion?

EXPLANATION The farmworkers were exploited because of their low wages and the lack of toilets and drinking water in the fields. Chávez was the leader because he was the one who dreamed the impossible, and he drew national attention to the movement with his hunger strike.

Practice 13

Read each of the following passages and write your own conclusions, indicating the reasons for each conclusion.

Passage 1

Many words are used to describe people who try to make careers in the arts: *dreamers, kooks, creative, flaky, immature,* and sometimes *irresponsible*. Regular nine-to-five workers cannot understand why these dreamers continue to work as waiters, avoiding predictable and comfortable career paths. The aspiring writers, artists, actors, musicians, and dancers often wonder the same thing, but they fight to stay focused. They struggle to answer a "higher calling": an inescapable need to create, an urge to build something from nothing and to explore different possibilities of expression. Ideally, few will readily take the advice offered by the novelist William Styron when asked what he would tell would-be writers: "Stop if you can."

Conclusion: _____

_____

What is the basis for this conclusion?

_____

Passage 2

An unsuspecting AOL user in Santa Barbara, California, received an official-looking e-mail offering her a month's free service to make up for recent phone difficulties. She replied with her user name and password. The next week she was accused of sending pornography over the Internet. She had been faked out by a dishonest porn-site operator who used her AOL account to "bounce" his mailings. If you are a victim of such a hoax, report it to hoaxcheck@hoaxkill.com.

Conclusion: _____

_____

What is the basis for this conclusion?

_____

Passage 3

Should you reach for a tissue or a decongestant at the first signs of a nasty cold and a runny nose? Although nose blowing may seem essential, some research suggests that blowing shoots mucus up into the sinuses along with the viruses and bacteria that it carries. As a result, even after the cold is cured, you will be left with a sinus infection.

Conclusion: _____

_____

What is the basis for this conclusion?

_____

Passage 4

Proctor and his cousin Gamble produced a soap that would form a rich lather even in the cold water of rivers and murky creeks in which Civil War soldiers were bathing. Their popular soap, however, was destined for an accidental improvement. One day a factory worker overseeing soap production vats took a lunch break and forgot to turn off the mixing machine. Upon returning, he realized that too much air had been whipped into the solution. The resulting product was the first floating soap. Immediately the factory was swamped with orders for this remarkable soap that bathers said saved them money.

7
Inf.

Conclusion: _____

_____

What is the basis for this conclusion?

_____

_____

Passage 5

The bubonic plague still occurs, with the last threatening outbreak taking place in India in 1994. The first deadly plague epidemic occurred in Constantinople in 542. During the peak period, more than 10,000 people died each week. In 1346, a second plague spread across Europe and Asia. More than 1,000 villages in England became void of human life. The third and last major epidemic killed more than 12 million people in Manchuria in 1890.

Conclusion: _____

_____

What is the basis for this conclusion?

_____

_____

_____

Passage 6

To use the **door-in-the-face** technique, first ask a friend to lend you $100; after being turned down, ask to borrow $5. Your friend may be relieved to give you the smaller amount. It works best if there is little time between requests.[2]

Conclusion: _____

_____

_____

What is the basis for this conclusion?

_____

_____

_____

Passage 7

American men and women spend more than $5 billion a year on cosmetics and beauty treatments. Interestingly, in ancient Egypt in 4000 B.C.E the art of

---

[2]Lester A. Lefton and Linda Brannon, *Psychology*, 8th ed., p. 447.

makeup was in demand and beauty shops flourished. King Tut even stocked his tomb for the afterlife with skin creams, lip color, and fragrances. In 1500 B.C.E the Assyrians were obsessed with spending money on hairstyling, and in 157 C.E. the noted physician Galen treated the wealthy royal women of Rome with cold creams for cleansing and skin softening.

Conclusion: _____

_____

What is the basis for this conclusion?

_____

_____

Small-Group EXPLORATION

Form a five-member group and select one of the following activities. Brainstorm and then outline your major points on a transparency. Choose a group member to present the group's findings to the class. Individual assignments can also be made.

- Create a joke about a rival college in your area.
- Write a positive description of your college using slanted language, similes, and metaphors.
- Outline the plot for a murder mystery that has an ironic twist at the end.
- Write a veiled letter of recommendation for an employee who has not been a willing worker.

7
Inf.

Net SEARCH

Jokes are funny when an inference is shared. But a joke about college students may not be funny to those who have not attended college because they do not share the experience that relates to the joke's implied meaning. Visit three of the following joke sites and select a joke from each. Explain the implied meaning that makes each joke funny.

Tasteful and Funny Jokes
pauline.berkeley.edu/colton/jokes.html

Attorney Jokes
www.apc.net/ia/law.htm

Airline Jokes
www.winn.com/bs/airlines.html

Bachelor Jokes
www.winn.com/bs/bachelor.html

Pizza Jokes
www.winn.com/bs/pizza.html

College Degree Jokes
www.winn.com/bs/degrees.html

Chapter

8

Point of View

8a   What Is the Author's Point of View?

What if the required student activity fee at your college were suddenly and dramatically increased? An article about this issue written by one of your classmates would probably differ from one written by the college president. The student article would probably question or protest the fee increase, whereas the one written by the president would probably justify and promote it. The two authors would have different opinions or positions on the fee issue, and thus each would be writing from a different **point of view**.

EXAMPLE   Read the following passage and use the choice of words and supporting information to identify the author's point of view.

The electromagnetic energy transmitted each day by radio and television signals does not stay neatly contained within the Earth's atmosphere. Just as scientists on Earth study signals from distant stars, beings from other planets can intercept our broadcast waves and collect data. The Super Bowl may, in fact, be the most easily detected signal from our planet because it is beamed simultaneously from more transmitters than any other signal we generate. When investigating aliens decide to stop in for a visit, they will certainly be surprised not to find people wearing helmets and shoulder pads and trying to knock one another down.

What is the author's point of view? Underline clues that suggest your answer.

_____

_____

EXPLANATION The author believes that aliens are studying our planet and would be surprised to find that we do not all play football. This is not a typical point of view.

Practice 1

Read each group of passages and answer the questions that follow it.

Group 1

Passage 1

To lower cholesterol levels and prevent heart attacks, the American Heart Association (AHA) suggests eating no more than two eggs each week. A single egg has 215 mg of cholesterol, which is more than most other foods with the same number of calories. As the AHA recommends that your dietary cholesterol intake not exceed 300 mg per day, egg consumption leaves little room for other healthy proteins that also contain cholesterol. Enjoy an egg-white omelet and discard the cholesterol-filled yolks.

Passage 2

Because eggs are a high-quality protein and a good source of essential amino acids and other nutrients, Dr. Robert Atkins recommends eating two eggs each day. Eggs do not raise cholesterol levels; carbohydrates and sugars do. Egg yolks contain more vital carotenes than any other foods. In addition, the lutein and zeaxanthin in eggs can lower the risk of developing macular degeneration, the leading cause of blindness in people over 50. It is a joke to pay extra for a yolk-free omelet and be robbed of most of the egg's essential nutrients.

1. What is the point of view of each author?

_____

2. What authorities are cited in each passage?

_____

3. How would you describe the support for each point of view?

_____

4. What is your view on eating eggs?

_____

5. What other information would you want before deciding whether to eat two eggs per day or two eggs per week?

_____

Group 2

Passage 1

In the aftermath of September 11, 2001, Homeland Security officials continue to evaluate options for a national identification system. Some officials recommend using biometric identification technology. In this system, both your fingerprint and a retinal scan of your eye—two unique features—are recorded on an identification card such as your driver's license. When this card is presented for a security check, a computer scans your eye and finger to instantly verify a match to your identification card. With this technology, forgery is difficult, innocent citizens are protected, and authorities have help in finding people who might have terrorist ties.

Passage 2

Lawyers of the American Civil Liberties Union oppose biometric identification cards. They claim that such a system prohibits the exercise of personal freedom guaranteed under the Constitution. The computer checking system gives authorities the ability to track citizens and build a database of their movements. Government officials could pull up a computer file revealing the checks you cash, the movies you see, and the concerts you attend. According to the ACLU, the government has no right to track its citizens.

8
Pt. of
View

1. What is the point of view of each author?

_____

2. What authorities are mentioned in each passage?

_____

_____

3. How would you describe the support for each point of view?

_____

_____

4. What is your view on biometric identification?

_____

5. What other information would you want before deciding to accept or reject biometric identification?

_____

The terms _point of view_ and _bias_ are very similar and are sometimes used interchangeably. When facts are slanted—though not necessarily distorted—toward the author's personal beliefs, the written material is said to reflect the author's **bias.** Thus a bias, like a point of view, is simply an opinion or position on a subject. As commonly used, however, _bias_ has a negative connotation that suggests narrow-mindedness and prejudice, whereas _point of view_ connotes more thoughtfulness and openness. Perhaps you would refer to your own opinion as a point of view and to those of others, particularly when they disagree with you, as biases!

Recognizing the author's point of view is a major part of understanding what you read. Sophisticated readers seek to identify the beliefs of the author in order to know where he or she "is coming from." When the point of view is not directly stated, you must be sensitive to the author's choice of words, facts, and opinions to detect it.

Practice 2

8
Pt. of
View

Read the following passages and use the choice of words and supporting information to identify each author's point of view.

Passage 1
During "sweeps weeks," periods when television networks are competing for audience attention to attract advertisers, even local news shows unleash torrents of sensational stories to boost viewership as high as possible. What the public needs, however, is not news as distraction, celebrity entertainment, or movie promotion. What is needed is honest news, news that thoughtfully gives the important facts of the day without sensationalizing for ratings.

What is the author's point of view? Underline clues that suggest your answer.

_____

_____

Passage 2

Behind the wholesome, family-oriented characters of Mickey Mouse, Donald Duck, and Snow White operates a calculating, media-savvy marketing machine. The marketing of Walt Disney's classic animated movies on video is a prime example. The films are movies for kids, but marketing is not a kid's game. Videos are offered as "limited release" items to create demand. The same videos, however, are continually rereleased on a seven-year timetable, which is coincidentally the same time it takes a kid to grow out of Disney's target group. Thus, there is always a "fresh" video ready for a new toddler. Promotions that say "This title will not be available on video again" should add "at least not for another seven years." This formula is as magical as the Seven Dwarfs.

What is the author's point of view? Underline clues that suggest your answer.

_____

_____

8b   What Is the Reader's Point of View?

The opinions we have affect how open we are to accepting or rejecting what we read. If our beliefs are particularly strong, sometimes we refuse to hear what is said—or we hear something that is not said. For example, if you were reading that air pollution should not be a concern for most Americans, would you "tune in" or "tune out"?

As a reader, you need to recognize your own prejudices as well as those held by an author. Don't let your own biases interfere with your reading comprehension. Open your mind to understanding new opinions, and then, having considered them, decide whether to accept or reject them.

8
Pt. of
View

EXAMPLE Read the following passage twice, first from the point of view of a believer in global warming and then from the point of view of a nonbeliever, and answer the questions.

When it comes to global warming, two sides express an opinion. Is the Earth heating up or isn't it? As you know, the term _global warming_ refers to the process by which the Earth's atmosphere is warmed by the release of "greenhouse gases" from the burning of fossil fuels such as gas, oil, and coal. Those who disagree with the whole global warming theory say that the Earth is going through a natural cycle; for thousands of years the Earth has undergone cycles of heating and cooling, and we are now in a heating cycle. The opposition is against industrial development. Environmentalists point out that 2,000 scientists and more than 100 countries agree that the current warming is caused by human activity. <u>The average temperature in Alaska has risen 2 to 4 degrees, and Alaskan glaciers are melting at the rate of 23 cubic miles of water run off each year, which has caused sea levels to rise. Wouldn't it make sense to err on the safe side and explore alternative fuels?</u> With increased wealth in China and India, the number of gas-guzzling cars will climb from 800 million today to 3.25 billion by 2050. <u>Will New York City be under water by then?</u>

1. Does the author believe in the theory of global warming? Underline the clues suggesting your answer.

   _____

2. What is your view on global warning?

   _____

3. Reading this passage as someone who believes that global warning is a threat, what message is conveyed to you?

   _____

   _____

   _____

4. Read this passage as someone who believes that global warming is a hoax or a lie dreamed up by environmentalists and evaluate the facts about Alaska.

   _____

   _____

   _____

5. What main point is the author trying to convey?

   _____

   _____

8
Pt. of
View

EXPLANATION The author's point of view supports the environmentalists who think we should err on the safe side. The increase in the number of the world's cars and the flooding of New York City add a fear factor to the author's point of view. The melting in Alaska, however, could be support for either a natural heating cycle or global warming.

Practice 3

Read the following passages and answer the questions about point of view.

Passage 1

Animal welfare groups are outraged that authorities in Australia's Outback plan to shoot thousands of wild camels from helicopters. With no natural predators, the Australian camel population has been expanding by 11 percent each year and is now endangering productive farmland. The wild camels are grazing the land and drinking the limited water that is needed for raising sheep and cattle. Scientists estimate that as many as 500,000 wild camels are now roaming the Outback.

Animal welfare leaders argue that the aerial shootings would create an inhumane bloodbath. From the air, it is impossible to be sure that every animal is killed outright. Some animals may linger in pain. Originally introduced into Australia to transport much-needed supplies across the desert, these beasts of burden were replaced by trains and trucks, and now they will be slaughtered by sharpshooters from helicopters. Progress can be cruel to those who bore the first burdens to achieve it.

1. What is the author's view of killing the camels from helicopters? Underline clues in the passage to support your answers.

   _____

2. What is the view of the ranchers on the camel issue?

   _____

   _____

   _____

3. What is your view on the camel issue? What has influenced your view?

   _____

4. What is the main point that the author is trying to convey?

   _____

   _____

   _____

Passage 2

Politicians face angry voters when debating a statewide smoking ban. On one side are health issues and on the other are personal freedoms and liberties. Since smoking and nonsmoking areas in restaurants are already designated, why is further restriction needed? Surely the nonsmoking public can avoid secondhand smoke by avoiding the restaurants and bars that welcome smokers. The harm, however, is that many low-paid workers, especially in food services or small businesses, have limited job opportunities. They are forced to work on job sites that are unsafe because of daily exposure to smoke. Secondhand smoke contains 4,000 chemical compounds, and 60 of the compounds are known or suspected of causing cancer. Since state laws have been passed to protect construction and road crews, shouldn't laws also protect food servers and office workers? Cancer is a big price to pay for personal freedom.

1. What is the author's point of view on a statewide smoking ban? Underline clues in the passage to support your answer.

_____

_____

2. What is your view on the states interfering with personal freedom and liberties?

_____

3. What is your view on a statewide smoking ban?

_____

4. What main point is the author trying to convey?

_____

_____

Passage 3

The women were beaten with clubs by the forty prison guards. By the end of the night the thirty-three women were barely alive. They beat Lucy Burn and left her hanging for the night with her hands chained to the cell bars over her head. They smashed Dora Lewis's head against an iron bed and knocked her unconscious. Alice Cosu suffered a heart attack because she thought Lewis was dead. This horror began on November 15, 1917, with the imprisonment of innocent women who were wrongly convicted of "obstructing sidewalk traffic." The warden at Occoquan Workhouse in Virginia ordered his guards to teach the suffragists a lesson because they dared to picket Woodrow Wilson's White House for the right to vote.

For weeks, the women drank dirty water from an open pail. Their food was infested with worms. Alice Paul, one of the leaders, went on a hunger strike. A tube was forced down her throat and liquid was poured into it until she vomited. This torture went on for weeks until word got out to the press. The HBO movie *Iron Jawed Angels* shows the courage and conflict of these brave women who struggled for the right of women to vote. If you are one of those lazy Americans who doesn't have the time or finds it inconvenient to vote, purchase a DVD of the film and watch it before voting day.

8
Pt. of
View

1. What is the author's view of people who do not vote? Underline clues in the passage to support your answer.

_____

_____

2. At the beginning of the passage, where did you think these actions were occurring? Why? At what point did you figure out that it happened in the United States? What is your view on the privilege of voting?

_____

_____

3. What main point is the author trying to convey?

_____

_____

8c   How Do Facts and Opinions Differ?

Your point of view, position, or belief on a subject has evolved over time and is probably based on both facts and opinions. For example, consider your positions on panhandling on city streets, pornography on the Internet, and vitamin therapy for cancer patients. Are your views on these issues supported solely by facts? Do you recognize the difference between fact and opinion in your thinking?

Both facts and opinions support positions. As a reader, your job is to determine which is which and then judge the issue accordingly. A **fact** is a statement based on evidence or personal observation; it can be proved to be either true or false. An **opinion,** on the other hand, is a statement of personal feeling or a judgment; it reflects a belief or an interpretation rather than an accumulation of evidence, and it cannot be proved true or false. Even if you feel an opinion is valid, it is still an opinion.

Authors mix facts and opinions, sometimes in the same sentence, to win you over to a particular point of view. Persuasive tricks include quoting sources who voice opinions and hedging a statement with "It is a fact that," followed by a disguised opinion. Recognize that both facts and opinions are valuable persuasive tools, but be able to distinguish between the two.

EXAMPLE

Fact: George Washington was the first president of the United States.

Opinion: George Washington was the best president of the United States.

Fact: The author states that George Washington was the best president of the United States.

Opinion: It is a fact that George Washington was the best president of the United States.

EXPLANATION The first and third statements are facts that can be proven true or false. The second and fourth are opinions even though the fourth tries to present itself as a fact. In psychology, it is a fact that Sigmund Freud believed that the personality is divided into three parts; however, it is only an opinion that there are three parts to the human personality. (Other experts may believe the personality should be divided into two or a dozen parts.)

Practice 4

Read each sentence following and indicate *F* for fact and *O* for opinion.

_____ **1.** A pair of women's stockings is made from one strand of nylon that is 4 miles long and knitted into 3 million loops.

_____ **2.** Originality and independence are the most difficult qualities to achieve; if they were easy, everyone would have them.

_____ **3.** Complimenting someone achieves such positive results that we should all try doing it more often.

_____ **4.** For operations prior to the use of anesthesia in 1846, patients were held down by several strong men, incapacitated with alcohol, or simply knocked unconscious.

_____ **5.** In Santa Fe, New Mexico, the burning of Zozobra, Old Man Gloom, is celebrated by burning a 40-foot marionette.

_____ **6.** The worst tropical storms are not hurricanes but rather cyclones that sweep out of the Bay of Bengal and attack India with 145-mile-per-hour winds and 20-foot waves.

_____ **7.** Queen Victoria was the first person in England to own a dachshund, a dog bred to fight badgers.

_____ **8.** In the 1600s attempts to transfuse animal blood into humans were always fatal and the practice was outlawed.

_____ **9.** Islam is the major religion in 48 countries, and it has the second largest number of adherents worldwide.

_____ **10.** The difference between weather forecasts of partly cloudy and partly sunny depends on your disposition.

8d   What Is the Author's Purpose?

Authors write with a particular **purpose** or **intent** in mind, and usually that purpose is to inform, persuade, or entertain. You might be instructed to write a paper on environmental pollution with the purpose of inspiring classmates to recycle. In writing the paper, you must both inform and persuade. Your overriding goal, however, is persuasion—you want to change minds, convince classmates to recycle, and move them to action. Therefore, you will use only those facts that support your argument. Your classmates will then carefully evaluate your scientific support, recognizing that your primary purpose was persuasion rather than education, and decide whether to recycle all or some combination of the paper, glass, aluminum, and plastic they toss out.

Author's Purpose

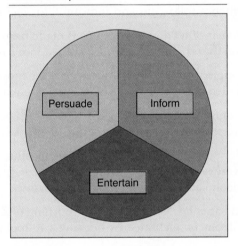

EXAMPLE For each of the following statements, decide whether the main purpose is to inform (*I*), to persuade (*P*), or to entertain (*E*).

_____ **1.** During a panic attack, the first symptoms are adrenaline and heart rate increases, followed by breathlessness, chest pains, sweating, shaking, dizziness, and extreme feelings of anxiety.

_____ **2.** Only a sophisticated duck would walk into a bar and tell the bartender to put the drink on his bill.

_____ **3.** Clean up before your guests arrive to show respect. Put all dishes in the washer, hang up clothes, and discard trash. Your guests will appreciate your efforts.

EXPLANATION The purpose of the first sentence is to inform or educate with a description of symptoms. The purpose of the second sentence is to entertain by making a play on words for a joke. The purpose of the last sentence is to persuade by offering advice for making house guests comfortable.

✓ Reader's TIP

Recognizing the Author's Purpose

The three common purposes for writing are:

■ **To inform**
Authors use facts **to inform, to explain, to educate,** and **to enlighten.** The purpose of textbooks is usually to inform or explain, but sometimes an author might venture into persuasion, particularly on topics like smoking or recycling.

■ **To persuade**
Authors use a combination of facts and opinions **to persuade, to argue, to condemn,** and **to ridicule.** Editorials in newspapers are written to argue a point and persuade the reader.

■ **To entertain**
Authors use fiction and nonfiction **to entertain, to narrate, to describe,** and **to shock.** Novels, short stories, and essays are written to entertain. Sometimes an author may adopt a guise of humor to entertain or to achieve a special result.

Practice 5

Identify the main purpose of each statement: to inform (*I*), to persuade (*P*), or to entertain (*E*).

_____ 1. Off-shore oil drilling platforms may be beneficial to oil companies, but they threaten coastal residents and the natural habitat of sea creatures. The oil industry can determine its profits and losses in dollars, but the potential cost to the coastline and its inhabitants cannot be measured.

_____ 2. Infrared satellite photographs offer clues to locations of significant oil reserves by detecting rocks containing manganese and chromium. The long-distance views provided by satellites can also reveal faults and other geological phenomena that indicate what might lie beneath the surface.

8
Pt. of
View

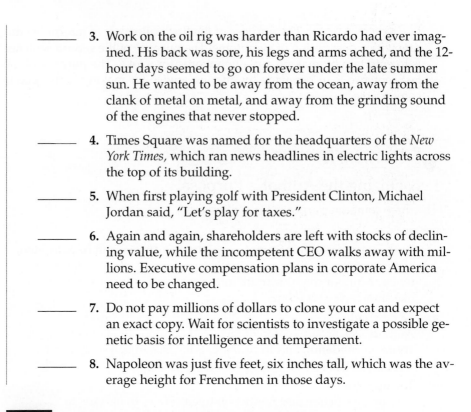

_____ **3.** Work on the oil rig was harder than Ricardo had ever imagined. His back was sore, his legs and arms ached, and the 12-hour days seemed to go on forever under the late summer sun. He wanted to be away from the ocean, away from the clank of metal on metal, and away from the grinding sound of the engines that never stopped.

_____ **4.** Times Square was named for the headquarters of the *New York Times*, which ran news headlines in electric lights across the top of its building.

_____ **5.** When first playing golf with President Clinton, Michael Jordan said, "Let's play for taxes."

_____ **6.** Again and again, shareholders are left with stocks of declining value, while the incompetent CEO walks away with millions. Executive compensation plans in corporate America need to be changed.

_____ **7.** Do not pay millions of dollars to clone your cat and expect an exact copy. Wait for scientists to investigate a possible genetic basis for intelligence and temperament.

_____ **8.** Napoleon was just five feet, six inches tall, which was the average height for Frenchmen in those days.

8e What Is the Author's Tone?

The **tone** of an author's writing is similar to the tone of a speaker's voice. For listeners, it is fairly easy to tell the difference between an angry, joyful, or romantic tone on hearing the speaker's voice. For an example of how tone in writing can vary, pretend you are waiting for a friend who is already a half-hour late. You can wait no longer, but you can leave a note. On your own paper, write your friend three different messages—one with a sympathetic tone, one with an angry tone, and one with a sarcastic tone. What would determine which message you would actually leave?

Detecting extremes such as anger and joy is easier than distinguishing among more sophisticated attitudes such as humor, sarcasm, and irony. Humorous remarks are designed to be comical and amusing, whereas sarcastic remarks are designed to cut or give pain. Ironic remarks sometimes express the exact opposite of what the words state. Noting these differences requires more than just listening to sounds; it requires a careful evaluation of what is said. Because the sound of the voice is not heard in reading, clues to the tone must come from the writer's presentation of the message. Your job is to look for clues to answer the question *What is the author's attitude toward the topic?*

8
Pt. of
View

✔ Reader's TIP

Recognizing the Author's Tone

The following words, listed with their meanings, can describe an author's tone or attitude.

- **Absurd, farcical, ridiculous:** laughable or a joke
- **Ambivalent, apathetic, detached:** not caring
- **Angry, bitter, hateful:** feeling bad and upset about the topic
- **Arrogant, condescending:** acting conceited or above others
- **Awestruck, wondering:** filled with wonder
- **Cheerful, joyous, happy:** feeling good about the topic
- **Compassionate, sympathetic:** feeling sorrow at the distress of others
- **Complex:** intricate, complicated, and entangled with confusing parts
- **Congratulatory, celebratory:** honoring an achievement or festive occasion
- **Cruel, malicious:** mean-spirited
- **Cynical:** expecting the worst from people
- **Depressed, melancholy:** sad, dejected, or having low spirits
- **Disapproving:** judging unfavorably
- **Evasive, abstruse:** avoiding or confusing the issue
- **Formal:** using an official style
- **Frustrated:** blocked from a goal
- **Gentle:** kind, or of a high social class
- **Ghoulish, grim:** robbing graves or feeding on corpses; stern and forbidding
- **Hard:** unfeeling, strict, and unrelenting
- **Humorous, jovial, comic, playful, amused:** being funny
- **Incredulous:** unbelieving
- **Indignant:** outraged
- **Intense, impassioned:** extremely involved, zealous, or agitated
- **Ironic:** the opposite of what is expected; a twist at the end
- **Irreverent:** lack of respect for authority
- **Mocking, scornful, caustic, condemning:** ridiculing the topic
- **Objective, factual, straightforward, critical:** using facts without emotions
- **Obsequious:** fawning for attention

(continued)

8
Pt. of
View

- **Optimistic:** looking on the bright side
- **Outspoken:** speaking one's mind on issues
- **Pessimistic:** looking on the negative side
- **Prayerful:** religiously thankful
- **Reticent:** shy and not speaking out
- **Reverent:** showing respect
- **Righteous:** morally correct
- **Romantic, intimate, loving:** expressing love or affection
- **Sarcastic:** saying one thing and meaning another
- **Sensational:** overdramatized or overhyped
- **Sentimental, nostalgic:** remembering the good old days
- **Serious, sincere, earnest, solemn:** being honest and concerned
- **Straightforward:** forthright
- **Subjective, opinionated:** expressing opinions and feelings
- **Tragic:** regrettable or deplorable mistake
- **Uneasy:** restless or uncertain
- **Vindictive:** seeking revenge

EXAMPLE Identify the tone of the following passage.

The officer standing at my door repeated the charge that my license plate number was the same as that of a car leaving the scene of an accident on the highway that afternoon. It didn't matter that my car was a different color and that I had been at lunch with friends at the time. I found myself suddenly being treated like a criminal. It wasn't fair.

The author's tone is:
  a. nostalgic
  b. ironic
  c. angry

EXPLANATION The details show that the speaker is resentful of the intrusion and the unfair accusation. The tone is angry.

Practice 6

Mark the letter that identifies the tone for each of the following sentences.

_____ **1.** If you took all his fitness efforts to exercise and eat healthy foods and laid them end to end, they would have stretched from the refrigerator to the couch and back again . . . twice.
  a. objective
  b. nostalgic
  c. humorous

8
Pt. of
View

_____ 2. Advances in technology have fulfilled the promise of hundreds of television channels and movies on demand. Unfortunately, these advances have not brought about an equivalent improvement in the content of what we watch. Where are the quality shows to go with the quality technology?
  a. optimistic
  b. ironic
  c. sentimental

_____ 3. In those gentler times, kids played outdoors until dinner was ready. Families ate together. Neighbors knew each other and people seemed to have more time to enjoy life without a hundred different concerns competing for their attention.
  a. objective
  b. nostalgic
  c. bitter

_____ 4. My daughter complimented my dinner and said it was so good she thought someone else had made it.
  a. melancholy
  b. cheerful
  c. comic

_____ 5. City property taxes continue to rise. Hopeless citizens accept that there is nothing they can do to stop the increases.
  a. pessimistic
  b. sensational
  c. prayerful

_____ 6. Our Russian ice skater is highly favored to win the Olympic gold. The training and competition in my country are superior to those in any country in the world.
  a. incredulous
  b. arrogant
  c. vindictive

_____ 7. I was asked to write a recommendation for Harold Davis. He worked at my company for the last two years, and I have seen him work.
  a. evasive
  b. straightforward
  c. irreverent

_____ 8. The apartment rental agent refused to return $150 of my deposit. I think landlords always keep money, claiming that you did not clean the refrigerator, stove, or toilet.
  a. ghoulish
  b. tragic
  c. cynical

8
Pt. of
View

_____ 9. When the great composer entered the room amid applause, I stood in disbelief that I would finally meet such an admirable talent.
   a. awestruck
   b. reticent
   c. compassionate

_____ 10. After the jury had found the defendant guilty of drunken driving and manslaughter, the judge's sentence fell far short of the expectations of the victims' families. Weekends in jail and community service show little respect for two dead sons.
   a. objective
   b. bitter
   c. arrogant

Small-Group EXPLORATION

Form a five-member group and select one of the following activities. Brainstorm and then outline your major points on a transparency. Choose a group member to present the group's findings to the class. Individual assignments can also be made.

■   List five facts and five opinions that could be used to support the argument that exercise reduces stress.

■   Outline a speech supporting school uniforms in public schools.

■   Outline a speech against requiring school uniforms in public schools.

■   Should Americans have a national identification card with biological data? Answer the question with an angry reply, an arrogant reply, and a nostalgic reply.

Net SEARCH

8
Pt. of
View

Search the Internet to find information on the two different points of view on global warming. Support each position with three facts, not opinions.

Chapter 9

Reading Graphics

9a   What Do Graphics Do?

If a picture is worth a thousand words, a graphic illustration is worth at least several pages of facts and figures. Graphics express complex interrelationships in visual form. Instead of plodding through repetitious data, you can glance at a chart, a map, or a graph and immediately see how everything fits together as well as how one part compares with another. Instead of reading several lengthy paragraphs and trying to visualize comparisons, you can study an organized design. The graphic illustration is a logically constructed aid for understanding many small bits of information.

Graphic illustrations are generally used for the following reasons:

- **To condense.** Many pages of repetitious, detailed information can be organized into a single explanatory design.
- **To clarify.** Processes and interrelationships can be more clearly defined through visual representations.
- **To convince.** Developing trends and gross inequities can be forcefully dramatized.

A familiarity with graphics is particularly important in an increasingly visual world. Graphics are used as tools to convey and emphasize meaning. They appear on the front page of every issue of *USA Today*, as well as on Web sites and in textbooks, business letters, corporate reports, and government studies.

9b   How Do You Read Graphic Material and Visual Aids?

There are five kinds of graphic illustrations: diagrams, tables, maps, graphs (including pie graphs;) bar graphs, and line graphs), and flowcharts. Deciding which is the best one to use will depend on the type and complexity of the material to be presented. This chapter contains explanations, examples, and practice exercises for the various types of graphic illustrations.

✓ Reader's TIP

Reading Graphics

- Read the title and get an overview. What is the graphic about?
- Read any text that accompanies the graphic.
- Look for footnotes and read introductory material. Identify the who, what, where, and how.
  How and when were the data collected?
  Who collected the data?
  If a survey is depicted, how many persons were included?
  Do the researchers seem to have been objective or biased?
  Considering the above information, does the graphic seem valid?
- Read the labels.
  What do the vertical columns and the horizontal rows represent?
  Are the numbers expressed in hundreds, thousands, or millions?
  What does the legend represent?
- Notice the trends and find the extremes.
  What are the highest and lowest rates?
  What is the average rate?
  How do the extremes compare with the total?
  What is the percentage of increase or decrease?
- Draw conclusions and formulate future exam questions.
  What does the information mean?
  What needs to be done with the information?
  What wasn't included?
  Where do we go from here?

Diagrams

A **diagram** is an outline drawing or picture of an object or a process. It shows the labeled parts of a complicated form such as the muscles of the human body, the organizational makeup of a company's management and production teams, or the directional flow of energy in an ecosystem. The diagram shown in Figure 9-1 labels the parts of the nearsighted and farsighted eye and shows how corrective lenses work; the diagram in Figure 9-2 on page 176 shows the process by which a coal-burning power plant converts the energy in coal to electrical energy.

FIGURE 9-1 | Diagram: How corrective lenses work

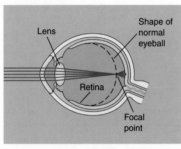 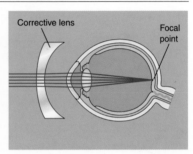

A. A nearsighted eye (eyeball too long)

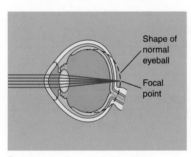 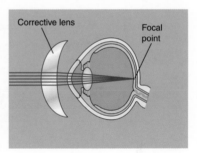

B. A farsighted eye (eyeball too short)

Source: Neil Campbell et al., *Biology Concepts and Connections,* 2nd ed.

Practice 1

Refer to Figure 9-1 to respond to the following statements with T (true), F (false), or CT (can't tell).

_____ **1.** The focal point of a nearsighted eye is too close to the lens of the eye, and the focal point of a farsighted eye is too far from the lens.

_____ **2.** The correct focal point of the eye should be on the retina directly opposite the lens.

_____ **3.** An astigmatism does not affect a nearsighted eye or a farsighted one.

_____ **4.** Farsightedness is easier to correct than nearsightedness.

FIGURE 9-2 | Diagram: Coal-burning power plant

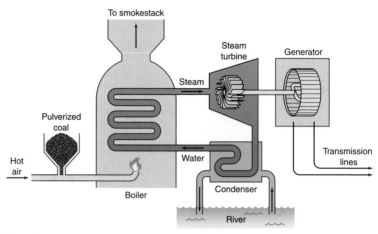

Source: John W. Hill, *Chemistry for Changing Times,* 8th ed.

_____ 5. Regardless of magnification, the shapes of corrective lenses are different for nearsighted and farsighted eyes.

6. The purpose of this diagram is to show

_____

_____

Practice 2

Refer to Figure 9-2 to respond to the following statements with *T* (true), *F* (false), or *CT* (can't tell).

_____ 1. Coal provides the fuel to create the steam.

_____ 2. Water turns to steam inside the boiler.

_____ 3. Water drives the turbine.

_____ 4. The water taken from the river damages the environment.

_____ 5. In this process, pollutants can escape through the smoke-stack when the boiler is turned off.

6. The purpose of this diagram is to show

_____

_____

Tables

A **table** is an organized listing of facts and figures in columns and rows for easy reference. Tables are commonly used in social science, business, and allied health texts to compare and classify information.

When you encounter a table in a piece of writing, first read the title to determine the topic. Next, read the footnotes to obtain additional information such as the source of the data, the statistical procedure used, or an explanation of terms. Read the column and row heads to determine what each represents. Finally, compare column and row entries to note how they interact.

Compare the items in the table shown in Figure 9-3. Can you draw any conclusions about what is being portrayed?

FIGURE 9-3	Table: Nutritional value of various meats

NUTRITIONAL GUIDE

If you like red meat *but could do with fewer calories and less fat and cholesterol, game meats may be just what it takes to have your steak and eat it, too:*

Meat 4-ounce raw serving size	Calories	Fat	Cholesterol
Bison	124	2 grams	20 mg
Beef bottom round	256	18 grams	74 mg
Beef tenderloin	179	9 grams	71 mg
Chicken breast	124	1 gram	73 mg
Ostrich	112	1 gram	72 mg
Pork tenderloin	139	4 grams	67 mg
Venison	143	5 grams	n/a

Source: Kathleen Zelman, spokeswoman for the American Dietetic Association.

Source: Marcia Langhenry, *Atlanta Journal and Constitution*, June 17, 1999.

Practice 3

Refer to Figure 9-3 to respond to the following statements with *T* (true), *F* (false), or *CT* (can't tell).

_____ **1.** The same amount of raw meat was compared for each item.

_____ **2.** Beef bottom round has the highest number of calories, grams of fat, and milligrams of cholesterol of any of the meats compared.

_____ **3.** Dieters are choosing bison over beef.

9
Graphics

_____   **4.** Venison is the red meat with the lowest number of fat grams.

_____   **5.** Chicken has more than three times as much cholesterol as bison.

6. The purpose of this table is

_____

Maps

Traditionally **maps,** such as road maps and atlas maps, have shown a geographic area, emphasizing differences in its physical terrain or *topography.* Maps found in history books show exploration routes into new territories, political changes in national boundaries, and patterns of industrial growth such as railroad expansion and areas of cotton production. In science, anthropology, and geography texts, maps can indicate ecological changes and population density.

A modern use of the map as a visual aid is to highlight nongeographic characteristics such as the *demographics,* or population distributions of a particular area. For example, a map of the United States might highlight all states with gun-control laws in red and all states without gun-control laws in blue. A map of the world might use red to show English-speaking countries, blue to show Spanish-speaking countries, and yellow to show French-speaking countries.

Begin by reading the title of the map and then notice the date, source, and distance scale if given. The *legend* of a map, which usually appears in a corner box, explains the meanings of symbols and colors (for example, color may designate a spoken language). Use the legend on the demographic map shown in Figure 9-4 to help you complete Practice 4.

✓ Reader's TIP
Reading an Atlas or a Road Map

- ■ Note the date of the map so that you can judge its currency; old maps may be obsolete.
- ■ Use the index to find the desired country or street.
- ■ See the legend for a key to translate symbols and colors representing such elements as boundaries, town size, parks, swamps, and toll roads.
- ■ Use the scale of distance to approximate mileage.
- ■ Orient yourself to the north, south, east, and west.

(continued)

- Use the broader maps to orient yourself to your specific area.
- Notice topographic features such as mountains, swamps, deserts, and coral reefs.
- For road maps, notice historical sites, campsites, information centers, service areas, highway numbers, and the mileage between towns.
- Use the insertions or enlargements for more details about a city or recreation area.

| **FIGURE 9-4** | Map: How urban is your state? The rural-urban makeup of the United States |

Note: The most urban state is New Jersey; the source reports that it is now 100 percent urban. The most rural state is Vermont, where 72.2 percent live in rural areas.
Source: James Henslin, *Sociology: A Down-to-Earth Approach,* 7th ed.

Practice 4

Refer to the map in Figure 9-4 to respond to the following statements with *T* (true), *F* (false), or *CT* (can't tell).

_____ 1. According to the map, North Carolina is more urban than Kansas.

_____ 2. The large states of Texas and California are both more than 83.9% urban.

FIGURE 9-5	Map: Texas and Louisiana

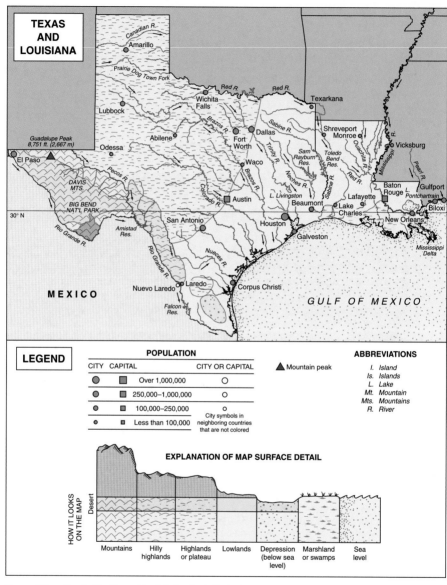

Source: Wynn Kapit, *The Geography Coloring Book*, 2nd ed.

_____ **3.** More than half of Montana is rural.

_____ **4.** More people live in Florida than live in Ohio.

_____ **5.** The northwestern states are more urban than the northeastern states.

6. The purpose of the map is

_____

_____

_____

Practice 5

Refer to the map in Figure 9-5 to respond to the following statements with *T* (true), *F* (false), or *CT* (can't tell).

_____ **1.** The most mountainous part of Texas is near El Paso.

_____ **2.** The capital of Louisiana is New Orleans.

_____ **3.** The Louisiana coast is considered marshland or swamp.

_____ **4.** The population of Fort Worth is greater than that of Waco.

_____ **5.** Texas has more productive farmland than Louisiana.

6. The purpose of the map is

_____

Pie Graphs

A **pie graph** is a circle that is divided into wedge-shaped slices. The complete pie or circle represents a total, or 100 percent. Each slice is a percentage or fraction of that whole. Budgets, such as the annual expenditures of federal or state governments, are frequently illustrated by pie graphs.

FIGURE 9-6	Pie Graph: Projections of the racial-ethnic makeup of the U.S. population

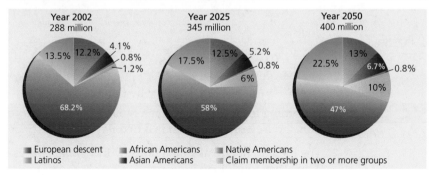

Source: James Henslin, *Sociology: A Down-to-Earth Approach,* 7th ed.

Practice 6

Refer to the pie graph in Figure 9-6 to respond to the following statements with *T* (true), *F* (false), or *CT* (can't tell).

_____ **1.** The percentage of Latinos in the U.S. population is projected to more than double between 2025 and 2050.

_____ **2.** According to the graph, the only group predicted to diminish as a percentage of the U.S. population is people of European descent.

_____ **3.** Between 2002 and 2050, African Americans will become a greater percentage of the U.S. population than are Asian Americans.

_____ **4.** The percentage of Native Americans in the U.S. population is not predicted to change from 2025 to 2050 because it did not change from 2002 to 2025.

_____ **5.** By 2050 fewer than 200 million people in the U.S. population will be of European descent.

6. The purpose of the pie graph is

_____

_____

_____

Bar Graphs

A **bar graph** is a series of horizontal or vertical bars in which the length of each bar represents a particular amount or quantity of whatever item is being discussed. Often, categories are shown on one axis and quantities on the other axis. You can quickly compare a series of different items by noting the different bar lengths. Figure 9-7 illustrates a vertical bar graph, and Figure 9-8 on page 184 is a horizontal bar graph.

Practice 7

Refer to the vertical bar graph in Figure 9-7 to respond to the following statements with *T* (true), *F* (false), or *CT* (can't tell).

_____ **1.** According to the graph, women typically do 7.5 hours a week more housework than men in a two-paycheck marriage.

_____ **2.** The men do not do as much housework as their wives because they work longer hours.

FIGURE 9-7 | Bar Graph: In two-paycheck marriages, who does the housework?

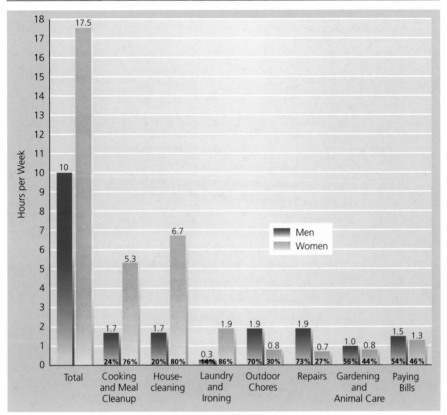

Source: James Henslin, *Sociology: A Down-to-Earth Approach*, 7th ed.

_____ 3. Women in two-paycheck marriages spend more than twice as much time in cooking and meal cleanup than men do.

_____ 4. Men and women in two-paycheck marriages spend an equal amount of time paying bills.

_____ 5. Men in a two-paycheck marriage spend twice as much time as women in doing outdoor chores and repairs.

6. The purpose of the bar graph is

_____

_____

FIGURE 9-8 | Percentage of ex-convicts who are rearrested

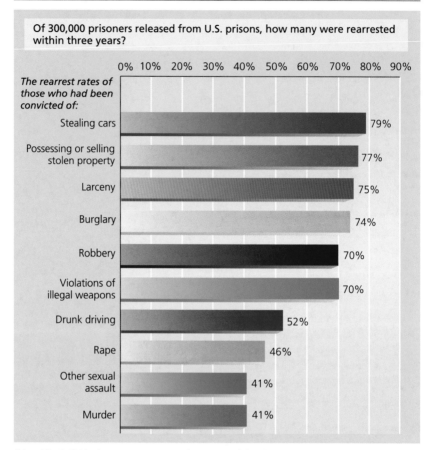

Of 300,000 prisoners released from U.S. prisons, how many were rearrested within three years?

The rearrest rates of those who had been convicted of:

- Stealing cars — 79%
- Possessing or selling stolen property — 77%
- Larceny — 75%
- Burglary — 74%
- Robbery — 70%
- Violations of illegal weapons — 70%
- Drunk driving — 52%
- Rape — 46%
- Other sexual assault — 41%
- Murder — 41%

(Note: The individuals were not necessarily rearrested for the same crime for which they had originally been in prison.)
Source: James Henslin, *Sociology: A Down-to-Earth Approach,* 7th ed.

Practice 8

Refer to the horizontal bar graph in Figure 9-8 to respond to the following with *T* (true), *F* (false), or *CT* (can't tell).

_____ **1.** Of the groups shown, the people who steal cars are the most likely to be rearrested within three years.

_____ **2.** Over half of those convicted of burglary stay clean of crime and are never arrested again.

_____ **3.** Those who commit murder are least likely to be rearrested because they are in jail the longest.

_____ 4. Those who are convicted of burglary are most likely to be re-arrested for similar crimes such as robbery and larceny.

_____ 5. Over half of those convicted of drunk driving are rearrested within three years.

6. The purpose of the bar graph is

_____

_____

Line Graphs

A **line graph** shows a continuous curve or *frequency distribution*. The horizontal scale (or *axis*) measures one aspect of the data (or *variable*) and the vertical scale measures another aspect, making it easy to see the relationship between the variables at a glance. As the data fluctuate, the line will change direction and, with extreme differences, become very jagged.

In the line graph shown in Figure 9-9 , notice that the horizontal axis measures the age of those dying and the vertical axis indicates the number of deaths. This graph shows different frequency distributions according to the number of cigarettes or cigars smoked per day.

FIGURE 9-9 | Line Graph: Lung-cancer deaths

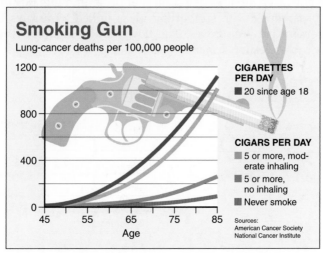

Source: "Smoking Gun," from *Time,* June 21, 1999. © 1999 Time, Inc.
Reprinted by permission.

Practice 9

Refer to the line graph in Figure 9-9 to respond to the following statements with *T* (true), *F* (false), or *CT* (can't tell).

———— 1. According to the graph, death from lung cancer at age 56 was statistically just as likely for those who smoked 5 cigars a day as for those who smoked 20 cigarettes a day.

———— 2. The graph shows that people who never smoked never got lung cancer.

———— 3. Cigar smokers who smoked and inhaled 5 cigars a day were more than three times as likely to die of lung cancer at age 85 as those who smoked but did not inhale 5 or more cigars a day.

———— 4. After 80 years of age, cigar smokers increased the number of cigars smoked each day.

———— 5. At age 65, more people died of lung cancer from cigarette smoking than from cigar smoking.

6. The purpose of the line graph is

_____

_____

Flowcharts

Flowcharts, which diagram relationships and sequences of elements or events, were first used in computer programming. Key ideas are stated in boxes, along with supporting ideas linked by arrows that show the movement between boxes. The flowchart in Figure 9-10 traces a company's job selection system.

FIGURE 9-10 | Flowchart: Job selection system

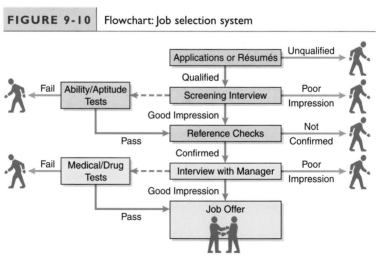

Source: Ronald Ebert and Ricky Griffin, *Business,* 4th ed.

Practice 10

Refer to the explanation and the flowchart in Figure 9-10 to respond to the following statements with *T* (true), *F* (false), or *CT* (can't tell).

_____ **1.** Applicants who are given drug tests are not offered jobs.

_____ **2.** All applicants are given aptitude tests.

_____ **3.** Reference checks are done after an interview with the manager.

_____ **4.** Applicants who make a poor impression do not move past the screening interview.

_____ **5.** Only one in seven applicants receives a job offer.

6. The purpose of the flowchart is

_____

Practice 11

On separate pieces of paper, use what you have learned in this chapter to construct a bar graph, a line graph, and a pie graph showing the following distribution of grades in your American History class.

A's = 8 students   B's = 14 students   C's = 12 students

D's = 4 students   F's = 2 students

Small-Group EXPLORATION

Form a five-member group and select one of the following activities. Brainstorm and then outline your major points on a transparency. Choose one group member to present the group's findings to the class. Individual assignments can also be made.

■ Create a pie graph showing an average student's expenses at your college for one semester. First, list the expenses; next, total them; then calculate the percentage of the total that each represents and create your graph.

■ Create a bar graph showing the number of birthdays in each month represented by students in the class.

■ Draw a map of your college campus. Insert building and street names.

■ Calculate the average number of sleep hours for your group members for each night of the past week. Create a frequency graph to show the daily averages.

9
Graphics

Net SEARCH

Search the Internet for a map that will help you to get to the home of a friend or relative who lives in another town. Printout each map, evaluate the information, and cite the source.

Part 2
Study Strategies

Chapter 10

Critical Thinking

10a What Is Critical Thinking?

Do you question what you read as truth? Can you evaluate and justify what you believe? If so, you are thinking critically. Deliberating in a purposeful, organized manner to assess the value of information, both old and new, is **critical thinking.** Critical readers and thinkers use all the skills described in the previous chapters to analyze the value and validity of what they are reading. They identify the issue or the main idea, select the relevant argument or supporting details, and question inferences. Then they go one step further and evaluate. Since critical thinking demands the systematic application of many well-learned skills, colleges rank it as an essential academic goal.

Overcome Barriers to Critical Thinking

Allow yourself to think critically, to be challenged, and to change. Recognize and avoid the following barriers to your own critical thinking:

1. **Existing Beliefs**—Do you refuse to consider or immediately reject ideas outside your belief system? We are culturally conditioned to resist change and feel that our own way is best.

   Example: You might refuse to look at the merits of something your belief system rejects, such as the advantages of marijuana.

✔ Reader's TIP
Thinking Critically

■ *Be willing to plan.* Think first and write later. Don't be impulsive. Develop a habit of planning.

■ *Be flexible.* Be open to new ideas. Consider new solutions for old problems.

■ *Be persistent.* Continue to work even when you are tired and discouraged. Good thinking is hard work.

■ *Be willing to self-correct.* Don't be defensive about errors. Figure out what went wrong and learn from your mistakes.

---

2. **Wishful Thinking**—Do you talk yourself into believing things that you know are not true because you *want* them to be true? Are you fooling yourself? Are you in self-denial?

   Example: If you like a prominent political figure, you might refuse to believe well-founded claims of moral corruption. You might be unwilling to think that a favorite celebrity could commit a crime.

3. **Hasty Moral Judgments**—Do you tend to evaluate someone or something as good or bad, right or wrong, and then remain fixed in this thinking? Such judgments are often prejudiced, intolerant, emotional, and self-righteous.

   Example: You might think it absolutely unquestionable that abortion should never be legal.

4. **Reliance on Authority**—Do you think for yourself? Many people let the government, doctors, religious leaders, and teachers do their thinking for them.

   Example: Do you question it when the government says you should consume more carbohydrates than recent low-carb diet books advise?

5. **Labels**—Do you ignore individual differences and lump people and things into categories? Labels oversimplify, distort the truth, stereotype, and usually incite anger and rejection.

   Example: To say that there are two kinds of people, those who love America and those who do not, will force others to take sides in reaction.

10
Crit.
Think.

|EXAMPLE| My doctor disagrees with the use of alternative medicines in the treatment of heart disease even though some of the reports are promising.

Is this wishful thinking, labeling, or reliance on authority?

EXPLANATION It involves reliance on authority, in this case a respected medical doctor. A critical thinker might investigate the promising reports.

Practice 1

Read the following statements and identify with *a, b, c,* or *d* the type of barrier each statement best represents.

    a. wishful thinking
    b. existing beliefs
    c. reliance on authority
    d. labels

_____ **1.** Herbal medications and alternative therapies are not covered by any major insurance company, so they cannot be beneficial.

_____ **2.** An only child in a family does not grow up having to share, so that child becomes a spoiled and self-centered teenager.

_____ **3.** He would never try to steal my girlfriend! We've been friends for too long for him to do something like that.

_____ **4.** Regardless of the benefits of a needle exchange program, it's wrong to distribute articles that contribute to drug activity.

_____ **5.** Although some men fear its side effects, the new drug for baldness has recently been approved by the federal Food and Drug Administration, and therefore it must be safe.

_____ **6.** Lawyers are paid liars who plead insanity for murderers who have no other possible defense.

10b | What Are the Steps in the Process of Critical Thinking?

You already know the steps in the process of critical thinking. They are the same steps that you have been using in the preceding chapters of this text. In thinking critically you are just using different terminology and going one step further to question truthfulness and logic in order to evaluate what you read. Rely on what you already know and do not let the terminology fool you. Use the following four-step procedure to guide your critical thinking:

1. Identify the issue. (What is the main idea?)
2. Identify the support for the argument. (What are the supporting details?)

3. Evaluate the support. (Are the supporting details relevant, believable, and consistent?)
4. Evaluate the argument.

An attorney presents her closing argument to the jury.

Step 1: Identify the Issue

Good readers pinpoint the central issue by asking *What is the debatable question?* The **issue** is an assertion or position statement. It is what the author is trying to convince you to believe or to do. For example, in the statement "Because rain is not in the forecast, you should water your grass" the issue is "You should water your grass." The support for the issue is "because rain is not in the forecast."

✓ Reader's TIP

Using Signal Words to Identify the Issue

The following key words and phrases are sometimes used to signal the central issue being argued:

should	consequently	therefore	for these reasons
thus	finally	it follows that	as a result

10
Crit.
Think.

To identify the issue in persuasive writing, use your main-idea reading skills. First ask yourself *What is the passage mainly about?* to determine the topic. Then ask *What main point is the author trying to convey about the topic?* Your answer will be a statement of the issue being argued, which could also be called the main point, the thesis, or the conclusion.

EXAMPLE Identify the central issue that is being argued in the following passage.

> In choosing a career path, many job seekers first examine the latest career trends and then try to package themselves for those jobs. For the best results, however, they should evaluate their own strengths and interests in order to create the career plan best suited to them. Because of the high interest connection, the job seeker will be more enthusiastic, work harder, and ultimately achieve greater success.

EXPLANATION The central issue is directly stated after the phrase "For the best results," and the word *should* signals that the author is trying to convince you to do something.

Practice 2

Read the following passages and underline the central issue that is being argued in each.

1. New pledges to sororities and fraternities are routinely forced to endure "hazing," a practice of ritualized actions that intentionally produce mental or physical discomfort. Although intended to prove a pledge's worthiness, hazing should be banned from the Greek scene because it is disrespectful and inappropriate in an institution of higher education.

2. Studies have shown that up to 2 million patients acquire infections while in the hospital each year. Prescription mistakes and adverse drug reactions kill at least 50,000 patients each year both in and out of hospitals. It is clear, therefore, that hospitals can be dangerous to patients.

3. Sea horses are agile and resemble miniature horses. They mate with one partner for a lifetime and greet each other in the morning with a dance. For these reasons, sea horses make interesting aquarium pets.

4. In ancient Asia the rare white elephant was regarded as holy. An owner had to provide special food and also serve pilgrims who came to worship it. Consequently, a displeased king would give a white elephant to someone he wished to ruin financially.

Step 2: Identify the Support for the Argument

The **points of support** form the argument. They are the reasons or the evidence offered as proof of the position being argued. In the example about watering the grass, only one reason was offered: "because rain is not in the forecast." Other reasons, such as "the grass will die without water" and "water is plentiful right now," would have added further support. In reality, the identification of supporting points is simply the identification of significant supporting details for the main point.

10
Crit.
Think.

✓ Reader's TIP

Using Signal Words to Identify Supporting Reasons

Key words and phrases that signal support in an argument are the same as those that signal significant supporting details. They include the following:

because	first . . . second . . . finally
since	assuming that
if	given that

EXAMPLE   Let's return to a previous passage to see how signal words can introduce supporting details. Identify the issue and the points of support.

> In choosing a career path, many job seekers first examine the latest career trends and then try to package themselves for those jobs. For the best results, however, they should evaluate their own strengths and interests in order to create the career plan best suited to them. Because of the high interest connection, the job seeker will be more enthusiastic, work harder, and ultimately achieve greater success.

EXPLANATION   The issue is that job seekers should evaluate their own strengths and interests to create the career plan best suited to them. The points of support are threefold and are signaled by *Because:* the job seeker will be more enthusiastic, work harder, and ultimately achieve greater success.

✓ Reader's TIP

Identifying Categories of Support in Arguments

- ■ *Facts:* objective truths
  Ask: How were the facts gathered, and are they true?
- ■ *Examples:* anecdotes to demonstrate the truth
  Ask: Are the examples true and relevant?
- ■ *Analogies:* comparisons to similar cases
  Ask: Are the analogies accurate and relevant?
- ■ *Authority:* words from a recognized expert
  Ask: What are the credentials and biases of the expert?
- ■ *Causal relationship:* saying one thing caused another
  Ask: Is it an actual cause or merely an association?

10
Crit.
Think.

(continued)

■ *Common knowledge claim:* assertion of wide acceptance
Ask: Is it relevant, and does everyone really believe it?

■ *Statistics:* numerical data
Ask: Do the numbers accurately describe the population?

■ *Personal experiences:* personal anecdotes
Ask: Is the experience applicable to other situations?

Practice 3

In the following passages, identify the central issue that is being argued and the supporting reasons. Place the letter *I* before the sentence or phrase containing the central issue and place the letter *S* before those containing supporting reasons.

1. To summarize the discussion, _____ Maria Inojosa's band would be the best choice for playing at the party. _____ Since they can play both salsa and merengue, everyone will be happy.

2. For the purposes of our discussion, _____ the octopus will become our perfect model for an alien body from another galaxy. An octopus _____ can see polarized light, and _____ its skin can change color and texture and give cues to certain "emotions."

3. _____ Disease plagued the builders of the Panama Canal. _____ The hot, moist climate was an excellent breeding ground for mosquitoes that caused yellow fever. _____ Therefore, the mosquitoes became the first obstacle that the canal builders needed to conquer.

4. _____ Frogs jump into water, but they do not drink. _____ They absorb water through their skin. _____ Consequently, you will never see a frog drinking from a birdbath.

Step 3: Evaluate the Support

Valid arguments have well-crafted reasons and evidence, but some arguments are supported by tricky reasons and evidence that might look good on the surface but have no real usefulness. Therefore, in evaluating the support for an argument, beware of *fallacies*. A **fallacy** is an inference that appears at first to be reasonable but on closer inspection proves to be unrelated, unreliable, or illogical. It is a tool used in constructing a weak argument. For example, to say that something is right because everybody is doing it is not a convincing reason for accepting an idea. Such "reasoning," however, can be compelling, and it is so frequently used that it has been labeled a *bandwagon* fallacy.

10
Crit.
Think.

Logicians have categorized, labeled, and defined more than 200 types of fallacies or tricks of persuasion. You do not need to memorize a long list of fallacy types, but you should understand how irrelevant reasoning techniques can manipulate logical thinking. Therefore, sensitize youself to the "tools" of constructing a weak argument.

Evaluate the support in every argument in three areas: *relevance, believability,* and *consistency.* The following list describes fallacies common to each area.

1. Relevance Fallacies.   Is the support related to the conclusion?

Testimonials: opinions of agreement from respected celebrities who are not experts on the subject

Example: A famous athlete endorses a cell phone company.

Transfer: an association with a positively or negatively regarded person in order to lend the same association to the argument

Example: A school superintendent quotes from Martin Luther King, Jr.'s "I Have a Dream" speech to suggest the same noble goals and vision for her plan to reorganize the school district.

Ad Hominem: an attack on the person rather than the issue, in the hope that if the person is opposed, the idea will be opposed

Example: Governor Wilson claims he wants the best education for the children of our state, but he has no children and he knows nothing about educating them.

Bandwagon: the idea that everybody is doing it and you will be left out if you do not quickly join the crowd

Example: If you do not take steroids as the other strong athletes do, you will eventually be cut from the team.

Straw Person: a setup in which a distorted or exaggerated form of the opponent's argument is introduced and then knocked down, making it appear weak or without merit

Example: After proposing moderate gun control measures, Simpson's opponents ran ads claiming that he was trying to make all gun ownership illegal and that a hunter would then need to use a bow and arrow or a slingshot.

Misleading Analogy or Faulty Comparison: a comparison of two things that suggests they are similar when in fact, they are distinctly different

Example: Musicians are just like toddlers; they're fine until you try to get them to conform to societal norms.

Red Herring: introducing an irrelevant issue to throw the thinker off track; this term originates from escaping prisoners who would drag a strong-smelling fish to confuse tracking dogs

10
Crit.
Think.

Example: During the Watergate investigations President Nixon refused to release personally damaging tapes on the basis of national security, saying that it was his job to protect the country.

2. Believability Fallacies.

Is the support believable or highly suspicious?

Incomplete Facts or Card Stacking: omission of factual details in an attempt to misrepresent reality

Example: Purchase this condominium time-share now because the units will soon be sold out and prices are sure to go up.

Misinterpreted Statistics: numerical data misapplied to unrelated populations that they were never intended to represent

Example: The number of people who suffer from a fear of flying has obviously decreased since the number of air travelers has dramatically grown over the past five years.

Overgeneralizations or Hasty Generalizations: examples and anecdotes asserted to apply to all cases rather than a select few

Example: Teenagers who constantly visit malls are training to shop but not training to work.

Questionable Authority: testimonial suggesting authority from people who are not experts

Example: Dr. Lin Song, a leading expert in astrology, asserts that life never could have existed on Mars.

3. Consistency Fallacies.

Does the support hold together or does it fall apart and contradict itself?

Appeals to Pity: pleas to support the underdog—that is, the person or issue that needs your help

Example: If you don't give me an extension on the deadline, I'll get another incomplete and be cut from the team just before the state championships.

Appeals to Emotion: highly charged language used for emotional manipulation

Example: These puppies and kittens did not ask to be abandoned or abused. A contribution of just $25 from you will help them find a new and caring home.

Oversimplification: reduction of an issue to two simple choices, without consideration of other alternatives or gray areas in between

Example: If you really cared about the truth, you would sign the petition to force the chancellor to resign.

Circular Reasoning: support for a conclusion that is merely a restatement of that conclusion

Example: Songs with obscene lyrics should not be played on the radio because the radio should not broadcast foul language to the public.

Begging the Question: the assertion that needs support is not proven, yet it is used as the conclusion in a manner similar to circular reasoning

Example: To answer your question, blueberries are considered a cancer-fighting food because the berries contain antioxidants that work to prevent cancer.

Slippery Slope: objecting to something because it will lead to greater evil and disastrous consequences

Example: If you support another private oceanfront development, you will soon find that you are not allowed on a beach in this state. Every grain of sand will be privately owned.

Non Sequitur: conclusion does not follow as a logical result of the facts presented

Example: Warren Beatty is an excellent actor, has championed worthy causes, and would make a great President of the United States.

Post Hoc Ergo Propter Hoc: implying that an event that follows another event was caused by the first event; the Latin words mean "after this, therefore because of this"

Example: Having an argument with your roommate caused you to forget your key and be locked out of the room.

Practice 4

Identify the type of fallacy in each of the following statements by indicating *a*, *b*, or *c*.

_____ **1.** When the students objected to the tuition increase, the administrator angrily complained that students want excellence for nothing and college is not their welfare program.
a. testimonials
b. *ad hominem*
c. bandwagon

_____ **2.** If Gloria Estefan recommends *Sparkle* shampoo for shiny hair, I'll use it.
a. *ad hominem*
b. misleading analogy
c. testimonial

10
Crit.
Think.

_____ **3.** If the activists save the whales, the next cry will be to save tuna and salmon. Then no one will be able to eat a tuna fish sandwich for lunch or go to a seafood restaurant for dinner.
a. misleading analogy
b. questionable authority
c. slippery slope

_____ **4.** Juan Costilla has the skills to be the best candidate for mayor because this city needs the skills that Costilla has.
a. begging the question
b. appeal to pity
c. appeal to emotion

_____ **5.** Health care reform is just like breathing. You won't live very long without either.
a. circular reasoning
b. appeal to emotions
c. misleading analogy

_____ **6.** Dr. Gloria May is an expert on genetic engineering because she wrote a best-selling book on the subject. If she wrote a book on it, then she is a top expert.
a. slippery slope
b. circular reasoning
c. _post hoc ergo propter hoc_

_____ **7.** Education is like a ladder. When you reach the top rung, it becomes unsafe.
a. misleading analogy
b. circular reasoning
c. red herring

_____ **8.** Amar scored 92 on the history test, while Julie scored 88. This result proves that Amar is smarter than Julie.
a. begging the question
b. red herring
c. _non sequitur_

_____ **9.** The advertisement points out that Japanese cars are purchased by everyone in America, including soccer moms, students, dentists, actors, and grandfathers.
a. card stacking
b. bandwagon
c. _non sequitur_

10
Crit.
Think.

_____ **10.** In reply to the criticism, the dictator stated that he did not permit general elections or political parties. He explained that the people had benefited immensely from his medical reforms.
   a. red herring
   b. appeal to pity
   c. misinterpreted statistics

Determine What Support Is Missing.   If you take a position, in an argument, you are not obliged to present evidence that could be used to support the opposite view. Thus, in analyzing any argument, ask yourself *What has been left out?* Think like the opposition and guess at evidence that could be presented. If much has been consciously omitted because it would weaken the argument, consider that in your evaluation.

Step 4: Evaluate the Argument

In deliberating, allow yourself enough time to evaluate arguments by weighing the support and looking at the issues from different perspectives. Remember, in critical thinking there is no "I am right, and you are wrong"; there are only strong and weak arguments. Relevant, believable, and consistent reasons build a good argument. Weigh the support, and make an informed evaluation.

Applying the Critical Thinking Steps 1–4

The following passage provides an example of how you can use the four-step format to evaluate an argument. Read the argument, respond briefly according to the directions for each step, and then read the explanation of how the critical thinking process was applied.

The Argument: Mandatory Military Service

Every high school graduate in the United States should be required to serve two years in the military. Leading experts agree that mandatory military service provides a valuable chance to learn about discipline and hard work. After this two-year opportunity for maturity, young men and women would be better equipped to succeed in college. To doubt this proposal is to question the value of our American youth.

Step 1: Identify the issue.
   What main point is the writer trying to convey? _____

_____

_____

10
Crit.
Think.

Step 2: Identify the support in the argument.
    What significant details support the central issue being argued? Briefly list them.

1. _____

_____

2. _____

_____

3. _____

_____

Step 3: Evaluate the support.
    Examine each supporting assertion separately for relevance, believability, and consistency. Can you identify any as fallacies that are intended to sell a weak argument? Also, list the type of supporting information that you believe is missing.

1. _____

2. _____

3. _____

What is missing? _____

Step 4: Evaluate the argument.
    Is this argument convincing? Why or why not? What do you think?

_____

Explanation of the Steps

Step 1: Identify the issue.
    The issue or main point is stated in the first sentence. Good critical thinkers would note, however, that "every" is always impossible to achieve and must be qualified.

Step 2: Identify the support in the argument.
    This argument contains three details offered in support.

1. Leading experts agree that mandatory military service provides a valuable chance to learn about discipline and hard work.

2. After this two-year opportunity for maturity, young men and women would be better equipped to succeed in college.

3. To doubt this proposal is to question the value of our American youth.

10
Crit.
Think.

Step 3: Evaluate the support.

The first supporting detail is a vague appeal to authority that does not reveal the leading experts. The second statement is vague and an over-simplification. The third is an overgeneralization. Scientific, psychological, and economic support for this argument seems to be missing.

Step 4: Evaluate the argument.

This is a weak argument. There may be good reasons for high school graduates to join the military before college, but this argument fails to give hard facts as evidence. The last sentence in the argument is a slippery slope statement that avoids logic.

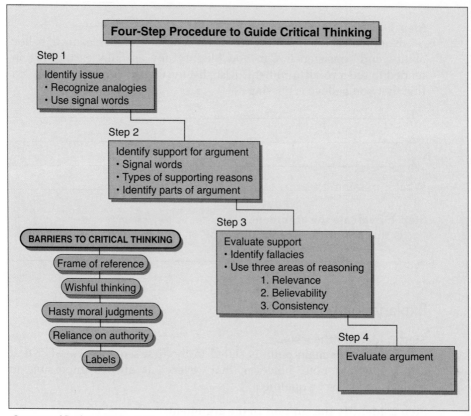

Courtesy of Professor Helen R. Carr, San Antonio College

Practice 5

10
Crit.
Think.

Read the following arguments and apply the four-step format for evaluation. State the issue, state the support, evaluate the support, and evaluate the argument.

Argument 1: Civility in the Classroom

The decline of civility in the classroom is directly related to the growth of a fast-food mentality in American society.   Consumers want instant hamburgers and are vocal in complaining if valuable minutes are wasted.   Similarly, students want a quick fix and have no tolerance for the long sentences of William Faulkner, the five-act plays of Shakespeare, or an extended classroom discussion.   The rudeness of the drive-in window threatens to disrupt the discourse that makes education possible.

Step 1: Identify the issue.

State the main point.

_____

_____

Step 2: Identify the support for the argument.

List the three details offered in support.

1. _____

_____

2. _____

_____

3. _____

_____

Step 3: Evaluate the support.

Examine each supporting assertion for relevance, believability, and consistency. Identify and label any fallacies. List missing support.

1. _____

_____

2. _____

3. _____

_____

What is missing? _____

Step 4: Evaluate the argument.

What is your overall evaluation, and why?

_____

_____

10
Crit.
Think.

Argument 2: Global Warming

Global warming is a real danger, and Americans should begin working against the threat that it poses to our environment. To illustrate visible warming, in the late 1800s Glacier National Park in Montana had 150 glaciers and now only 35 glaciers are left. Rock Winn, the star of *Coastal Warming*, summarized the ultimate danger by saying, "When the Arctic melts, New York City will be under water." Americans can look to eventually vacating the coastlines and heading for the interior to set up housekeeping.

Step 1: Identify the Issue.

State the main point.

_____

_____

Step 2: Identify the support for the argument.

List the three details offered in support.

1. _____

2. _____

3. _____

_____

Step 3: Evaluate the support.

Examine each supporting assertion for relevance, believability, and consistency. Identify and label any fallacies. List missing support.

1. _____

2. _____

3. _____

What is missing? _____

_____

Step 4: Evaluate the argument.

What is your overall evaluation, and why?

_____

_____

10
Crit.
Think.

Small-Group EXPLORATION

Form a five-member group and select one of the following activities. Brainstorm and then outline your major points on a transparency. Choose one group member to present the group's findings to the class. Individual assignments can also be made.

■ Demonstrate that you understand the barriers to critical thinking by writing four sentences explaining why you do not wish to discuss the topic of binge drinking in college. The sentences should be written to reflect the following barriers: wishful thinking, existing beliefs, reliance on authority, and labels.

■ Create an advertisement for a new shampoo. To sell the product, write a testimonial, a misleading analogy, an overgeneralization, and a misinterpreted statistic.

■ Outline an argument to support a proposal that 100 hours of community service be required for college graduation. Give four sound reasons to support your argument, and avoid fallacious thinking.

■ Outline an argument to support a proposal that each student at your college be required to have a computer. Support your argument with fallacies that include transfer, overgeneralization, questionable authority, and circular reasoning.

Net SEARCH

Advertisers use many techniques to promote and sell their products, including the use of celebrities as spokespeople. Search the Internet for three examples of celebrity endorsements or testimonials. Assess whether each testimonial is credible or a fallacy. Provide support for your conclusion.

10
Crit.
Think.

Chapter

11

Reading Rate

11a What Is Your Reading Rate?

When asked what they would like to change about their reading, many students answer that they read too slowly and would like to improve their reading speed. Whether you are reading a magazine or a textbook, reading 150 words per minute takes twice as long as reading 300 words per minute. Understanding the factors that contribute to your reading rate can both reduce anxiety and help increase reading efficiency.

Assess Your Reading Rate

How many words do you read, on average, each minute? To find out, read the following selection at your usual reading rate, just as you would have read it before you started thinking about speed. Time your reading of the selection so that you can calculate your rate. Read carefully enough to answer the ten comprehension questions that follow the selection.

Practice 1

Time your reading of this selection so that you can compute your words-per-minute rate. To make the calculation easier, begin reading on the exact minute, with zero seconds. In other words, begin when the second hand points to 12 or use a digital watch. Record your starting time in minutes and seconds and, when you have finished reading, record your finishing time in minutes and seconds. Then answer the questions that follow. Remember, read the selection at your normal rate.

Starting time: _____ minutes _____ seconds

Thanksgiving

Though the Pilgrims held the first Thanksgiving dinner, our celebration of the holiday today is due in large part to the efforts of a female magazine editor.

After a four-month journey, the 102 Pilgrims on board the *Mayflower* landed at Plymouth, Massachusetts, on December 11, 1620. The winter was se-
5   vere and deadly. A plague killed hundreds of local Indians and forty-six Pilgrims. The hard work of the spring and summer, however, brought a bountiful autumn harvest. Food was finally abundant. The survivors were grateful and particularly appreciated the help of an Indian named Squanto.

As a boy, Squanto had been captured by explorers to America and sold
10   into slavery in Spain. He escaped to England, spent several years working for a wealthy merchant, and then returned to his native Indian village just six months before the Pilgrims landed. He helped them build houses and grow crops. In that first autumn the Pilgrims elected a governor and then proclaimed a day of thanksgiving in their small town.

15   A feast was prepared for ninety Indians and fifty-six settlers, who celebrated with a parade, games, and fellowship.

The six women who prepared the first Thanksgiving Day meal produced a menu that has become our traditional holiday fare. The wild turkeys, however, might have been guinea fowl or any other wild bird that hunters could have
20   shot in the woods. The menu also included venison, wild plums, corn, and dried berries. Pumpkin was boiled. There was probably no pumpkin pie since the flour stored on the ship had been eaten. The fifteen young boys in the settlement gathered wild cranberries, which the women boiled and mashed into a sauce.

The following year brought a poor harvest and no feast. The Pilgrims never
25   regularly celebrated Thanksgiving Day.

More than a hundred years after the Pilgrims, the first national Thanksgiving proclamation was issued by President George Washington in 1789. The celebration, however, was not embraced by the new nation. Many Americans in the newly united thirteen colonies were against honoring the
30   hardships of only one colony in the northeast. The feeling was that the brave new nation had nobler events that merited celebration.

About forty years later, in 1827, Sarah Josepha Hale started a one-woman crusade for a Thanksgiving celebration. She was the editor of the extremely popular Boston *Ladies' Magazine*; her editorials argued for the national holiday,
35   and she encouraged subscribers to write to local politicians with requests.

National events helped make Mrs. Hale's request a reality in 1863. Victory for the Union in the Civil War seemed possible after the bloody Battle of

Gettysburg, where thousands of Union and Confederate soldiers lost their lives. In response, Mrs. Hale wrote an impassioned plea for unity and a national
40 day to give thanks. President Abraham Lincoln responded by setting aside the fourth Thursday in November as a national Thanksgiving Day. Only once, thanks to Franklin Roosevelt, was that date changed to the third Thursday in November. When millions protested, the holiday date was returned to the fourth Thursday.[1]

(500 words)

Finishing time: _____ minutes _____ seconds

Reading time in minutes: _____

Words per minute from chart: _____

Time (minutes)	Words per Minute	Time (minutes)	Words per Minute
1:00	500	2:30	200
1:10	429	2:40	188
1:20	375	2:50	176
1:30	334	3:00	167
1:40	300	3:10	158
1:50	272	3:20	150
2:00	250	3:30	143
2:10	231	3:40	136
2:20	214		

Mark each statement with *T* for true or *F* for false.

_____ **1.** In the fall of 1621, fewer than 75 Pilgrims remained.

_____ **2.** In that first year many Pilgrims were killed by Indians.

_____ **3.** Because of his past experiences, Squanto probably spoke some English.

_____ **4.** Six months prior to the Pilgrims' landing, Sqanto returned to America as a slave.

_____ **5.** The author implies that the first Thanksgiving feast celebrated both the bountiful harvest and the election of a governor.

_____ **6.** The Pilgrims' first Thanksgiving menu included turkey, pumpkin pie, and cranberries.

_____ **7.** The author implies that regional rivalry or jealousy played a part in the lack of popularity for a national Thanksgiving Day during George Washington's presidency.

[1]Adapted from Charles Panati, *Panati's Extraordinary Origins of Everyday Things.*

_____ **8.** Sarah Hale launched a lengthy campaign in her *Ladies' Magazine* for a national holiday to celebrate Thanksgiving.

_____ **9.** Thanksgiving has been celebrated annually as a national holiday in America from its beginning in 1621.

_____ **10.** The author implies that Abraham Lincoln's primary reason for proclaiming Thanksgiving a national holiday was his desire to honor the Pilgrims from Massachusetts.

Comprehension (% correct): _____%

Evaluate Your Rate

Reading specialists say that the average adult reading speed on relatively easy material is approximately 250 words per minute with 70 percent comprehension. The reading rate on the same type of material for college students tends to be a little higher, averaging about 300 words per minute with 70 percent comprehension. However, these figures are misleading for a number of reasons.

Anyone who says *My reading rate is 500 words per minute* is not telling the whole story. One question immediately comes to mind: Is that the rate for reading the newspaper or a physics textbook? For an efficient reader, no one reading rate serves for all purposes or all materials.

"You did very well. The first chapter
is always the most difficult."

Vary Your Rate According to Prior Knowledge, Difficulty, and Purpose

If you already know a lot about a topic, you can usually read about it at a faster rate than if you were exploring a totally new subject. For example, a psychology major will work through a chapter on deviant behaviors at a faster rate than he or she would read a chapter on a less familiar topic such as supply-side economics. At the beginning of the economics chapter, the student may need to slow to a crawl so as to understand the new concepts. Toward the end of the chapter, as new ideas become more familiar, the same student's reading rate is likely to increase.

The difficulty level of reading material is measured by a formula that combines the length of the sentences and the number of syllables in the words. Complex sentences are more difficult to read than simple ones, and unfamiliar technical vocabulary can bring a reader to a complete stop. In addition, sometimes the difficulty is increased by the complexity of the ideas expressed and—perhaps unnecessarily—by the author's writing style.

Before reading, ask yourself, *Why am I reading this material?* Based on your answer, vary your speed to best suit your purpose. Do you want 100 percent comprehension (studying for a nursing exam), 70 percent (reading a newspaper article), or 50 percent (flipping through a magazine in the doctor's office)? In other words, figure out what you want to know when you've finished, and read accordingly.

11b What Are the Techniques for Faster Reading?

Concentrate

Fast readers, like race-car drivers, need to concentrate on what they are doing. Although you use your eyes, you actually read with your mind. If your attention is veering off course, you lose some of that mental alertness necessary for success.

Distractions that interfere with concentration fall into two categories, external and internal. External distractions—the physical happenings around you—are easy to control with a little assertiveness. You can turn off the television, go to another room, ask people not to interrupt, or choose a place to read where interruptions will be minimal. Internal distractions—the irrelevant ideas that pop into your head while reading—are more difficult to manage. Use a notepad to jot down reminders for action on nagging concerns, so that your mind will be clear for reading.

Stop Regressing

During your initial reading of material, have you ever realized halfway down a page that you have no idea what you just read? Your eyes were engaged, but your mind was not. To resolve this problem, did you go back and reread sentences or paragraphs? This type of rereading is called **regression.**

Regression can be a crutch that allows you to make up for wasted time. If you have this problem, analyze when and why you are regressing. If you discern that your regression is due to wandering thoughts, deny yourself that privilege to break the habit. Tell yourself, *Okay, I missed that paragraph because I was thinking of something else, but now I'm going to start paying close attention.*

Rereading because you do not understand, by contrast, is a legitimate correction strategy used by good readers who monitor their own comprehension. Rereading because your mind was asleep is a waste of time; daydreaming is a habit caused by lack of involvement with the material. Be demanding of yourself and expect 100 percent attention to the task. Visualize the incoming ideas and relate the new material to what you already know. Don't just read the words; *think the ideas.*

Expand Fixations

Your eyes must stop to read. These stops, called **fixations,** last a fraction of a second. On average, 5 to 10 percent of reading time is spent on fixations. Thus, reading more than one word per fixation will reduce your total reading time.

Research on vision shows that the eye is able to see about one-half inch on either side of a fixation point. Thus a reader can see two or possibly three words per fixation. To illustrate, read the following phrase:

in the car

Did you make three fixations, or two, or one? Now read the following word:

entertainment

This word can be read automatically with one fixation. A beginning reader probably stopped for each syllable, giving a total of four fixations. If you can read *entertainment,* which has 13 letters, with one fixation, you can certainly read the eight-letter phrase *in the car* with only one fixation.

Use your peripheral vision on either side of the fixation point to help you read two or three words per fixation. In expanding your fixations, take in phrases or thought units that seem to go together. To illustrate, the following sentence has been grouped into thought units with fixation points:

After lunch,   I studied   in the library   at a table.
      •   •   •   •

By expanding your fixations, you can easily read the sentence with four fixations rather than ten, thereby reducing your total reading time.

Monitor Subvocalization

Subvocalization is the little voice in your head that reads for you. Some experts claim that subvocalization is necessary for difficult material, whereas others say that fast readers are totally visual and do not need to hear the words. Good college readers will probably experience some of both. On easy reading tasks you may find yourself speeding up to the point that you are not hearing every word, particularly the unimportant filler phrases. However, with more difficult textbook readings, your inner voice may speak every word. The voice seems to add another sensory dimension to help you comprehend. Because experts say that the inner voice can read up to about 400 words per minute, many college students can make a considerable improvement in speed while still experiencing the inner voice.

Some readers move their lips while reading, as if to pronounce each word. This immature habit, called *vocalization*, should be stopped. If you find yourself vocalizing, putting a slip of paper or a pencil in your mouth while reading will alert you to lip movement and inspire you to stop.

Preview

Size up your reading assignment before you get started. If it is a chapter, glance through the pages and read the subheadings. Look at the illustrations and notice the italicized words and boldfaced print. Make predictions about what you think the chapter will cover. Activate your prior knowledge on the subject. Pull out your mental computer chip and prepare to blend your experience with the printed page.

Use Your Pen as a Pacer

The technique of using your pen or your fingers as a pacer means pointing under the words in a smooth, flowing motion, moving back and forth from line to line. Although as a child you might have been warned never to point to words, this technique is very effective for improving reading speed. It offers several benefits. First, it improves concentration by drawing your attention directly to the words. In addition, the forward motion of your pen tends to keep you from regressing because rereading would interrupt your established rhythm. What's more, by pulling your eyes down the page, the pen movement helps set a rapid, steady pace for reading and encourages you to shift from word-by-word reading to phrase reading.

You cannot read an entire book using your pen as a pacer, but you can start out with this technique. Later, if you notice yourself slowing down, use your pen again to get back on track. The technique is demonstrated in the following passage. Your pen moves in a Z pattern from one side of the column to the other. Because you are trying to read several words at each fixation, your pen does not have to go to the extreme edges of the column.

> Rapid reading requires quick thinking
> and intense concentration. The reader
> must be alert and aggressive. Being
> intrested in the subject helps improve speed.

As you begin to read faster and become more proficient with the Z pattern, you will notice the corners starting to round into an S. That is, the Z pattern is turning into a more relaxed S swirl. When you get to the point of using the S swirl, you will be reading for ideas and not reading every word; you are then reading actively and aggressively, with good concentration. Use the Z pattern until you find your pen or hand movement has automatically turned into an S.

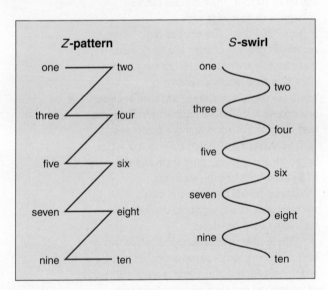

Push and Pace

Be alert and aggressive and try to read faster. Sit up straight and attack the text. Force yourself to hurry. Changing old habits is difficult; you will never read faster unless you make a conscious effort to do so.

Set goals and pace yourself. Count the number of pages in your homework assignments and estimate according to your reading rate how many pages you can read in 30 minutes. Use a paper clip or a sticky note to mark the page you are trying to reach. Push yourself to achieve your goal.

Practice 2

The following passages are written in columns with approximately six words on each line for the first passage and nine for the second. Using your pen as a pacer, read each passage and try to make only two or three fixations per line. A dashed line has been placed down the middle of the column to help you with the fixations. Record your time for reading each passage and then answer the comprehension questions. Since both passages are 200 words long, you can determine your reading rate for one from the same chart.

Passage 1: The Whale Shark

The largest shark is the
massive whale shark. Little is known
about these giants, some of which
have been estimated at sixty feet long
5   and up to 20 tons. Their mouths can be
as large as six feet wide with
at least 7,000 teeth. Contrary to the
reputation of some of their smaller cousins,
these animals are not considered dangerous
10   since they feed mostly on plankton,
which are microscopic organisms such as algae,
protozoans, animal larvae, and worms. They also
feed on small fish, squid, and tiny octopuses.
To feed, sharks take in large quantities of water
15   by mouth and then use their teeth and gills
to filter, thus pushing the water out
and leaving behind plankton and other
sea creatures. This is similar to the feeding
techniques used by whales.
20   There have been reports that whale sharks
have overturned small native boats, but it is
widely believed that the sharks were in the middle
of feeding and not even aware of the boats.
In all other reports, whale sharks have shown
21   themselves to be docile and friendly to humans.
Their natural curiosity has brought them
very close to small boats. They have even
allowed scuba divers to "ride" them.

(200 words)

Reading time: _____

Words per minute: _____ (See time chart on page 217.)

Mark each statement *T* for true or *F* for false.

_____ **1.** The mouth of a whale shark can be six feet wide.

_____ **2.** According to the passage, whale sharks turn over fishing boats in an attempt to eat humans.

Passage 2: The Ice Business

Before refrigeration was invented, ice was a lucrative business. During the winter months, it was cut into large blocks from frozen ponds and stored in well-insulated buildings called ice houses. Before delivery
5   to customers, workers cut the ice into smaller blocks that would easily fit into the family ice box. An iceman made home deliveries to the family's ice box, a heavy wooden chest with three or four doors on the front for easily accessing food. The inside was lined
10   with metal to contain water as the ice melted.
    A typical New England icehouse was built next to a pond with the inner wall 10 inches from the outer wall for insulation. Sawdust or hay was spread on the floor and over the ice for additional insulation, allowing
15   the ice in some places to last for the entire year.
In the mid 1800s, a thriving Alaskan ice company owned seven steamers and hired over 200 workers to cut and store the ice for summer shipment. Ice from Alaska was shipped as far as South America, and ice from New
20   England was shipped as far as the Caribbean.
By the 1870s, innovations in cooling made the ice business obsolete.

(200 words)

Reading time: _____

Words per minute: _____

Mark each statement *T* for true or *F* for false.

_____ **1.** Sawdust was used as insulation in the family ice box.

_____ **2.** Ice was shipped from Alaska by steamers during the summer months.

Time Chart for Passages 1 and 2			
Time (minutes)	Words per Minute	Time (minutes)	Words per Minute
0:20	600	1:00	200
0:30	400	1:10	171
0:40	300	1:20	150
0:50	240		

11c Why Skim?

Skimming is a technique of selectively reading for the main idea. Because it involves processing material at rates of around 900 words per minute, some experts do not define it as reading. Skimming involves skipping words, sentences, paragraphs, and even pages. It is a method of quickly overviewing material to answer the question *What is this about?*

Skimming and previewing are very similar in that both involve getting an overview. Previewing sets the stage for a later careful reading, whereas skimming is a substitute for a complete reading. Skimming is useful for getting the gist of material that you want to know about but don't have enough time to read carefully. For example, you might want to skim supplemental articles that have been placed on reserve in the library. If your professor is interested only in your understanding the main idea of each article, a complete reading of each article would be unnecessary. At other times, you may want to pick up a book just to "get the idea" but not read it completely.

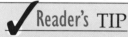 Reader's TIP

Using Skimming Techniques

1. Read the title, subheadings, italics, and boldfaced print to get an idea of what the material is about.

2. Get an insight into the organization of the material to help you anticipate the location of important points. Some of the organizational patterns and their functions are as follows:
   a. *Listing:* explains items of equal value
   b. *Definition and examples:* defines a term and gives examples to help the reader understand the term
   c. *Time order or sequence:* presents items in chronological order
   d. *Comparison-contrast:* compares similarities and differences among items
   e. *Description:* explains characteristics of an item
   f. *Cause and effect:* shows how one action produces another
   g. *Problem-solution:* explains the causes and effects of a problem; suggests a solution
   h. *Opinion-proof:* states an opinion and then supports it with evidence

3. If the first paragraph is introductory, read it. If not, skip to a paragraph that seems to introduce the topic.

(continued)

4. Move rapidly, letting your eyes float over the words. Try to grasp the main ideas and the significant supporting details.

5. Notice first sentences in paragraphs and read them if they seem to be summary statements.

6. Skip words that seem to have little meaning, such as *a, an,* and *the.*

7. Skip sentences or sections that seem to contain the following:
   a. Familiar ideas
   b. Unnecessary details
   c. Superfluous examples
   d. Restatements or unneeded summaries
   e. Material irrelevant to your purpose

8. If the last paragraph of a section is a summary, read it if you need to check your understanding.

11d   Why Scan?

Because **scanning** is a process of searching for a single bit of information, it is more a locating skill than a reading skill. When you look up a number in a telephone book, you are scanning. When scanning for information, you do not need to understand the meaning of the material; you merely want to pinpoint a specific detail. Suppose that after reading a chapter on pricing in your marketing textbook, you cannot recall the definition of *price lining.* You would not reread the entire chapter, but scan it to find the phrase and its definition. You use this same scanning technique with a glossary and an index, as well as doing online research on the Internet.

Researchers use a combination of skimming and scanning. If you are working on a research paper on paranoia, you might have 30 sources to investigate. Instead of a complete reading of each reference, you can scan to locate the information relevant to your topic and skim to get the main idea.

✓ Reader's TIP
Using Scanning Techniques

■ Figure out the organization of the material. Predict which section will probably contain the information you are seeking.

■ Know specifically what you are looking for. Decide on a key expression that will signal your information, but be ready to switch to a related idea if your first choice doesn't work.

(continued)

- Repeat the phrase and hold the image in your mind. Concentrate on the image so that you will recognize it when it comes into view.
- Move quickly and aggressively. Remember, you are scanning, not reading.
- Verify through careful reading. After locating your information, read carefully to make sure you have really found it.

Small-Group EXPLORATION

Form a five-member group and select one of the following activities. Brainstorm and then outline your major points on a transparency. Choose one group member to present the group's findings to the class. Individual assignments can also be made.

- Create a Top Ten list of suggestions for improving your reading speed.
- Create a Top Ten list of reasons why students have trouble concentrating on what they are reading.
- List reasons why prior knowledge influences reading rate.
- List reasons why students should not expect to read a textbook at the same reading rate as a novel.

Net SEARCH

Do you think your reading is more efficient with a book or on the computer screen? Search the Internet for an online speed reading test. Take the test and compare your efficiency. Summarize your reactions to the online timed reading. Do you think it was an accurate assessment? What seemed to be the motivation behind online timed reading selections?

Chapter

12

Techniques for Remembering Textbook Information

12a How Do You Organize College Textbook Reading?

During your years in college, you will encounter a variety of textbooks in several academic areas. As you work through these textbooks, it will be important for you to make sense of the material you read and to remember important points made by each author. In this chapter we cover strategies that you can use to organize textbook material so that you can better understand it.

12b What Is Annotating?

Do you view your textbook as a treasure to be preserved for resale? If so, change your thinking and look at it as a learning tool. Your job is to

✔ Reader's TIP

Reading College Textbooks

■ Preview the chapter before reading. Take advantage of any signposts: opening questions, introductory stories, outlines, subheadings, italics, boldfaced print, numbers, and concluding summary.

■ Integrate knowledge while reading: predict, picture, relate, monitor, and correct.

■ Recall and self-test.

■ Organize material for future study by summarizing, annotating, note-taking, outlining, and/or mapping.

■ Control distractions by choosing an environment conducive to study. Sit at a table or desk instead of on the bed. Let your phone pick up messages.

■ Control internal distractions. Free your mind by writing a daily checklist of things you need to do.

FAST FACT

George Miller of Harvard University found that people can store only approximately seven listed items in memory. Hence we have seven-digit telephone numbers.

make sense of textbook information and to select the important points to remember.

Annotating is a method of highlighting main ideas, significant supporting details, and key terms. The word *annotate* means "to add marks," not just to color the book yellow. Using a system of symbols and notations, you mark the text on the first reading so that a complete rereading will not be necessary. Your markings should indicate pertinent points to review.

You can use a colored marker for highlighting, but you will also need a pen for notations. Mark after a unit of thought has been completed. This may mean after a single paragraph or after three pages; marking varies with the material. When you are first reading, every sentence seems of major importance as each new idea unfolds, and the tendency is to annotate too much. But overmarking is not useful and wastes both reading and review time. Students who annotate will probably also want to list terms and ideas on a separate sheet for review and self-testing. At the end of the course, your textbook should have a worn but well-organized look.

Example of Annotating

Notice in the passage on page 223 how the notations highlight main ideas and significant supporting details that you may need to know for a test. This same passage will be used throughout this chapter to demonstrate each of the five methods of organizing textbook material.

✓ Reader's TIP

Annotating Your Textbook

Develop a system of notations. Use circles, stars, numbers, and whatever else helps you put the material visually into perspective. Anything that makes sense to you is a correct notation. An example follows.

Main idea	( )
Supporting material	————
Major trend or possible essay exam question	*
Important smaller point to know for multiple-choice item	✓
Word that you must be able to define	⬭
Section of material to reread for review	{ }
Numbering of important details under a major issue	(1), (2), (3)
Didn't understand and must seek advice	?
Notes in the margin	Ex., Def., Topic
Questions in the margin	Why signif.?
Indicating relationships	⌒
Related issues or idea	← R

Skin Cancer: Save Your Skin

Def.   A golden suntan means damaged skin and an increased risk of skin cancer. Every year more than 7,300 people die from a deadly form of skin cancer called melanoma. The ultraviolet rays of the sun penetrate the skin and injure pigment cells. If detected while still confined to the upper skin layer, however, melanoma is 100% curable.

Prevent   First, practice prevention. (1) Avoid the strongest rays by staying out of the sun as much as possible during midday between 10 am and 4 pm. At least a half-hour before going into the sun, apply (2) a sunscreen with an SPF (Sun Protection Factor) of 15 or higher and reapply every two hours. When possible, wear loose (3) clothing to cover your skin.

Check   Check your skin regularly for signs of cancer. Use the American Academy of Dermatology's ABCD checklist to monitor moles and freckles. If any of the following features are present, you have the potential for cancer: (1) **Asymmetry** such that one half looks different from the other. (2) **Borders** that are ragged and irregular. (3) **Color** variations, and (4) **Diameter** that is greater than the size of a pencil eraser.

Practice 1

Using a variety of notations, annotate the following passage as if you were preparing for a quiz on the material.

Conflict-Induced Stress

Conflict is unsettling and causes stress. Such a conflict does not have to be an argument with others but can be a struggle within yourself to make decisions that best satisfy your goals. If you are faced with positive goals that you wish to approach and negative goals that you wish to avoid, your conflict may fall into any of the following categories:

Approach-approach conflicts: You are torn between two excellent choices, but yet you agonize over making the right decision. For example, you may have two appealing job opportunities, one in Houston and one in New York City. When you accept one, you lose the other.

Avoidance-avoidance conflicts: You are faced with two alternatives, each of which is negative and punishing. You feel trapped. Perhaps you are deciding between an easy course with a boring professor and a difficult course with an interesting one. Both have negative aspects to consider.

Approach-avoidance conflicts: In this conflict you are considering only one goal, but it has both positive and negative aspects. For example, you want to go to the football game with your friends on Saturday, but you do not want to sit in the cold wind on the upper-level seats for which they have tickets. What should you do? When faced with the many alternatives in life, not just one but multiple approach-avoidance conflicts can be common.

Review your annotations. Have you sufficiently highlighted the main idea and the significant supporting details?

12c What Is Summary Writing?

A **summary** is a brief, concise statement of the main idea of a piece of writing and its significant supporting details. The first sentence should state the main idea or thesis, and subsequent sentences should include the significant details. Minor details and material irrelevant to your purpose as a learner should be omitted. A summary should take the form of a paragraph and should always be shorter than the material being summarized.

When you write a research paper, summarizing is an essential skill. As you research sources, you may be consulting as many as ten articles, four books, and ten Internet sites over a period of a month or two. After each reading, take notes that will enable you to write your paper without returning to the library or the Internet for another look at the original reference.

 Reader's TIP

Summarizing

- Keep in mind the purpose of your summary. Your projected needs will determine which details should be included.
- Make the main idea the first sentence in your summary.
- Include as many major ideas and significant supporting details as your purpose demands.
- Do not include irrelevant or repeated information in your summary.
- Use appropriate transitional words and phrases to show relationships between points.
- Use paragraph form.

Example of Summarizing

Reread the passage on skin cancer on page 223 as if you were researching the topic for a term paper and needed to write a summary on a note card. Mark key terms that you would include in your summary. (They will probably be the same terms that you have annotated.) Before reading the example below, anticipate what you would include in your own summary.

> **Skin Cancer**
> Sun exposure increases the risk of melanoma, a deadly skin cancer. Practice prevention by avoiding midday sun, applying a SPF sunscreen of 15, and covering your skin. Check your moles and freckles for asymmetry, borders, color, and diameter.

Practice 2

Summarize the key ideas in the passage on conflict-induced stress on page 224 as if you were creating a research note card. Use your annotations to summarize.

12d What Is Notetaking?

Notetaking simply means jotting down important ideas from the text for future study. Students who prefer this method say that working with pencil and paper while reading keeps them involved with the material and thus improves concentration. Notetaking takes longer than annotating, but there will be times, even if you have already annotated the text, when you may feel the need to organize information further into notes. Your decision on whether to take this step will be based on later testing demands, time, and the complexity of the material.

 Reader's TIP

Taking Notes

One of the most popular systems of notetaking is called the **Cornell Method.** The steps are as follows:

1. Draw a line down your paper 2½ inches from the left side to create a 2½-inch margin for noting key words and a 6-inch area on the right for writing sentence summaries.

2. After you have finished reading a section, tell yourself what you have read and jot down sentence summaries in the 6-inch area on the right side of your paper. Use your own words, and make sure you have included both main ideas and significant supporting details. Be brief, but use complete sentences.

3. Review your summary sentences and underline key words. Write these key words in the column on the left side of your paper. These words can be used later to stimulate your memory.

Because of time constraints, some students write in phrases rather than complete sentences. The following example applies the Cornell Method of notetaking to the passage on skin cancer that you have already read.

> *Skin Cancer*
>
> | Melanoma | Sun exposure increases risk of skin cancer. |
> |---|---|
> | Prevention | Practice prevention by avoiding midday sun, using SPF 15 sunscreen, & covering skin. |
> | Detection | Check your moles and freckles for asymmetry, borders, color, & diameter. |

Practice 3

Use the Cornell Method to take notes on the passage on conflict-induced stress on page 224 as if you were preparing for a quiz on the material.

12e   What Is Outlining?

An **outline** organizes major points and subordinates items of lesser importance. The Roman numerals, letters, numbers, and indentations quickly show how one idea relates to another and how all aspects relate to the whole. The layout of the outline is simply a graphic display of main ideas and significant supporting details.

The following example is a picture-perfect version of the basic outline format. In practice, however, your working outline would probably not be as detailed or as regular as this one is. Use the tools of the outline format, *especially the indentations and numbers,* to devise your own outlining system for organizing information.

Title
  I. First main idea
    A. Supporting idea
      1. Detail
      2. Detail
      3. Detail
        a. Minor detail
        b. Minor detail
    B. Supporting idea
      1. Detail
      2. Detail
    C. Supporting idea

II. Second main idea
  A. Supporting idea
  B. Supporting idea

Don't worry about creating an absolutely perfect outline. Do use numbers, letters, and indentations to show levels of importance. A quick look to the far left of an outline indicates the topic, with subordinate ideas indented underneath. Good outliners use plenty of paper so that the levels of importance are evident at a glance.

Another use of the outline is to organize notes from class lectures. While listening to a class lecture, you must almost instantly receive, synthesize, select, and record material for future reference. Focus on the big picture rather than every small detail. Use a modified outline form and include stars, circles, and underlines for emphasis.

Professors say that they can look around a classroom at student lecture notes and tell how well each person understood the lesson. The errors most frequently observed fall into four categories:

- Poor organization
- Failure to show importance
- Writing too much
- Writing too little

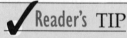 Reader's TIP

Avoiding Pitfalls in Outlining

The most important thing to remember in outlining is *What is my purpose?* You don't need to include everything, and you don't need a picture-perfect version for study notes. Include only what you will need to remember later, and use the numbering system and the indentations to show how one idea relates to another.

Other important guidelines to remember are:

- Get a general overview before you start. How many main topics do there seem to be?
- Use short phrases rather than sentences.
- Put it in your own words. If you cannot paraphrase, do you really understand?
- Be selective. Are you organizing or completely rewriting?
- Review your outline and highlight key terms in yellow to make them highly visible for later review and self-testing.

Example of Outlining

In the following study outline for the skin cancer passage on page 223, notice how the numbers and letters, as well as the indentations, show levels of importance of ideas.

Skin Cancer

   I. Melanoma
      A. Kills more than 7,300 annually
      B. If early detection, 100% curable

   II. Prevention
      A. Avoid midday sun
      B. Use SPF 15 sunscreen
      C. Cover skin

   III. Detection
      A. Asymmetry
      B. Borders
      C. Color
      D. Diameter

✓ Reader's TIP

Taking Class Lecture Notes

■ Show levels of importance. Make use of numbers, stars, and indentations.

■ Write on only one side of your notebook. Use the other side for inserting clarifications, later discussion, and review questions.

■ Spread out. Paper is inexpensive compared to your college investment.

■ Write in pen, not pencil. You'll need to read it many weeks later.

■ **Always** review your class lecture notes before the next class. Do so within 24 hours. This review takes time initially but saves time later. Note gaps of knowledge and follow up with class questions.

Practice 4

Outline the key ideas in the passage on conflict-induced stress (see page 224 as if you were planning to use your notes to study for a quiz. Use your annotations to outline.

12f What Is Mapping?

Mapping is a visual system of condensing ideas to show relationships and importance. A map is a diagram of the major points, with their significant subpoints, that support a topic. The purpose of mapping as an organizing strategy is to improve memory by grouping material in a highly visual way.

A map provides a quick reference to overviewing an article or a chapter, and it can be used to reduce notes for later study. Maps are not restricted to any one pattern but can be formed in a variety of creative shapes, as the diagrams here illustrate.

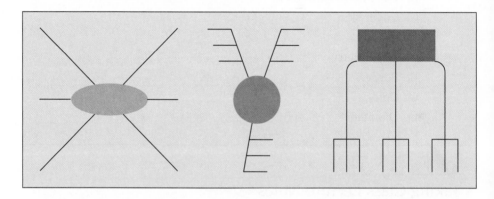

The next map diagrams the passage on skin cancer. Notice how the visual display emphasizes the groups of ideas that support the topic.

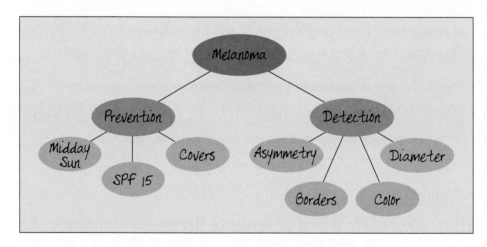

✓ Reader's TIP

Drawing Maps

Follow these steps for mapping:

1. Draw a circle or a box in the middle of a page. In it, write the subject or topic of the material.
2. Determine the main ideas that support the subject. Write them on lines radiating from the central circle or box.
3. Determine the significant details. Write them on lines attached to each main idea. The number of details you include will depend on the material and your purpose.

Practice 5

Create a map for the key ideas in the passage on conflict-induced stress (see page 224). Use your annotations and outline to help. Experiment with several different shapes for your map pattern.

12g What Are Mnemonics?

Mnemonics are techniques or tricks to help you organize and recall. You use pictures, sounds, rhythms, and other mental tricks to create sensory "handles" or hooks to arrange and retrieve information. If given a list of 12 nouns to remember, students who link them in a story will remember more than students who just try to memorize them as unrelated items. Weaving such a story is called *narrative chaining* because the technique links, organizes, and gives meaning to unrelated items. Several mnemonic techniques are suggested for college learning.

Study Out Loud. Although you may not think of this approach as a mnemonic, you are using additional senses when you read or study out loud. Your eyes *see* the material on the page, and your ears *hear* the information. Your mouth, tongue, lips, and throat *feel* the sensation of speaking the words. This technique is particularly effective for studying lecture notes after class or before an exam.

Write It Down. Writing works in a similar way to studying aloud because you feel your hand transcribing the information. Thus, summarizing, annotating, notetaking, outlining, and mapping add sensory steps to learning. Always take class lecture notes to reinforce the spoken informa-tion. Translate or paraphrase what the professor says into your own words.

Create Acronyms.   Create words using the first letter of each word you want to remember. A well-known example of this technique is using *HOMES* to remember the Great Lakes: *H*uron, *O*ntario, *M*ichigan, *E*rie, *S*uperior.

Create Acrostics.   Form a sentence in which the first letter of each word corresponds to the first letter of each word in a list you want to remember. For example, *Members must promise justice unless neighbors enlist very soon* is an acrostic for remembering the nine planets in our solar system: *M*ercury, *M*ars, *P*luto, *J*upiter, *U*ranus, *N*eptune, *E*arth, *V*enus, *S*aturn. If you need to remember the planets in the order they orbit the sun, create a different sentence. Silly and unusual acrostics can be easy to remember.

Use Rhythms, Rhymes, and Jingles.   Use rhythm and rhyme to create additional "handles" for your brain to use to process and retrieve information. Most young students never forget the year Christopher Columbus discovered America because they learned the rhyme "In fourteen hundred and ninety-two, Columbus sailed the ocean blue."

FAST FACT

In caves, remember *stalagmites* as "mounds (as the *m* in *mites*) on the floor" and *stalactites* as "holding on tightly (sounds like *tights*) to the top of the cave."

Make Associations.   Make a connection between seemingly unrelated ideas by using pictures, nonsense ideas, or connected bits of logic. For example, two easily confused words are *stationary*, which means "standing still," and *stationery*, meaning "letter-writing paper." To remember the difference, note that *stationary* is spelled with an *a*, which relates to the *a* in "standing still," while *stationery* is spelled with an *e*, which relates to "letters."

Use Your Imagination.   Create a picture, perhaps a funny picture, just as you would on a vocabulary concept card. For example, picture a *voracious* reader as a shark greedily eating a book.

Use Key Word Images.   To learn foreign language vocabulary, use the sound of the new word to relate to an image of a known word. For example, the Spanish word for horse is *caballo*, which is pronounced *cab-eye-yo*. Associate *eye* as the key word, and picture a horse with only one large eye.

Reader's TIP
Remembering Information

- Understand it by studying aloud and writing it down.
- Hook it to strengthen retrieval cues.
- Link it through letter, word, and narrative associations.
- Sense it in pictures, rhythm, or rhymes.
- Rehearse it to reinforce the links.

12
Text-
books

Practice 6

1. Create an association to remember that *cereal* is a breakfast food and *serial* means "arranged in a series, rank, or row."

_____

_____

2. Create an acrostic or an acronym to remember the elements that make up the vast majority of molecules in living things: carbon, hydrogen, nitrogen, oxygen, phosphorus, and sulfur.

_____

_____

3. Create a rhyme or a jingle to remember that World War II ended in 1945.

_____

_____

Small-Group EXPLORATION

Form a five-member group and select one of the following activities. Brainstorm and then outline your major points on a transparency. Choose one group member to present the group's findings to the class. Individual assignments can also be made.

- Review lecture notes that classmates have taken in other classes. Make a list of strengths and suggestions for improvement.
- Conduct an experiment with the class using a story as a mnemonic. To prepare, create two lists of 12 different nouns. Create no story for the first list, but for the second list make up a story that links the 12

nouns in a meaningful narrative. Now you are prepared for your class presentation. Give the first 12 nouns without a story to the class, allow one minute for memorizing, and then ask classmates to write down the 12 nouns. Tally results. Next, present the second list of 12 nouns with its linking narrative. Again, allow one minute for rehearsal, and then ask students to write the nouns. Compare the results. Did the addition of a narrative improve memory?

■ Create mnemonics for remembering the names of the members of your group and present them to the class.

■ Devise three different mnemonic techniques, other than reading aloud and writing, for remembering the following facts about your two blood pressure measurements:

Blood moves in waves, and the systolic pressure is the pressure at the height of the blood wave when the ventricles contract. The diastolic pressure is the pressure within the arteries when the ventricles are at rest. An average healthy blood pressure is 120/80. The systolic is reported above the diastolic.

Net SEARCH

Search the Internet for mnemonic techniques to help you recall and organize information. List at least five examples of mnemonics that have helped others remember information.

Part 3
Reading in the Disciplines

Chapter
13

Reading in the Humanities

13a   What Are the Humanities?

Colleges group core curriculum courses into areas such as the humanities, social sciences, natural sciences, and mathematics and computer science. For graduation in any major, you are usually required to take a minimum number of credit hours in each area.

Humanities courses typically include literature, composition, languages, history, philosophy, fine arts, and communication. The name for the area is taken from *human,* which means "mankind." The courses focus on the culture of human beings, which includes ideas, art, and history. Through studying the humanities, we learn about ourselves by connecting with all who have gone before us and contributed to our heritage.

13b   How Is History Interpreted?

You will almost certainly take at least one history course during your college career, maybe even more. History tells stories—stories of real people—and not just the rich and powerful, but the poor and ordinary as

237

well. History shows us who we are and where we might be going by reflecting on what we have thought and done, how we have changed, and how we have remained the same. History is a story of people told by people, and your history textbook is a record accumulated over many years. Your textbook and your professor will help you interpret historical events and appreciate the stories told in them.

✓ Reader's TIP

Using History Textbook Reading Aids

■ **Timelines.** Familiarize yourself with chronologies to get an idea of the sequence of important events to be covered in each chapter. Study timelines to get an overall picture of parallel or overlapping events.

■ **Regional Maps.** Familiarize yourself with maps of the region being studied. What areas do different cultures cover? What separates cultures—mountains, plains, rivers? How have the regions changed?

■ **Opening Scenarios.** Build your curiosity about the coming chapter topics by reading the chapter-opening vignettes or stories.

■ **Feature Essays.** Relate the past to the present as you read the in-depth, people-oriented feature essays on topics such as "Birth Control in the Early United States" or "Brutality and Corruption in College Football in 1910."

■ **Boxed Features.** Reflect on how the cause-and-effect relationship between popular culture and ordinary citizens influences politics by reading special boxed features such as "Politics and Film."

■ **Conclusions.** Compare your conclusions with the historian's conclusions found at the chapter's end. Do you agree or disagree with the interpretation?

Recognize Different Patterns of Organization

History textbook paragraphs employ all twelve patterns of organization discussed in Chapter 6 but rely most heavily on two types: (1) time order/narrative and (2) cause and effect. On the first page of *Making a Nation: The United States and Its People*, by Jeanne Boydston et al., you can see both the following well-known chronological order of events and also the promise of many cause-and-effect connections.

Time Order.   Columbus and his crew of 89 men—divided among three ships: the *Santa Maria*, the *Niña*, and the *Pinta*—departed the Spanish port of Palos on August 3, 1492. They reached what he mistakenly thought was an island off the coast of China on October 12.

Cause and Effect. Columbus's arrival in the Western Hemisphere dramatically and irreversibly changed the worlds into which he and the Indians had been born. The encounter in effect fused their two worlds into one Atlantic world that Europeans and Indians—as well as Africans—would inhabit and transform together.

Recognize Different Historical Perspectives

History can be told from many different perspectives—cultural, political, military, economic, religious, diplomatic, and social history. In your textbooks, however, you will find the focus mainly on two perspectives: (1) the significant **political events** and **people** of the day, which are the happenings, and (2) the **social changes** of daily life, which are the effects. The following passages from *America and Its Peoples*, by James Kirby Martin et al., illustrate the difference in a political and social perspective.

13
Hum.

Political Perspective
For the Allies in World War II, the D-Day landing on June 6, 1944, was the long-planned, long-anticipated blow against Nazi Germany. Originally scheduled for 1942, it had been pushed back first to 1943 and finally to 1944. Although both the Soviet Union and impatient Americans had clamored for an earlier invasion, Prime Minister Winston Churchill of Great Britain, who remembered the difficulties of Dunkirk, counseled caution.

—James Kirby Martin et al., *America and Its Peoples*

Social Perspective
Seldom has technology so dramatically transformed so much of people's lives in a single generation. Bewildering as the changes sometimes were in the late nineteenth century, the public generally welcomed new inventions with wide-eyed wonder and nationalistic pride. Innovations in communication, for example, unified a collection of island communities into a nation.

—Martin, *America and Its Peoples*

Practice 1

Read the following history textbook passages and then circle the correct historical perspective and circle or explain the pattern of organization.

Passage 1
Immigration and native sources fueled the urban explosion. Most of the late-nineteenth-century immigrants came from rural communities, but they settled in America's industrial heartland. For every industrial worker who moved to the countryside, 20 farmers moved to urban America. As in Europe and Asia, rural opportunities in the United States were dwindling at the same time that the population was growing. Thus, for each farm son who became a farm owner, 10 farm sons moved to the cities.

—Martin, *America and Its Peoples*

1. political or social?
2. time order or cause and effect?

Passage 2

During World War I, France held out against the Germans for four years. This time, French resistance lasted two weeks. Germany began its assault on France June 5; its troops entered Paris June 14; and on June 22, a new French government, made up of pro-German sympathizers, was set up at Vichy. In just six weeks, Germany had conquered most of continental Europe.

—Martin, *America and Its Peoples*

3. political or social?
4. time order or cause and effect?

Passage 3

During the Great Depression, Hollywood played a valuable psychological role, providing reassurance to a demoralized nation. Even at the depths of the depression, 60 to 80 million Americans attended movies each week. In the face of economic disaster, the fantasy world of the movies sustained a traditional American faith in individual initiative, in government, and in a common American identity rising above social class.

—Martin, *America and Its Peoples*

5. political or social?
6. time order or cause and effect?

Passage 4

Equally frightening was the impact of overcrowding on the morals of tenement dwellers. The number of prison inmates in the United States increased by 50 percent in the 1880s, and the homicide rate nearly tripled, most of the rise occurring in cities. Driven into the streets by the squalor of their homes, slum youths formed gangs bearing names like Alley Gang, Rock Gang, and Hell's Kitchen Gang.

Slums bred criminals—the wonder was that they bred so few. They also drove well-to-do residents into exclusive sections and to the suburbs. From Boston's Beacon Hill and Back Bay to San Francisco's Nob Hill, the rich retired into their cluttered mansions and ignored conditions in the poorer parts of town.

—John Garraty, *The American Nation*

7. political or social?
8. What is the cause-and-effect relationship?

Learn the Usefulness of Dates

Dates organize history; they provide a framework for grouping and understanding events much like an outline provides a framework for writing. To understand relationships as a student of early American history, you must know that Columbus landed in America in 1492, that the *Mayflower* arrived in 1620, and that the Declaration of Independence was signed in 1776. Thus, you can make connections with cattle coming to New England in 1624, Anne Hutchinson being banished from Boston for her sermons in 1638, and the Boston Tea Party in 1773.

Dates are markers that stretch across cultures to help you see how events are connected. The American Revolution (1776) had a cause-and-effect influence on the French Revolution (1789). The Great Depression of the 1930s ended when the United States entered World War II in 1941; because factories had to produce war goods for the troops in Europe, the sagging economy began to grow.

Memorize the dates that will provide you with an adequate framework for making connections. Major turning points and landmark events are usually important to remember. If you are unsure of which dates are important, ask your instructor and check the chronological lists of events for each chapter.

13
Hum.

Landmark Dates in United States History	
1492	Columbus discovers America
1620	*Mayflower* lands English Pilgrims in Plymouth, Massachusetts
1776	Declaration of Independence signed
1863	Emancipation Proclamation issued
1865	Civil War ends
1918	World War I ends
1929	Stock market crashes; Great Depression starts
1945	World War II ends
1955	Rosa Parks refuses to give up her seat on the bus: starts Civil Rights Movement
1965	Voting Rights Act signed into Law

✓ Reader's TIP

Studying for History Exams

■ Identify possible questions by noting what is stressed in your lecture notes, syllabus, study questions, and table of contents.

(continued)

- Know the *who, what, when, where,* and *why significant* for people, places, documents, and events.
- Outline answers to possible essay questions. Supply evidence to support your interpretations. Use historical facts. Demonstrate how other interpretations are less believable than yours.

13c Are Speech and Communication More Than Just Words?

13 Hum.

In the area of the humanities, one of the fastest-growing departments is **communications.** Majors are offered in speech, journalism, film, and video. Courses range from those that prepare you for a telecommunications or public relations career to those that help you develop your own style of communication.

The main part of human communications is *you.* Introductory communications texts are interactive, encourage application, and ask you for ongoing self-assessment. They lead you to ask yourself these questions:

- How can I improve as a communicator and a conversationalist?
- How do I react to other people? Am I open to new ideas?
- How can I become a more valuable group member or a more productive group leader?
- Am I afraid to speak in public? How can I gain confidence?
- What are the rules for opening and closing a speech?

Areas of Communications

Communications textbooks usually center on three main areas of study: interpersonal communication, small group communication, and public speaking. The following exercises will give you practice in each of the areas.

Practice 2

Interpersonal communication involves two people with an established connection. This type of communication occurs in an interview, a discussion with a friend, a fight with your mother, or an interchange between customer and clerk.

EXAMPLE

The first step is to open the conversation, usually with some kind of greeting: "Hi. How are you?" "Hello, this is Joe." The greeting is a good example of *phatic* communication. It is a message that establishes a connection between two people and opens up the channels for more meaningful interaction.

At the second step, you usually provide some kind of *feedforward*, which gives the other person a general idea of the conversation's focus: "I've got to tell you about Jack" or "Did you hear what happened in class yesterday?"

At the third step, you talk "*business*," the substance or focus of the conversation. You converse to learn, relate, influence, play, or help.

—Joseph DeVito, *The Interpersonal Communication Book*

1. What are the three steps of interpersonal communication?

_____

Small-group communication involves a small number of people with a common purpose who operate under a set of governing rules. It occurs in a family, a class project team, a club membership, a social group, or a group of colleagues.

EXAMPLE

Cohesive groups offer their members greater returns, or rewards, for their personal investment in the group. For example, in an academic situation, a professor may give the same grade to all students working on a group project, regardless of their individual contributions.

—Larry Barker and Deborah Roach Gaut, *Communication*

2. What is cohesion?

_____

FAST FACT

A poll of 3,000 Americans indicated that "speaking before a group" is what Americans fear most, even more than snakes and spiders.

Public speaking involves a speaker, in front of a large audience, whose purpose is to inform or persuade the group. *Informative* speeches demonstrate or explain something and usually include visual aids. *Persuasive* speeches strive to influence or change the beliefs of the audience by presenting evidence, reasonable arguments, and emotional appeals in addition to visual aids. For example, an urban planner might give an informative speech about a new public transit system, and a politician might give a persuasive speech to get some money for the new transit system.

EXAMPLE

A speech should say something of lasting value. Even a talk intended to entertain, full of fluffy humor, should be built around a significant point. A speech needs both content and style; without the former, the latter is empty.

One veteran speechwriter for a large corporation and an influential trade organization applies what he calls the "Door Test" to the speeches he writes. After hearing a dinner speaker, the listeners go out the door of the banquet room and on entering the doors of their homes are greeted by their spouses and asked what the dinner speaker said. In reply, the listeners give the essence of the speech as they remember it. Was there a message clear and concise enough to remember? Did the speech pass the Door Test?

—Dennis Wilcox et al., *Public Relations*

3. What are two elements of a good speech?

✓ Reader's TIP

Questions to Ask While Reading Communications Textbooks

- How can I improve as a communicator and a conversationalist?
- How do I react to other people? Am I open to new ideas?
- How can I become a more valuable group member or a more productive group leader?
- Am I afraid to speak in public? How can I gain confidence?
- What are the rules for opening and closing a speech?

13d What Is English Composition?

Because of the vital importance of written communication in every career, all college majors require at least one course in English composition. With e-mail, your written communication becomes your "business suit." You may communicate daily with colleagues in other parts of the country whom you never personally meet. They will judge you and your aptitude for success by your written messages.

Composition courses train you to present your ideas logically and accurately in written form. English composition courses usually require two types of books: a handbook and a reader.

English Writing Handbook

The *handbook* is a reference or how-to book with guidelines on topic selection, writing style, and research documentation. It also includes rules and examples of grammar, punctuation, and sentence structure. Keep your English handbook forever as a reference; ten years after graduation, you may find you need to check whether the comma goes inside or outside the quotation marks. The following handbook excerpt provides an example of writing instructions.

> *Tone and level of formality.* Note how the words listed in each of the following groups have approximately the same meaning, but each word conveys a tone different from that of others in the group.
>
> *Child:* kid, offspring, progeny
> *Friend:* pal, buddy, chum, mate, comrade
> *Jail:* prison, slammer, can, cooler, correctional institution
> *Angry:* ticked off, furious, mad, fuming, wrathful
>
> Words like *kid, pal,* and *ticked off* are not appropriate in formal academic writing or business letters, but they will raise no eyebrows in journalism, advertising, and e-mail. Overusing words such as *progeny, comrade,* and *wrathful,* on the other hand, could create an overly formal tone that does not sound natural and genuine.
>
> —Ann Raimes, *Keys for Writers*

Another handbook excerpt shows sample punctuation rules.

> Use commas after introductory subordinate clauses. Subordinate clauses are signaled by words such as *although, if, when, because, as, after, since, unless,* and *while.*
> Although the vote was close, we passed the motion.
> While the military band played taps, the flag was lowered.
>
> —Maxine Hairston et al., *The Scott, Foresman Handbook for Writers*

✓ Reader's TIP
Using Your Handbook

- Locate general concepts in the table of contents. Concepts have a page number, section number, and letter such as the following:

  23. Problems with Pronoun Reference   401
      A. Pronouns lack antecedents   401
      B. Pronoun references ambiguous   403

- Use the index to locate specifics.
  whose

      in adjective clauses, 248
      as possessive of *who*, 428
      as relative pronoun, 248, 259

(continued)

13
Hum.

■ Learn from the examples.

Remember that the possessive of *who* is *whose*. Don't mistake *whose*, the possessive, for *who's* which is the contraction for *who is* or *who has*.

Possessive	Whose teammate is on first base?
Contraction	Who's on first?

—Maxine Hairston et al., *The Scott, Foresman Handbook for Writers*.

13e English Composition Reader

The *reader* is a collection of essays, offering models for writing and subject matter for inspiration. These essays are usually organized under themes or controversial issues or patterns of organization in writing. Throughout, you will be encouraged to develop compositions that have a strong *introduction, body,* and *conclusion*.

■ The **introduction** is usually a single paragraph in which you state your thesis by telling your readers what you intend to discuss. A good introduction captures the reader's attention.

■ The **body** is the longest part of the composition—usually several paragraphs—and contains the details. It provides logical proof, examples, and explanations for each of the points made in the introduction.

■ The **conclusion** is very general and signals closure to the reader by summarizing the main points or suggesting future action on the reader's part.

Small-Group EXPLORATION

Form a five-member group and select one of the following activities. Brainstorm and then outline your major points on a transparency. Choose one group member to present the group's findings to the class. Individual assignments can also be made.

■ Consider the history of the American Revolution from both political and social perspectives. Write a separate sentence that reflects each perspective.

■ In surveys about fears, people have rated the fear of public speaking higher than the fear of death. List reasons why people fear public speaking.

■   List suggestions for overcoming the fear of speaking in public.

■   List the top ten grammatical errors that you hear most frequently.

Net SEARCH

Find a Web site that lists rules for grammar and punctuation. Print an example of each and share with classmates.

13
Hum.

Chapter 14

Reading Literature and Contemporary Fiction and Nonfiction

14a What Is Literature?

Literature is the art form of language. Its purpose is to entertain an audience, to explore the human condition, and to reveal universal truths through shared experiences. As you read a work of literature, you are allowed inside the minds of characters, and you feel what they feel. You learn about life as the characters live it. Two types of literature are essays and fiction. Although essays and fiction differ in intent and style, they share many of the same elements.

Understand Literary Elements

In literary writing, the writer has carefully engineered every detail to give pleasure and suggest meaning. To enjoy a literary work and find its deeper meaning, you need to understand the following elements.

Plot.   The **plot** describes the action in a story. It is a sequence of incidents or events linked in a manner that suggests their causes.

These incidents in the story build progressively to reveal and explain conflict to the reader. The **conflict** is a struggle or a clash of ideas, desires, or actions. Stories can have more than one conflict. Conflicts can take any of several forms:

- *Main character versus another character,* such as a daughter who wants to leave her parents and live in an apartment while at college.

- *Main character versus a group,* such as a lawyer opposing factory pollution.

- *Main character versus himself or herself,* such as a student who is trying to break a drug habit.

- *Main character versus external forces,* such as a mountain climber who battles the elements to reach the summit.

As the plot moves forward, **suspense** builds because the reader is concerned about the character's well-being. The conflict intensifies to a peak or **climax,** which comes near the end of the story and is the turning point, for better or worse. The **denouement,** or the outcome of the main dramatic complication in the work, follows the climax. Then the action falls and leads to a **resolution,** that answers any remaining questions and explains the outcome (see the diagram below).

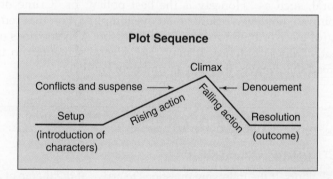

Characters.   In real life, you can observe behavior directly but you can merely guess at people's inner thoughts and feelings. In literature, however, you are not only aware of their actions, you are also told what they think and feel. You "live through" significant events with the character and learn to feel the joy and pain of others.

14
Fiction/
Non-
Fiction

You learn what kind of person the character is by noting what the character does and says, as well as what others say about the character. **Characters** should be consistent or predictably the same in their behavior, and they should grow and change according to their experiences in the story. Rather than being simply good or bad, main characters are *round*—complex, lifelike people who have strengths and weaknesses, ideally with the good points emerging to combat the weak ones. *Flat,* static, or one-dimensional minor characters sometimes form a backdrop for the actions of the main characters.

Tone. The **tone** is the writer's attitude toward the subject or the audience. When friends speak, we recognize their tone of voice. In stories, however, we must rely on the author's choice of words to suggest attitudes. Word clues may suggest that the author is being humorous. Cutting remarks, on the other hand, may suggest *sarcasm,* which is an expression of disapproval designed to cause pain. The author's tone may be gloomy, anxious, or sentimental toward the subject. The author's emotional and intellectual attitude toward the subject also describes the **mood,** or overall feeling of the work.

Setting. The **setting** is the backdrop for the story and the stage for the characters. All stories exist in a time and place. Details must be consistent with the setting or else they distract your attention.

Theme. The theme is the heart or soul of the work. The **theme** is the main idea, central insight into life, or universal truth. This message is never preached; rather, it is revealed to your emotions, senses, and imagination through powerful shared experiences. Stating the theme tests your understanding of the literary work, and thus it is not always an easy task. In some cases you may understand the events but not know what they mean. All too often readers want to reduce the theme to a one-sentence moral, such as "Honesty is the best policy" or "Crime does not pay." Doing so, however, results in an oversimplification that reduces a meaningful piece of literature to a narrow lesson. A theme does not need to fit neatly into a sentence. It may take several sentences to tie together a thread that weaves through a number of conflicts.

✓ Reader's TIP

Determining the Theme

Ask yourself the following questions to arrive at the theme of a narrative:

- What is the central conflict?
- How has the main character changed?

(continued)

- What has the main character learned during the story?
- What insight into life does the story reveal?

Also keep in mind the following:

- The theme, like a statement of the main idea, must be expressed in a complete sentence to convey the complete thought.
- The theme is the central and unifying idea in the story.
- The theme is a generalization or truth about life.
- The theme should not be stated as a cliché, an overused expression that has lost its originality. Settling for a trite phrase, such as "You can't teach an old dog new tricks," shows a lazy attitude and an aversion to deep thinking. Do not try to force refreshing new insights into an old formula. Be expressive and imaginative.

14
Fiction/
Non-
Fiction

14b What Is an Essay?

An **essay** is a short work of nonfiction that discusses a specific topic. An essay does not develop as a story does, and it lacks characters and a plot. Examples include speeches and sermons, as well as expository or explaining, argumentative, critical, and personal pieces of writing. Much of your own college writing will follow an essay format.

The *title* of the essay gives you the first clue to its contents. The theme, thesis, or main idea is usually, but not always, stated in the *introduction*. The *body* of the essay discusses and proves the thesis by presenting a series of ideas and supporting evidence. These details unify the theme and reveal, sometimes through inferences, the author's *tone*, or attitude toward the subject. The writing style can be formal or informal, and essayists may use *symbols* to create pictures or images. The *conclusion* is a summary of the main points and may be stated in a manner to provoke further thought on the subject.

The following are the most common essay types and their purposes.

- **Expository essay:** to inform or explain
- **Argumentative essay:** to convince the audience to agree or disagree with a position on an issue
- **Critical essay:** to critique and evaluate a piece of writing, a play, or an author's style
- **Personal essay:** to reveal personal experiences and reflections

Reader's TIP

Understanding an Essay

Ask yourself the following questions:

- What is the theme, thesis, or main idea?
- How do the details and examples develop the theme?
- How does the title aid in understanding the essay?
- What is the author's tone or attitude toward the subject?
- What images contribute to the theme and tone of the essay?
- What is the conclusion? How is it significant?

Practice 1

This critical essay is an example of the type of essay you might write in a literature class. Read the essay and answer the questions that follow it.

Two Reflections of Helen of Troy

By Julie Wakefield Smith

Helen, the wife of King Menelaus, was admired in ancient Greece for her beauty. Her sudden abduction by the Trojan prince Paris started the bloody Trojan War. Two poems about this legendary woman, "To Helen" by Edgar Allan Poe and "Helen" by Hilda Doolittle, express contrasting viewpoints on her
5 worthiness and her effect on Greece.

The first poem, "To Helen," is romantic and graceful. The poem is a soldier's ode to the famous beauty. The "way-worn wanderer" has returned to the "glory" of Greece and feels fulfilled, having fought for Helen across the "desperate seas." His tone is admiring, expressing love and devotion. The author's word
10 choice shows an admiration for Helen's "hyacinth hair," "classic fall," and "statue-like" presence. To the soldier, she is the perfect picture of beauty and love, the reason that wars should be fought.

The second poem, "Helen," is filled with hate for Helen as the figure who caused the Trojan War and, thereby, caused great destruction. The poet de-
15 scribes Helen impersonally, concentrating on her physical appearance, her "still eyes" and her "wan and white" face. Even her legendary smile, which was regarded as breathtakingly beautiful, is described with disgust. At the conclusion of this poem the author decides that the Greeks will be able to love her only once she is dead and buried.

20 The endings of both poems highlight the differences in the authors' perspectives. In the first poem Helen is "Psyche," a mythological princess loved by Cupid, and in the second she is the beauty who could be loved only in "white ash amid funereal cypresses."

1. What is the main idea or thesis of this essay?

---

2. What details develop the theme?

---

3. What pattern of organization is suggested by the title?

---

4. What is the author's tone or attitude?

---

5. What is the conclusion?

14
Fiction/
Non-
Fiction

14c What Is Fiction?

The word *fiction* comes from the Latin root *fingere,* which means "to feign or pretend." In fiction an author creates an illusion of reality in order to share an experience and communicate lasting truths about the human condition. Because a work of fiction is created deliberately, each element has a meaning that is subject to interpretation on many levels. Short stories and novels entertain and enlighten by engaging you in the lives of other human beings.

Short Story.   A **short story** is a brief work of fiction ranging usually from 500 to 15,000 words. It is a narrative with a beginning, a middle, and an end that tells about a sequence of events. The plot of the story involves characters in one or more conflicts. As the conflict intensifies, the suspense rises to a *climax,* or turning point, which is followed by the *denouement,* or unraveling. Then the action falls for a *resolution.* Because a short story is brief, the author makes every element important. For a true appreciation, some literary experts recommend reading a short story three times: first to enjoy the plot, second to recognize the elements, and third to appreciate how the elements work together to support the theme. (To practice your skills, read the two short stories in Part 5.)

Novel. The **novel** is an extended fictional work that has all of the elements of a short story. Because of its length, a novel usually has more characters and more conflicts than a short story. You become involved in the lives of the characters and learn from them.

✓ Reader's TIP

Understanding a Short Story or a Novel

Ask yourself the following questions:

14
Fiction/
Non-
Fiction

- How would you describe the main character? What other characters are well developed? What is the purpose of the "flat" characters? What do the characters learn? How do the characters change?

- What is the main conflict in the story? What are the steps in the development of the plot? What is the climax? What is the resolution?

- What is the theme of the story? What universal truth did you learn from the story?

- When and where is the story set? How does the setting affect the theme?

- Who is telling the story? How does this point of view affect the message?

- What is the tone of the author? What mood is the author trying to create?

- What symbols provide vivid images that enrich the theme?

- What is your evaluation of the author's work?

Practice 2

Read this short story and answer the questions that follow it.

The Getaway

By John Savage

Whenever I get sleepy at the wheel, I always stop for coffee. This time, I was going along in western Texas and I got sleepy. I saw a sign that said GAS EAT, so I pulled off. It was long after midnight. What I expected was a place like a bunch of others, where the coffee tastes like copper and the flies never sleep.

5   What I found was something else. The tables were painted wood, and they looked as if nobody ever spilled the ketchup. The counter was spick-and-span. Even the smell was OK. I swear it.

Nobody was there, as far as customers. There was just this one old boy— really only about forty, getting gray above the ears—behind the counter. I sat

10   down at the counter and ordered coffee and apple pie. Right away he got me started feeling sad.

I have a habit: I divide people up. Winners and losers. This old boy behind the counter was the kind that they *mean* well; they can't do enough for you, but their eyes have this gentle, far-away look, and they can't win. You know? With
15   their clean shirt and their little bow tie? It makes you feel sad just to look at them. Only take my tip: Don't feel too sad.

He brought the coffee steaming hot, and it tasted like coffee. "Care for cream and sugar?" he asked. I said, "Please," and the cream was fresh and cold and thick. The pie was good too.

20   A car pulled up outside. The old boy glanced out to see if they wanted gas, but they didn't. They came right in. The tall one said, "Two coffees. Do you have a road map we could look at?"

"I think so," the old boy said. He got their coffee first, and then started rooting through a pile of papers by the telephone, looking for a map. It was easy
25   to see he was the type nothin's too much trouble for. Tickled to be of service.

I'm the same type myself, if you want to know. I watched the old boy hunting for his map, and I felt like I was looking in a mirror.

After a minute or two, he came up with the map. "This one's a little out of date, but . . ." He put it on the counter, beside their coffee.

30   The two men spread out the map and leaned over it. They were well dressed, like a couple of feed merchants. The tall one ran his finger along the Rio Grande and shook his head. "I guess there's no place to get across, this side of El Paso."

He said it to his pal, but the old boy behind the counter heard him and lit
35   up like a light bulb. "You trying to find the best way south? I might be able to help you with that."

"How?"

"Just a minute." He spent a lot of time going through the papers by the telephone again. "Thought I might have a newer map," he said. "Anything recent
40   would show the Hackett Bridge. Anyway, I can tell you how to find it."

"Here's a town called Hackett," the tall one said, still looking at the map. "It's on the river just at the end of a road. Looks like a pretty small place."

"Not any more. It's just about doubled since they built the bridge."

"What happens on the other side?" The short one asked the question, but
45   both of the feed merchant types were paying close attention.

"Pretty fair road, clear to Chihuahua. It joins up there with the highway out of El Paso and Juarez."

The tall man finished his coffee, folded the map, put it in his pocket, and stood up. "We'll take your map with us," he said.

50   The old boy seemed startled, like a new kid at school when someone pokes him in the nose to show him who's boss. However, he just shrugged and said, "Glad to let you have it."

The feed merchants had a little conference on the way out, talking in whispers. Then they stopped in the middle of the floor, turned around, reached

14
Fiction/
Non-
Fiction

55 inside their jackets, and pulled guns on us. Automatic pistols, I think they were. "You sit where you are and don't move," the tall one said to me. "And *you*, get against the wall."

Both of us did exactly what they wanted. I told you we were a lot alike.

The short man walked over and pushed one of the keys of the cash regis-
60 ter. "Every little bit helps," he said, and he scooped the money out of the drawer. The tall man set the telephone on the floor, put his foot on it, and jerked the wires out. Then they ran to their car and got in. The short man leaned out the window and shot out one of my tires. Then they took off fast.

I looked at the old boy behind the counter. He seemed a little pale, but he
65 didn't waste any time. He took a screw-driver out of a drawer and squatted down beside the telephone. I said, "It doesn't always pay to be nice to people."

He laughed and said, "Well, it doesn't usually cost anything," and went on taking the base plate off the telephone. He was a fast worker, actually. His tongue was sticking out of the corner of his mouth. In about five minutes he
70 had a dial tone coming out of the receiver. He dialed a number and told the Rangers about the men and their car. "They did?" he said. "Well, well, well ... No, not El Paso. They took the Hackett turnoff." After he hung up, he said, "It turns out those guys robbed a supermarket in Wichita Falls."

I shook my head. "They sure had me fooled. I thought they looked per-
75 fectly all right."

The old boy got me another cup of coffee, and opened himself a bottle of pop. "They fooled me, too, at first." He wiped his mouth. "Then I got a load of their shoulder holsters when they leaned on the counter to look at the map. Anyway, they had mean eyes, I thought. Didn't you?"
80 "Well, I didn't at the time."

We drank without talking for a while, getting our nerves back in shape. A pair of patrol cars went roaring by outside and squealed their tires around the Hackett turnoff.

I got to thinking, and I thought of the saddest thing yet. "You *knew* there
85 was something wrong with those guys, but you still couldn't keep from helping them on their way."

He laughed. "Well, the world's a tough sort of place at best, is how I look at it."

"I can understand showing them the map," I said, "but I'm damned if I'd
90 have told about the bridge. Now there's not a snowball's chance in hell of catch-ing them. If you'd kept your mouth shut, there'd at least be some hope."

"There isn't any—"

"Not a shred," I went on. "Not with a car as fast as they've got."

The way the old boy smiled made me feel better about him and me. "I
95 don't mean there isn't any hope," he said. "I mean there isn't any bridge."

1. Who is telling the story and how does that affect your point of view?

_____

_____

2. Describe the narrator and his attitude toward life and people.

_____

_____

_____

3. In a short psychological story, the main character changes. Who is the main character? How do we hope he changes as a result of the events in the story?

_____

_____

4. Why is the conflict "man versus himself" rather than "man versus man"?

_____

_____

_____

5. What is the theme of this story?

_____

_____

6. This story has an unexpected twist at the end. Were you as short-sighted as the narrator? At what point did you correctly predict the ending?

_____

_____

14d   What Are the Different Types of Contemporary Novels?

Over the years, writers have experimented with form and expanded the novel into many different types. The following list highlights types of contemporary novels.

Mainstream.   Mainstream novels are set in reality. The settings are usually real places and real locations on the map. Although these novels do not focus on actual people, the characters are realistic, with problems common to modern people or those of the recent past. For example, in the novel *Sula* by Toni Morrison, Sula and Nel have been best friends who grew up together in a poor Ohio town. Sula leaves for ten years and on her return is upset to find that her friend has married and accepted conditions that the friend previously found unacceptable. When you read a mainstream novel, think about how the characters and the events that affect them are related to your life and the world around you. What can you learn from them?

Horror.   Horror novels have a deadly force or evil character at their center, usually one that terrorizes the main character, or *protagonist*. The evil presence can be a human, a monster, or a supernatural being. Stephen King's *Pet Sematary* (1983) is a horror novel about a plot of land that has the power to resurrect the dead. When the main character buries his son there, the son comes back to life possessed by an evil spirit. There is nothing like a good haunted house story for pleasurable reading on the bus or at the beach. You'll savor the thrill of being frightened!

14
Fiction/
Non-
Fiction

Science Fiction.   Science fiction novels rely on imaginary futuristic worlds as the setting. Often the science fiction author tries to predict what the world and the universe will be like far into the future. Philip K. Dick's *Do Androids Dream of Electric Sheep?* is about a futuristic bounty hunter who is hired to hunt down and kill a group of artificially created beings called androids who have escaped the mining planet where they worked and are now threatening Earth. If you are in the mood to "escape" to another universe, pick up a science fiction novel.

Fantasy.   Often associated or confused with science fiction, fantasy novels take place in lands invented by the writer. Rather than being predictions about the future, however, they are tales of imagination and magic. For example, in the *Harry Potter* series by J. K. Rowling, Harry attends Hogwarts, a school for magic, and is victorious over superhuman villains.

Western.   One of the most formulaic types of novels is the Western. Louis L'Amour wrote many such novels, which are always set in the western United States in the 1800s, during the time of the expansion westward. Usually the central character is a lone stranger passing through the area. When you read a Western novel, think about the conflict between good and evil.

Mystery.   The action of a mystery novel (sometimes called a whodunit or detective novel) hinges on a crime, usually a murder. Although Edgar Allan Poe wrote the first mystery story, "The Murders in the Rue Morgue," Agatha Christie perfected the English murder mystery. She wrote 78 crime novels that have sold more than 2 billion copies in 44 different languages. Popular authors today who have written series of blockbuster mysteries are Mary Higgins Clark, James Patterson, and Nora Roberts.

Action.   Action novels involve a hero's battling against great odds and a great force—but not superhuman forces. For example, in Tom Clancy's novel *Cardinal of the Kremlin,* heroes of the intelligence network pit their skills in the Cold War against the Soviet KGB.

Romance.   Romance novels involve a love affair between two people. These novels are often set in times considered more romantic than the present day. A recurrent theme in romance novels is that love conquers obstacles such as family feuds and the divisiveness of war. In Danielle Steel's *Granny Dan,* a motherless young girl becomes a great Russian ballerina, but an extraordinary man, an illness, and a revolution force her to make heartbreaking choices.

Practice 3

For practice in identifying types of novels, insert in the blank the novel type implied by each of the following sentences.

Mystery	Science fiction	Western	Horror	Romance

_____ 1. As Lance rode into town, he heard a shot at the Longhorn Saloon and then saw the cowboy with the blood red bandana slip quietly out the side door and onto his horse.

_____ 2. Rita had been surprised last night at Juan's charm, and today she could feel herself reluctantly draw toward him as the others left the room.

_____ 3. Sergo struggled to explain to Kolon that his planet was in grave danger of destruction if the intergalactic warriors from Nolls could not be intercepted.

_____ 4. Warming the cold night, the fire crackled and, to my surprise, her chair began to rock gently as if she were still sitting in it, telling us the haunting story of finding the Farrows dead in the basement.

_____ 5. Kristen and Lee worked quickly to inspect the marks in the sand, knowing that nightfall and the incoming waves would wash away the clues and lessen their chances of connecting Brad to the scene of the crime.

What Are the Different Types of Contemporary Nonfiction?

Earlier in this chapter we said that *fiction* is writing that has been invented from the author's imagination. *Nonfiction,* by contrast, is writing that is based on actual events.

Historical Nonfiction

All writers both report and invent. For historical novels and biographies, the dialogue between two historical characters may be invented, based on known facts about the actual people and events of a given time. Thus, authors of nonfiction add a degree of fiction when they interpret historical facts. The following are literary genres that incorporate history.

Memoir. A memoir is a dramatized narrative of the author's own life, often looking far back into the past. Memoirs can read very much like mainstream fiction. *The Diary of Anne Frank* is a memoir of a Jewish girl's last days hiding from the Nazis during World War II. The heartbreaking aspect of the diary is Anne Frank's charm and cheerfulness in the face of what turned out to be her death.

Biography. Biographies dramatize the life—or a portion of the life—of a historical figure or group of people. In *Lindbergh* by A. Scott Berg, the author describes the life and achievements of the popular hero who in 1927 piloted the first solo flight across the Atlantic.

Historical Chronicle/Interpretation. Thousands of books that are not novels have been written about global events such as World War II. These historical chronicles have no plot; they simply retell and interpret events, based on documents, interviews, and research. In *Citizen Soldiers,* Stephen Ambrose chronicles the U.S. Army's movements from the Normandy beaches to the surrender of Germany.

Other Nonfiction

Nonfiction books that are not biography or history may lack both plot and characters. They are generally divided into chapters by ideas and then further divided by subheadings. The label *nonfiction* includes books about travel, art, music, decorating, computers, cooking, and other interests. Two of the most popular instructional types of nonfiction are self-improvement and how-to books.

Self-Improvement. Do you want to be more assertive, make millions on the stock market, lose weight, get relief from pain, or find a spouse? Self-improvement books report the relevant research, offer many convincing anecdotes, and then make suggestions. They also tend to repeat themselves, saying in a 200-page book what could be stated in a 20-page article. Use the table of contents to read selectively. Current examples include Stephen Covey's *Seven Habits of Successful People* and Suze Orman's *The Courage to Be Rich*.

How-To. Do you want to know how to master your computer, plan a wedding, create a garden, or remodel a house? How-to books break down such activities into easy steps with specific directions. For example, the popular series "Complete Idiot's Guide" and the yellow "Dummies" books analyze virtually anything from hiking to Web design to fat burning, providing lighthearted and interesting instruction.

14f   What Should You Consider When Selecting a Book?

Remember the adage "Don't judge a book by its cover." Book jackets are slick marketing tools designed by experts who use pictures, testimonials, and exaggeration to entice you to make a purchase.

If you want to know what books other people are buying, consult a best-seller list. Your bookstore may display "Paperback Favorites," or your city newspaper may publish a list. If not, the *New York Times* best-seller list is nationally respected. Similar to a listing of top-grossing movies, a best-seller list indicates quantity but not necessarily quality. When you find a book that looks interesting, investigate further by using these strategies:

- Read the book jacket. Do the quotes from reviewers seem valid or clipped out of context? Do the blurbs introducing the book arouse your interest? Has the author written other books that you have enjoyed? If the work is nonfiction, what are the author's credentials?

- Read the first page and at least one other page. Do you like the writing style? Is it comfortable for you to read? Does the first page grab your attention?

- If the book is nonfiction, look at the illustrations and read the captions. Are you intrigued? Review the table of contents and scan the index. Is this something you want to learn more about?

Small-Group EXPLORATION

Form a five-member group and select one of the following activities. Brainstorm and then outline your major points on a transparency. Choose one group member to present the group's findings to the class. Individual assignments can also be made.

- Select a recent movie of Academy Award quality that all group members have seen. List the characters, discuss the plot, and state the theme of the movie.

- Create an outline for a short story that has this theme: *Not only hard work, but also the sacrifice and support of others, will help a single person achieve success.* Describe the characters, setting, plot, conflict, climax, and resolution of your story.

- Create a list of the top ten advantages for an educated person of having read good literature.

- What ten books would you most like to read?

Net SEARCH

Search the Internet for at least two best-seller lists. How do the lists differ? Are books categorized differently on each list? What books would you like to read?

Chapter
15

Reading in the Social Sciences

15a What Are the Social Sciences?

The **social sciences**—psychology, sociology, anthropology, and political science—address social problems such as mental illness, crime, violence, and poverty. Social scientists try to understand the causes, apply theories, and find solutions. They assume that social problems have causes that can be explained through careful investigation.

Understand the Scientific Method

Although the problems studied by social scientists are social and cultural, the method of inquiry is scientific. The common thread for testing truth in all sciences is an investigative process called the **scientific method.** In the social sciences, as well as the life and natural sciences (see Chapter 16), the scientists observe, make predictions or hypothesize, and predict future behaviors. Then they test their predictions through further research and observation in order to propose theories.

Throughout social science, life science, and business textbooks, articles on scientific studies are referenced to confirm facts and offer details for further research. You will see the names of authors and the dates of publications cited as shown in this example from a psychology textbook.

EXAMPLE

Levels-of-processing theory suggests that the deeper the level at which information was processed, the more likely it is to be committed to memory (Craik and Lockhart, 1972; Lockhart and Craik, 1990). If processing involves more analysis, interpretation, comparison, and elaboration, it should result in better memory.

—Philip Zimbardo and Richard Gerrig, *Psychology and Life*

EXPLANATION In this example, the same two authors wrote two articles on the topic: one article published in 1972 with Craik as the first (sometimes called *senior*) author, then another article in 1990 with Lockhart as the leading author. The articles describe two separate (but possibly similar) experiments. If you want to examine the actual articles, refer to the references list (sometimes called the *Bibliography*) in the back of the textbook for detailed publication information.

**15
Soc.
Sci.**

15b What Is Psychology?

Psychology is the study of the behavior and the mental processes of human beings and animals, focusing on observable action as well as thoughts and feelings. As a psychologist, you might train athletes to mentally improve their performance, compose profiles of serial killers, administer tests to evaluate academic skills, treat clients with mental illnesses, or evaluate job applicants. Regardless of your major, psychology can help you know yourself and understand and predict the behavior of others.

Practice 1

The study of psychology can take various perspectives, ranging from treating patients for personality disorders to investigating how children learn. Introductory textbooks usually include at least one chapter or major section on each of the following psychological perspectives. Study the perspectives and answer the question that follows each.

Psychodynamic Perspective

What inner needs are you trying to satisfy with your actions? What happened in your childhood that is now causing emotional distress and tension? These principles of motivation were developed by Sigmund Freud (1856–1939), who believed that behavior is determined primarily by unconscious forces that he described as the *id* (biological instincts), the *ego* (sense of self), and the *superego* (conscience differentiating right and wrong). The following textbook passage has a psychodynamic perspective.

Passage 1

The ego tries to satisfy the id's desire for pleasure and the superego's strict demands, in a way that is realistically possible. For instance, suppose your id urges you to eat two large pizzas by yourself—for pleasure—and your super-ego urges you not to eat any pizza because it is fattening and not very healthy. Your ego might balance those desires by directing you to eat only a moderate amount. Hence, the ego, which neo-Freudian psychodynamic theorists empha-size more than Freud did, is responsible for making rational decisions.

—Laura Uba and Karen Huang, *Psychology*

1. What is the role of the ego?

Behavioral Perspective

What stimulus in the environment triggers your response? The re-searchers Ivan Pavlov (in the early 1900s) and B. F. Skinner (in the mid to late 1900s) believe that behavior can be manipulated through rewards and punishments. The following passage has a behavioral perspective.

Passage 2

The first time Pavlov turned on the light and then presented the food to one of his dogs, the dog didn't instantly learn that the light indicated that food was coming. The light was initially a neutral stimulus—dogs don't naturally sali-vate when someone turns on a light. When the light was turned on shortly be-fore the presentation of the food on several occasions, the light lost its neutral-ity and became a cue that food was coming. The combination of turning on the light and presenting the food had to occur several times for the dog to become conditioned (see Figure 15-1).

—Uba and Huang, *Psychology*

1. When conditioned, the light meant what to the dog?

Psychologists with a social learning perspective subscribe to behav-iorists' stimulus and response theories, but they also go beyond them by recognizing that feelings and interpretations affect how one responds to a stimulus. They also believe that people learn through observing others.

Cognitive Perspective

How do you think? Cognitive psychologists investigate thinking, memory, and the way material is stored in the mind, as in learning theo-ries and concepts such as *schema* and *metacognition* (see Chapter 2). The following example takes a cognitive perspective.

15
Soc.
Sci.

FIGURE 15-1 | Classical conditioning

Before conditioning occurs, a UCS (food) automatically causes a UCR (salivating). During the classical conditioning process, a CS (turning on the light) signals that a UCS (food) is coming. Classical conditioning has taken place when the CS triggers the CR.

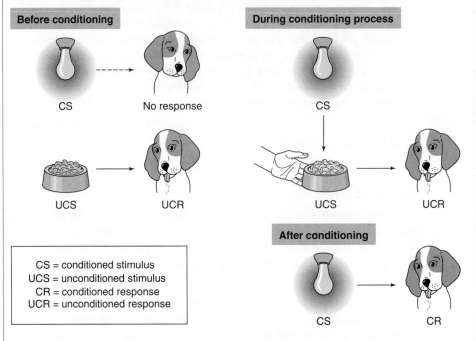

Before conditioning

CS — No response

UCS → UCR

During conditioning process

CS

UCS → UCR

After conditioning

CS → CR

CS = conditioned stimulus
UCS = unconditioned stimulus
CR = conditioned response
UCR = unconditioned response

Passage 3

Children in the concrete operations stage (ages 7 to 12 years) begin to develop many concepts and show that they can manipulate those concepts. For example, they can organize objects into categories of things: balls over here, blocks over there, plastic soldiers in a pile by the door, and so on. Each of these items is recognized as a toy, ultimately to be put away in the toy box and not in the closet, which is where clothes are supposed to go.

—Josh Gerow, *Psychology*

1. What is the concrete operations stage?

_____

Humanistic Perspective

Can you be anything you want to be? According to the humanists, among them Carl Rogers (1902–1987) and Abraham Maslow (1908–1970), people have choices in life. They believe that you are limited only by your desire and motivation, rather than by your genetic history or your environment. The following is an example of a text with a humanistic perspective.

Passage 4

Suppose you want to become a more sensitive person than you are. A humanistic psychologist would suggest that you honestly recognize the ways in which you are insensitive. You can then work on increasing your awareness and growing in your potential. Humanistic psychologists Abraham Maslow and Carl Rogers have broadened our perspective on how people might accept their existential freedom and what they do with it.

—Uba and Huang, *Psychology*

1. What would a humanist believe your potential to be?

_____

Practice 2

Name the perspective illustrated in each of the following interpretations.

_____ **1.** The smell of bacon cooking made me want a hearty protein breakfast rather than a bagel and cream cheese.

_____ **2.** Excessive emphasis on details, sometimes referred to as an anal personality, can be caused by earlier difficulties in potty training.

_____ **3.** Students are better able to remember ten unrelated nouns if the words are connected in a creative narrative.

_____ **4.** Inner strength and motivation can transform a child of poverty into a successful multimillionaire.

15
Soc.
Sci.

15c What Is Sociology?

Do opposites attract? Does absence make the heart grow fonder—or is it out of sight, out of mind? Sociological researchers go beyond anecdotal data and seek real answers to such questions. They use logic and the scientific method to observe and explain interpersonal interaction, group membership, and social institutions. Students majoring in **sociology** may concentrate on family and community services, social justice, urban issues, or gerontology (the study of issues of aging).

Understand the Organization of Sociology Textbooks

Most introductory sociology textbooks begin with chapters explaining how to think like a sociologist and end with a few chapters about future challenges such as increased population, environmental pollution, and urbanization. In the middle are usually three large sections with chapters focusing on the individual within society, social inequalities, and social institutions.

Practice 3

Read each passage and answer the questions that follow.

Sample Discussion about the Individual and Society

Overall drug use in the United States has steadily declined since the late 1970s. But beginning in 1992, drug use among teenagers began to increase sharply. This upsurge may have resulted from a number of factors: First, many parents of today's teen drug users are reluctant to offer stern warnings about the dangers of drugs because they themselves used drugs in their youth. Second, movies, television shows, and MTV often glamorize and glorify drug use. And third, the U.S. government has substantially reduced funds for drug education and treatment programs (Goldberg, 1996; Wren, 1996).

—Alex Thio, *Sociology*

1. What is the cause-and-effect relationship explained in the first factor?

_____

_____

Sample Discussion of Social Inequities

Shocking as it may be, adult slavery is not uncommon today. According to Britain's Anti-Slavery International, the world's oldest human rights organization, there are more than 100 million slaves. This old-fashioned human bondage, called chattel slavery, can be found in the North African country of Mauritania, where some 100,000 black Africans live as the property of Arab-descended Berbers.

Most slaves today, however, are victims of debt bondage, which forces whole families to work, sometimes for generations, in fruitless efforts to pay off loans. Such human bondage will cease only if poor countries are able to achieve social mobility in the global stratification system.

—Thio, *Sociology*

2. How would social mobility through economic opportunity reduce slavery?

_____

Sample Discussion of Social Institutions

Most Hispanic families are nuclear, with only parents and children living together, but they do have the characteristics of an extended family. There exist strong kinship ties, as various relatives live close to one another and often exchange visits, emotional support, and economic assistance (Vega, 1992).

Imbued with strong family values, Hispanics generally have lower divorce rates compared with Anglos (people of European descent).

—Thio, *Sociology*

3. What is a nuclear family?

_____

4. What is the stated cause of the lower Hispanic divorce rate?

_____

Reader's TIP

Studying Psychology and Sociology

- Seek to understand key terms and concepts through examples. Even if certain definitions are vague or confusing, the illustrating examples can be concrete and easy to visualize.

- Relate the discussion in the text to yourself and to people you know. Visualize characters from your own background.

- Connect names with theories. Know the names of the researchers as well as the characteristics and examples of each theory.

- Compare and contrast theories. For example, how do the social learning theorists differ from the behaviorists?

- Reduce your notes to visual diagrams. For example, to study personality theories, draw charts to list comparative elements.

- Test yourself by turning each boldfaced heading into a question and reciting your answer.

- Memorize key terms along with a possible application of each, especially when preparing for multiple-choice exams. For example, be able to identify the conditioned response in a sample research study.

15
Soc.
Sci.

15d   What Is Political Science?

Who are the two U.S. senators from your state? What are their senatorial duties? How much money does it take to get elected to the Senate? **Political science** is the study of politics and government—how politicians get elected and how the country is ruled. Most introductory U.S. political science textbooks begin with a description of the Constitution and a history of the political forces behind it. Textbooks explain political parties and elections, as well as the manipulation of public opinion. All books explain the powers and rules regarding the presidency, Congress, and the federal court. Shining through every page, the American values of liberty, equality, and democracy are presented with an underlying optimism that students who learn about our government will then become enlightened, participating citizens.

The predominant pattern of organization is description, with an emphasis on one thing's leading to another in a cause-and-effect manner. Examples from two political science textbooks follow.

Practice 4

Read each sample passage and answer the questions that follow.

The Constitution

In order to understand American politics today, it is extremely important to know and understand the Constitution of the United States. To be sure, the document has been formally amended 27 times, and some very important things have changed in it because of judicial interpretations and political practices. But the major outlines of our present-day government are expressed in, and substantially determined by, the Constitution that was written in Philadelphia. The U.S. Constitution, in fact, can be considered one of the major structural factors that has influenced the evolution of American government and continues to shape politics today.

—Edward Greenberg and Benjamin Page, *The Struggle for Democracy*

1. What is the purpose of this passage?

_____

2. What sense of pride comes through in this passage?

_____

Institutions

One thing is certain: Staff members have to speak accurately for the President. They must do what the President wants, or what he *would* want if he knew the details. The ideal staffer knows exactly what the boss wants and does it, with or without being told; otherwise, he or she won't last long. Of course, it can be useful for a President to create the *impression* that staff members are acting on their own, particularly when they are doing something unpopular or even illegal. One of Eisenhower's favorite hidden-hand techniques was to have Sherman Adams take the heat for tough decisions.

—Greenberg and Page, *The Struggle for Democracy*

15
Soc.
Sci.

3. What does the passage imply about Sherman Adams?

_____

_____

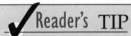

Reader's TIP

Learning Political Science

- Understand the Constitution and how it can be—and has been—amended.
- Relate the laws of the United States to the Constitution.
- Connect the cause-and-effect relationships of events, political changes, and laws.
- Know the rules and powers of the President, Congress, and federal courts, and how they have changed over the years.
- Be able to trace how people get elected or appointed to different public offices.
- Understand why U.S. democracy has worked when other governments have failed.
- Understand your "citizen's role" in American government.
- Keep up with the news and relate current events to what you are learning about politics and government.

15
Soc.
Sci.

15e For Further Practice: Extended Reading Selection in Psychology

Sleep Deprivation and Disorders of Sleep

We are a nation in need of a good night's sleep. On average, Americans get about 1.5 hours less sleep each night than they need. This reflects an average reduction in nightly sleep of nearly 20 percent over the last century—due to a myriad of factors, including demands of the workplace, school, home, and family.

5 "A good night's sleep" is the amount of sleep that will allow a person to awaken without the use of some device or environmental influence such as an alarm clock. If a person does not get an adequate amount of sleep, he or she will be less alert and less able to function well the next day. What is particularly troubling is that sleep loss accumulates from one night to the next as a "sleep debt."

10 The more sleep lost each day, the greater the debt, and the more severe the consequences.

Most sleep deprivation studies—in which humans or animals are awakened so as to disrupt their sleep—show remarkably few long-term adverse side effects. Even if sleep is disrupted over several nights, there are few lasting changes in a person's reactions, particularly if the person is in good physical and psychological health to begin with. If, after deprivation, a task is interesting enough and if it is not lengthy or time-consuming, there is little impairment of intellectual functioning. At least, up to a point, we can adapt to deprivation, perhaps by taking little catnaps while we're awake. Very short episodes of sleep, called microsleeps, can be found in the EEG records of waking subjects, both animal and human. These microsleep episodes increase in number when normal sleep is disrupted.

That is not to say that there aren't any effects of being deprived of sleep. Some people show marked signs of depression and irritability when their sleep is interrupted. People deprived of REM sleep for a few nights and then left alone will spend long periods REMing, as if to catch up on lost REMs. This REM rebound effect is generally found only for the first night after deprivation; then patterns return to normal. There is some evidence that NREM sleep also rebounds. When, in 1965, 17-year-old Randy Gardner set the world record by going without sleep for nearly 266 hours, he slept for 14 hours the first night after deprivation, but by the second night he returned to his normal 8 hours of sleep. The current record holder for sleeplessness, Maureen Weston, went nearly 19 days without sleep and similarly experienced no lasting effects once given the opportunity to reduce her sleep debt.

Some people have no difficulty sleeping. Others experience problems, either in getting to sleep in the first place, or during sleep itself.

Insomnia

At some time or another, each of us has suffered from a bout of insomnia—the inability to fall asleep or stay asleep when we want to. We may be excited or worried about something that is going to happen the next day. We may have overstimulated our autonomic nervous systems with drugs such as caffeine. However, most people who chronically (regularly) suffer from insomnia haven't the slightest idea why they are unable to get a good night's sleep. Chronic, debilitating insomnia afflicts nearly 30 million Americans, women more commonly than men and the elderly about 1.5 times as often as younger adults.

Prescribing sleeping pills (common in nursing home settings) and using over-the-counter medications to treat insomnia may cause more problems than it solves. The medication (usually sedatives or depressants) may have a positive effect for a while, but eventually dosages have to be increased as tolerance builds. When the medications are discontinued, a rebound effect occurs that makes it more difficult to get to sleep than it had been before.

Narcolepsy

Narcolepsy involves going to sleep even during the day, without any intention to do so. Symptoms include excessive sleepiness, brief episodes of muscle weakness or paralysis precipitated by strong emotion, paralysis upon falling asleep, and dreamlike images that occur as soon as one goes to sleep (in a nar-

15
Soc.
Sci.

coleptic episode, one immediately goes into REM sleep). No one knows exactly
55   what causes narcolepsy, and the disorder seems resistant to treatment.

Sleep Apnea

Apnea means a sudden stoppage in breathing, literally "without breath."
Episodes are usually short, and long-term effects are few. When apnea episodes
are longer—say, a minute or two—carbon dioxide in the lungs builds to such a
level that the sleeper is awakened, draws a few gasps of air, and returns to sleep,
60   probably oblivious to what just happened.

Sleep apnea is a prime suspect in the search for a cause of Sudden Infant
Death Syndrome, or SIDS. In this syndrome, young infants, apparently without any
major illness, but sometimes with a slight cold or infection, suddenly die in their
sleep. Such sudden death occurs at a rate of about two infants per thousand.

—Josh Gerow, *Psychology*

Comprehension Questions.   Label the following items with *T* (true)
or *F* (false).

_____   1. The main idea of this passage is that Americans are sleeping
less because they are troubled by sleeping disorders.

_____   2. According to the author, a sleep loss of one hour each night
for three nights creates a total "sleep debt" of one hour.

_____   3. According to the author, you can use the weekend to "catch
up" on the sleep lost during the week.

_____   4. Webb has been involved in more than one published research study on sleep deprivation.

_____   5. Maureen Weston stayed awake for more than six days longer
than Randy Gardner.

_____   6. The findings of the research studies quoted in this passage indicate that prolonged sleep deprivation can damage your health.

_____   7. The passage offers encouraging treatment for the three major
sleep disorders.

_____   8. The sleeping problems of insomnia and narcolepsy are opposite in nature.

_____   9. The author suggests that SIDS may be caused by a carbon
dioxide buildup in the lungs.

10. What is the pattern of organization in the second half of the
passage beginning with the *Insomnia* subheading?

_____

_____

15
Soc.
Sci.

Critical Thinking Question. From the information presented in this passage, is it possible Randy Gardner and Maureen Weston could have taken microsleeps? How could researchers have controlled for that event?

Small-Group EXPLORATION

Form a five-member group and select one of the following activities. Brainstorm and then outline your major points on a transparency. Choose one group member to present the group's findings to the class. Individual assignments can also be made.

- What household jobs do you consider to be more appropriate for a male than for a female? List the jobs according to your beliefs about gender roles.

- Why might discussing your thoughts with a friend have a positive effect on your health? List the reasons.

- Why do more women than men bear the burden of poverty in the United States, to the point that sociologists refer to the "feminization of poverty"? List the reasons.

- How does society benefit from an educated citizenry? List the reasons.

15
Soc.
Sci.

Net SEARCH

Why do some young people commit crimes? Many theories attempt to explain juvenile delinquency. Some are based on psychology and others are based on sociology. Search the Internet for both a psychological theory and a sociological theory of juvenile delinquency. Explain each.

Chapter

16

Reading in the Life and Natural Sciences

16a What Are the Life and Natural Sciences?

Science appeals to the curious. Scientists ask questions such as *How do hummingbirds fly across the Gulf of Mexico?* and *Why does a weight lifter need protein?* Explaining the *how* and *why* of natural phenomena is like solving a puzzle, one that ultimately connects all living organisms.

Whether a scientist studies a tiny piece of the puzzle, such as a protein, or a huge piece, such as a killer whale sickened by pollution, the parts of this gigantic puzzle are all interconnected. Why does the destruction of the Amazon rain forest affect a family in Ohio? How can the growth on another continent of a tiny organism like the AIDS virus drastically alter American lives? How does the application of technological advances for space travel influence your choice of a winter jacket? The discoveries, the interconnections, and the applications give rise to the beauty and the power of science.

Life and natural scientists study biological organisms (life forms) and the natural phenomena affecting them. Their areas of study include biology, agriculture, chemistry, physics, astronomy, environmental sciences, and allied health sciences. Scientists rigorously apply the **scientific method,** the same investigative techniques used by social scientists.

16b   What Is Biology?

Biology is the science of living organisms and life processes. A biology major might become a genetic engineer, a soil conservationist, a fish and game manager, a mortician, or a zoo curator. A biology degree also provides a foundation for further study in medical, dental, or veterinary school.

Recognize the Organizational Patterns of a Biology Text

Introductory biology textbooks either begin with the small such as atoms and molecules and move to the large such as biosphere and ecosystems (micro to macro), or they start with the large and move to the small (macro to micro). These two approaches refer to the organization of life forms into different levels of size and complexity The levels, in ascending order, are shown below.

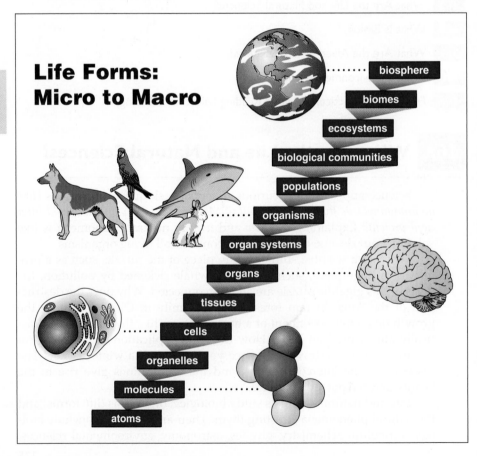

Life Forms: Micro to Macro

biosphere
biomes
ecosystems
biological communities
populations
organisms
organ systems
organs
tissues
cells
organelles
molecules
atoms

In biology textbooks, typical paragraphs tend to be a mixture of organizational patterns. You may find a simple listing of terms, each defined with examples explaining cause-and-effect results in real life. A photograph or drawing often further supports the text explanation.

> The critical experiments of Italian physician Francesco Redi (1621–1697) beautifully demonstrate the scientific method and also help illustrate the principle of *natural causality*, on which modern science is based. Redi investigated why maggots appear on spoiled meat. Before Redi, the appearance of maggots was considered to be evidence of **spontaneous generation,** the production of living things from nonliving matter.
>
> Redi observed that flies swarm around fresh meat and that maggots appear on meat left out for a few days. He formed a testable *hypothesis:* The flies produce the maggots. In his *experiment,* Redi wanted to test just one variable: the access of flies to the meat. He left one jar open (the *control* jar) and covered the other with gauze to keep out flies (the *experimental* jar). He did his best to keep all other variables the same (for example, the type of jar, the type of meat, and the temperature). After a few days, he observed that maggots swarmed over the meat in the open jar, but no maggots appeared on the meat in the covered jar. Redi concluded that his hypothesis was correct and that maggots are produced by flies, not by the meat itself. Only through controlled experiments could the age-old hypothesis of spontaneous generation be laid to rest.
>
> —Teresa Audesirk, Gerald Audesirk, and Bruce E. Byers, *Biology: Life on Earth*

**16
Nat.
Sci.**

Practice 1

Answer the following questions regarding the preceding passage.

1. As signaled in the text by boldfaced print or italics, what terms might you later need to be able to define?

_____

_____

2. Why was spontaneous generation rejected?

_____

3. What is the definition of a variable?

_____

4. What connections are made to everyday life?

_____

Knowledge of biology is cumulative; you will build and network your understanding. For example, do not leave the cellular reproduction

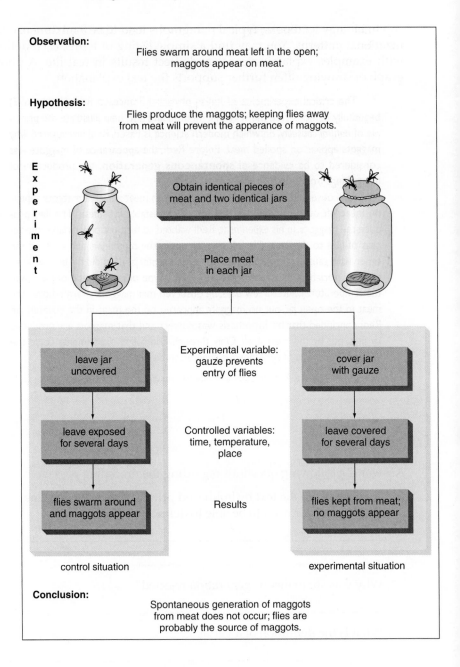

Observation:
Flies swarm around meat left in the open;
maggots appear on meat.

Hypothesis:
Flies produce the maggots; keeping flies away
from meat will prevent the apperance of maggots.

Experiment

Obtain identical pieces of
meat and two identical jars

Place meat
in each jar

leave jar
uncovered

Experimental variable:
gauze prevents
entry of flies

cover jar
with gauze

leave exposed
for several days

Controlled variables:
time, temperature,
place

leave covered
for several days

flies swarm around
and maggots appear

Results

flies kept from meat;
no maggots appear

control situation

experimental situation

Conclusion:
Spontaneous generation of maggots
from meat does not occur; flies are
probably the source of maggots.

chapter until you understand the difference between *mitosis* and *meiosis*; you will find both terms again later in the text.

No part of nature can be understood in isolation; parts must be connected to be meaningful. In the following passage, you can see the cause-

and-effect nature of science and the way a single tiny organism can destroy human life.

> Streptococcus is a common bacterium, the one that causes strep throat, and everyone is exposed to it every day. There are perhaps 75 kinds of strep A bacteria, but one type, perhaps infected by a virus that takes over its metabolic machinery, produces a very powerful poison that can cause toxic shock syndrome—when many of the systems of the body simply shut down—or necrotizing fasciitis.
>
> In necrotizing fasciitis, the bacteria destroy human tissue, particularly fat and muscle, at the rate of about an inch an hour. Once it has reached this stage, there is often nothing to do but cut away the infected tissue and, in many cases, amputate any affected limbs while administering heavy doses of antibiotics. Even then, death may follow in three to four days.
>
> The problem is not new. Perhaps 15,000 people come down with group A every year and about 3,000 die, a remarkably high mortality rate. However, early treatment could drastically lower that rate. The germ is spread from person to person and usually enters through a cut, but it can be spread by coughs and handshakes.

—Robert A. Wallace, *Biology*

✓ Reader's TIP

Using the Signposts in a Biology Textbook

■ *Preview the chapter* by reading initial learning objectives or outlines. Use them later to test your comprehension.

■ *Arouse your interest* in the topic by reading the opening case studies and personal anecdotes.

■ *Use illustrations* as reading tools to clarify the text.

■ *Walk step-by-step* through complicated processes such as the path of blood flow through the cardiovascular system. *Recite* the steps in the processes.

16
Nat.
Sci.

Practice 2

Answer the following questions regarding the preceding passage.

1. How do bacteria enter the system?

_____

2. How has the strep bacteria been altered?

_____

3. What is necrotizing fasciitis?

_____

4. What are the human consequences of infection?

_____

✔ **Reader's TIP**

Studying Biology

- Master a concept by explaining it in your own words.
- Draw your own biological structures and processes to reinforce learning them. Your notes should have lots of pictures.
- Know the theories you are applying in the lab and their significance.
- Blend lecture, lab, and textbook notes. List connections.
- Use illustrations as review tools before exams.
- Use chapter summaries as study checklists to be sure you have reviewed all the chapter material.
- Think like a scientist at the textbook website by participating in virtual research activities.
- Use mnemonics to memorize. Remember the example for the five kingdoms: *Many People Find Parachuting Alarming.*

Use Mnemonics

Many new names and facts must be memorized in science. Use *mnemonics,* or memory tricks such as creating words, sentences, rhymes, or songs, to enhance your memory (see Chapter 12). For example, all living organisms are divided by common traits into five classification groups called *kingdoms:* monera, protests, fungi, plants, animals.

How can you remember this list? A mnemonic device can help to memorize the kingdoms in order. In a sentence like *Many People Find Parachuting Alarming,* each word represents one kingdom. Finally, rehearse, recite, and even write. Memory links can save you lots of time in the long run.

16c What Are the Allied Health Sciences?

The **allied health sciences** promote the mental and physical well-being of the population. Careers in the allied health sciences include nurse, physician, physician's assistant (PA), dentist, pharmacist, chiropractor, nutritionist, therapist, radiologic technician, and paramedical technologist. Each job function demands that you collaborate with other professionals to deliver quality health care. For example, in a follow-up visit after a broken bone has been treated, a nurse will take your vital signs, a lab technician will take X-rays, a doctor will assess your progress, and a physical therapist will show you how to regain strength and mobility.

Critical thinking is vital in the health sciences field. You must be prepared for unexpected emergencies such as a frightened patient or a person who is near death. You must be able to recognize signs and use critical analysis to take the appropriate actions. The choices you make can be life-and-death decisions.

Recognize the Organizational Patterns of a Health Text

Introductory health textbooks include discussions on ethics, psychology, and teaching, as well as explanations of illnesses, medical assessment, and procedural steps. The following passage from a nursing textbook explains the proportions of body fluid in humans.

Proportions of Body Fluid

The proportion of the human body composed of fluid is surprisingly large, considering that the external appearance suggests mostly solid tissue such as muscle and bone. Fluid makes up about 47% to 55% of the average healthy adult's weight (see the table below). In healthy people, this volume (about 40
5   liters) of body fluid remains relatively constant. In fact, a healthy person's weight varies less than 0.5 lb in 24 hours, regardless of the amount of fluid ingested. Some diseases cause serious excesses or deficiencies of body fluid. For example, a client with heart failure can retain fluid in the tissues and may suffer a fluid excess. A person with kidney disease may not be able to excrete the required
10   amount of urine and also suffer a fluid excess. Another person with a mouth injury may not be able to drink and may suffer a fluid loss.

Fluid as Percentage of Body Weight (by age)	
Age	Percentage of Fluid*
Full-term newborn	70 to 80
1 year	64
Puberty to 39 years	52 to 60
40 to 60 years	47 to 55
Over 60 years	46 to 52

*Generally, men have a slightly higher percentage of fluid than women.

The percentage of total body fluid varies according to the individual's age, body fat, and sex. Infants have the highest proportion of fluid; fluid constitutes 70% to 80% of their body weight. As people grow older, the proportion
15   decreases. Body fat is essentially free of fluid. For example, a thin man's body may be 70% fluid, whereas an obese man's may be only 53%. This variable, body

fat, also accounts for the difference in total body fluid between the sexes. After adolescence, women have proportionately more fat than men. Thus they have a smaller percentage of fluid in relation to total body weight than do men.

—Barbara Kozier et al., *Fundamentals of Nursing*

Practice 3

Mark the following statements regarding the previous passage *T* (true) or *F* (false).

_____ **1.** According to the passage, a healthy person can gain more than one pound in 24 hours by drinking excessive amounts of water.

_____ **2.** The average percentage of total body fluid decreases with age.

_____ **3.** People with more body fat have a smaller percentage of total body fluid.

_____ **4.** On the average, women tend to have a higher percentage of body fluid than men.

_____ **5.** Heart failure can cause a patient to retain excess fluids.

16
Nat.
Sci.

Much of the material in health textbooks is organized into lists with definitions and in sequential patterns. Many of the procedural passages that explain how to examine patients for illnesses are lengthy and complex. The following passage from a nursing textbook is a short and simple example of a time-order or sequence pattern for cleaning and disinfecting objects in a hospital or home setting.

The following steps should be followed when cleaning objects in a hospital or in a home where infectious agents exist.

1. Rinse the article with cold water to remove organic material. Hot water coagulates the protein of organic material and tends to make it adhere. Examples of organic material are blood and pus.

2. Wash the article in hot water and soap. The emulsifying action of soap reduces surface tension and facilitates the removal of dirt. Washing dislodges the emulsified dirt.

3. Use an abrasive, such as a stiff-bristled brush, to clean equipment with grooves and corners. Friction helps dislodge foreign material.

4. Rinse the article well with warm-hot water.

5. Dry the article; it is now considered clean.

6. Clean the brush, gloves, and sink. These are considered soiled until they are cleaned appropriately, usually with a disinfectant.

—Kozier et al., *Fundamentals of Nursing*

Other typical passages have assessment checklists like the following example for testing and grading muscle strength. They are usually accompanied by charts or diagrams (see below).

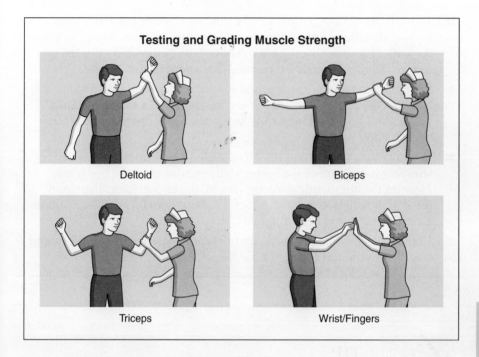

Testing and Grading Muscle Strength

Deltoid

Biceps

Triceps

Wrist/Fingers

Muscle/Activity

Deltoid: Client holds arm up and resists while nurse tries to push it down.

Biceps: Client fully extends each arm and tries to flex it while nurse attempts to hold arm in extension.

Triceps: Client flexes each arm and then tries to extend it against the nurse's attempt to keep arm in flexion.

Wrist and finger muscles: Client spreads the fingers and resists as the nurse attempts to push the fingers together.

—Kozier et al., *Fundamentals of Nursing*

Practice 4

Mark the following statements regarding the two previous passages *T* (true) or *F* (false).

_____ **1.** To clean infectious objects, begin with hot water.

_____ **2.** Use a disinfectant to clean your cleaning equipment.

_____ **3.** Push against the client to check deltoid and triceps.

✔ Reader's TIP

Reading a Health Science Textbook

- To learn procedures, stop and recite the equipment needed and step-by-step directions. Use diagrams and pictures for visualizing. Know the patient assessment signals to notice both before and after the procedure. Predict possible exam questions about the procedure.

- For tables and charts, understand the connection and interaction between the columns and the rows. In a table of joint movements, understand how the major muscle groups cause the range of motion in each body part listed.

- In a diagram, understand how the labeled parts interrelate. When studying a diagram of the homeostatic regulators of the body, ask, How do the autonomic nervous system, the endocrine system, and the specific organ systems interact? Or, how does blood flow through a cardiovascular system diagram?

- Connect textbook concepts to lab or clinical experiences to give added meaning to the text ideas.

✔ Reader's TIP

Study Tips for the Health Sciences

- *Memorize medical abbreviations and symbols* using recitation, writing, and flashcard techniques. For example, *pc* means "after meals"; # can mean "number" or "fracture."

- *Draw your own diagrams* to reinforce learning medical processes. For example, draw a diagram of the chain-of-infection cycle, moving from parasite to susceptible host.

- *Think critically* by considering your actions in potential clinical problems. Typically, "What Would You Do?" boxes propose situations such as the following: After starting an intravenous infusion, you notice a small amount of blood on your forearm as you are removing your gloves. *What would you do?*

- *Learn the dos and don'ts* of clinical behavior. Frequently, boxes include proper "Clinical Guidelines" such as, "Always identify the patient verbally and by bracelet before administering any intervention."

16d   What Is Environmental Science?

Environmental scientists are specialists in biology, chemistry, geology, geography, or other fields who collaborate as a team to solve problems that threaten our planet. In an effort to halt the decline of the Earth's natural resources, they study pollution, overpopulation, the agricultural revolution, global warming, and alternative energy sources.

Because we are upsetting the balance in our ecosystem with industrial pollution, deforestation, and toxic waste dumping, **ecology**—the study of the interrelationship of organisms and their environment—is rapidly becoming an extremely important area.

Environmental science incorporates knowledge from other sciences. Apply study tips and textbook reading suggestions on the previous pages.

Practice 5

Read the following passage from an environmental science textbook and mark the statements that follow *T* (true) or *F* (false).

Surface impoundments are simple excavated depressions ("man-made ponds") into which liquid wastes are drained and held. They were the least expensive and hence most widely used way to dispose of large amounts of water carrying relatively small amounts of chemical wastes. As waste is discharged into the pond, solid wastes settle and accumulate while water evaporates (see

16
Nat.
Sci.

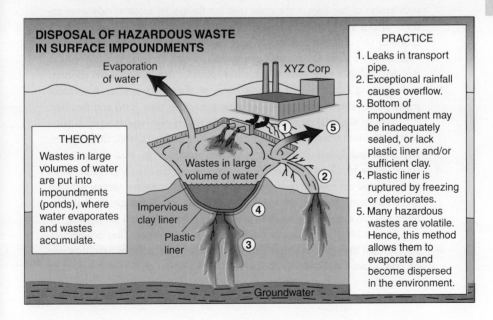

DISPOSAL OF HAZARDOUS WASTE IN SURFACE IMPOUNDMENTS

Evaporation of water

XYZ Corp

THEORY

Wastes in large volumes of water are put into impoundments (ponds), where water evaporates and wastes accumulate.

Wastes in large volume of water

Impervious clay liner

Plastic liner

Groundwater

PRACTICE

1. Leaks in transport pipe.
2. Exceptional rainfall causes overflow.
3. Bottom of impoundment may be inadequately sealed, or lack plastic liner and/or sufficient clay.
4. Plastic liner is ruptured by freezing or deteriorates.
5. Many hazardous wastes are volatile. Hence, this method allows them to evaporate and become dispersed in the environment.

the figure). If the pond bottom is well sealed and if evaporation equals input, impoundments may receive wastes indefinitely. However, inadequate seals may allow wastes to percolate into groundwater, exceptional storms may cause overflows, and volatile materials can evaporate into the atmosphere, adding to air pollution problems and eventually falling down with rain to contaminate water in other locations.

—Bernard Nebel and Richard Wright, *Environmental Science*

_____ 1. The diagram illustrates five ways in which the impoundments can be dangerous to the environment.

_____ 2. The passage indicates that groundwater contamination is less serious than air pollution.

_____ 3. In theory, evaporation should allow for indefinite use of impoundment ponds.

16e For Further Practice: Extended Reading Selection in Biology

Firefly Flashes

Fireflies live in many parts of the world. In the eastern United States, for example, the flashes of fireflies in a field are a common sight on a summer night. Males do most of the flashing.

5　　When a female sees flashes of light from a male of her species, she reacts with flashes of her own. If the male sees her flashes, he automatically gives another display and flies in the female's direction. Members of both sexes are responding to particular patterns of light flashes characteristic of their species. Mating occurs when the female's display leads a male to her, and most females stop flashing after they mate. But in a few species, a mated female will continue

10　to flash, using a pattern that attracts males of *other* firefly species. A veritable *femme fatale,* she waits until an alien male gets close, then grabs and eats him.

Each of the 2000 or so species of firefly has its own way to signal a mate. Some flash more often than others or during different hours, while other species give fewer but longer flashes. Many species produce light of a characteristic

15　color: yellow, bluish-green, or reddish. In areas where fireflies congregate—often on lawns, golf courses, or open meadows—you can usually see several different species signaling. Because the insects respond instinctively to specific flash patterns, you can even attract males to artificial light if you flash it a certain way.

From a biological standpoint, fireflies are poorly named. They are beetles,

20　not flies, and their light is almost cold, not fiery. In fact, in emitting light, they give off only about one hundred-thousandth of the amount of heat that would be produced by a candle flame of equal brightness.

What happens in a firefly that makes this light? The light comes from a set of chemical reactions that occur in light-producing organs at the rear of the insect. Light-emitting cells in these organs contain an acidic substance called *luciferin* and an enzyme called *luciferase* (both named from the Latin for "light bearer"). In the presence of oxygen (O_2) and chemical energy from ATP molecules, luciferase catalyzes the conversion of luciferin to a molecule that emits light.

The luciferin-luciferase system is one example of how living cells put energy to work by means of enzyme-controlled chemical reactions. Light is a form of energy, and the firefly's ability to make light energy from chemical energy is an example of life's dependence on energy conversion.

Many of the enzymes that control a cell's chemical reactions, including the firefly's luciferase, are located in membranes. Membranes thus serve as sites where chemical reactions can occur in an orderly manner.

—Neil A. Campbell, Lawrence Mitchell, and Jane Reece, *Biology: Concepts and Connections*

Comprehension Questions.   Answer the following statements or questions with true (*T*), false (*F*), or a written response.

_____   1. Mating is the primary purpose of the flashes of light from fireflies.

_____   2. According to the passage, females eat males of the same species.

_____   3. The main idea of this passage is that fireflies are cannibalistic.

_____   4. The flash of the firefly is species-specific, which means that there are more than 2,000 uniquely different flashes.

_____   5. The fireflies could not flash without oxygen.

_____   6. According to the author, fireflies are categorized as beetles because they emit cold light.

_____   7. Energy reactions occur in membranes.

8. What is the pattern of organization in the fifth paragraph, which begins "What happens in"?

_____

9. From the context of the passage, define *catalyzes* in the phrase, "luciferase catalyzes the conversion of luciferin to a molecule that emits light."

_____

16
Nat.
Sci.

10. This passage on fireflies begins a chapter in a biology text-book. What would you predict that the chapter will be about?

_____

_____

_____

Critical Thinking Question. Why have firefly flashes evolved to be species-specific?

Small-Group EXPLORATION

Form a five-member group and select one of the following activities. Brainstorm and then outline your major points on a transparency. Choose one group member to present the group's findings to the class. Individual assignments can also be made.

■ What can you do to diminish the chances that you will catch a cold? List your precautionary strategies.

■ Assume that you are a laboratory biologist. List potential money-making invention opportunities for the twenty-first century.

■ What is needed for life as we know it to exist on other planets? How might such life help or hurt us?

■ What environmental issues are of greatest concern in your local area? List the top ten concerns—and the culprits, if you can identify them.

Net SEARCH

As a world-renowned environmental scientist, you have been asked to brief the President on overpopulation and the environment. The President would like to know (1) what the current world population is, (2) how overpopulation harms the environment, and (3) how overpopulation can be controlled.

Search the Internet for the answers to these questions, then prepare a one-page summary of your findings. Be sure to cite the sources of your information.

Chapter

17

Reading in Mathematics and Computer Science

17a How Can You Get the Most from Your Mathematics Textbook?

Mathematics is the foundation for many college courses and a primary tool in many professions. What do civil engineers, automobile designers, doctors, pharmacists, landscape architects, and artists all have in common? *Math skills* is the answer. In fact, you will probably use some math in whatever career you choose.

Math is also essential in your personal life. You need math skills to figure your monthly budget, sports statistics, and an appropriate tip for the server in a restaurant. Determining whether your cell phone bill is correct and furnishing an apartment are other examples of the practical use of math.

What's more, math is used in ways you probably never thought about. How about a skydiver's calculating free-fall time and average speed, a scuba diver's considering depth when estimating maximum time underwater, or a foreign student's calculating exchange rates? Math is not just for school use; you use it everywhere, even when you're having fun.

Some people have come to believe that they can't do math, and therefore they experience fear or "math anxiety." The strategies in this chapter will help you overcome any such problem by explaining the strategies for success with math.

Learn the Language of Mathematics

Similar to a foreign language, mathematics requires you to learn unfamiliar symbols and terms. Even previously known words like *absolute* and *origin* have different meanings in mathematics. Thus, you must master the language of mathematics in order to understand its abstract ideas.

Symbols. Each of the following symbols has a specific meaning:

+ add	− subtract
(+3) positive 3	(−4) negative 4
≠ not equal to	× or ( ) multiplied by / divided by
√ square root	> greater than < less than
ab *a* times *b*	

(+8)/(−2) divide positive 8 by negative 2

Practice 1

Using the explanation of mathematical symbols, translate the following mathematical terms into words and sentences.

1. $ab - 8$

_____

2. $7 + \sqrt{240}$

_____

3. $x/7$

_____

4. $(2x)(3y) - 5$

_____

_____

5. $(+2) + (+4) = (+6)$

_____

6. $(+8) / (-2) = (-4)$

_____

_____

17
**Math/
Comp.
Sci.**

✓ Reader's TIP

Speaking the Language of Mathematics

■ **Memorize.** Use 3×5 cards for definitions of symbols and vocabulary. Recite and repeat aloud to involve your sense of hearing. Exact definitions are vital in mathematics. To stress the importance of memorizing definitions, in some simple cases you can prove a theorem simply by writing the definitions of terms.

■ **Translate.** Express mathematical terms in words and sentences.
   Example $x - 8 = 12$
   Explanation A number, x, decreased by 8, is equal to 12.

■ **Look around.** Use the glossary and previous chapters to clarify terminology.

■ **Use the language.** Speak and write in mathematical terms whenever you communicate about mathematics.

Take the Time to Understand Examples and Explanations

In mathematics textbooks, the primary pattern of organization is that of definition and example. Terms, theorems, and formulas are first defined and then demonstrated through examples.

Mathematics is *cumulative*, meaning that each chapter builds on another. In other words, you probably can't do problems in Chapter 6 if you have forgotten something in Chapter 4. Thus, flip back to clarify and use your glossary for definitions and formulas.

Read mathematics textbooks slowly and even read aloud when confused. Seek to understand all the information in each sentence before moving on. Rephrase newly learned ideas in your own words as you read.

**17
Math/
Comp.
Sci.**

✓ Reader's TIP

Learning from Your Mathematics Textbook

■ **Preview.** Get an overview of how the chapter is presented. If you get stuck on a concept, you'll know if additional coverage appears later in the chapter.

■ **Read slowly.** Mathematics texts are filled with compressed information. Each sentence is important. Seek to understand all the information in each sentence before moving on.

(continued)

■ **Repeat to yourself.** Rephrase each newly learned idea in your own words as you read.

■ **Use visualization.** Substitute letters or pictures in your mind for symbols or procedures. Draw your own diagrams, numbered lines, or tables. Do whatever helps you to "see" the concept.

■ **Use cards to memorize.** Read with 3 × 5 cards to record definitions. Use mnemonics like "*P*lease *E*xcuse *M*y *D*ear *A*unt *S*ally" whenever possible. The first letter in each word explains the order of operations when solving problems, which is Remove "*P*arentheses from the inside out in the order of *E*xponents, *M*ultiplication, *D*ivision, *A*ddition, and *S*ubtraction."

■ **Take translated notes.** Rewrite mathematical expressions in your own words as you read to get comfortable with their meanings.

Examples $x^2 = 9$ The square of a number, x, is equal to 9.
$(x)(y) = 35$ The product of two numbers x and y, is equal to 35.

■ **Work all examples as you read.** Examples help you understand how and why each step of a procedure is done. Remember to write questions about any unclear steps, and be sure to ask these questions later in class.

Use Lecture Notes to Your Best Advantage

When in a class lecture, remember that you will later be doing your homework alone. In class you may think that you will never forget what your professor clearly said, but don't bet your grade on it. Write down *every step of all examples*, even if you already understand them. Inject your own everyday words to connect ideas. Ask questions and take lots of notes to stay focused.

Review your notes immediately after class to clear up any fuzzy areas while the information is still fresh in your mind. Use two brains by reviewing with a classmate.

Review all of your notes on a regular basis to strengthen your knowledge networks. Since mathematics is a linear science, new material can be learned only when you have a solid understanding of previous material.

Use Homework to Get Ahead in Mathematics

Homework is a critical process in remembering. Working independently with new material helps transfer information from short-term memory to long-term memory.

Never skip assigned homework exercises. Each new problem builds on what you already know. With practice you will become faster at calculating, and complex problems will then become easier.

17
Math/
Comp.
Sci.

Do some mathematics homework every day. Like a foreign language, mathematics needs to be reinforced on a regular basis. Frequent short sessions are better for learning than infrequent long sessions. Always quiz yourself on the main concepts you have learned.

Improve Your Mathematics Study Skills

Mathematics builds new information on previous information. If you skip something in mathematics, you will not be able to grasp new material before first learning the material you skipped. That is why it is important to keep up with your mathematics homework and reviews. Once you get behind, it can prove difficult to catch up.

"An unprecedented blizzard has buried the Eastern Seaboard under one hundred and fifty-eight inches of snow. That's, let's see . . . twelve into fifteen goes once, two from five is three, bring down the eight, twelve into thirty-eight goes three times with two left over . . ."

17
Math/
Comp.
Sci.

If mathematics is your most difficult subject, study it first while you are fresh. Cover new material at the beginning of your session. Save review for the end, when you may be tired. Also, alternate left-brain (logical) and right-brain (intuitive) subjects in your study order to give one side of your brain a rest after each subject. For example, don't follow mathematics with another left-brain subject such as statistics, accounting, or computer science. Choose a right-brain subject such as history, English, or Spanish instead.

Don't try to learn new material just before a test. This time should be used for *review only.*

✓ Reader's TIP

Using Studying Strategies for Mathematics

- ■ Study your *most difficult subject first*. For you that may not be mathematics. Because of the demanding nature of the subject however, it might be wise to study mathematics first before you tire.
- ■ Study mathematics *every day* to reduce the amount of forgetting.
- ■ *Alternate* left-brain (logical) and right-brain (intuitive) *subjects* in your study order.
- ■ Review regularly to prepare for tests.
- ■ Seek expert help in the mathematics lab.

Create 3 by 5 index cards to record definitions, symbols, theorems, and formulas. Review them weekly, not only the night before a test. Include diagrams or tables to help you "see" the concept.

Take advantage of the *mathematics lab*, which may have computer programs that enable you to practice solving problems. The mathematics lab tutor may have a different explanation that finally helps you "get it."

To improve your success in mathematics, use the problem-solving strategies of *flexibility, generalizability*, and *reversibility.*

Flexibility. How many ways can you solve a problem? There may be *several* correct ways to solve a problem. This is especially handy to know when a homework exercise does not exactly match either the instructor's example or the examples in the book. By being flexible, you can usually find another way to solve the problem.

EXAMPLE Lisa's favorite new CD is on sale for 20 percent off the original price of $15. How much will she have to pay for the CD?

Method I	Method 2
The CD will cost ($15)(100% − 20%)	The discount is ($15)(20%)
$x = 15(.80)$	$x = 15(.20)$
$x = 12 = $ cost $= \$12$	$x = 3 = $ discount $= \$3$
	$\$15 - \$3 = $ cost $= \$12$

Generalizability. Do you see a pattern here?

Mathematics is a science of patterns. Learning to look for patterns and understanding the rules behind them will save you time. Then you will not start from scratch on each new problem you attempt to solve. Remember to think about what you already know before starting to solve a problem.

> EXAMPLE If $x + 3 = 5$ and $x + 4 = 6$, then x must be 2.

Reversibility.   Can you work a problem backwards?

Reversibility enables you to work forward or backward when you are given any part of a problem. You can work forward to a solution or backward to obtain the original problem. Many applications are worked this way in the real world; we know the answer, and we have to figure out how we got there. You can also use reversibility to check your work.

> EXAMPLE If $3 + 3 + 2 = 8$, then subtract the first three numbers from 8 to get zero.

17b How Can You Get the Most from Your Computer Science Textbook?

According to experts, computer science is still in its infancy, and we have seen only the tip of the information technology iceberg. We are experiencing an exploding information society. The pioneers with vision who lead us to the new frontiers will likely have taken computer science courses. For all jobs, computer competency is both maninstream (considered "cool") and mandatory (necessary). You need computer knowledge to get, keep, and advance in good jobs. With a portable personal computer, you have your own command center, and you can be at work in any location. You can keep in touch, learn, shop, and make money at your computer. What more incentive is needed to embrace computer technology?

Introductory **computer science** courses focus on explaining, defining, and connecting. Advanced studies in computer science rely heavily on mathematics and physics. A systems analysis text may be written in a narrative style with many diagrams to show how information flows through the system and at what points the information is processed. Programming and data management textbooks assist the reader with key concept boxes, flowchart diagrams, marginal notes, and tables defining commands.

As you do with your mathematics textbook, use the glossary of a computer science textbook as a valuable reference. Two sections often found in computer science books deal with these application areas:

- **Case studies.** One or more real-world projects offer an opportunity to problem-solve, applying each new area of knowledge on a continuing basis. For example, one project might be to design and implement an inventory system for a video rental store.

- **Common errors and debugging.** This section may appear at the end of each chapter to point out concepts that are often misunderstood. Tips may be offered for avoiding programming code errors and for debugging in advance of a need to do so.

Learn the Language of Computer Science

Computer science has its own vocabulary, signs, and symbols to learn in addition to all the mathematical language you have already learned.

Vocabulary. As in mathematics, familiar terms such as *mouse, bus,* and *port* take on new meanings. Certain terms are frequently used:

- **Syntax:** the grammar of a programming language; the specific order of grouping commands and symbols in a line of code.

- **Binary system:** a system of ones and zeros used to represent numbers that have been assigned to alphanumeric characters. It is the computer's way of handling all data—a system of switches either *on* or *off* to represent a one or a zero.

Symbols. Most of the symbols in computer science are made up of one or more alphanumeric characters. Some look like abbreviations, such as *char* for *character,* and some look like acronyms, such as *bfs* for *big file scanner.* Symbols that look familiar— { , [ ], $, and #—may be used in very specific ways depending on the syntax of the programming language being used.

Signs. Arithmetic signs usually have the same meanings in computer science that they have in mathematics.

17
Math/
Comp.
Sci.

Use Mathematics Strategies to Study Computer Science

Computer science *is* problem solving; you will need to apply your mathematical problem-solving strategies of *flexibility, generalizability,* and *reversibility* (see pages 294–295). For example, if you are writing a computer program, you may be flexible in *what* you tell the computer to do but not in *how* you tell the computer to do it. You must follow precise rules in the coding process.

Study strategies for mathematics apply to computer science as well. Like mathematics, computer science is cumulative; you must expect to refer back to previous chapters. Because the material is condensed, you should read slowly, taking care to understand each sentence and build your knowledge.

17c For Further Practice: Extended Reading Selection in Computer Science

Don't be confused by the big words in the following passage. You already understand these concepts. Read slowly to build meaning; visualize and relate to known examples to understand.

The Study of Algorithms

We begin with the most fundamental concept of computer science—that of an algorithm. Informally, an algorithm is a set of steps that defines how a task is performed. For example, there are algorithms for constructing model airplanes (expressed in the form of instruction sheets), for operating washing ma-
5 chines (usually displayed on the inside of the washer's lid), for playing music (expressed in the form of sheet music), and for performing magic tricks.

Before a machine can perform a task, an algorithm for performing that task must be discovered and represented in a form that is compatible or well-suited with the machine. A machine-compatible representation of an algorithm is
10 called a **program.** Programs, and the algorithms they represent, are collectively referred to as **software,** in contrast to the machinery itself, which is known as **hardware.**

The study of algorithms began as a subject in mathematics. The search for algorithms was a significant activity of mathematicians long before the develop-
15 ment of today's computers. The major goal of that search was to find a single set of directions that described how any problem of a particular type could be solved. One of the best-known consequences of this early search for algorithms is the long division algorithm for finding the quotient of two multiple-digit numbers. Another example is the Euclidean algorithm, discovered by the ancient
20 Greek mathematician Euclid, for finding the greatest common divisor of two positive integers.

Once an algorithm of performing a task has been found, the performance of that task no longer requires an understanding of the principles on which the algorithm is based. Instead, the performance of the task is reduced to the
25 process of merely following directions. We can follow the long division algorithm to find a quotient or the Euclidean algorithm to find a greatest common divisor without understanding why the algorithm works. In a sense, the intelligence required to perform the task is encoded in the algorithm.

It is through this ability to capture and convey intelligence by means of al-
30 gorithms that we were able to build machines that display intelligent behavior. Consequently, the level of intelligence displayed by machines is limited by the intelligence that can be conveyed through algorithms. Only if we find an algorithm that directs the performance of a task can we construct a machine to perform that task. In turn, if no algorithm exists for performing a task, then the perfor-
35 mance of that task lies beyond the capabilities of machines.

A major undertaking throughout the computing field, then, is the development of algorithms, and consequently a significant part of computer science is

17
Math/
Comp.
Sci.

concerned with issues relating to that task. One such issue deals with the question of how algorithms are discovered in the first place—a question that is
40 closely related to that of problem solving in general. To discover an algorithm for solving a problem is essentially to discover a solution for the problem.

Once an algorithm for solving a problem has been discovered, the next step is to represent the algorithm so it can be communicated to a machine or to other humans. This means that we must transform the conceptual algorithm
45 into a clear set of instructions and represent these instructions in an unambiguous or crystal clear manner. Studies emerging from these concerns draw from our knowledge of language and grammar and have led to an abundance of algorithm representation schemes, known as programming languages, which are based on a variety of approaches to the programming process, known as pro-
50 gramming paradigms.

—J. Glenn Brookshear, *Computer Science: An Overview*

Comprehension Questions.   Answer the following statements or questions with true (*T*), false (*F*), or a written response.

_____ **1.** The purpose of this passage is to explain the importance of algorithms in computer science.

_____ **2.** You cannot follow an algorithm without understanding it.

_____ **3.** The author would probably consider the steps in problem solving to be an algorithm for problem solving.

_____ **4.** Companies that duplicate existing products copy rather than create algorithms.

_____ **5.** The major reason people have difficulty working a VCR is that they do not understand the algorithm.

_____ **6.** Programming is not limited by the capability of the hardware.

_____ **7.** Algorithms are created for computers, not created by them.

_____ **8.** Programmers translate algorithms for hardware.

9. What is an algorithm?

_____

10. How is an algorithm related to a program?

_____

_____

11. What is the pattern of organization in the first paragraph?

_____

12. From the context of the passage, define the term *paradigms* in the sentence, "We consider some of these languages and the paradigms on which they are based."

_____

_____

Critical Thinking Question.   What is the algorithm for course registration at your college?

Small-Group EXPLORATION

Form a five-member group and select one of the following questions. Brainstorm and then outline your major points on a transparency. Choose one group member to present the group's findings to the class. Individual assignments can also be made.

■ In several studies on retention, the SAT mathematics score was found to be one of the few predictors of success in college. List reasons why you think mathematical knowledge would predict college success.

■ List the top ten reasons why students fail mathematics.

■ List ten reasons why "Because I'm not good in math" is not an appropriate reply.

■ Create examples to demonstrate the problem-solving strategies of flexibility, generalizability, and reversibility.

Net SEARCH

Search the Internet for articles on *math anxiety*. Define math anxiety and list ways to overcome it.

Chapter

18

Reading in Business and Vocational Technology

18a   What Are the Goals of Business Courses?

What are your career goals? Do you want to be your own boss and open a small business? Would you like to own a video production company, a Domino's Pizza franchise, or an industrial cleaning service? Or would you prefer to work for a large corporation such as Microsoft or Coca-Cola, perhaps as a manager for computer services, an international marketing expert, or a strategic planner for future expansion? For all of these jobs you will need the skills necessary to handle predictable and unpredictable business career situations. Business courses will teach you these skills.

Differentiate Among the Business Disciplines

Most business majors are required to take one or more introductory courses in management, marketing, economics, finance, and accounting, which can be differentiated as follows:

Management.   You *plan, organize, lead,* and *control* activities to accomplish company objectives. For example, if you owned a Smoothie King store, you would work with others to set sales goals, hire, train, and motivate workers, order materials, attract customers, and strive for a profit.

Marketing.   You *price* and *promote products.* Sometimes you plan the creation of a new product to fit company and consumer needs. If you worked for Clinique, for example, you might be in charge of launching a new lipstick product line by pricing the products, naming the colors, and supervising the advertising campaign.

Accounting.   You *record, classify, summarize,* and *report financial data* to measure business performance. You may work for a large or small accounting firm and be in charge of tax preparations for wealthy clients, small companies, or large corporations.

Economics.   You *use formulas to predict supply and demand, plot trends,* and *monitor inflation.* If you were an economic forecaster, you might analyze job growth to predict apartment occupancy in a city for the upcoming year.

Finance.   You *plan to control the inflow and outflow of an organization's monetary resources.* As a financial officer of a large corporation, you might plan how the company would borrow $50 million to open 12 new warehouses for the faster and more profitable distribution of goods.

Recognize the Organization in Business Textbooks

The patterns of paragraph organization most prevalent in business textbooks are definition and example, as well as a simple listing pattern. Business concepts are introduced, often in a list, and then defined and expanded with real-world examples that show how those concepts relate to modern organizations. Solutions, actions, and reasons may be listed in no particular order of importance in other paragraphs.

18b What Are the Features of Business Textbooks?

Although every textbook has a somewhat different approach, certain learning features are fairly typical of business books. In addition to chapter opening scenarios, listed learning objectives, and related Web sites, certain common features are intended to heighten your interest.

Boxed Presentations.   Boxed material explores subjects or issues that call for expanding applications into new areas, such as the natural environment, new technologies, the global economy, and ethics. For

18
Bus.
Tech.

example, within a discussion of managing costs, the following boxed material reveals some problems with new technologies.

EXAMPLE

Technology Jail

Today's demanding business environment continually forces companies to find ways not only to cut costs but to improve customer service at the same time. An increasingly popular means of achieving both goals is voice mail—a computer system capable of answering the telephone, directing calls to various destinations, and storing messages in individual "voice mailboxes."

By replacing receptionists, voice-mail systems can help a company reduce payroll expenses. Perhaps more importantly, they can also answer incoming calls promptly.

Despite all of its advantages, however, voice mail seems to be capable of creating as many problems as it solves. "The phone," admits technology consultant Judith Cole, "is the lifeline of most businesses these days." But, she warns, "if you implement voice processing badly, you can find yourself losing business and losing customers." Sometimes, for instance, customers become frustrated when they get trapped in so-called "voice-mail jail"—a technology limbo where electronic systems refer them to other electronic systems and no other human voice.

—Ronald Ebert and Ricky Griffin, *Business*

Practice 1

1. What positive and negative experiences have you had with voice-mail systems?

_____

2. When do you think the benefits of voice mail outweigh the potential backlash from customers who react negatively?

_____

18
Bus.
Tech.

Summary of Learning Objectives.   The learning objectives stated at the beginning of a chapter are frequently repeated and answered at the end of the chapter. Use them to review the material.

EXAMPLE

Discuss the importance of job satisfaction and employee morale in the workplace. Good *human relations*—the interactions between employers and employees and their attitudes toward one another—are important to business because they lead to high levels of *job satisfaction* (the degree of enjoyment that workers derive from their jobs) and *morale* (workers' overall attitude toward their workplace). Satisfied employees generally exhibit lower levels of absenteeism and turnover. They also have fewer grievances and engage in fewer negative behaviors.

—Ronald Ebert and Ricky Griffin, *Business Essentials*

Practice 2

1. If you are the boss, why should you be concerned about employee morale?

2. How do companies boost the morale of low-paid employees?

Teamwork Exercises and Case Studies. These features help you collaborate with classmates to solve real problems faced by real companies and to apply the concepts taught in the chapter to everyday management concerns. Some textbooks have companion videos that further explain the corporate situation. Read the following example and collaborate with another student to respond to the answers.

> EXAMPLE
>
> Like Chick-fil-A, Dallas-based Southwest Airlines has an annual employee turnover rate that is the envy of the industry. At only 7.5 percent, Southwest's turnover rate is considered "amazingly low." Not surprisingly, Southwest can point to many of the same motivating factors as Chick-fil-A:
>
> *Job security and opportunities for growth.* Southwest's strategy of slow growth has allowed it to be the best—though not necessarily the biggest—airline in its markets. According to Sherry Phelps, Director of Corporate Employment, "We won't staff up for peak and then furlough people once the peak season is over." Many employees pass up higher-paying jobs with other airlines because they want the security and growth opportunities that Southwest offers.
>
> *Compensation.* Like Chick-fil-A, Southwest has devised a unique compensation package that enables employees to earn more than they are likely to earn at comparable firms. The difference in earning power derives from employee involvement in Southwest's profit sharing plan. Employees are vested in the plan after only five years, and because Southwest has shown a profit for 24 straight years, many employees have become wealthy.
>
> *Perks.* Another incentive is free or discounted travel. Employees with perfect attendance and on-time records for just three months receive two free airline tickets to any city the airline serves (as long as there's an empty seat).

18
Bus.
Tech.

A strong corporate culture. Southwest's strong corporate culture deemphasizes hierarchy while encouraging employees to take the initiative in improving quality and performance. "If people in the field have a great idea for something," says Phelps, "they can go directly to that department head and say, 'Have you ever thought about this?'"

—Ebert and Griffin, *Business Essentials*

Practice 3

1. How does Southwest Airlines illustrate that money is only one factor in motivating workers?

_____

_____

2. Why do some companies give employees stock in the company? How does that practice affect employee motivation?

_____

_____

18c Why Choose a Vocational or Technical School?

Vocational and technical schools offer certificate and diploma programs that can usually be completed in two years or less. These programs train students for specific jobs in a variety of fields: horticulture, electronics (including computer information systems), automotive technology, allied health, criminal justice, travel agency operation, aviation, and restaurant management. In the health care field you can train to be a radiologic technologist, a diagnostic medical sonographer, a respiratory therapist, or an emergency medical technician. Rather than begin with a general college curriculum that includes English, history, sociology, and psychology courses, a student at a vocational or technical school would focus primarily on courses within the chosen major.

Because of the nature of their disciplines, technical schools must rapidly adapt to advances in technology and the changing demands of the workplace. Classrooms are often set up to simulate the actual work environment. Some schools, in fact, work directly with corporations to train employees for specific jobs within those companies. Such arrangements have flourished in South Carolina, for example, where companies such as Mercedes-Benz work in partnership with schools and offer jobs to

18
Bus.
Tech.

their graduates. If you have chosen a vocational or technical school, you have probably made a definite career choice.

Vocational and technical courses can be complicated. They require attention to details and an ability to remember processes and procedures. Much of the hands-on work in the courses is designed to reinforce these details. To get the most out of your textbook, become familiar with its index and table of contents; it may continue to prove to be a useful resource once you are in the workplace. Blend your experiences with your textbook study to visualize and connect as you learn.

18d   What Are Electricity, Electronics, and Computer Technology?

Electronics is the branch of science that applies the principles of **electricity** to the behavior of electrons, especially in electronic devices. Therefore, a knowledge of electricity is a prerequisite to learning electronics. Electronics technology programs train technicians to install, maintain, and repair various electronic systems, including those found in computers. Employment can be found in the fields of telecommunications, utilities, broadcasting, robotics, and aviation and space manufacturing.

Computer technology, or information systems technology, is among the most rapidly growing areas in the electronics field. You can study programming to learn to write application programs for mainframes or microcomputers. You may be interested in installing and maintaining computer systems—or in entering the fields of desktop publishing, graphic design, creating Web pages, or computer security. Opportunities in these areas will continue to grow.

Recognize the Organization of Electricity and Electronics Texts

In addition to patterns for listing definitions and characteristics, electronics textbooks use many diagrams to help you visualize complex circuits, directional flow, and procedures that must be performed in a definite order. Use these diagrams to cross-reference your reading. If the information is extremely complex, you may need to read the material more slowly, at a sentence-to-sentence pace, to understand it. The following passage from an electricity textbook explains a graphic on the *service entrance*.

18
Bus.
Tech.

The Service

The connection between the incoming utility supply conductors and the building electrical equipment is called the *service entrance*. The exact equipment used for the service entrance varies with the type of supply—underground or overhead—and the total electrical demand.

FIGURE 18-1	Typical overhead service

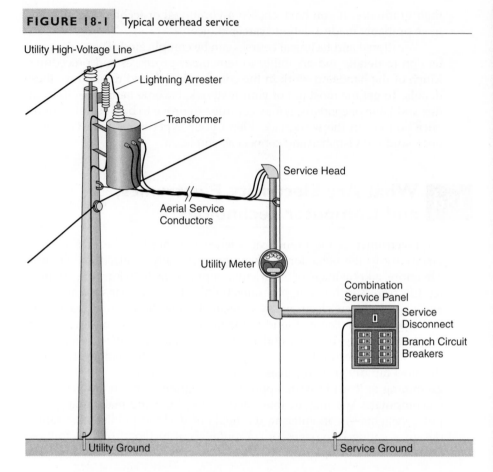

Regardless of size of the service, the incoming energy must be measured by the *utility metering* equipment. The service conductors must pass through the metering equipment before they connect to the electrical system inside the building. On smaller buildings this may be an external meter socket mounted in the service conduit or cable run. The service conductors connect to jaws inside the meter socket. The upper set of jaws are the line side, meaning they connect to the utility supply, and the lower set are the load side, meaning they connect to the building load. When the meter is installed—it plugs into the jaws of the socket—it completes the circuit from the utility supply into the building. On services supplied from aerial conductors, the service cable or conduit must be cut so the meter can be installed. A typical overhead service is shown in Figure 18-1. On underground services, the meter socket serves as the junction point between the underground supply conductors and the conductors that carry power through the wall of the building to the service equipment inside.

—Timothy Alton, *Electricity for Heating, Ventilation, Air Conditioning, and Related Areas*

Practice 4

Mark the following statements *T* (true) or *F* (false).

_____ **1.** The service head is located on the utility pole.

_____ **2.** One function of the utility measuring equipment is measurement.

_____ **3.** According to the diagram of service, the transformer contains the circuit breakers.

_____ **4.** Transformers on a utility pole reduce voltage.

_____ **5.** The service cable must be cut to install the meter.

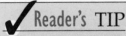 Reader's TIP

Reading Electricity and Electronics Textbooks

■ Carefully examine the diagrams. Diagrams condense and clarify written details, showing how devices work and how current flows. Ask the following questions as you study the diagrams:

What is the diagram illustrating?

What does the prose say about the diagram?

What are all the labeled parts?

Can I visualize the drawing three-dimensionally?

Can I trace the flow of electrical current through the diagram?

What possible exam question could be asked about this diagram?

■ Duplicate the simpler diagrams from memory to reinforce learning.

■ Read slowly and reread sections until they become clear. The complicated details of electronics cannot usually be grasped on only one reading.

18
Bus.
Tech.

18e What Is Automotive Technology?

Automotive technology programs train technicians for entry-level positions in modern automotive electronics and mechanics industries. Technicians are knowledgeable in areas of engines, brakes, suspension and steering, transmissions, electrical systems, fuel and exhaust systems, and heating and air conditioning. Trained technicians may take the National Automotive Service Excellence (NASE) certification exam to enhance their training and employability. Some programs have a working relationship with a manufacturer such as Ford or General Motors to train and certify technicians for specific positions.

Recognize the Organization of Automotive Texts

Automotive texts are very specialized, relying heavily on definitions and sequence to explain technical procedures. Cause-and-effect paragraphs or tables are used for explaining diagnostics. Graphics usually accompany the prose to help you visualize and translate. In the following example from an automotive textbook, the accompanying diagram (see Figure 18-2) aids comprehension of the material.

An internal combustion gasoline engine works because of the strokes of the pistons within the cylinders of the engine. The basic four-stroke engine cycle works repeatedly as described here:

FIGURE 18-2 | The four-stroke cycle

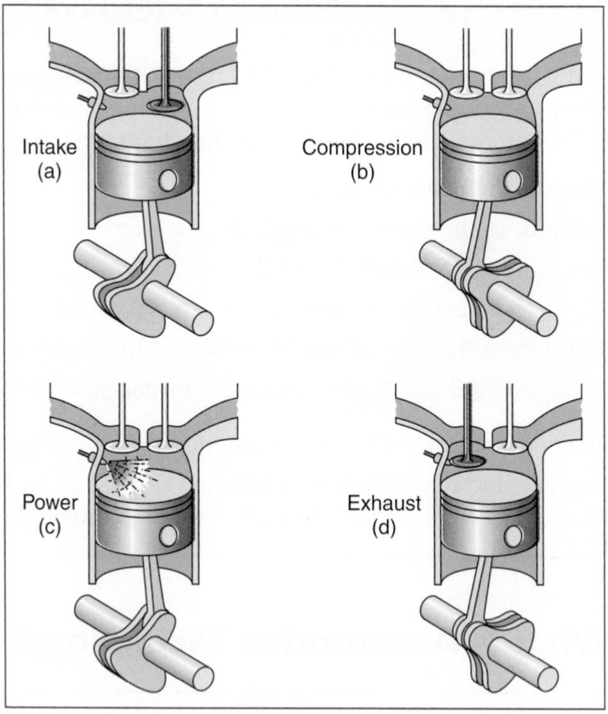

Intake
(a)

Compression
(b)

Power
(c)

Exhaust
(d)

The Four-Stroke Cycle

Automotive engines, with few exceptions, operate on a four-stroke cycle. An air-fuel mixture is drawn into a cylinder, compressed, and ignited. Upon ignition, gases expand and force the piston downward in the cylinder. Force and motion are transmitted from the piston through the connecting rod to the crankshaft. In this manner, reciprocating, or up-and-down, motion at the piston

18
Bus.
Tech.

is changed to rotary motion at the crankshaft. The relationship of valves, piston, and crankshaft is as follows:

1. On the intake stroke, the intake valve is open and the piston travels downward. The air-fuel mixture is forced into the cylinder because of low pressure in the cylinder and higher atmospheric pressure outside the engine (see Figure 18-2a).

2. On the compression stroke, both intake and exhaust valves are closed and the piston travels upward in the cylinder. The piston travel compresses the air–fuel mixture and then ignition occurs (see Figure 18-2b).

3. On the power stroke, both intake and exhaust valves remain closed. Upon ignition of the air-fuel mixture, the expansion of burning gases forces the piston to travel downward in the cylinder (see Figure 18-2c).

4. On the exhaust stroke, the exhaust valve is open and the piston travels upward in the cylinder. Burned gases are forced through the exhaust valve by the piston (see Figure 18-2d).

Keep in mind that one stroke requires one-half turn or 180 degrees of crankshaft rotation. Four strokes require two full turns, or 720 degrees of crankshaft rotation. All cylinders, regardless of the number of cylinders in the engine, complete the four-stroke cycle in two crankshaft revolutions.

—Gary Lewis, *Engine Service*

Practice 5

Based on the workings of the four-stroke gasoline engine, place the following descriptions in proper sequential order from 1 to 4.

_____   1. Matter explodes.

_____   2. Matter moves to fill a void.

_____   3. Matter is expelled.

_____   4. Matter becomes compact and flammable.

✓ Reader's TIP

Reading an Automotive Textbook

Understanding the *diagrams* is essential to understanding automative technology. Each individual automotive system's complicated details are clearly illustrated. Ask the following questions as you read and study the provided diagrams:

1. What is the diagram illustrating?
2. What are all the labeled parts?

(continued)

3. Can I explain the workings of the system? *Example:* Power steering operates under hydraulic pressure pumped into a cylinder where a piston does the steering work.

4. Where in the vehicle can the illustrated system be found? *Example:* A steering system is found beneath the steering column and under the front of the vehicle.

5. How does this system interrelate with other systems in the vehicle? *Example:* The steering system is connected to the wheels through the steering linkage. Improper wheel alignment can negatively affect steering control.

18f   For Further Practice: Extended Reading Selection in Business

Bankruptcy Law

At one time, individuals who could not pay their debts were jailed. Today, however, both organizations and individuals can seek relief by filing for **bankruptcy**—the court-granted permission not to pay some or all of their debts.

5   Hundreds of thousands of individuals and tens of thousands of businesses file for bankruptcy each year and their numbers continue to increase annually. Filings have doubled since 1985. Why do individuals and businesses file for bankruptcy? Cash-flow problems and drops in farm prices caused many farmers, banks, and small businesses to go bankrupt. In recent years, large enter-
10   prises like Continental Airlines and R. H. Macy have sought the protection of bankruptcy laws as part of strategies to streamline operations, cut costs, and regain profitability.

Generally speaking, there are perhaps three main reasons for the increase in bankruptcy filings:

15   1. The increased availability of credit;

2. The "fresh-start" provisions in current bankruptcy laws; and

3. The growing acceptance of bankruptcy as a financial tactic.

In some cases, creditors force an individual or firm to **involuntary bankruptcy** and press the courts to award them payment of at least part of what is
20   owed them. Far more often, however, a person or business chooses to file for court protection against creditors. In general, individuals and firms whose debts exceed total assets by at least $1,000 may file for **voluntary bankruptcy.**

The first step in filing for voluntary bankruptcy is filing a petition in bankruptcy court. By law, businesses filing for bankruptcy must file in federal court;
25   individuals can use state courts. The petition must provide a thorough and honest picture of the filer's assets, income, and liabilities. It must also include a plan

for dealing with creditors. Business and personal bankruptcy cases are generally similar, but there are a few important differences.

Business Bankruptcy

A business bankruptcy may be resolved by one of three plans:

30 1. Under a *liquidation plan,* the business ceases to exist. Its assets are sold and the proceeds used to pay creditors.

2. Under a *repayment plan,* the bankruptcy company simply works out a new payment schedule to meet its obligations. The time frame is usually extended, and payments are collected and distributed by a court-appointed trustee.

35 3. *Reorganization* is the most complex form of business bankruptcy. The company must explain the sources of its financial difficulties and propose a new plan for remaining in business. Reorganization may include a new slate of managers and a new financial strategy. A judge may also reduce the firm's debts to ensure its survival. Although creditors naturally dislike debt reduc-
40 tion, they may nevertheless agree to the proposal; after all, 50 percent of one's due is better than nothing at all.

Personal Bankruptcy

When an individual files for bankruptcy, reorganization is not an option. Instead, a repayment plan is worked out and a budget is imposed by the court. Almost all the filer's assets are sold for repayment of debt. Some assets, how-
45 ever, are considered "exempt." The definition of exempt assets varies from state to state, but people are usually allowed to keep equity in homes and cars. Frequently, they can also keep furniture, clothes, and other personal property, as well as professional tools and prescribed health-related items. Finally, the court often allows them to keep other assets if they are not excessive and if debts
50 can still be repaid on a regular basis.

—Ebert and Griffin, *Business*

Comprehension Questions. Answer the following statements and questions with true (*T*), false (*F*), or a written response.

_____ 1. The main purpose of this passage is to explain the advantages and disadvantages of declaring bankruptcy.

_____ 2. Bankruptcy is a court-granted permission to avoid 100 percent debt repayment.

_____ 3. Voluntary bankruptcy is forced by creditors.

_____ 4. According to the passage, a company with assets of $10,000 and debts of $9,000 can legally declare bankruptcy.

_____ 5. In a liquidation plan, the bankruptcy creditors receive a payment based on the selling price of the company assets, which could be five cents on the dollar.

18
Bus.
Tech.

_____ **6.** In a successful bankruptcy repayment plan, creditors may agree to a payment that is less than the amount of the money originally owed.

_____ **7.** Creditors view bankruptcy as a very positive system for usually obtaining 100% debt repayment.

_____ **8.** In a personal bankruptcy, family savings are always protected from creditors.

9. What two patterns of organization are most prevalent in this passage?

_____

10. According to the passage, why do the rules for personal bankruptcy vary more than the rules for business bankruptcy?

_____

_____

Critical Thinking Question. Why has bankruptcy replaced jail as the court's method of dealing with debt?

Small-Group EXPLORATION

Form a five-member group and select one of the following questions. Brainstorm and then outline your major points on a transparency. Choose one group member to present the group's findings to the class. Individual assignments can also be made.

■ You receive 80 to 100 e-mail messages a day. Many are from coworkers who send you copies of messages directed to other employees. What steps would you take to reduce this information overload?

—Ebert and Griffin, *Business Essentials*

■ As an upper-level manager, you are responsible for evaluating 14 employees whom you supervise. They are also managers, and each is in charge of a branch bank in the local area. Establish and list the criteria you would use to evaluate the performance of each of these managers.

■ If you had the knowledge and the financial backing, what business would you like to start on the Internet? Make a list of six new businesses that you think would be successful.

■ In industry, why has the ability to work in groups to problem-solve and make decisions become increasingly important?

18
Bus.
Tech.

Net SEARCH

Select three career fields that require a business, vocational, or technical education. Search the Internet for salary information in each of these fields. Consider the information that you find, and explain which field you might choose, if any, and why.

Chapter
19

Reading Scholarly
Reference Works

19a | How Do You Find Relevant Research References?

19b | What Is the Format of Scholarly Articles?

19c | What Other Reference Works Are Available?

19a | How Do You Find Relevant Research References?

Are you writing a term paper or locating facts for a speech? Where do you start? As a researcher, you first decide on your topic, and then you look for leads, redefine your focus, and seek more leads. You want to find relevant and reliable data to support your final conclusions. The reference material you use for support will depend on your project, your goals, and the research tools available to you.

Consult Encyclopedias

General encyclopedias such as the *Americana*, *Colliers*, and the *Britannica* may be helpful in your preliminary efforts at defining your research topic. Other, more subject-specific encyclopedias such as the *Encyclopedia of African American Religions* and *Encyclopedia of Earth Sciences* can provide background information about your particular topic, define key words used in the field, and even identify the important researchers in that area. The following list describes several interesting encyclopedias that may surprise you.

- *Encyclopaedia Britannica* is the oldest and largest encyclopedia in English, first published in 1768–1771.

- *Encyclopedia of Popular Music* is an extensive encyclopedia covering rock, pop, and jazz articles from the 1900s to the present.

- *World Encyclopedia of Cartoons* surveys the international field of cartooning, including caricature, editorial and political, sports, syndicated, and animated cartoons. It includes historical, ideological, aesthetic, sociological, cultural, and commercial aspects of the cartoon.

- *Notable Black American Women* covers the achievements of African-American women from colonial times to the present. The subjects range from social, political, and civil rights activists to literary figures and performing artists.

- *Encyclopedia of Television* includes biographies of actors, producers, filmmakers, writers, journalists, and media executives, as well as articles on notable programs of all genres and entries on the business and social aspects of television.

Your college or university library probably subscribes to several encyclopedias on the Internet. Three popular ones are:

- *Encarta* (www.encarta.msn.com)
- *Encyclopaedia Britannica* (www.eb.com)
- *Grolier*(www.grolier.com)

Keep in mind that free online general encyclopedias are not as comprehensive as subscription-based online encyclopedias or printed encyclopedias.

✓ Reader's TIP

Defining Your Topic

To define your research topic, consider the following:

- **Geography:** Pick a specific area.
- **Time Frame:** Limit the time period under examination.
- **Interest Groups:** Narrow your research by appropriate descriptors such as age, gender, and occupation.
- **Academic Discipline:** What college or department would study this subject?

19
Ref.

Use Indexes to Scholarly Articles

After narrowing your research topic, you will next want to locate articles in the *periodical literature*. **Periodical** is a term used to describe all publications that come out on a regular schedule. They include popular sources (newspapers and magazines) and scholarly journals (scientific studies). For popular magazines, *Reader's Guide to Periodical Literature* is a well-known index. Such indexes are listings of author, title, and subjects of published articles, in alphabetical order. For most college research, however, you will reference scholarly journals.

To find appropriate articles on your topic, use periodical indexes (listings) to guide your search. Computer-based indexes are also referred to as **databases.** A single article may be listed under several topics and may appear in several different indexes.

Many academic libraries offer dozens of periodical indexes that focus on a specific academic area. For example, the *Sociological Abstracts Index* lists journal articles that were published in sociology journals, and the *ERIC* index lists articles that were published in education journals. A reference librarian can help you determine which indexes are appropriate for your topic.

Choose Articles Based on Database Entries

Each database entry will display a **citation** of the article that includes the title, author(s), name of the periodical, volume and page numbers, issue date, and descriptive notes or key search terms (see Figure 19-1). The entry may also include notes on technical information (whether the article includes references, graphics, tables), other search topics under which

FIGURE 19-1 | Examples of a citation and art abstract

TITLE: ①Peer Pressure Can Be Useful

AUTHOR: ②Graciella Russo

PUBLICATION: ③*Journal of Developmental Psychology* | v. 48(3) | June 99 | pp. 35—41

NOTES: ④article | ⑤feature article | ⑥English | ⑦table | ⑧ISSN: 0020-4852

SUBJECTS: ⑨Drug abuse, Prevention. | Peer influence. | Peer teaching.

⑩ ABSTRACT: Peer pressure is usually viewed as an undesirable dynamic leading to drinking, smoking, early sexual activity, and undesirable social behaviors. A number of schools and civic/social organizations, however, are offering programs in which peers demonstrate how positive behaviors offer desirable outcomes. Individuals who receive this peer input develop a more positive self-image and are likely to improve their academic/social skills and behaviors and, in turn, offer the same kind of assistance to other at-risk students.

19
Ref.

the article has been categorized, and, often, an abstract.

If the article title and the date look appropriate to your search, read the abstract. The **abstract** is a short paragraph that summarizes the article, stating the premise the authors set out to prove, the subjects or location of the project, and the conclusions (see Figure 19-1). If the abstract sounds relevant to your research, print the entry page or record the information so that you can locate a copy of the article. In some cases, the database will provide a link to the complete text of the article. Remember, however, that the best articles for your topic may not be available electronically, but they may be easily accessible in the library collection.

In the abstract in Figure 19-1, the circled numbers represent the following:

1. Title of the article.

2. Author of the article.

3. It is a journal article, rather than a book.

4–6. It is a feature article rather than a paragraph or two; it is written in English.

7. A table is included in the article.

8. The ISSN (International Standard Serial Number) is the counterpart to a book's ISBN. This unique number enables you to identify the correct journal when looking for a cited article.

9. The key terms or subjects under which this article is abstracted.

10. The abstract.

✓ Reader's TIP

Searching Indexes

- Select appropriate descriptive search terms. Most online indexes allow you to enter more than one term.

- When you find an appropriate article, look at the subject terms listed to see if those terms would aid your search.

- Try several databases; the quality of the indexing systems varies, and various databases index different periodicals.

- Don't waste time, If the title doesn't fit, move to the next entry.

- Seek articles with current publication dates.

- Read the abstract and decide whether the article fits your topic.

- Print or write down the complete citation for each article you choose.

19
Ref.

Practice 1

1. Would the article abstracted in Figure 19-1 be relevant if you were developing a teen peer group for your church as part of an effort to promote healthy social behaviors?

_____

2. For this field, would this article still be considered current enough to be useful?

_____

3. What key words could you use to find articles on teenage alcohol abuse?

_____

_____

4. Where are the programs described offered?

_____

_____

Search the Internet

There are both advantages and limitations to using the Internet for research. The advantages are up-to-date coverage and easy access. You can use a **search engine,** an index of World Wide Web locations, to find a list of current Web sites that include your search term(s). The Web sites listed will vary depending on which search engine you use. (See Chapter 20 for Internet search directions.)

Because the Internet is open to everyone, you should always question the accuracy, reliability, and bias of online information. With the Internet, there are no gatekeepers. In contrast, scholarly journals have editors, usually a group of experts in the field, who decide what deserves to be published.

19 Ref.

19b What Is the Format of Scholarly Articles?

Once you have decided which articles are most appropriate to your research, use the organization of the article to guide your reading. Scholarly articles follow a different—but standard—format that is both predictable and helpful. This format organizes material into sections: *abstract, review of the literature, method, results, discussion, conclusion,* and *references.*

Abstract. A paragraph that gives a concise overview of the content of the article. Even though you may have already read the abstract during your search, you may want to reread it to refresh your memory.

Review of the Literature. An introductory section that explains why the research was done and gives historical background on other studies and books that relate to the topic. For a researcher on a similar topic, this section can be particularly valuable; the summaries of previous studies provide a wealth of leads for your own investigation.

Method. The method section explains exactly how the authors set up the study, how many people participated, who they were, where they lived, what they did, how their actions or responses were measured, and how those measurements were analyzed. If you are conducting a similar experiment, you will benefit from knowing the exact procedures used in this study.

Results. The results section gives the raw measurements and numbers obtained from the procedures explained in the method section. Charts and graphs are typically used in this section to organize the responses.

Discussion. In this analysis of the results, the author attempts to explain why different groups of people in the study responded as they did. An analysis may categorize the results of participants by gender, age, ethnicity, or economic level and then examine the differences.

Conclusion. The conclusion section summarizes the significance of the study, suggests practical applications for the findings, and points to related areas that need further research. In the peer pressure abstract example, the conclusion of the article might discuss the emotional and economic benefits of setting up peer counseling programs in middle schools by engaging students before their negative behaviors cause trouble with police and the court system.

References. A references section provides a bibliography or complete list of all resource materials used to prepare the article. It contains precise documentation so that you can seek further information from those books, articles, periodicals, and Web sites. A typical reference entry is shown in Figure 19-2.

19
Ref.

FIGURE 19-2   A typical reference entry

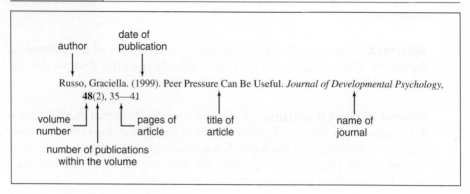

Practice 2

Indicate which of the following sections of a journal article would contain the listed information:

review of the literature	method	results
discussion	conclusion	references

1. The sample consisted of 200 freshmen who were taking both Psychology 101 and Biology 101.

2. X, M. (1992). *The Autobiography of Malcolm X.* New York: Ballantine Books.

3. Keimig (1983) developed a hierarchy of learning programs that includes four levels.

4. An item analysis shows that 99 percent of the freshmen tested answered the first two items correctly, but only 22 percent of the males and 24 percent of the females answered the third item correctly.

5. The researchers recommend that writing be incorporated into the teaching of mathematics because the findings indicate that the ability to explain the concepts correlates with the ability to solve an equation.

19c   What Other Reference Works Are Available?

Reference works are incredible works of scholarship. They include specialized dictionaries, books of lists, books of household tips, consumer buying guides, and many more informative and entertaining creations.

Annual Record Books

An **almanac** contains millions of current facts about countries, cities, census data, astronomy tables, foreign exchange rates, election and sports results of the previous year, and much more. If you are writing a paper on El Salvador, for example, you could look in an almanac to find the names of the current leaders, population statistics, exports estimated in dollars, the embassy address, and details as small as the number of televisions and telephones per person in the country. Popular almanacs include *The World Almanac, The New York Times Almanac, The Wall Street Journal Almanac,* and *The Time Almanac.*

The Guinness Book of World Records, which is also published annually, contains current record-breaking facts presented in an entertaining style. For pinpointing specific facts, use the index. Did you know that the golfer Tiger Woods holds the record for the highest single season's earnings on the U.S. PGA tour ($9,188,321) or that Jerry Seinfeld has the highest-ever annual earnings for a TV actor ($267 million)? What was the most expensive dress ever purchased?

> A flesh-colored beaded gown worn by Marilyn Monroe when she sang "Happy Birthday" to President Kennedy on May 19, 1962, is the world's most valuable dress. It was auctioned on October 27, 1999, for $1,267,000 at Christie's in New York City to dealers Robert Schagrin and Peter Siegel. It originally cost $12,000.
>
> —*The Guinness Book of World Records 2002*

Books of Quotations

Do you need a quote for a paper or a speech? Depending on your topic, look into *Power Quotes,* by Daniel Baker; *Outstanding Women of the Twentieth Century,* edited by Tracey Quinn; or *The Guinness Book of Poisonous Quotes.* The following examples are from several quotation books:

From *Bartlett's Familiar Quotations:*

Anna Eleanor Roosevelt
"No one can make you feel inferior without your consent." (p. 654)

> —*This Is My Story,* 1937

19
Ref.

From *The Great Thoughts*, compiled by George Seldes:

Alex Haley, 1921–1992, American writer
"History is written by the winners." (p. 190)

—Television interview, 1972

From *Famous Last Words*, compiled by Jonathon Green:

Adam Smith, Scottish political economist, author of *The Wealth of Nations*, died 1790
"I believe we must adjourn this meeting to some other place." (p. 95)

From *The Speaker's Sourcebook II*, by Glenn Van Ekeren:

On Personality: "He has the personality of a dial tone."

—Phyllis Diller, p. 283.

Practice 3

Answer the following questions about the preceding examples.

1. Why does Alex Haley's quote on history make sense?

_____

2. What is the most expensive dress sold at auction?

_____

3. What is the meaning of Anna Eleanor Roosevelt's quotation?

_____

Small-Group EXPLORATION

Form a five-member group and select one of the following activities. Brainstorm and then outline your major points on a transparency. Choose one group member to present the group's findings to the class. Individual assignments can also be made.

19
Ref.

- List the top ten questions you would like to ask a librarian about the use of the library.
- List the reasons why you think a college library intimidates some students.
- List the differences between a college library and a public library.
- Outline how you would research the classic Broadway musical, *Man of La Mancha*.

Net SEARCH

Search the Internet to locate three online encyclopedias. Choose a topic such as fencing, hawks, or diamonds, and then search each source. Print the information that you find. Compare and contrast the quality, type, and level of information that each site provides. Begin your own search, or start with the following sites:

Encyclopedia.com
www.encyclopedia.com

Encyclopaedia Britannica Online
www.eb.com

World Book Encyclopedia
www.worldbook.com

Encarta
www.encarta.msn.com

Part 4

Reading in Everyday Life

Chapter

20

Reading Print and Electronic Media

20a How Are Newspapers Organized and What Are Their Elements?

Newspapers are divided into predictable sections: national and international news; local or regional news; business; sports; entertainment and the arts (including movies and television); classified ads; and editorials. The front page will have the most important stories from all categories. What do you usually read first in your daily newspaper?

Understand the Evolution of Newspaper Style

To appreciate the organization of a newspaper, you must first understand the evolution of newspaper writing, or **journalism.** Journalistic style developed as a response to technology. Words and sentences are short, and a paragraph may be only one sentence long. The most important

327

information is included in the first paragraph or two. In news stories the typical order of storytelling—with the punch line at the end—is reversed.

The first newspapers were published in the 1700s. They were small—only four letter-size pages—and they were published just once or twice a week. Colonial readers, thirsty for information, generally read every word. By 1833, new technology allowed newspapers to expand into a larger, tabloid format. By the 1840s, the new telegraph system offered reporters the capacity for instant communication from distant locations. Unfortunately, telegraph service was expensive (it charged for each word) and the system could be interrupted or break down at any time.

To make communication more complicated, in a small town with a breaking news story, all reporters had to use the same telegraph operator. For the sake of order and equity, a system developed by which reporters took turns by sending one paragraph at a time in rotation. After each had sent the first paragraph of a story, each then sent a second paragraph, and so on. This continued until the story was completed, the telegraph service was interrupted, or a publication deadline elapsed.

As protection against a communication breakdown or a deadline cut-off, and to ensure that readers received the most important parts of the news story, reporters got into the habit of including only the most important points in the first paragraphs. The major and minor details of the story were then placed in the following paragraphs in descending order of importance. The result was the **inverted pyramid** format of newswriting. Although technology has improved dramatically, this format persists. Today, if space is a last-minute problem, editors can cut a news story from the bottom with minimal loss of content.

Recognize the Variety of Newspaper Articles

Modern newspapers expand far beyond headline news and include all of the following elements:

News Stories. News stories are the general articles that report the facts in descending order of importance. The **lead** is the first paragraph, which catches the reader's attention, summarizes the essential points of the story and establishes a focus. The lead answers the five *W*'s and one *H*: *who, what, when, where, why,* and *how.* Think of the first paragraph as a condensed version of the event; if you don't have the interest or the time, you won't read beyond the first paragraph of a news story.

Subsequent paragraphs present details in descending order of importance. A news story has no ending; rather, it tapers from major details to minor ones in that inverted pyramid style. Your level of interest will determine how far you read. Figure 20-1 is an example of a news story in the inverted pyramid format.

✓ Reader's TIP

Reading a News Story

- Get an overview from the headline and photographs.
- Expect to find answers to the five *W*'s and the *H*.

  Who is the story about?
  What happened?
  When did it happen?
  Where did the event or events take place?
  Why did this event occur?
  How did this happen?

- Continue to read according to the amount of detail desired.

FIGURE 20-1 | A news story in the inverted pyramid format

THE **DAILY REPORTER**

95¢   Friday, May 26, 2005

FBI Cracks Down on Movie Downloads
The Associated Press

Most important points

Washington — Federal raiders. Internet pirates. Intergalactic screen adventures. The government announced a crackdown Wednesday on the theft of movies and other copyrighted materials with elements of a movie plot. Federal agents shut down a Web site that they said allowed people to download the new "Star Wars" movie even before it was shown in theaters.

Major details

The Elite Torrents site was engaging in high-tech piracy by letting people download copies of movies and other copyrighted material for free, authorities said.
The action was the first criminal enforcement against individuals who are using cutting edge BitTorrent technology, Justice and Homeland Security Department officials said.

Minor details

Elite Torrents had more than 133,000 members and 17,800 movies and software programs in the past four months, officials said. Among those titles was "Star Wars: Episode III—Revenge of the Sith," which was downloaded more than 10,000 times in the first 24 hours.
People trying to access the elitetorrents.org Web site on Wednesday were greeted with a warning about the penalties for copyright infringement, although officials said the investigation is focusing on those who originally offered the pirated materials.
Authorities served search warrants in 10 cities against computer users accused of being the first to offer copyrighted materials to other BitTorrent users on the Web site, Homeland Security's Customs and Immigration Enforcement agency said. The cities are Austin, Texas; Erie, Pa; Philadelphia; Wise, Va; Clintonwood, Va; Germantown, Wis; Chicago; Berea, Ohio; Anthem, Ariz.; and Leavenworth, Kan.
Authorities said the warrants were still under seal.

20
Print/ Elect. Media

Practice 1

Read the news story in Figure 20-1 and answer the following questions.

1. What are the answers to the 5 *W*'s and the *H*?

   Who: _____

   What: _____

   When: _____

   Where: _____

   Why: _____

   _____

   How: _____

   _____

2. If you were a *Star Wars* fan, how would you feel about this news?

   _____

3. If you were a criminal justice major, how would you feel about this news?

   _____

All news reporting should be *objective,* meaning that only factual details are given, without opinions or judgments (Unless those opinions *are* the news being reported). Personal views of the reporter should not appear in a news article.

Feature Stories.   **Feature stories** differ from news stories in their timeliness, style, and length. News stories cover breaking news—events or activities in which time is of the essence, such as conflict in the Middle East. In contrast, the profile of an actor and an account of new decorating trends are less time-sensitive and could appear today or five days from now. Unlike the inverted pyramid style of news stories, a beginning, a middle, and an end usually characterize feature stories.

Feature writers may engage in "judgment journalism" by injecting their own opinions and evaluations into a story. Sometimes opinions or controversial ideas are included as quotes from "an unidentified authority." (See Chapter 10, Critical Thinking, for more on credibility.) Be wary of undisclosed sources.

Figure 20-2 is an example of a feature story.

20
Print/
Elect.
Media

FIGURE 20-2 | A feature story

Latex vs. Soap

Gloved hands may not be more sanitary than bare ones.

By Rosie Mestel/Los Angeles Times

There's something reassuring about watching restaurant workers handle our food with gleaming gloves, but the appearance of extra cleanliness may be no more than that—appearance. That's what a team of Oklahoma scientists suggests after studying hundreds of tortillas purchased at fast-food eateries in Oklahoma and Kansas.

The tortilla testing team, led by Robert Lynch, an occupational and environmental health professor at the University of Oklahoma, was addressing a meaty debate among food-safety scientists—whether donning gloves lowers the chance that germs end up in food and thus the chance that customers will come down with food poisoning.

The case for gloves: They keep food away from bare hands, which are constantly touching items such as money, raw food, door handles, and faucets—places illness-causing microbes can end up.

The case against gloves: They're only squeaky clean if they're new, and they won't help matters if they foster a culture of complacency and backsliding on hand washing.

In the study, published in the Journal of Food Protection, Lynch and co-workers chose tortillas as a test case and purchased 371 of them, one at a time, at 140 restaurants from four fast food chains in Wichita, Kan; Oklahoma City and Tulsa, Okla.

Roughly half the samples were collected from gloved workers, the others from ungloved.

The disconcerting news: There was no statistical difference between glove-handled tortillas and ones that were touched by human flesh. Tortillas handled with gloves gave rise to microbe growth 9.6 percent of the time; those touched with hands, 4.4 percent of the time. But the sample size was not large enough to establish that the rates were truly different.

Source: Rosie Mestel, the *Los Angeles Times*, 2/14/05.

Practice 2

Read the feature story in Figure 20-2 and answer the following questions.

1. What does the headline have to do with the content of the story?

_____

_____

2. Do you think this article is part of an organized public relations campaign to encourage people to wash their hands properly? Why or why not?

_____

Editorials. Unlike news stories, editorials are subjective—that is, they express the opinion of a person or an organization. A newspaper's editorial pages present the views of its management, editors, and guest columnists. Subjects for these pieces are usually related to particular local, national, or international news stories.

✓ Reader's TIP

Reading a Feature

- ■ How does the angle or focus of the story differ from that of a straight news story?
- ■ How credible are the sources cited?
- ■ Is the story factual or sensationalized?
- ■ Does the reporter show a bias?
- ■ Does the reporter judge, or do you decide?

✓ Reader's TIP

Reading Editorials

- ■ What event prompted the editorial?
- ■ What thesis or opinion is being promoted?
- ■ Do the details support the thesis?
- ■ Is the author liberal or conservative?
- ■ What is being left out?
- ■ Are the sources, facts, and other supporting details credible?

Although the styles of editorials vary, the basic format is usually the same. After giving some background, the writer states and supports a position. Alternative ideas and solutions may be offered, as well as the writer's prediction of what will happen if the current situation does not change. Figure 20-3 provides an example of an editorial.

Remember that editorials *always express opinions* and, regardless of how persuasive the writer's argument might be, you are free to accept or reject it. Readers are encouraged to express their own opinions—either for or against editorials—in "Letters to the Editor."

Practice 3

Read the editorial in Figure 20-3 and answer the following questions.

1. What does the writer describe to introduce the main idea?

_____

_____

20
Print/
Elect.
Media

FIGURE 20-3 | An editorial

National TV Turnoff Week:
Turn off the TV and Turn on Life

For the past decade, National TV Turnoff Week has occurred during April to encourage people to go without television for seven days. This effort, with supporters such as the American Academy of Pediatrics, recognizes the benefits of imagining, interacting, exercising, reading, conversing, playing, celebrating, meditating, entertaining, and relishing found time.

My own experience of going without television occurred 14 years ago, and the change occurred because of a haunting conversation with a student in my night class.

At the time, I had been preaching about the importance of turning off the TV and reading. "If we could get our parents to read to their preschool children 15 minutes a day, we could revolutionize the schools," I quoted Ruth Love, former superintendent of Chicago public schools. "Just think," I continued, "if you turned off the television and read 15 minutes a day, you could revolutionize your life."

Later, during the break in our evening class, one of my students shyly approached me.

"I'm 28 years old," Sebastian said, "and I have a 15-year-old son. I wish someone had talked to me about reading when I was younger. I was a football player then, and I figured I would never have to excel in academics. But I've had four back surgeries so far, and I'll be lucky if I can walk when I'm forty. What I want now is to become a good student to make something of my life."

His words stunned me. When I arrived home that night, I explained to my husband and three children that our evenings would be a little different during the school year. The children looked eager. My husband looked confused. I told them about my conversation with Sebastian, and then I explained that during the rest of the school year, no one in the house would watch TV from Monday through Thursday. The children looked confused. "Monday night football?" my husband said pitifully.

"*No one* in the house will watch TV Monday through Thursday," I repeated. We followed that regimen each school year. Instead of wasting time passively in front of the TV, we spent time around the dinner table. We talked and enjoyed our meals. Afterward I read aloud to everyone.

The experiment was a valuable one. The children's grades improved. Their conversations became more stimulating.

Why not try turning off the TV for one week? According to the National TV Turnoff Week Web site, there are several reasons to try the experiment. First, children in the United States log an average of 1,023 hours a year in front of the television but only 900 in school. In addition, 40 percent of Americans report frequently watching TV during dinner—a tradition that negatively impacts quality family communication.

Turn off the TV. Turn off the video games. Leave the computer games for one week. Challenge yourself and make connections instead.

At the same time, remember my former student Sebastian who prompted this experiment with my own family. He recently earned his master's degree. Fourteen years later, he exemplifies someone who reclaimed his time and revolutionized his life.

Source: Susan Pongratz, *Daily Press*, April 24, 2005.

2. What is the writer's main idea?

---

3. What one example does the writer give that would help readers understand the main idea?

---

4. What is the author's job?

---

5. Is the author's advice that your life will be better if you turn off the TV a fact or an opinion?

_____

6. What is your opinion about turning off the TV for a week?

_____

Service Information.   Newspapers also provide weather reports, stock market prices, sports scores, television schedules, and obituary notices. These day-to-day constants provide a service for readers.

20b   How Do You Choose a Newspaper?

Different types of newspapers target different audiences. Your own areas of interest may determine which of the following newspapers you read.

The _New York Times_ and the _Washington Post_ are large, powerful publications with international staff. Both are known for their detailed reporting and analysis of international and national events. The _New York Times_ in particular sees itself as the "paper of record" for nearly every subject it covers, and it is generally regarded as an authoritative source of information. The _Wall Street Journal_ specializes in business and financial news

Big-city newspapers focus on local, state, and regional events and on how national and international developments affect their local areas. Community newspapers cover issues of interest to residents of particular neighborhoods.

Weekly **tabloids,** the type of newspaper you see at the checkout counter in the supermarket, sensationalize the news. They prey on celebrities, report questionable gossip, and print photographs taken by stalking paparazzi. Be very cautious in believing what is printed in these papers; they are frequently sued for libel. Figure 20-4 is an example of a tabloid article.

Practice 4

Read the tabloid article in Figure 20-4 and answer the following questions.

1. Why would you question the validity of this story?

_____

2. Why would you question the sources on the healing power of the water?

_____

FIGURE 20-4 | A tabloid article

Miracle in Minnesota

"I've never seen anything like this before. I have absolutely no explanation for it at all."
Dr. Jaime Suarez, Oncologist

A medical miracle—a real-life fountain of youth—may have been found in Algonquin, Minnesota, 45 minutes outside St. Paul.

William and Patricia Elliot and their three children, ages 7, 11, and 14 live just outside of Algonquin in Chaddup County. As a result, they rely on their own well rather than the city system for their water supply. The family didn't make much of a connection between that seemingly insignificant fact and their own excellent health until Patricia's mother, Eileen, came to live with them after doctors discovered a cancerous tumor in her right lung.

Despite doctors' gloomy prognoses for her condition, during the 18 months since Eileen came to live with her daughter and son-in-law, her tumor inexplicably shrank and eventually disappeared. Eileen's oncologist, Dr. Jaime Suarez, said simply, "I've never seen anything like this before. I have absolutely no explanation for it at all."

Unnamed sources believe the Elliots' well is tapped into an underground spring that also feeds nearby Fulton Creek. The creek water has historically been found to have higher than average levels of certain minerals like magnesium and zinc. They also have surmised that residue from certain healthful herbs that grow wild in the area may have leached through the soil and into the underground spring, making it a kind of disease prevention and treatment cocktail.

Patricia's mom, Eileen, says, "I came here expecting to live out the last of my days on earth. Instead, I'm looking forward to the whole rest of my life!"

3. What scientific facts are given to support these assumptions?

_____

4. Why are people attracted to reading such accounts?

_____

Practice 5

Examine a copy of *USA Today*. How does it differ from your local big-city newspaper? Why do you think this paper is particularly popular in airports? What do you like and dislike about *USA Today*?

20c How Do You Use Online Newspapers?

Most major national and city newspapers offer free online services. You can check out the latest news in the *New York Times* (www.nytimes.com), *USA Today* (www.usatoday.com), and the *Atlanta Journal Constitution* (www.ajc.com). When you log onto the site, you are presented with the major headlines of the day and maybe a one-sentence summary. Clicking on a headline will take you to the complete article, but before doing this you will probably need to register at the site.

Although the online news services are presently free, most newspapers want some background information on the users. Thus, on your first Web site visit you will probably need to enter your age and other information in order to create a screen name and get a password. On later visits you will just enter your screen name and password.

To pull up articles from other sections of the paper, use the index, which is usually on the left side of the web page. For example, click on *business* if you want to see the business headlines or *sports* for game scores. These newspaper Web sites tend to be amazingly engaging, with lots of interesting information that you never would have imagined and pictures to attract your attention. You can get weather, stock quotes, or movie reviews instantly.

If you want to search for articles for that day or for months past, you can enter keywords in the *Search* window and the relevant headlines will appear for you to reclick for the complete article. Most of these services are free, but some papers may charge a small fee for printing articles from past years.

Practice 6

Compare the Web sites and services of two popular online newspapers. Go to the *New York Times* (www.nytimes.com) and to *USA Today* (www.usatoday.com). Explore the links for each and compare the quality and the services. Which do you like better, and why?

20d How Do You Differentiate Magazines?

Browse through the magazine section of a local store, and enjoy the variety of specialty magazines ranging from computer programming to scuba diving. Covers sell magazines, so check out the contents before purchasing.

News Magazines

There are three main news magazines in the United States: *Time, Newsweek,* and *U.S. News & World Report.* Although *Time* and *Newsweek* provide more coverage of popular culture than *U.S. News & World Report,* all three follow a similar format: reviews of international and national developments, coverage of noteworthy events in business, science, the arts, and lifestyle/social trends, and columnists' essays. *U.S. News & World Report* tends to be more politically conservative than the other two, but all contain news stories, feature stories, editorials, essays, and **critiques** or reviews of new movies, plays, music CDs, and books. Figure 20-5 is an example of a critique.

FIGURE 20-5 | A critique

Arts & Leisure

Movie Review

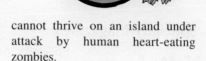

Deadly Depths

A budding romance takes a second seat as suspicion turns to fear when an island paradise is threatened by restless zombies. Simon Lane (Paul Mills) and Regina Wood (Jessica Johnson) fear for innocent islanders as evidence of the supernatural emerges from the dead victims of nightly raids.

While scuba diving on offshore reefs, Simon and Regina find unsettling clues in the disappearance of three island fishermen. Seeking an open police investigation proves fruitless. Greedy executives with business goals first try to dissuade and then to silence the inquisitive two who have come to know too much. Needless to say, tourism, gambling, and increased profits cannot thrive on an island under attack by human heart-eating zombies.

Simon and Regina dodge sharks on land and demons at sea to save the island and themselves from evil. Simon, who is a hunk at sea, proves less crafty with his above-water dialogue. Equally, the beautiful Regina gives an unconvincing performance as a stockbroker who needs a break from the goons on Wall Street, only to sidestep goons at sea. Don't hold your breath for the sequel. Unless you are thirteen years old and very bored, you may want to hold your nose underwater for this summer thriller.

Practice 7

Read the critique in Figure 20-5 and answer the following questions.

1. At what point do you recognize whether this critique is a positive or a negative one?

   _____

2. What does the author of the critique think of the leading actors?

   _____

3. Why would you decide to see (or not see) this movie?

   _____

Practice 8

Review current issues of *Time, Newsweek, U.S. News & World Report,* and *People* to answer the following questions.

1. Which magazine would you prefer to subscribe to and why?
2. What is the feature story in each, and why is each noteworthy?
3. Is *People* a news magazine? How would you categorize the stories in *People?*

Specialty Magazines

FAST FACT

John Johnson started *Ebony* in 1945 to inform and build ethnic pride for returning African-American World War II veterans.

Specialty magazines cover almost every imaginable subject: fashion, business, technology, decorating, hobbies, health, and entertainment. Such publications can be very precise in their focus—not just arts and crafts, but quilting; and not any type of guitar, but acoustic guitars. Specialty magazines often use *jargon,* or specialized insider vocabulary that might be unfamiliar to a new reader. Usually there are columns and articles written expressly for beginners.

If you are unfamiliar with a particular magazine, read the Letters to the Editor section. These letters, sent in by readers, will refer to past stories and can give you an idea of the audience to which the magazine appeals. Can you identify with the ideas and issues that seem to be important to the letter writers?

Specialty magazines are often openly subjective. Support for particular products, processes, technologies, and methods may be directly expressed because readers frequently seek advice. As you read, decide whether the facts are presented correctly and the conclusions are well supported.

Magazines gain most of their revenue through selling advertising pages. The wider the circulation a publication enjoys, the more advertisers it attracts. If a major advertiser's products and services always receive overwhelmingly positive reviews within the feature stories, take extra care to decide for yourself whether the findings are warranted. With some magazines, particularly fashion magazines, ask yourself if the publication is more interested in informing its readers or in maintaining its advertising dollars.

✓ Reader's TIP

Choosing a Magazine

- Read the lead article headlines and the table of contents to find articles of interest to you.
- Flip through the magazine and read article titles and boxed article excerpts.
- Use article subheadings to preview.
- Read the captions of photos that interest you.
- Read Letters to the Editor.
- Decide, purchase, and enjoy!

Practice 9

Visit a magazine stand or your community or college library and select four magazines to which you would like to subscribe if money were not an issue. For each magazine, do the following:

1. Evaluate the quality of the feature articles.

_____

_____

_____

2. Estimate the ratio or percentage of news and feature stories to advertisements.

_____

_____

_____

3. Which regular articles are particularly appealing to you?

_____

_____

_____

20e How Do You Navigate the World Wide Web?

The **Internet** is an electronic system of more than 25,000 computer networks using a common language that connects millions of users around the world. It was initially developed by the United States Defense Department in the 1960s to protect the flow of strategic information in case a nuclear attack destroyed the usual lines of communication. Other defense-related organizations, as well as universities, gradually became part of the network. As technology advanced, the Internet became the backbone for an information network that is now commonly called the **World Wide Web (WWW)** or, more simply, "the Web." The Internet is actually the networked system that allows the Web to function, but the two terms are frequently used interchangeably.

The WWW is similar to an enormous library; Web sites are like books, and **Web pages** are like pages in books. These pages can contain written text, photographs, graphics, music, sound effects, movies, and animation. The systems for delivering this information are called _e-mail_ for electronic messages; _Web pages_ for the locations or "sites" of information provided by individual people, businesses, educational institutions, and other organizations; _listservs_ for subscription electronic mailing lists based on specific topics; and _newsgroups_ for discussions and news about particular subjects.

For finding your way on the Web, you need specific directions, just as you need an address with a zip code to mail a letter. A **Uniform Resource Locator (URL)** routes you to a source of information called a _Web page_ or _Web site_. URLs are made up of several parts, as can be seen in the address for the Web site for the Emory University Health Sciences Center Library shown in Figure 20-6.

The following is a key to the components of the URL shown in Figure 20-6.

1. **Protocol**—This is standard for Web addresses; it stands for _Hypertext Transfer Protocol_, the type of language computers use on the Internet to communicate with each other. It is not always necessary to type "http://" before "www" when navigating the Web.

20
Print/
Elect.
Media

| **FIGURE 20-6** | The URL for the Emory University Health Sciences Center Library. Numbers indicate the sections of the URL, which are named and explained in the text. |

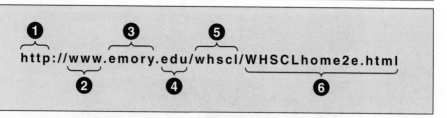

2. **Server name**—This indicates the computer network over which you will "travel" to reach the desired location. In most cases, it will be the World Wide Web.

3. **Domain name**—This is a name registered by the Web site owner.

4. **Domain type**—This indicates the category to which the site owner belongs.

5. **Directory path**—This indicates a particular location within the Web site's host computer.

6. **File name**—This indicates a specific file within the host's directory.

Addresses for Web pages sometimes go no further than the domain type. Such an address will take you to the site's **home page,** which can be thought of as the main terminal through which other areas of the site can be reached. As you move to other parts of the site, more detailed information on directory path and file names will be displayed in the *Location* line on your screen.

URLs must be typed without mistakes. Any misspelling, incorrect capitalization, or incorrect punctuation could result in an error message indicating that the address cannot be found.

Locate a Web site

After you have entered the URL and reached the desired Web site, you can get an overview of what the site offers by scanning headlines, graphics, buttons, animation, category headings, and tables of contents (see Figure 20-7). By clicking on any of them, you can usually move to another, more specific location within the Web site. **Hypertext links** appear as blue, sometimes bold, underlined text. Clicking on them will not only move you from one page to another within the site, but can also send you to other related Web sites.

FIGURE 20-7	The home page of the "Get Caught Reading" Web site illustrates the effective use of topic headings, graphics, and hypertext links.

Source: www.getcaughtreading.com/getcaughtreading/index.html.

After you have viewed several pages within a Web site or investigated several sites, you can return to any of the pages without reentering the URL. By clicking icons provided by your **browser,** the software that searches to find the URL, you can retrace your steps as shown in Figure 20-8.

FIGURE 20-8	Sample Web toolbar commands. Numbers indicate the icons representing the commands that are named and explained in the text.

1. *Back*— This command moves you to the page that precedes the one currently shown on your screen.
2. *Forward*— This command moves you to the page that follows the one currently shown on your screen. If you are already on the last page, this button will be inactive.

3. *Stop*— This command causes a Web page to stop downloading immediately. It is useful if you have accidentally clicked on a link to another location. If you have already moved from your previous location before clicking the Stop button and your screen is blank, clicking the Back button will take you to the previous page again.

4. *Reload* (or *Refresh*)— If you encounter a problem while a Web page is downloading, you will often see obvious "symptoms," such as text or graphics that are unreadable or a delay in visualization of the page. These problems can sometimes be taken care of by clicking the Reload (or Refresh) button so that the information can be sent again and received without error.

5. *Home*— Clicking this icon will automatically take you back to the home page of your Internet service provider.

Practice 10

Go to the Smithsonian Institute's Web site (http://www.SI.edu) and examine the headings. Then go to the appropriate page to find the year the museum was established.

1. _____

Next, find out what time the museum opens and the admission fee.

2. _____

Conduct a Search

Conducting a successful search can be like solving an intriguing mystery. Follow these steps to organize your search:

FAST FACT

The first computer bug was real. In 1945, according to Grace Hopper, the Mark I came to a halt and the computer personnel found a moth inside the machine. They removed the bug and the computer was fine. Henceforth, any mysterious problem or glitch was called a *bug*.

1. **Make a Plan.** Locating information on the Web requires using a **search engine,** a program that looks throughout the Internet for information. Companies that offer their own versions include Yahoo!, AltaVista, Excite, Infoseek, Google, Dogpile, and Lycos (see the following list). No matter which one you choose, it will require you to enter a key word (or words) in a search text box to describe the information you want. The search engine will search the Internet for sites that contain the word or phrase and will display a list of the first 10 to 25 sites, called *hits*. The more specific your description, the better the results. For example, entering "Michelangelo" will list a large number of sites about the artist and his work, many more than you can examine.

Popular Search Engines and Their URLs

Google: www.google.com

Dogpile: www.dogpile.com

Excite: www.excite.com

Infoseek: www.infoseek.com

Webcrawler: www.webcrawler.com

Yahoo!: www.yahoo.com

Lycos: www.lycos.com

2. **Search and Search Again.** Your initial search may be so specific that you get very few hits, or it may be so general that you get thousands of hits, many of which are not appropriate to your research. Either way, you may have to try several searches before finding what you need. Scan a few of your initial hits and make a list of related terms. For example, terms related to *Michelangelo,* such as *Sistine Chapel, statue of David, Renaissance art,* and *Medici family,* might help you get started.

3. **Read Selectively.** Read selectively to narrow the scope of your research. When you go to a particular Web site, read titles, subtitles, links, tables of contents, outlines, or introductory paragraphs to determine whether the information is appropriate to your research.

4. **Record Your Sources.** As you progress in your search, keep track of key words and phrases you have used as well as the results they produced. When you find a site to which you would like to return or one that you would like to use as a reference in your research, you have several options:

   ■ Record the URL next to the term used to find it so you can return to it later. You can cut and paste this onto a word-processing page.

   ■ *Print* the Web site material. This step will provide a hard (paper) copy to keep, usually with the URL shown at the top of the printout.

   ■ *Bookmark* or save the site. **Bookmarking** (or adding to *Favorites,* depending on your particular Web browser) lets you return quickly to the Web site with just one or two mouse clicks. If you will not have access to the same computer in the future, saving (or *exporting,* depending on your Web browser) a copy of the text of the Web page to a disk will enable you to take it with you as a reference on a different computer.

✔ Reader's TIP
Searching the Web

■ *Limit your search.* Entering **AND** between each word of your search or putting the words of a key phrase in quotation marks will narrow the search by making it more specific. For example, using the words *Apple Computer* for your search will turn up thousands of hits that include not only sites about the company, but also sites related to "apple" (the fruit) and sites about computers in general. Using *AND* in your key phrase (*Apple AND Computer*) will return only sites that contain both words in the phrase. By contrast, using **OR** will broaden a search (*Apple OR Computer* will return sites that contain information about either apples or computers). Using **NOT** can also be helpful (*Apple AND Computer NOT fruit* will excludes sites that mention fruit).

■ *Seek reliable sources.* Many websites include advertising and promotional material created by companies with products and services to sell. Not all of this information is accurate or objective. It can be misleading, unfounded, intended as marketing material, or based on personal opinions rather than facts. Examine information carefully to determine who is providing it and whether that source and the information are reliable. Data from sites such as news stations, libraries, city newspapers, government databases, academic databases, and educational institutions are probably more reliable than obscure sites with no obvious signs of credibility.

✔ Reader's TIP
Using Institutional Indexes

Indexes are *databases* that categorize articles according to topic for easy access. Check with your library for the following popular college databases, which are paid for by your institution:

Galileo
Periodical Abstracts
Newspaper Abstracts
Lexis-Nexis Academic Universe
MLA Bibliography
ABI Inform
Psyc FIRST
Social Science Abstracts
ERIC
Medline

20
Print/
Elect.
Media

Practice 11

Using the search engine of your choice, locate three Web sites with information on Condoleezza Rice and her accomplishments. List each site and briefly describe its focus and its strengths.

1. _____

   _____

   _____

2. _____

   _____

   _____

3. _____

   _____

   _____

20f How Do You Read Electronic Material Critically?

For researching anything from recent movie reviews to Shakespeare's plays, the Internet has the advantage of offering easy access to up-to-date information. The disadvantage of Internet information, however, is that you must always question its reliability and its credibility. Unlike the periodicals in libraries whose content have been reviewed by experts, there are no gatekeepers on the Internet. Anyone from a Nobel Prize–winning scientist to a paramilitary fanatic can purchase a Web site for approximately $130, self-publish, sound like an expert, and turn up in your search. Be prepared to use your critical thinking skills (see Chapter 10) to evaluate Internet material. Question not only what is said, but also who wrote it and who paid for it. See Figure 20-9 for a sample Web site.

✓ Reader's TIP

Evaluating Electronic Material

- What are the author's credentials in the field? Is the author affiliated with a university? Check this by noting professional titles in the preface or introduction, finding a biographical reference in the library, or searching the Internet for additional references to the same author.

(continued)

- Who paid for the Web page? Check the home page for an address, as well as the end of the electronic address for *edu, gov, org,* or *com.* Depending on the material, this could lend credibility or raise questions.

- What is the purpose of the Web page? Is the purpose to educate or to sell a product, a service, or an idea? Check the links to look for hidden agendas.

- How do the biases of the author and the sponsor affect the material? Is the reasoning sound? Check the tone, assumptions, and evidence. What opposing views have been left out?

FIGURE 20-9   A sample Web site

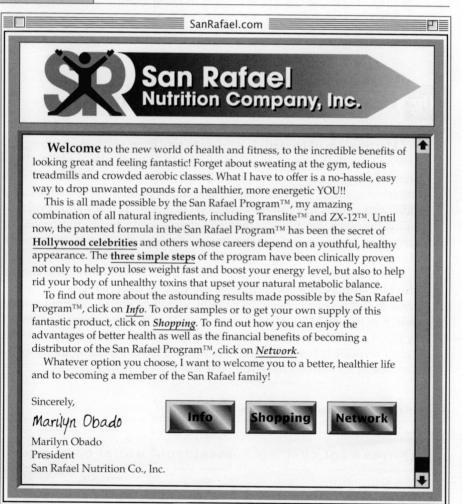

Practice 12

Examine Figure 20-9 and answer the following questions.

1. What is the purpose of this site?

_____

2. What are the credentials of the author?

_____

3. Who paid for the site?

_____

4. Why are you inclined to believe or not believe the information in the letter?

_____

20g How Can You Manage Your E-mail?

Electronic mail (e-mail) is a message sent from one person or organization to another person or group of people using the World Wide Web. These messages can be read, printed, saved, forwarded to someone else, and/or discarded. Document files, graphic or photographic images, and video and audio clips can be "attached" to e-mail. Privacy and confidentiality, however, are not guaranteed. Your e-mail can be intercepted or viewed by others as it navigates its way through the enormous network of computers that make up the Web.

Do you already have a free e-mail address or one through a service provider such as AOL or Earthlink? You may be required to get a free address through your college. In general, e-mail addresses use the format shown in Figure 20-10. Note that the *user ID* or mailbox name is followed by the @ symbol, the name of the *service provider* or institution where the e-mail account is handled, and a period (called a *dot*), and that it ends with one of six suffixes indicating particular types of *domains*.

FIGURE 20-10 | Sample e-mail address format

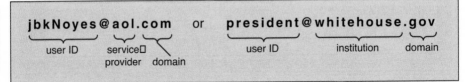

20
Print/
Elect.
Media

Reader's TIP

Electronic Domains

In the United States, the following are the most common domains.

- **.edu**—educational institution
- **.com**—commercial organization
- **.gov**—government organization
- **.mil**—military institution
- **.org**—nonprofit organization
- **.net**—Internet service provider

Reader's TIP

Free E-mail Providers

Hotmail
www.hotmail.com
Bigfoot
www.bigfoot.com
Excite
www.excite.com
Mail.com
www.mail.com
Yahoo!
www.my.yahoo.com

Check Your E-mail

Your online mailbox lists messages in the order in which they were received, indicating the date of the message, the sender's user ID, and the subject—as shown in Figure 20-11. Your options typically include the following:

- *Read*—Double-click to read the message or highlight the message line and click the Read button.
- *Keep as New*—After reading a message, highlight the desired e-mail and then click this option. The message will be displayed as a newly received e-mail the next time you open your mailbox.
- *Save*—Click this option after highlighting the desired e-mail notification. The message can be saved in a file of your choice.

20
Print/
Elect.
Media

FIGURE 20-11 A sample on-line mailbox

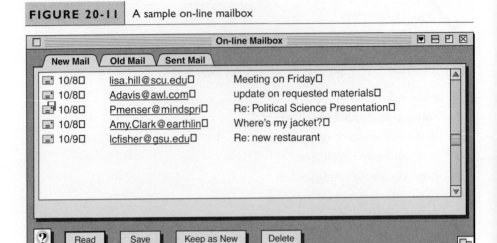

■ *Delete*—Highlight the message line and choose this option to remove it completely from your mailbox. Unless your service provider offers storage (such as a personal filing cabinet), you will be unable to retrieve the e-mail message once it is deleted. Note that this option is useful for getting rid of unsolicited e-mail ads and offers without reading them.

Sending E-mail

Know your options when sending e-mail messages, and strive for maximum efficiency.

Subject—Always insert a phrase to introduce the topic. This display line shows the reader the importance of the message.

CC—These letters refer to *carbon copy,* a term used with typewritten letters to indicate who is being sent a copy of the message. Send such a copy if someone else needs to be aware of what you sent.

Blind Copy—This option enables you to secretly send a copy of your message to someone other than the designated recipient.

Message—Keep it brief and to the point.

Files or Attachments—You can send lengthy files or attachments. Keep in mind that your receiver will need to **download** the attachment to view it. Thus, when possible, cut and paste the download information into the original message to save the receiver time and increase the chances that it will be read.

Replying to E-mail

After reading your e-mail message, you can print it, copy it, save it to another file, delete it, or use one of the following options to respond to the message:

Reply—Click this option to automatically respond to the sender. The "To," "From," and "Subject" lines are filled in; all you need to do is type your response in the "Message" area.

Reply All—This option works just like "Reply," but it sends your answer to everyone who received the original—that is, everyone shown in the "To" and "CC" lists.

Forward—This option automatically fills in the "From" and "Subject" lines and inserts the original message you received in the "Message" section. You must fill in the address of the new recipient, and you can add your own message to the one you are forwarding.

A Note About Computer Viruses—Do not download any attachment from an unknown source. Most Internet service providers will warn you of this danger each time you download a file. Computer *viruses,* which are programs designed to attack and ruin your files and your computer, can enter your computer through downloaded attachments as well as unsolicited e-mail messages.

Spam—Don't waste your time on unwanted e-mail. Delete when you do not recognize the sender or the subject line sounds like a sales pitch.

Respect the Rules of Netiquette

The word *etiquette,* meaning "proper manners," has been humorously altered for the Internet as *netiquette.* The message is the same, however, and these are the suggested rules:

■ Be appropriately formal or informal with language, grammar, and punctuation. An e-mail to friends and family can be casual and use slang, but a message to anyone you do not know well should be more formal. For business correspondence, use formal grammar and punctuation.

■ Use emoticons carefully. **Emoticons** are symbols sometimes used to represent emotions in a lighthearted way. They are not appropriate for formal correspondence but are sometimes used in personal e-mail messages, instant messages, and newsgroups. Common examples:

:-) "smiley face"—happy

;-) "winking smiley"

:-(sad

20
Print/
Elect.
Media

- Do not type all uppercase letters; in electronic communication this is interpreted as yelling. To place emphasis on a word, enclose it in *asterisks.*

- Do not engage in personal attacks. This practice, known as **flaming,** is most likely to occur in a newsgroup or listserv situation. Disagreeing with an opinion or fact is acceptable, but criticizing the person who expressed the opinion or fact is bad manners.

- Consider your audience when using abbreviations. Some people argue that "insider" abbreviations such as BTW (by the way), KISS (keep it simple, stupid), and IMHO (in my humble opinion) tend to exclude those who are not "in the know."

- Do not reply unless necessary; you don't want to junk up everyone's e-mail box.

- Avoid attachments if you can because the receiver may not have a compatible system.

- Scan attachments before sending them so that you don't inadvertently send a file with a virus.

Small-Group EXPLORATION

Form a five-member group and select one of the following activities. Brainstorm and then outline your major points on a transparency. Choose one group member to present the group's findings to the class. Individual assignments can also be made.

- List the reasons that the members of your group read newspapers.

- List the magazines that the members of your group would like to subscribe to or buy frequently. Describe the appeal of each magazine.

- During the next ten years, what improvements would you like to see in the Internet?

- List ways in which you predict daily life will change over the course of the next ten years because of the Internet.

Net SEARCH

Locate the Web sites for three major newspapers on the Internet. Record the front-page news stories for each paper on the same day. How does the list differ, and what do the selections reflect about the papers?

The *New York Times*
www.nytimes.com

20
Print/
Elect.
Media

The *Washington Post*
www.washingtonpost.com

1,800-Plus Newspaper Links
hem.passagen.se/gumby/newspapers

Links to More Than 5,000 Newspapers
www.onlinenewspapers.com

20
Print/
Elect.
Media

Chapter
21

Workplace and Personal Reading

21a How Should You Manage Your Professional and Personal Reading?

FAST FACT

The average American works two months more per year than most Europeans. Four-week vacations are mandated by law in Switzerland and Greece, five weeks in France and Spain, and almost eight weeks per year in Sweden.

Experts urge individuals to follow three rules for efficiently meeting reading demands in the workplace and at home. Rule #1 is to set reading priorities. For example, memos may need to be read immediately, but annual reports can probably wait until later. Rule #2 is to handle a piece of paper only once. In other words, do not open a letter and then set it aside to be handled later. If you open a letter, follow through to finish the job. Rule #3 is to finish by taking one of the three action options: (1) respond to it, (2) throw it in the trash, or (3) file it to be used later with other material on the same subject. Use this expert advice to budget your time and energy effectively.

21b What Are the Different Types of Workplace Reading?

Work-related documents usually make points quickly, have a serious tone, and are written to inform rather than to entertain. Which documents are most important? Only you can answer this question because it depends on how a document affects your job performance.

In this section we will examine a variety of business documents: memos, letters, newsletters, minutes, reports, instructions, procedures, employment forms, contracts, and leases.

Memos

A **memo** is a brief message intended to update co-workers, announce meetings, ask questions, request assistance, or announce decisions. Memos are written in a concise, direct style and can be formal or informal. Most memos are now sent by e-mail. When used correctly, memos are internal messages among company employees, rather than communicatons with people outside the organization.

The standard format for a memo makes it easy to determine who sent it and what it is about (see Figure 21-1). The most important information is given at the beginning. Take care to notice dates, times, places, and requests for a response or action.

TO: Lists the person or group of people to whom the memo was sent.

FROM: Indicates who wrote the memo.

DATE: Shows when the memo was written.

CC: Lists the name of anyone not shown in the "TO" line who also received a copy. This recipient may be a superior who needs to know what is happening. "CC" stands for "carbon copy."

RE: (or SUBJECT:) Indicates the topic of the memo. "RE" is an abbreviation for "regarding." It can be used interchangeably with "SUBJECT."

Practice 1

Read the memo in Figure 21-1 and answer the following questions.

1. What is the reason for the memo?

_____

2. What is the necessary action?

_____

FIGURE 21-1	Example of a memo

Memorandum

TO: Lee Designs Personnel
FROM: Alex Rodriguez, Director of Personnel Services
DATE: March 1 , 2005
CC: Bob Hamilton, General Manager
RE: Direct Deposit of Paychecks

Please note that beginning with the second pay period in April, all nonsalaried employees will have the option of direct deposit of their paychecks. To take advantage of this option, you must fill out a Direct Deposit Request Form (sample is attached) and return it to the Accounting Department no later than March 15. Implementation of the direct deposit option will be delayed one month for those who submit their requests after that date.

If you have any questions, please contact me at extension 225.

Business Letters

A **business letter** is more formal than a memo and is therefore more appropriate for communication outside a company. A letter can give or request information, congratulate or express appreciation, register complaints, or emphasize an action. Like memos, business letters are relatively short and are written in a concise, direct manner. A typical business letter format includes the following (see Figure 21-2.)

1. **Letterhead or return address.** The letterhead or return address is where you will find the information needed to respond to the sender.
2. **Date.** It indicates when the letter was written.
3. **Recipient's address.** The recipient's name or department name may be included here, along with his or her company's mailing address.
4. **Salutation.** This greeting will appear either as "Dear:" or "To Whom It May Concern:"
5. **Text.** This is the body of the letter, in which the sender gives information, asks questions, or both.
6. **Closing.** In business letters it usually appears as "Yours truly," "Sincerely," or some variation of the two. The sender's printed full name and business title appear just below the sender's handwritten signature.

FIGURE 21-2 | Example of a business letter

❶  **SFI**≣ **Southern Factoring Incorporated**
1812 New England Dr. • Greensboro, NC 27403

Mr. Bruce Chen
Director of Human Resources

❷ October 5, 2005

❸ Ms. Marianne Parker
28 West Post Trail
Atlanta, GA 30327

❹ Dear Ms. Parker:

❺ I enjoyed our meeting last week. Your background in product design is quite impressive and after speaking with our management team to evaluate budget and salary concerns, I am delighted to offer you the position of Assistant Manager, New Product Development. This position would start at the beginning of next month, so please contact me by October 18 with your decision.

I have taken the liberty of including brochures from several realtors and new housing developments in the area as well as information from the Chamber of Commerce. These may be helpful as you consider this offer.

I hope to hear from you as soon as possible and look forward to welcoming you as part of the Southern Factoring Inc. team.

❻ Sincerely,

Bruce Chen

Bruce Chen
Director of Human Resources

❼ cc: Alphonse Di Lallo, Manager, New Product Development
     Susan Pratt, National Sales Manager

❽ Enclosures

7. **CC.** If copies of the letter have been distributed to anyone besides the person to whom it is addressed, the names are listed here.

8. **Attachments or enclosures.** If other documents or copies of documents are being sent along with the letter, one of these terms will appear. *Attachments* indicates that the other documents are clipped

or stapled to the letter; *enclosures* indicates that they are included in the same envelope or package with the letter. These terms help the reader determine whether all the material intended to accompany the letter actually arrived.

✓ Reader's TIP

Reading Memos and Letters

- Determine who sent the correspondence.
- Figure out the subject of the correspondence by reading the subject line of a memo or the first paragraph of a letter.
- Pay special attention to items that are emphasized through the use of numbers, bullets, boldface or italic type, or capital letters.
- Determine what action or response is appropriate and the date that it is due.

Practice 2

Read the letter in Figure 21-2 and answer the following questions.

1. What is the purpose of the letter?

_____

2. What action is requested?

_____

3. How many days will Ms. Parker have to respond?

_____

Newsletters

Newsletters are documents published by businesses, organizations, clubs, and schools that combine news, editorial columns, letters, stories, and graphics on subjects of interest to group members. They look like mini-newspapers or multiple-page, stapled letters. The purpose of a newsletter is to build group spirit, bind members together, recognize member achievement, and chronicle group events. Each member of the particular group usually receives the newsletter automatically.

Newsletters are basically *promotional material* (public relations information) for the organization. They tend to report on the past and rarely contain critical information that demands action. If the newsletter has a table of contents, use it to guide your reading. If not, read the headings and beginning paragraphs to determine what you care to read.

 **Reader's TIP**

Reading Newsletters

- Read selectively. You may want to read all of the newsletter or none of it.
- Read critically. You cannot consider the information in a newsletter to be objective because it is beneficial only to the company or organization. Unflattering information is not included, so the coverage is not balanced.
- Note items that are highlighted, those that are set off by numbers, bullets, or capital letters, and those in boldfaced or italic type.

Committee Minutes and Reports

Minutes form the official records of formal meetings in which employees create policies, make reports, and develop action plans. The minutes list the people attending and briefly describe what happened at the meeting. Minutes usually have subheadings to indicate the topics under discussion (see Figure 21-3). For an employee, committee minutes serve two purposes: (1) to verify what was decided for later reference if questions arise, and (2) to record what occurred at a meeting for the benefit of those who did not attend.

Reports, which may be the work of a subcommittee, are frequently summarized at committee meetings. The full report may be available for you to read later on a Web site, or it may be attached to the minutes. Use the subheadings to find the parts of the report that interest you.

Reader's TIP

Reading Minutes and Reports

- Use subheadings to guide your reading.
- Confirm the accuracy of any statements attributed to you.
- Double-check the wording of decisions that affect your department.

Practice 3

Read the minutes in Figure 21-3 and answer the following questions.

1. Who gave reports at the committee meeting?

FIGURE 21-3 | Example of committee minutes

Minutes of the University Planning and Development Committee

Members Present: Angelo, Briggs, Cole, Hall, King, Lopez, Mann, Soto, Vega

October 12, 2005

The meeting was called to order at 1:00 by Chair Tony Angelo.

The minutes of the September 10 meeting were approved with one correction in the third paragraph to specify 15 new lights, rather than 12.

Classroom Renovation
Margaret Mann reported that the second floor of Jaramillo Hall is being renovated. Fourteen classrooms will be ready for use by spring semester. Nine of these will be equipped with 26 computer terminals each.

Banners
Foster King reported that the installation of banners with the university logo has been completed in the Student Center. Installation in the library, however, has been delayed because the poles that were shipped were defective. They will be replaced at no cost to the university and should arrive by November 1.

Science Building
Laura Cole reported that faculty and students are still discussing the plans for meeting and group study rooms in the new science building. The subcommittee will meet with the architects on October 18 and present a plan at the next meeting. Juan Soto requested that noise control should be considered in assigning space.

The meeting adjourned at 2:25.

---

2. What seems to be the responsibility of this committee?

_____

_____

Instructions and Procedures

Both instructions and procedures documents provide sequential steps for successfully completing a project or an action. *Instructions* usually refer to the directions for executing a specific task, such as bicycle assembly, computer installation, fax machine usage, or DVD player operation (see Figure 21-4). *Procedures,* by contrast, describe the course of action to be followed in particular circumstances—for example, how to file insurance claims if you are injured on the job, how to request vacation time,

FIGURE 21-4 Example of instructions

The Utilities Disk for your Macintosh computer can be run from the disk itself or installed on your hard drive. YOU WILL NEED AT LEAST 128 MB OF RAM AND OPERATING SYSTEM 9.0 OR HIGHER FOR THE PROGRAM TO OPERATE SUCCESSFULLY.

To operate from the CD:
1. Insert the Utilities Disk into the CD-ROM drive.
2. Restart the computer while holding down the letter "C" key on the keyboard. This will tell the computer to start from the Utilities Disk instead of the usual start-up disk.
3. After start-up is complete, double-click on the Repair icon in the Utilities main window.
4. In the Repair window, select the item that needs attention and follow the on-screen instructions.
5. Once the repair process is complete, you will see an American flag icon on the screen. From here, you will have the options of repairing another item, quitting the program, or installing the Utilities program on your hard disk if it is not already installed.

 Reader's TIP

Reading Instructions and Procedures

- Preview the instructions/procedures to estimate time, predict tools, and "get the big picture."
- Assemble the required tools or authorization forms before starting.
- Follow each step in order. Never skip ahead.
- Match what you are reading with the diagrams and figures.
- Pay particular attention to capitalized, boldfaced, or italicized text.
- If a sentence is unclear, reread it until you understand exactly what you are being instructed to do. Reading the sentence aloud may help.
- If all else fails, seek help from someone who has experience with the task at hand or likes details, or call the toll-free number.

or how to respond to customer complaints. To respond to either successfully, pay attention to every single detail. If you miss one minor detail or perform a step out of order, your bicycle may not work or your insurance claim may not be processed.

Practice 4

Read the instructions in Figure 21-4 and answer the following questions.

1. What two items are required for the Utilities Disk to work properly?

_____

2. After inserting the disk, what is the first step that is to be completed?

_____

3. How will you know the repair process is finished?

_____

Employment Forms

Employment forms require specific information and are similar to tax forms, employment verification forms, and insurance forms. All must be filled out accurately and legibly. They request personal information such as your home address, Social Security number, work history, personal and business references, and salary history. Insurance forms require similar information, as well as information about illnesses, injuries, and doctors' telephone numbers. Because responding to most such forms is time-consuming, keep photocopies of completed forms in an ongoing file marked "Employment Forms." You will then have old information at your fingertips when you need it for new purposes.

✓ Reader's TIP

Responding to Employment Forms

- Begin by carefully reading all instructions, questions, and requests for information before starting to fill in any form or application.
- Photocopy the form and fill out this copy first for practice and accuracy. Then use it to complete the original.
- On employment applications, answer honestly and accurately, but do not volunteer any negative information if not specifically requested.
- Keep your photocopied forms in a file for later reference.

Practice 5

Fill out the employment application in Figure 21-5 and put it in your files. Why is the "Notice to Applicants" section included?

_____

FIGURE 21-5 | Sample employment application

ACTION **Team Inc.**   **An Equal Opportunity Employer**

Please complete all requested information. Use ink and print.

GENERAL INFORMATION

Name _____   Telephone _____

Address _____   Social Security # _____

Have you ever applied to work at our company previously? _____ Are you 18 years of age? _____ Are you a U.S. citizen? _____

AVAILABILITY

Position desired _____   Minimum salary desired _____

Date available for work _____   Full time or part time _____

Indicate the hours you are available to work both days and evenings. _____

WORK EXPERIENCE List employment, beginning with your most recent position.

EMPLOYER _____

Address _____

Telephone _____   Supervisor's name _____

Your position _____   Dates of employment _____

EMPLOYER _____

Address _____

Telephone _____   Supervisor's name _____

Your position _____   Dates of employment _____

REFERENCES

REFERENCE (not related to you) _____   Job title _____

Address _____   Telephone _____

How acquainted and for how long _____

REFERENCE (not related to you) _____   Job title _____

Address _____   Telephone _____

How acquainted and for how long _____

EDUCATION

TYPE OF SCHOOL	NAME & LOCATION	YEARS ATTENDED	DEGREE

PERSONAL INFORMATION

Why do you want to work for our company? _____

_____

What did you dislike about your previous jobs? _____

_____

Notice to Applicants

In completing this application I understand and agree that:

1. Acceptance of this application does not mean that the company has agreed to hire me.
2. If employed, my employment is "at will," meaning that I do not have a contract for a definite period of time and that my employment can be ended with or without cause and with or without notice.
3. All information in this application is accurate. I understand that false information can result in dismissal.
4. I authorize the company to contact my previous employers and references for full information regarding my employment history.

DATE _____   SIGNATURE OF APPLICANT _____

Contracts and Leases

A *contract* is a binding legal agreement between two parties in which the terms or conditions of the agreement are stated in writing. The signatures of both parties indicate their mutual consent to the terms or conditions of the

FIGURE 21-6 | Example of a lease

LEASE

This agreement made this 23rd day of May, 2003, is between Leonard Allen (hereinafter called "management") and Lotte Rivera (hereinafter called "resident").

Management leases to resident, and resident rents from management the dwelling located at 1845 Rosewood Ave., San Francisco, CA, under the following conditions:

TERM: 1. The initial term of this lease shall be 12 months beginning April 1, 2004, and ending March 31, 2005.

RENT: 2. Rent is payable monthly in advance at a rate of $735 per month, during the term of this agreement on the first day of each month at the office of management or at such other place management may designate.

LATE CHARGE: 3. Time is of the essence in this agreement. If management elects to accept rent after the 5th day of the month, a late charge of $5.00 per each late day will be due as additional rent.

SECURITY DEPOSIT: 4. Management acknowledges receipt of $735 as security for resident's fulfillment of the conditions of this agreement. Deposit will be placed in Account #45-827-3578 at Sun Trust Co. Bank. Deposit will be returned to resident within thirty (30) days after apartment is vacated if

   a) Lease term has expired or agreement has been terminated by both parties; and
   b) All monies due management by resident have been paid; and
   c) Apartment is not damaged and is left in its original condition, normal wear and tear
      expected.

Deposit may be applied by management to satisfy all or part of resident's obligations and such act shall not prevent management from claiming damages in excess of the deposit. Resident may not apply the deposit to any rent payment without approval of management.

SUB-LET: 5. Tenant may sublease apartment.

PROPERTY LOSS: 6. Management shall not be liable for damage to resident's property of any type for any reason or cause whatsoever, except where such is due to management's negligence.

EARLY TERMINATION: 7. Resident may terminate this agreement before the expiration of the original term by:

   a) Giving management thirty (30) days written notice; plus
   b) Paying all monies due through date of termination; plus
   c) Paying an amount equal to one month's rent; plus
   d) Returning dwelling in a clean, ready-to-rent condition.

PETS: 8. No animals, birds, or pets of any kind shall be permitted in the dwelling without written consent of management.

RULES AND REGULATIONS: 9. a) Locks: Resident is prohibited from adding or changing locks installed on the doors of dwelling, without the written permission of management.

   b) Storage: No goods or materials of any kind or description which are combustible or would increase fire risk will be taken or placed in storage areas.

   c) Guests: Resident shall be responsible and liable for the conduct of guests. Acts of guests in violation of this agreement or management's rules and regulations may be deemed by management to be a breach by resident.

SPECIAL STIPULATIONS: 10. The following special stipulations shall control in the event of conflict with any of the foregoing:

   a) Resident is responsible for yard maintenance and payment of all utilities.
   b) A $20.00 fee will be charged for a check returned for insufficient funds.
   c) Management may terminate this agreement by giving 30 days written notice.

_____   _____
Management   Resident

contract. A *lease* (see Figure 21-6) is a particular type of contract in which one party (the lessor) lends real estate or equipment for a specified time period and price to the other party (the lessee).

Contracts and leases are lengthy documents written in legal terminology that can be confusing but should be examined carefully. Capitalized and/or boldfaced headings begin each section and indicate the topic. Although the reading may be difficult, be sure that you understand all points for which you are legally responsible and all charges or payments that affect you. Be clear on the circumstances under which you can legally terminate the contract.

The same tips that apply to your workplace reading for tasks such as reviewing a service contract for the copy machine or responding to a rental lease for additional warehouse space also apply in your personal life. Use the same reader's tips when signing a lease to rent an apartment or a contract to buy a house. Not understanding the legalities can cost you money. When anything is unclear, ask questions.

✔ Reader's TIP

Reading a Contract or Lease

- What is the payment or cost commitment?
- What are the consequences of termination?
- What are the restrictions?
- What penalties are possible?
- Who is legally responsible for what?

Practice 6

Answer the following questions regarding the lease in Figure 21-6.

_____ 1. How much is the resident responsible for paying the lessor by April 5, 2004?

_____ 2. How many days' written notice must the resident give to terminate the lease early?

_____ 3. How many days' notice must management give to terminate the lease early?

_____ 4. Are pets allowed?

_____ 5. Who is responsible for yard maintenance and utilities?

_____ 6. If Ms. Rivera pays the rent on the 7th of the month, how much money does she owe?

21c How Should You Respond to a Letter?

It's likely your mailbox is often filled with advertisements, bills, and institutional letters. To manage them, use the same efficient system that you would use for business correspondence: Set priorities, handle a piece of paper only once, and then either reply to it, discard it, or file it.

Personally addressed letters from government agencies, institutions, or other organizations usually call for action, and your failure to reply can result in a penalty or a problem. For example, if your college notifies you by letter to take a specific test before graduation and you fail to take action or reply, your graduation date might be delayed. Other examples are vehicle registration forms, calls to jury duty, tax return queries, and insurance questions.

Such letters are short and to the point, first paragraph stating the purpose, the second paragraph stating the deadlines and consequences, and the third politely asking for compliance or offering assistance (see Figure 21-7). If there is anything you do not understand in the letter, contact the officer or agency that sent the correspondence and ask for clarification.

After responding to a letter, record in your daily planner the time and place of any action you must take in the future. In some cases, you may also want to photocopy your response to keep in your files.

Practice 7

Read the letter in Figure 21-7 and answer the following questions.

1. Exactly what does the letter request?

_____

_____

2. By what date must the information be returned to the Office of Scholarship Administration?

_____

3. What will happen if Thaddeus does not respond in time?

_____

21d What Are the Different Parts of a Bill?

If you have a cell phone, credit cards, or cable TV, you receive bills every month. Although bills are formatted differently, most include the same key features (see Figure 21-8).

FIGURE 21-7 | Example of a letter

Office of Scholarship Administration
Penmore College
2600 Elkmont Ave.
Warwick, CA 90426

December 6, 2005

Thaddeus Carver
1622 Lattimore Circle—Apt. 2F
Warwick, CA 90427

Dear Mr. Carver,
It has come to my attention that this office has not received any
record of your work-study hours for last semester. As you know,
verification of your completing the necessary work-study hours is
one of the requirements for maintaining your Hirsch Scholarship.

If I have not received the completed log of last semester's hours
signed by your academic advisor by January 6, 2006, you will become
ineligible for further consideration as a Hirsch Scholar.

Please make every effort to correct this oversight so that you may
continue your studies without interruption.

Sincerely,

Annette Hightower

Annette Hightower
Financial Officer

1. **Your account number.** This number identifies you to the company
   sending the bill. Write it on your check payments and all correspondence with the company.

FIGURE 21-8   Example of a bill

② Closing Date	① Account Number(s)	New Balance	Minimum Payment	③ Payment Date	Amount Enclosed
04/15/05	59-242-588-787	179.38	9.00	05/13/05	$ _____

YOU MAY AVOID ADDITIONAL **FINANCE CHARGES** ON PURCHASES BY PAYING THE **NEW BALANCE** BY **PAYMENT DATE**.

Make check payable to *Sloan's*

ELLIOT SWARTZBERG
1515 PARKWAY DR.
BALTIMORE, MD 21209

PO BOX 18425
WILMINGTON DE 19886-18425

⑨

5924258878799 0566798100000000018

Please detach here and return top portion with your payment. Do not staple or clip your check to the form.

DATE	STORE	REF #	DEPT	TRANSACTION DESCRIPTION	CHARGES	PAYMENTS & CREDITS
03/23	14	164566	6446	MENS DRESS SHIRT	28.17	
03/23	14	889455	0379	COOKWARE	132.64	
03/25	14	464657	6446	RETURN—MENS DRESS SHIRT		−28.17
04/09	10	100073		PAYMENT—THANK YOU		25.00

ACCOUNT NUMBER	59-242-588-787	④ PREVIOUS BALANCE		43.46
ACCOUNT TYPE	156-REV	TOTAL PURCHASES AND CHARGES		160.81
PAYMENT DUE DATE	05/13/05	⑤ TOTAL CREDITS		28.17
BILL CLOSING DATE	04/15/05	TOTAL PAYMENTS		25.00

Telephoning about billing errors will not preserve your rights under federal law. To preserve your rights, write to the address shown for Customer Service on the reverse side.

⑥ **FINANCE CHARGE**   3.28
⑦ NEW BALANCE   179.38
MINIMUM PAYMENT DUE NOW   9.00

⑧
FOR 24 HOUR CUSTOMER SERVICE CALL 1-888-445-4545

Periodic Rate	Annual Percentage Rate	Balance Subject to Finance Charge
.05918% DAILY	21.60	179.38

2. **Billing period or closing date.** The date(s) shown indicate the time period covered by the bill. Any charges occurring after the date of the bill will appear on the following month's statement. For services that

are billed in advance, such as paging and security, the billing period may cover the upcoming month.

3. **Due date or payment date.** This is the date by which your payment must be received, *not* postmarked. If you miss this deadline, late charges or finance fees will usually be added to the amount still owed.

✓ Reader's TIP

Paying Bills

- Check numbers for accuracy.
- Call for clarification if needed.
- Write your account number on payment checks.
- File paid bills, even if you use a shoebox with dividers. Keep them for one year in case of discrepancies and for personal financial planning purposes.

---

4. **Previous balance.** The amount of your last bill from the company will be shown here. If you had no previous balance, this space will show zeros or it will be blank.

5. **Payments received or credits.** Payments made since the last bill will appear here. On credit card bills, "credits" will indicate returned items.

6. **Finance charges, fees, or adjustments.** Any amounts shown here reflect additional money the company is charging you. Late payment fees can be either a standard amount or a percentage of the amount you owe. You may be charged for checks returned for insufficient funds or for additional company service fees. "Adjustments" can cover a variety of items, ranging from refunds for inadequate service to additional expenses charged to you that the company categorizes differently from finance charges.

7. **Total amount due or new balance.** This amount is how much you owe the company after all new charges, previous balances, credits, finance charges, fees, and adjustments have been added together.

8. **Customer service contact.** If you have questions or problems concerning your bill, call this telephone number for assistance.

9. **Payment coupon.** This coupon is usually the top or bottom portion of the first page of the bill. Tear it along the perforated edge and include it in the payment envelope with your check. Write the amount of your check in the designated space on the coupon.

Practice 8

1. In the bill shown in Figure 21-8, what is the total amount owed and

   when is it due? _____

2. What is the minimum amount that must be paid? _____

3. What amount was paid last month? _____

4. What was the finance charge last month? _____

5. What is the account number? _____

6. What adjustment was made on this bill? _____

   _____

7. What is the annual percentage rate for finance charges? _____

21e How Do You Respond to Direct Mail Advertisements?

Do not let unsolicited advertising waste your time. More than half of your mail may fall into this nuisance or "junk" category. If you have no interest in a piece of advertising, throw it away. If you are interested, remember the saying, "If it sounds too good to be true, it probably is."

Some ads and promotions arrive in official-looking envelopes that have the appearance of mail from government agencies. This resemblance is meant to grab your attention and get you to open and read the enclosed material. Be wary.

Decipher Promotions

Do not succumb to glitz. Recognize that if you do not really need the product or service, saving 40 percent is meaningless. If you are interested, however, read carefully to clarify your total commitment and exactly what you will receive in return. Read the fine print.

Credit Cards. Credit card promotions (see Figure 21-9) have become such a problem at colleges that some institutions have banned the advertisers from campuses. You have probably already received many promotions saying that you are preapproved for a certain credit limit. Some students, enticed by the easy credit and low monthly payments, charge themselves into serious debt by accumulating crippling finance fees that take years to repay. The misuse of credit cards can be devastating.

Proper use of a credit card, by contrast, can be extremely convenient. Before committing yourself to one, be certain that you have the means and the discipline to pay your bill before the due date. If you always pay promptly, your only cost for this financial convenience will be the annual fee, which is typically $50 or less.

College students are bombarded with offers of easy credit.

✓ Reader's TIP

Evaluating a Credit Card Offer

- How much is the annual fee for the card?
- What is the finance charge rate? Annual rates can run from 18 to 22 percent, so finance charges can add up quickly.
- Does the rate start low and rise after an initial introductory period? The balance may be subject to a higher interest rate after the initial period with the low rate expires.
- Why do you need the card? If you already have one card, why do you need another?

21
Home/
Work

| **FIGURE 21-9** | Example of a credit card promotion |

(NOTE: ALL OF THIS INFORMATION IS VALID EVEN IF THE OFFER INDICATES YOU HAVE BEEN PREAPPROVED.)

3.99%
Introductory APR

THE CARD YOU'VE BEEN WAITING FOR
THE BENEFITS YOU NEED
THE RATE YOU WANT

Dear Stephanie Albert,

This card is not for everyone. It's for people like you who are just starting out and have already demonstrated responsibility with their credit. Because you've shown that kind of special care, Hamilton Bank can make this special offer to you—a Hamilton Premier MasterCard.

The rate shown above is one of the lowest of any major credit card issuer. There's no gimmick here—the fixed rate of 3.99% is yours for nine months and will not increase if the Prime Rate changes.* After nine months, you'll still save with a variable Annual Percentage Rate as low as Prime +5.49%—right now that's only 13.24%.*

This rate saves you money on new purchases and on outstanding balances, too. Move those high rate balances to your Hamilton Premier MasterCard—who knows how much you'll save?

With a Hamilton Premier MasterCard, you'll also enjoy these benefits:
- Credit line up to $ 100,000
- No annual fee
- Optional Travel Accident Insurance, Lost Luggage Insurance, Auto Rental Insurance, Credit Card Registration and Merchandise Protection

*By filling out the following application, you agree that we reserve the right, based upon our evaluation, to open a Hamilton Standard MasterCard account if you do not qualify for a Hamilton Premier MasterCard account or, if you do not qualify, not to open any account. If we do not open an account, we may submit your application to our subsidiary, Hamilton Southwest, which will consider you for an Excel or Regular MasterCard account with the pricing terms shown below.

HAMILTON BANK SUMMARY OF TERMS

Annual Percentage Rate for Purchases	Variable Rate Information
Preferred Pricing: 3.99% Introductory APR for 9 months. Thereafter, for Hamilton MasterCard: 13.24% if your balances are greater than or equal to $2,500/15.24% if your balances are less than $2,500. For Hamilton MasterCard: 17.24%. **Non-Preferred Pricing:** 22.74%	Annual Percentage Rate is fixed at 3.99% for the first 9 months your account is open. Thereafter, your Annual Percentage Rate may vary. For Hamilton Premier MasterCard, the rate is determined monthly by adding 5.49% if your balances are greater than or equal to $2,500 or 7.49% if balances are less than $2,500 (for Hamilton Standard MasterCard: 9.49% for all balances), to the Prime Rate as published in *The Wall Street Journal.* **Non-Preferred Pricing:** Your Annual Percentage Rate may vary. The rate is determined monthly by adding 14.99% to the Prime Rate. This rate will not be lower than 19.8%.

HAMILTON SOUTHWEST SUMMARY OF TERMS

Annual Percentage Rate for Purchases	Variable Rate Information
Preferred Pricing: For Excel MasterCard: 23.15%. For Regular MasterCard: 27.15%. These rates will not be lower than 21.9% or higher than 29.9%. **Non-Preferred Pricing:** Fixed 29.9% APR.	**Preferred Pricing:** Your Annual Percentage Rate may vary. For Excel MasterCard accounts, the rate is determined quarterly by adding 15.4% to the Prime Rate as published in *The Wall Street Journal.* For Regular MasterCard accounts, the rate is determined quarterly by adding 19.4% to the Prime Rate.

Practice 9

Examine the credit credit card promotion in Figure 21-9 and answer the following questions.

1. How long will the introductory rate be available on this credit card?

_____

2. After the introductory period, what is the lowest annual percentage rate (APR) you could get if your account balance is less than $2,500?

_____

3. If your application is transferred to Hamilton Southwest, what is the highest fixed APR you might have to pay?

_____

CD, DVD, Tape, and Book Club Offers.   These promotions offer attractive packages. Who wouldn't want to get 10 or 15 CDs for a penny? In reality, these introductory items are "loss leaders." In other words, the company loses money by giving you so much up front, but it makes that money back (and more) by requiring you to purchase other merchandise in the future. Typically, you are sent a notice of a new selection every month. If you don't want the selection, you must return the notice form within a limited time period. However, if you neglect to send it back or are late, you will receive the product and be charged for it. Because shipping and handling fees are added, you may pay a higher price than you would at a local retailer or on the Internet.

If you are considering membership in one of these clubs, do the math and determine whether the number of "free" (or almost free) items you get up front will still be a bargain after you figure in the price of additional items that you are required to buy in the future. Carefully examine the types of movies, music, or books the club has to offer. Is there a large selection that interests you? Also, pay attention to how current the selections are. Often the most desirable new releases will not be available through the clubs until well after they have been shipped to regular retail stores.

Small-Group EXPLORATION

Form a five-member group and select one of the following activities. Brainstorm and then outline your major points on a transparency. Choose one group member to present the group's findings to the class. Individual assignments can also be made.

■ Write a follow-up letter to thank an important business colleague for writing a job recommendation for you. Compliment the person and state your continued interest in employment. Follow the letter format shown in this chapter (see Figure 21-2).

■ List the top ten reasons why students get into overwhelming credit card debt.

■ Estimate the number of personal mailings you have received in the past month, and categorize the nature of the correspondence.

■ What bills do you pay each month? What do you find confusing about each?

Net SEARCH

You have just interviewed for a job and are interested in pursuing career opportunities with the company. Write a follow-up business letter expressing your thanks and your interest in the position. Before you begin, search the Internet for tips on writing an effective business letter, or start with one of the following sites:

The Small Business Journal
www.tsbj.com/articles

Useful Phrases for Business Letter Writing
esl.about.com/library/weekly/aa041399.htm

Writing Business Letters and Addressing Envelopes
www.ais.msstate.edu/aee/Tutorial/busletters.html

Business Writing Tips
www.basic-learning.com/tips0529.htm

Part 5

Reading Selections

Reading Selections

Practice the reading and thinking skills that you have learned on the ten selections of writing that appear in the following pages. These selections represent the kind of reading that college students do; they include essays, short stories, excerpts from textbooks, newspaper and magazine articles, and a Web page. Each selection is followed by questions on the main idea, details, inference, and vocabulary. One selection has questions on graphic illustrations.

Use the progress sheet for Part 5 to record your scores and monitor your learning. For any incorrect answers, make explanatory notes in your book as reminders for success. If you need to refresh your knowledge on a skill, return to and review the chapter in which the skill was introduced.

Use your own paper to complete the *Think and Write* questions at the end of each section. These questions ask you to recall, react, reflect, connect, and think critically. You will also be applying the reading to your own life as well as linking old and new ideas.

Selection 1 Health

What are the benefits of daily exercise? Can exercise send endorphins to the brain and give you a feeling of well-being? Does exercise prevent diseases? Research shows that exercise helps maintain bone health, moderate blood pressure, relieve depression, and may influence hormone levels to prevent some cancers. Recent studies show that breast-cancer patients who walked three–to–five hours a week lived 50 percent longer than inactive patients. If exercise has such overwhelming health benefits, why don't 100 percent of the people in America exercise daily?

Personal Fitness

Shawn hasn't ever been physically active. In high school he didn't enjoy physical education classes because he didn't have the fitness level or skills needed for competitive activities like basketball and soccer. Now 20-years-old and a sophomore in college, Shawn typically drives
5 his car to campus rather than walking the six blocks from his apartment. His idea of a complete meal is a large pepperoni pizza delivered to his door and washed down with a large soda. To relax, he'll play a computer game. Recently Shawn heard about the adverse health effects of a sedentary lifestyle and no longer wants to be a couch potato.

10 Now that Shawn is ready for a more active lifestyle, how should he begin? After years of inactivity, what types of exercises should he choose? Should Shawn see a physician before he starts his exercise program? How soon will he notice positive effects?

A century ago in the United States, simple survival required per-
15 forming physical labor on a near-daily basis. Few people had the op-portunity to concern themselves with how to spend their leisure time, for they had none. But over the course of the twentieth cen-tury, an extraordinary number of scientific and technological discov-eries dramatically changed society as we know it. In the new millen-
20 nium, leisure time is plentiful, with many exciting new ways to enjoy it. Yet the majority of adults in our country lead sedentary lifestyles, and little or no physical labor or exercise makes up part of their daily routine. According to the Centers for Disease Control, more than 60 percent of American adults currently do not exercise enough, and 25
25 percent do not engage in any form of exercise whatsoever.

Most people would agree that modern life is preferable to those rugged and uncertain times in 1900, when the average life ex-pectancy was just 38 years. Medical and technological advances have more than doubled the average life expectancy in the United States.
30 But paradoxically, the growing percentage of Americans who live sedentary lives has been linked to dramatic increases in the inci-dence of chronic disease. According to authors Booth and Gordon, heart disease is a cause of death almost 30 times more frequently to-day than it was in 1900. Between 1958 and 1993, a sixfold increase
35 in incidence of type 2 (non-insulin-dependent) diabetes occurred.

Now is an excellent time to make a break with the past and de-velop exercise habits that can increase both the quality and duration of your life. Especially when combined with a healthy diet, regular physical activity reduces risk of heart disease, high blood pressure,
40 type 2 diabetes, and colon cancer.

Only 24 percent of American adults engage in at least 30 minutes of light to moderate physical activity five or more times per week, while fewer than 10 percent exercise at the frequency and intensity needed to improve cardiorespiratory fitness. Use the following infor-
45 mation to create your own exercise program to improve your level of physical fitness now and maintain it throughout your lifetime.

Improving Cardiorespiratory Fitness

Cardiorespiratory fitness refers to the ability of the circulatory and respiratory systems to supply oxygen during sustained physical activity.
50 The primary category of physical activity known to improve car-diorespiratory endurance is *aerobic exercise*. The term *aerobic* means "with oxygen" and describes any type of exercise, typically performed

at moderate levels of intensity for extended periods of time, that increases your heart rate. Aerobic activities such as walking, jogging,
55 bicycling, and swimming are among the best exercises for improving
overall health status as well as cardiorespiratory fitness. A person
said to be in "good shape" has an above-average *aerobic capacity*—a
term used to describe the current functional status of the cardiorespiratory system (i.e., heart, lungs, blood vessels).

Improving Flexibility

60   *Flexibility* is a measure of the range of motion, or the amount of
movement possible, at a particular joint. Improving your range of
motion through stretching exercises will enhance your efficiency
of movement and your posture. In addition, flexibility exercises have
been shown to be effective in reducing the incidence and severity of
65 musculo-tendinous injuries. (See Figure 1.1.)

A regular program of stretching exercises can enhance psychological as well as physical well-being. *Tai chi* is an ancient Chinese
form of exercise that combines stretching, balance, coordination, and
meditation; it is widely practiced in the West today. *Yoga,* which
70 originated in India and also combines stretching, coordination, balance, and meditation, is even more widely practiced. Both are excellent for improving flexibility. Many factory workers in the United

FIGURE 1-1 | Stretching exercises to improve flexibility

Use these general-purpose stretching techniques as part of your warm-up and cool-down. Hold
each stretch for at least 10 seconds, and repeat four times on each limb. After only a few weeks
of regular stretching, you'll begin to see improvements. (Drawings adapted from *Stretching, 20th
Anniversary Edition* by Bob Anderson, illustrated by Jean Anderson.)

Sel.
1

States now begin their workdays with simple forms of flexibility exercises, a concept introduced from Japan.

Improving Muscular Strength and Endurance

75   *Muscular strength* refers to the amount of force a muscle is capable of exerting. The most common way to assess strength in a resistance exercise program is to measure the maximum amount of weight you can lift one time. This value is known as the *one repetition maximum* and is abbreviated *IRM. Muscular endurance* is defined as a mus-
80 cle's ability to exert force repeatedly without fatiguing. The more repetitions of a certain resistance exercise you can perform successfully (e.g., a bench press of one half your body weight), the greater your muscular endurance.

Principles of Strength Development

    There are three key principles to understand if you intend to
85 maximize muscular strength and endurance benefits from your *resistance exercise program*. Unless you follow these principles, you are likely to be disappointed in the results of your program.

    The Tension Principle. The key to developing strength is to create tension within a muscle. The more tension you can create in a
90 muscle, the greater your strength gain will be. The most common recreational way to create tension in a muscle is by lifting weights. While weight lifting is one method of producing tension in a muscle, any activity that creates muscle tension—for example, riding a bike up a hill—will result in greater strength. It really does not matter
95 what type of equipment you choose to develop tension in your muscles; what matters is that you use the equipment in a way that produces the desired strength and endurance.

    The Overload Principle. The overload principle is the most important of the three key principles for improving muscular strength.
100 Everyone begins a resistance training program with an initial level of strength. To increase that level of strength, you must regularly create a degree of tension in your muscles that is greater than they are accustomed to. This overloading of your muscles will cause your muscles to adapt to the new level of overload. As your muscles respond to
105 a regular program of overloading by getting larger (*hypertrophy*), they become capable of generating more tension. Figure 1-2 illustrates how a continual process of overload and adaptation to the overload improves strength.

    Some women avoid resistance exercise because they fear that
110 they'll develop large "bulky" muscles, while others are frustrated because their weight-lifting efforts in the gym don't produce the results they see in their male friends. The main reason for this difference is the hormone *testosterone*. Before puberty, testosterone levels in blood are similar for both boys and girls. During adolescence,

FIGURE 1-2 | The overload principle

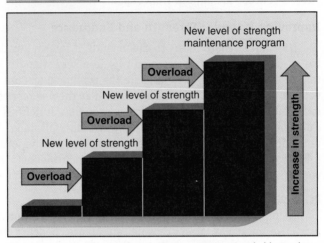

The overload principle contributes to an increase in strength. Notice that once the muscle has adapted to the original overload, a new overload must be placed on the muscle for subsequent strength gains to occur. (From *One Rep Max: A Guide to Beginning Weight Training* by Phillip A. Sienna.)

115   testosterone in men increases about tenfold to its adult level; testosterone in women remains at prepubertal levels throughout adulthood. Women's muscles will achieve hypertrophy from regular exercise but typically not to the same degree as in adult males. Using the exceptional muscular development of elite female body-builders as
120   our example, we know that considerable muscle hypertrophy is possible among women. Most likely, many of these women used anabolic steroids to increase their muscle mass and development. The difference in maximum attainable hypertrophy between men and women (without the aid of anabolic steroids) is not currently known.

125   ***The Specificity of Training Principle.*** This principle refers to the manner in which a specific body system responds to the physiological demands placed upon it. According to the specificity principle, the effects of resistance exercise training are specific to the area of the body being exercised. If the overload you impose is designed to improve
130   strength in the muscles of your chest and back, the response to that demand (overload) will be improved strength in those muscles only.

(1,356 words)

—Rebecca J. Donatelle, *Access to Health*, 7th ed.

Comprehension Questions. After reading the selection, answer the following questions with *a, b, c,* or *d.*

Main Idea

_____ 1. The best statement of the main idea of this selection is
   a. Eat less to keep fit.
   b. Exercise to keep fit.
   c. Exercise seems to keep away diseases.
   d. Walking is the best exercise.

_____ 2. The main idea of the third paragraph ("A century ago ... ") is
   a. Labor was physical and thus keeping fit was not an issue 100 years ago.
   b. Only 40% of the population engaged in regular physical activity.
   c. Americans need physical labor to remain healthy.
   d. Americans were healthier 100 years ago.

_____ 3. The main idea of the fourth paragraph ("Most people would agree ... ") is
   a. The average life expectancy in 1900 was 38 years of age.
   b. Health costs have increased because Americans are sick and living longer.
   c. Since the early 1900s, both life expectancy and chronic diseases have dramatically increased.
   d. Heart disease and diabetes are the number one health risks in the United States.

_____ 4. The main idea of the last paragraph ("This principle refers ... ") is
   a. The muscles of the body respond to overload.
   b. Training is improved if a specific muscle is targeted.
   c. If you are properly exercising specific muscles, strength in those muscles will increase.
   d. Resistance exercises meet specific training needs better than overload exercises.

_____ 5. In supporting the main idea of improving flexibility through certain exercises, Tai Chi and Yoga are
   a. major details.
   b. minor details.

Details

_____ 6. According to the Centers for Disease Control
   a. 40% of Americans exercise enough.
   b. 25% of Americans exercise enough.
   c. 85% of Americans do not exercise enough.
   d. 60% of Americans do not exercise enough.

_____ 7. Cardiorespiratory fitness refers to all of the following except
a. jumping.
b. running.
c. lifting weights.
d. skating.

_____ 8. The greater number of times you can lift a weight is technically described as
a. flexibility.
b. muscular strength.
c. muscular endurance.
d. hypertrophy.

**Sel.
1**

_____ 9. Women in resistance training do not develop the large "bulky" muscles of men primarily because women
a. lift lighter weights.
b. have lower testosterone levels.
c. do not experience hypertrophy after adolescence.
d. are not affected by anabolic steroids.

Inference

_____ 10. The primary purpose of the opening paragraph about Shawn is
a. to suggest that physical education should begin in high school.
b. to heighten interest and relate the issues to a college student.
c. to show that nutrition plays a part in physical fitness.
d. to argue that the car and the computer work against physical fitness.

_____ 11. The reader can conclude all of the following except
a. effective flexibility exercises should include meditation.
b. the ability to use oxygen is a positive factor in building physical fitness.
c. a level of muscle strain is involved in the overload principle.
d. People today are living longer than in 1900 and thus the 30 times increased frequency of heart disease-related deaths may be affected by age.

_____ 12. The statement that "Tai chi is an ancient Chinese form of exercise that combines stretching, balance, coordination, and meditation" is
a. fact.
b. opinion.

_____ **13.** The pattern of organization in the last section under "Principles of Strength Development" is
 a. definition and example.
 b. simple listing.
 c. cause and effect.
 d. comparison and contrast.

_____ **14.** The primary purpose of this selection is to
 a. entertain.
 b. educate.
 c. narrate.
 d. condemn.

_____ **15.** The reader can conclude that in order to most efficiently increase flexibility and muscular strength, you should
 a. jog and lift weights.
 b. do yoga and swim.
 c. do tai chi and walk.
 d. do yoga and lift weights.

Vocabulary. Use sentence context clues and word parts to select meaning for boldfaced words. Indicate *a, b, c,* or *d* for the 1–5 and insert a written response for 6–10.

_____ **1.** "In the new **millennium**, leisure time is plentiful . . . "
 a. ten years
 b. fifty years
 c. hundred years
 d. thousand years

_____ **2.** "respiratory systems to supply oxygen during **sustained** physical activity . . . "
 a. heavy
 b. strenuous
 c. prolonged
 d. moderate

_____ **3.** "stretching exercises will **enhance** your efficiency of movement . . . "
 a. improve
 b. lessen
 c. restrict
 d. satisfy

_____ 4. "Muscular strength refers to the amount of force a muscle is capable of **exerting**."
   a. increasing
   b. feeling
   c. changing
   d. using

_____ 5. "the exceptional development of **elite** female body-builders . . ."
   a. thin
   b. heavy
   c. top ranked
   d. muscular

6. The slang phrase **couch potato** means _____

_____

7. From the context in the fourth paragraph, the reader can conclude

that the word **paradoxically** means _____

_____

8. As in **hypertrophy**, the prefix of **hyperactivity** means _____

_____

9. What does **cardio** mean in **cardiorespiratory**? _____

10. The bottom of a coffee cup may contain some sediment of coffee grinds. What does the word **sediment** mean and how does it relate

to **sedentary**? _____

_____

Your instructor may choose to give you a true–false comprehension and vocabulary review.

Think and Write

1. Experts recommend 30 minutes of moderate-intensity activity each day? How do you measure up? How can you incorporate 30 minutes of exercise into your daily schedule? What is your plan for cardiorespiratory, flexibility and muscular fitness?

2. Why have Americans become more sedentary? What environmental factors work against us getting physical activity?

3. What are the hidden costs of a nation that is out of shape? Should the government become involved in encouraging fitness? If so, how?

Net Search. You probably know someone who has had breast, colon, or prostate cancer. Explore the research on the benefits of exercise in cancer recovery and prevention. List five compelling statistical facts that you discover about the relationship of exercise and cancer that might persuade someone to exercise regularly.

Sel.
1

Selection 2 History

The 1920s were a time of prosperity in the United States. Government had a hands-off attitude, and businesses boomed. The United States was producing more electricity than the rest of the world combined, and industrial output doubled. Inventions and technological advances led to improved products such as radios, refrigerators, and vacuum cleaners. Producers made their products more attractive and advertisers created new demands. The automobile fueled growth, and daring aviation feats caught national attention. In the following textbook selection, historian and Columbia University Professor John Garraty shows how the new products and prosperity influenced economic expansion in *The American Nation*.

The "New Era" of the 1920s

Despite the turmoil of the times and the dissatisfactions expressed by some of the nation's best minds, the 1920s were an exceptionally prosperous decade. Business boomed, real wages rose, and unemployment declined. The United States was as rich as all Europe;
5   perhaps 40 percent of the world's total wealth lay in American hands. Little wonder that business leaders and other conservatives described the period as a "New Era."

Undoubtedly the automobile had the single most important impact on the nation's economy in the twenties. The auto industry created industries that manufactured tires and spark plugs and other products. It consumed immense quantities of rubber, paint, glass, nickel, and petroleum products. It triggered a gigantic road-building program. Thousands found employment in filling stations, roadside stands, and other businesses catering to the motoring public. The tourist industry profited, and the shift of population from the cities to the suburbs was accelerated.

Henry Ford

The person most responsible for the growth of the automobile industry was Henry Ford, a self-taught mechanic from Greenfield, Michigan. In 1908 he designed the Model T Ford, a simple, tough box on wheels. In a year he sold 11,000 Model Ts. Thereafter, relentlessly cutting costs and increasing efficiency by installing the assembly-line system, he expanded production at an unbelievable rate. By 1925 he was turning out more than 9,000 cars a day, one approximately every ten seconds, and the price of the Model T had been reduced to below $300.

Ford's profits soared along with sales; since he owned the entire company, he became a billionaire. He also became an authentic folk hero: His homespun style, his dislike of bankers and sophisticated society, and his intense individualism endeared him to millions. He stood as a symbol of the wonders of the American system—he had given the nation a marvelous convenience at a low price, at the same time enriching himself and raising the living standards of his thousands of employees.

Unfortunately, Ford had the defects of his virtues in full measure. He paid high wages but refused to deal with any union. When he discovered a worker driving any car but a Ford, he had him dismissed.

Success made Ford stubborn. The Model T remained essentially unchanged for nearly 20 years. Other companies, notably General Motors, were soon turning out better vehicles for very little more money. Customers, increasingly affluent and style-conscious, began to shift to Chevrolets and Chryslers. Although his company continued to make a great deal of money, Ford never regained the dominant position he had held for so long.

The Airplane

Henry Ford also manufactured airplanes, and although the airplane industry was not economically important in the 1920s, its development led to changes in lifestyles and attitudes at least as important as those produced by automobiles. The internal combustion gasoline engine with its high ratio of power to weight made the airplane possible, which explains why the first "flying machines" and

Sel.
2

50 "gas buggies" were built at about the same time. Wilbur and Orville Wright made their famous flight at Kitty Hawk, North Carolina, in 1903, five years before Ford produced his Model T. Another pair of brothers, Malcolm and Haimes Lockheed, built one of the earliest commercial airplanes (they used it to take passengers up at five dol-
55 lars a ride) in 1913.

The great event of the decade for aviation, still an achievement that must strike awe in the hearts of reflective persons, was Charles A. Lindbergh's nonstop flight from New York to Paris in May 1927. It took more than 33 hours for Lindbergh's single-engine *Spirit of St.*
60 *Louis* to cross the Atlantic, a formidable physical achievement for the pilot as well as an example of skill and courage. When the public learned that the intrepid "Lucky Lindy" was handsome, modest, un-interested in converting his new fame into cash, and a model of pro-priety (he neither drank nor smoked), his role as American hero was
65 assured. It was a role Lindbergh detested—one biographer has de-scribed him as "by nature solitary"—but could not avoid.

Lindbergh's flight enormously increased public interest in flying, but it was a landmark in aviation technology as well. The day of rou-tine passenger flights was at last about to dawn. Two months after the
70 *Spirit of St. Louis* touched down in France, William E. Boeing of Boeing Air Transport began flying passengers and mail between San Francisco and Chicago, using a plane of his own design and manufacture.

In retrospect the postwar era seems even more a period of tran-sition than it appeared at the time. Rarely had change come so
75 swiftly, and rarely had old and new existed side by side in such profusion.

(777 words)

—John Garraty, *The American Nation*, 8th ed.

Comprehension Questions.   After reading the selection, answer the following questions with *a, b, c,* or *d.*

Main Idea

_____ **1.** The best statement of the main idea of this selection is
   a. In the "New Era" of the 1920s wages rose and unemploy-ment declined.
   b. The "New Era" of the 1920s was a business boom and a time of change driven by the automobile.
   c. Business leaders described the period as the "New Era" of the 1920s.
   d. In the "New Era" of the 1920s the United States had 40 percent of the world's wealth.

_____ 2. The main idea of the second paragraph is
    a. The auto industry created industries that manufactured tires and spark plugs.
    b. The auto industry triggered a gigantic road-building program.
    c. The auto industry caused a shift in population to the suburbs.
    d. The automobile had the single most important impact on the nation's economy in the twenties.

_____ 3. The main idea of the third paragraph is
    a. The person most responsible for the growth of the automobile industry was Henry Ford.
    b. The Model T Ford was a simple box on wheels.
    c. Henry Ford was a self-taught mechanic.
    d. Henry Ford worked to reduce the cost of the Model T to below $300.

_____ 4. The main idea of the seventh paragraph (begins "Henry Ford also manufactured") is
    a. The Wright bothers made their first flight at Kitty Hawk in 1903.
    b. The Lockheed brothers built one of the first commercial airplanes.
    c. Significant events led to the development of the airplane, which spurred important changes in lifestyles and attitudes.
    d. Henry Ford manufactured airplanes as well as automobiles.

_____ 5. The main idea of the eighth paragraph (begins "The great event") is
    a. Lindbergh was nicknamed "Lucky Lindy" for his brave achievement.
    b. Lindbergh embraced his role as national hero.
    c. Lindbergh's nonstop flight was filled with dangers, isolation, and conflict.
    d. The appealing Lindbergh's first nonstop flight from New York to Paris was the great event of the decade in aviation.

Details

_____ 6. All of the following are true about the Model T Ford except
    a. the cost went below $300.
    b. an assembly-line system of union workers built the car.
    c. 9,000 cars were produced a day.
    d. one car was produced every 10 seconds.

Sel.
2

_____ 7. According to the author, the Model T Ford lost its dominant
position in the auto industry because
a. Ford was stubborn and would not change.
b. Chevrolet and Chrysler were building autos for a lower
price.
c. General Motors built smaller and more fuel-efficient
cars.
d. Fords were not as fuel-efficient as Chevrolet and Chrysler.

_____ 8. According to the author, airplane flights were made possible
by
a. a low ratio of power to weight.
b. the Lockheed brothers.
c. the internal combustion gasoline engine.
d. Henry Ford's manufacturing of airplanes.

_____ 9. Charles Lindbergh is described as being all of the following
except
a. handsome.
b. eager to made money from his new fame.
c. nonsmoking.
d. courageous.

_____ 10. Passenger and mail flights began
a. with routes to San Francisco, Chicago, and France.
b. when the first Boeing aircraft was built.
c. on the day "Lucky Lindy" became a national hero.
d. two months after Lindbergh's historic flight.

Inference

_____ 11. Readers can infer that the auto had the single most
important impact on the nation's economy in the twenties
because
a. its manufacture and popularity started other businesses.
b. people could move to the suburbs.
c. wealthy Americans were ready to spend money on
technology.
d. 40 percent of Americans could afford to buy an
automobile.

_____ 12. The only statement of fact among the following is
a. It trigged a gigantic road-building program.
b. His intense individualism endeared him to millions.
c. He paid high wages.
d. When he discovered a worker driving any car but a Ford,
he had him dismissed.

Sel.
2

_____ **13.** The overall pattern of organization of this selection is
   a. comparison and contrast.
   b. classification.
   c. cause and effect.
   d. definition and examples.

_____ **14.** The author's tone in the eighth paragraph (begins "The great event") is
   a. arrogant.
   b. respectful.
   c. angry.
   d. pessimistic.

_____ **15.** The purpose of this selection is
   a. to argue.
   b. to entertain.
   c. to narrate.
   d. to educate.

Vocabulary.   Use sentence context clues and word parts to select the correct meaning of boldfaced words. Indicate *a, b, c,* or *d* for items 1–5 and respond in your own words to items 6–10.

_____ **1.** "The 1920s were an exceptionally **prosperous** decade."
   a. entertaining
   b. energetic
   c. wealthy
   d. promising

_____ **2.** "He also became an **authentic** folk hero"
   a. genuine
   b. humorous
   c. rich
   d. handsome

_____ **3.** "Still an achievement that must strike **awe** in the hearts of reflective persons."
   a. relief
   b. love
   c. jealousy
   d. wonder

_____ **4.** "To cross the Atlantic, a **formidable** physical achievement for a pilot"
   a. welcoming
   b. challenging
   c. unbelievable
   d. responsible

_____ 5. "It was a role Lindbergh **detested**."
  a. hated
  b. wanted
  c. played
  d. disguised

6. **Homespun,** as in "His homespun style," is a colloquial or invented word. What does it mean? It means _____.

7. What two suffixes have been added to form **relentlessly** in "relentlessly cutting costs"? What does the word mean? _____

_____

8. What is the suffix in **individualism,** as in "his intense individualism endeared him to millions"? What does the word mean? _____

_____

_____

Sel.
2

9. Lindbergh was described as "by nature solitary." What word is derived from the same root and denotes a card game that you play by yourself? _____

10. In "The day of routine passenger flights was at last about to dawn," what other meaning can the word **dawn** have? _____

_____

Your instructor may choose to give you a true–false comprehension and vocabulary review.

Think and Write.

1. How were Ford and Lindbergh nationally popular in different ways?
2. Although it is not stated, what have been the economic effects of the development of commercial aviation?
3. Similar to the impact of the automobile and the airplane, what new technology is generating massive social and economic change today? What are those far-reaching changes?

Net Search. Charles Lindberg was a greatly beloved and respected national hero. After his historic transatlantic flight, multimillionaire Harry Guggenheim sponsored Lindberg on a popular three-month tour of the United States to promote aviation. Later, on a goodwill trip to Mexico, Lindbergh met and married Anne Morrow, the American ambassador's daughter. He taught Anne to fly, and the adventurous couple chartered new airline routes throughout the world. The Lindbergs had two sons. Unfortunately, tragedy struck this happy family. Search the Internet for details in the disappearance of Charles Augustus Lindberg, Jr. Summarize the unfortunate events.

Selection 3 Essay

What excuses have you heard students offer for missing assignments and late work? Can the excuses be proven? Have you ever given an excuse that was less than truthful? Do you think teachers believe or disbelieve the excuses? Once I had a student who missed class to go to Florida because his grandfather was hospitalized and perhaps dying. Later the grandfather died and the student missed several classes in order to accompany the body back from Florida to Atlanta. The following essay by Carolyn Foster Segal, an English professor at Cedar Crest College in Allentown, Pennsylvania, addresses such excuses. The essay was first published in the *Chronicle of Higher Education,* a newspaper for college faculty and administrators in 2000.

The Dog Ate My Disk, and Other Tales of Woe

Taped to the door of my office is a cartoon that features a cat explaining to his feline teacher, "The dog ate my homework." It is in-

tended as a gently humorous reminder to my students that I will not accept excuses for late work, and it, like the lengthy warning on my
5 syllabus, has had absolutely no effect. With a show of energy and creativity that would be admirable if applied to the (missing) assignments in question, my students persist, week after week, semester after semester, year after year, in offering excuses about why their work is not ready. Those reasons fall into several broad categories:
10 the family, the best friend, the evils of dorm life, the evils of technology, and the totally bizarre.

The Family

The death of the grandfather/grandmother is, of course, the grandmother of all excuses. What heartless teacher would dare to question a student's grief or veracity? What heartless student would
15 lie, wishing death on a revered family member, just to avoid a deadline? Creative students may win extra extensions (and days off) with a little careful planning and fuller plot development, as in the sequence of "My grandfather/grandmother is sick"; "Now my grandfather/grandmother is in the hospital"; and finally "We could all see it
20 coming—my grandfather/grandmother is dead."

Another favorite excuse is "the family emergency." Which (always) goes like this: "There was an emergency at home, and I had to help my family." It's a lovely sentiment, one that conjures up images of Louisa May Alcott's little women rushing off with baskets of food
25 and copies of *Pilgrim's Progress*, but I do not understand why anyone would turn to my more irresponsible students in times of trouble.

The Best Friend

This heartwarming concern for others extends beyond the family to friends, as in, "My best friend was up all night and I had to (a) stay up with her in the dorm, (b) drive her to the hospital, or (c)
30 drive to her college because (1) her boyfriend broke up with her, (2) she was throwing up blood [no one catches a cold anymore; everyone throws up blood], or (3) her grandfather/grandmother died."

At one private university where I worked as an adjunct, I heard an interesting spin that incorporated the motifs of both best friend
35 and dead relative: "My best friend's mother killed herself." One has to admire the cleverness here: A mysterious woman in the prime of her life has allegedly committed suicide, and no professor can prove otherwise! And I admit I was moved, until finally I had to point out to my students that it was amazing how the simple act of my assign-
40 ing a topic for a paper seemed to drive large numbers of otherwise happy and healthy middle-aged women to their deaths. I was careful to make that point during an off week, during which no deaths were reported.

The Evils of Dorm Life

These stories are usually fairly predictable; almost always feature
45 the evil roommate or hallmate, with my student in the role of the innocent victim; and can be summed up as follows: My roommate, who
is a horrible person, likes to party, and I, who am a good person, cannot concentrate on my work when he or she is partying. Variations
include stories about the two people next door who were running
50 around and crying loudly last night because (a) one of them had
boyfriend/girlfriend problems; (b) one of them was throwing up
blood; or (c) someone, somewhere, died. A friend of mine in graduate
school had a student who claimed that his roommate attacked him
with a hammer. That, in fact, was a true story; it came out in court
55 when the bad roommate was tried for killing his grandfather.

The Evils of Technology

The computer age has revolutionized the student story, inspiring
almost as many new excuses as it has Internet business. Here are just
a few electronically enhanced explanations:

- The computer wouldn't let me save my work.
60 - The printer wouldn't print.
- The printer wouldn't print this disk.
- The printer wouldn't give me time to proofread.
- The printer made a black line run through all my words, and I
  know you can't read this, but do you still want it, or wait, here,
65   take my disk. File name? I don't know what you mean.
- I swear I attached it.
- It's my roommate's computer, and she usually helps me, but she
  had to go to the hospital because she was throwing up blood.
- I did write to the newsgroup, but all my messages came back to me.
70 - I just found out that all my other newsgroup messages came up
  under a diferent name. I just want you to know that its really me
  who wrote all those messages, you can tel which ones our mine
  because I didn't use the spelcheck! But it was ours truly :)
  Anyway, just in case you missed thos messages or don't belief its
75   my writing, I'll repeat what I said: I thought the last movie we
  watched in clas was boring.

The Totally Bizarre

I call the first story "The Pennsylvania Chain Saw Episode." A
commuter student called to explain why she had missed my morning class. She had gotten up early so that she would be wide awake
80 for class. Having a bit of extra time, she walked outside to see her
neighbor, who was cutting some wood. She called out to him, and
he waved back to her with the saw. Wouldn't you know it, the

safety catch wasn't on or was broken, and the blade flew right out
of the saw and across his lawn and over her fence and across her
85 yard and severed a tendon in her right hand. So she was calling
me from the hospital, where she was waiting for surgery. Luckily,
she reassured me, she had remembered to bring her paper and a
stamped envelope (in a plastic bag, to avoid bloodstains) along
with her in the ambulance, and a nurse was mailing everything to
90 me even as we spoke.

That wasn't her first absence. In fact, this student has missed
most of the class meetings, and I had already recommended that she
withdraw from the course. Now I suggested again that it might be
best if she dropped the class. I didn't harp on the absences (what if
95 even some of this story were true?). I did mention that she would
need time to recuperate and that making up so much missed work
might be difficult. "Oh, no," she said, "I can't drop this course. I had
been planning to go on to medical school and become a surgeon, but
since I won't be able to operate because of my accident, I'll have to
100 major in English, and this course is more important than ever to me."
She did come to the next class, wearing—as evidence of her recent
trauma—a bedraggled Ace bandage on her left hand.

You may be thinking that nothing could top that excuse, but in
fact I have one more story, provided by the same student, who sent
105 me a letter to explain why her final assignment would be late.
While recuperating from her surgery, she had begun corresponding
on the Internet with a man who lived in Germany. After a one-week,
whirlwind Web romance, they had agreed to meet in Rome, to rendezvous (her phrase) at the papal Easter Mass. Regrettably, the time
110 of her flight made it impossible for her to attend class, but she
trusted that I—just this once—would accept late work if the pope
wrote a note.

(1,278 words)

—Carol Foster Segal, The Chronicle of Higher Education.

Comprehension Questions. After reading the selection, answer the
following questions with *a, b, c,* or *d.*

Main Idea

_____ **1.** The best statement of the main idea of this selection is
   a. Students have hardships that require sympathy.
   b. Teachers do not show enough sympathy for students.
   c. Students offer predictable excuses for missing assign-
      ments that are unbelievable.
   d. Family and friends frequently interfere with students'
      meeting their assignment demands.

_____ 2. The main idea of the paragraph titled "The Evils of Dorm Life" is
   a. The student missing the assignment is the innocent victim of another evil student.
   b. Campus partying interferes with completing assignments.
   c. Little can be done to escape the conflicts of dorm life.
   d. True stories can sometimes pop up among the dishonest excuses.

_____ 3. The main idea of the paragraph titled "The Evils of Technology" is
   a. No work could be done on the assignment because of a machine.
   b. Technology prevents students from achieving.
   c. The Internet has both advantages and disadvantages for completing assignments.
   d. Students blame technology for preventing proper delivery of the completed assignment.

_____ 4. The main idea of the essay is best inferred from the
   a. first paragraph.
   b. second paragraph.
   c. third paragraph.
   d. last paragraph.

Details

_____ 5. The number of excuse categories the author describes is
   a. three.
   b. four.
   c. five.
   d. six.

_____ 6. The author's policy for not accepting late work is
   a. discussed in class but not stated.
   b. stated in the syllabus.
   c. suggested by a cartoon but not stated.
   d. considered unfair by college administrators.

_____ 7. The author told students of her concern that her assignments were killing off happy middle-aged women
   a. immediately after hearing of an alleged suicide as an excuse.
   b. on the first day of class before excuses were offered.
   c. during a week when no deaths were reported.
   d. during the week prior to exams.

_____ **8.** The only excuse that the author acknowledges as true is
   a. "The Pennsylvania Chain Saw Episode."
   b. the Easter Mass in Rome story.
   c. the roommate throwing up blood story.
   d. the roommate attacked me with a hammer story.

_____ **9.** Although several patterns are used, the overall pattern of organization for this essay is
   a. cause and effect.
   b. simple listing.
   c. time order.
   d. comparison and contrast.

_____ **10.** All of the following were reported about the student who used "The Pennsylvania Chain Saw Episode" as an excuse except
   a. she was a commuter student.
   b. she was planning on becoming a surgeon.
   c. she went to Rome to meet a man from Germany.
   d. the pope wrote her an excuse for the late paper.

Inference

_____ **11.** The reader can infer that the author repeats the excuse that a grandparent died several times because it is
   a. the most overused and least believed excuse.
   b. the most likely to actually happen and prevent work.
   c. the most creative.
   d. the most bizarre and least expected.

_____ **12.** By saying, "With a show of energy and creativity that would be admirable if applied to the (missing) assignments in question, my students persist," the author implies all of the following except
   a. her students have worked hard on creating interesting excuses.
   b. she would have liked that much energy and creativity applied to the assignment.
   c. she admires the energetic and creative excuses from students.
   d. admirable students complete assignments without excuses.

_____ **13.** The tone of this essay is
   a. sympathetic.
   b. angry.
   c. humorous.
   d. formal.

_____ **14.** The primary audience for whom the author is writing is
a. students.
b. teachers.
c. parents.
d. taxpayers.

_____ **15.** "The death of the grandfather/grandmother is, of course, the grandmother of all excuses" is a statement of
a. fact.
b. opinion.

Vocabulary. Use sentence context clues and word parts to select the correct meaning of boldfaced words. Indicate *a, b, c,* or *d* for items 1–5 and respond in your own words to items 6–10.

_____ **1.** "Taped to the door of my office is a cartoon that features a cat explaining to his **feline** teacher, 'The dog ate my homework.'"
a. strong
b. catlike
c. puzzled
d. ugly

_____ **2.** "At one private university where I worked as an **adjunct**"
a. teacher's aide
b. substitute teacher
c. full-time professor
d. part-time instructor

_____ **3.** "A mysterious woman in the prime of her life has **allegedly** committed suicide"
a. supposedly
b. certainly
c. suddenly
d. unluckily

_____ **4.** "I did mention that she would need time to **recuperate**."
a. feel guilty
b. recover wellness
c. learn to be honest
d. return to class

_____ **5.** "After a one-week, whirlwind Web romance, they had agreed to meet in Rome, to **rendezvous** (her phrase) at the papal Easter Mass." (corrected spelling)
a. pray
b. entertain
c. wed
d. meet

6. What is the suffix and meaning of *heartless* as used in "What **heartless** teacher would dare to question a student's grief?" _____

_____

7. What are the two suffixes in *truthfulness* as used in "What heartless teacher would dare to question a student's grief and **truthfulness?**"

_____

8. What is the prefix and meaning of *irresponsible* as used in "I do not understand why anyone would turn to my most **irresponsible** students in times of trouble"? _____

9 What is the root and meaning of *revolutionized* as used in "The computer has **revolutionized** the student story"? _____

_____

10. What is the meaning of *harp* in "I didn't **harp** on the absences," and what is another meaning of *harp?* _____

_____

Your instructor may choose to give you a true–false comprehension and vocabulary review.

**Sel.
3**

Think and Write

1. Explain what the title of the essay means and why the cartoon caption is humorous. How does the title set the tone for the essay?
2. How does the writing style of the author add to your enjoyment of the essay? Why does the author misspell words in the last bulleted item on the evils of technology and repeat certain excuses? Why is her multiple-choice format particularly entertaining? How does the author avoid "preaching and teaching"?
3. Why do students enter college expecting that late work will be accepted and excuses for missing assignments will be believed? How do you think professors should handle late work in their courses?

Net Search. Is there truth in the essay or has the author totally exaggerated? The missing homework excuse has long been a popular subject for humorists. Search the Internet for other excuses. List five of your favorites to share with classmates.

Selection 4 Short Story

Do you remember your first weeks of school? Did you have an easy time or did you have trouble adjusting? Were your parents concerned and involved in your schooling? Did your parents frequently communicate with your teacher? Think of your own reactions to settling down to the expectations of classroom learning as you read the following story written in 1948. The author, Shirley Jackson, is a master of surprise and has written numerous novels and short stories. You may have also read her famous story, "The Lottery," in which being the winner in a small New England town has an unexpected negative twist.

Charles

The day my son Laurie started kindergarten he gave up corduroy overalls with bibs and began wearing blue jeans with a belt. I watched him go off the first morning with the older girl next door, seeing clearly that an era of my life was ended. My sweet-voiced
5 nursery-school tot was replaced by a long-trousered, swaggering character who forgot to stop at the corner and wave good-bye to me.

He came home the same way, the front door slamming open, his cap on the floor, and the voice suddenly become raucous shouting, "Isn't anybody *here*?"

10   At lunch he spoke rudely to his father, spilled his baby sister's milk, and remarked that his teacher said we were not to take the name of the Lord in vain.

"How *was* school today?" I asked, elaborately casual.

"All right," he said.

15   "Did you learn anything?" his father asked.

Laurie regarded his father coldly.

"I didn't learn nothing," he said.

"Anything," I said. "Didn't learn anything."

"The teacher spanked a boy, though," Laurie said, addressing his 20 bread and butter. "For being fresh," he added, with his mouth full.

"What did he do?" I asked. "Who was it?"

Laurie thought. "It was Charles," he said. "He was fresh. The teacher spanked him and made him stand in a corner. He was awfully fresh."

25   "What did he do?" I asked again, but Laurie slid off his chair, took a cookie, and left, while his father was still saying, "See here, young man."

The next day Laurie remarked at lunch, as soon as he sat down, "Well, Charles was bad again today." He grinned enormously and 30 said, "Today Charles hit the teacher."

"Good heavens," I said, mindful of the Lord's name, "I suppose he got spanked again?"

"He sure did," Laurie said. "Look up," he said to his father.

"What?" his father said, looking up.

35   "Look down," Laurie said. "Look at my thumb. Gee, you're dumb." He began to laugh insanely.

"Why did Charles hit the teacher?" I asked quickly.

"Because she tried to make him color with red crayons," Laurie said. "Charles wanted to color with green crayons so he hit the 40 teacher and she spanked him and said nobody play with Charles but everybody did."

The third day—it was Wednesday of the first week—Charles bounced a see-saw onto the head of a little girl and made her bleed, and the teacher made him stay inside all during recess. Thursday 45 Charles had to stand in a corner during story-time because he kept pounding his feet on the floor. Friday Charles was deprived of black-board privileges because he threw chalk.

On Saturday I remarked to my husband, "Do you think kinder-garten is too unsettling for Laurie? All this toughness, and bad gram- 50 mar, and this Charles boy sounds like such a bad influence."

"It'll be all right," my husband said reassuringly. "Bound to be people like Charles in the world. Might as well meet them now as later."

On Monday Laurie came home late, full of news. "Charles," he shouted as he came up the hill; I was waiting anxiously on the front steps. "Charles," Laurie yelled all the way up the hill, "Charles was bad again."

"Come right in," I said, as soon as he came close enough. "Lunch is waiting."

"You know what Charles did?" he demanded, following me through the door. "Charles yelled so in school they sent a boy in from first grade to tell the teacher she had to make Charles keep quiet, and so Charles had to stay after school. And so all the children stayed to watch him."

"What did he do?" I asked.

"He just sat there," Laurie said, climbing into his chair at the table. "Hi, Pop, y'old dust mop."

"Charles had to stay after school today," I told my husband. "Everyone stayed with him."

"What does Charles look like?" my husband asked Laurie. "What's his other name?"

"He's bigger than me," Laurie said. "And he doesn't have any rubbers and he doesn't ever wear a jacket."

Monday night was the first Parent-Teachers meeting, and only the fact that the baby had a cold kept me from going; I wanted passionately to meet Charles's mother. On Tuesday Laurie remarked suddenly, "Our teacher had a friend come to see her in school today."

"Charles's mother?" my husband and I asked simultaneously.

"Naaah," Laurie said scornfully. "It was a man who came and made us do exercises, we had to touch our toes. Look." He climbed down from his chair and squatted down and touched his toes. "Like this," he said. He got solemnly back into his chair and said, picking up his fork, "Charles didn't even *do* exercises."

"That's fine," I said heartily. "Didn't Charles want to do exercises?"

"Naaah," Laurie said. "Charles was so fresh to the teacher's friend he wasn't *let* to do exercises."

"Fresh again?" I said.

"He kicked the teacher's friend," Laurie said. "The teacher's friend told Charles to touch his toes like I just did and Charles kicked him."

"What are they going to do about Charles, do you suppose?" Laurie's father asked him.

Laurie shrugged elaborately. "Throw him out of school, I guess," he said.

Wednesday and Thursday were routine; Charles yelled during story hour and hit a boy in the stomach and made him cry. On Friday Charles stayed after school again and so did all the other children.

With the third week of kindergarten Charles was an institution in our family; the baby was being a Charles when she cried all afternoon;
100 Laurie did a Charles when he filled his wagon full of mud and pulled it through the kitchen; even my husband, when he caught his elbow in the telephone cord and pulled telephone, ashtray, and a bowl of flowers off the table, said, after the first minute, "Looks like Charles."

During the third and fourth weeks it looked like a reformation in
105 Charles; Laurie reported grimly at lunch on Thursday of the third week, "Charles was so good today the teacher gave him an apple."

"What?" I said, and my husband added warily, "You mean Charles?"

"Charles," Laurie said. "He gave the crayons around and he
110 picked up the books afterward and the teacher said he was her helper."

"What happened?" I asked incredulously.

"He was her helper, that's all," Laurie asked, and shrugged.

"Can this be true, about Charles?" I asked my husband that
115 night. "Can something like this happen?"

"Wait and see," my husband said distrustfully. "When you've got a Charles to deal with, this may mean he's only plotting."

He seemed to be wrong. For over a week Charles was the teacher's helper; each day he handed things out and he picked things
120 up; no one had to stay after school.

"The P.T.A. meeting's next week again," I told my husband one evening. "I'm going to find Charles's mother there."

"Ask her what happened to Charles," my husband said. "I'd like to know."

125 "I'd like to know myself," I said.

On Friday of that week things were back to normal. "You know what Charles did today?" Laurie demanded at the lunch table, in a voice slightly awed. "He told a little girl to say a word and she said it and the teacher washed her mouth out with soap and Charles
130 laughed."

"What word?" his father asked unwisely, and Laurie said, "I'll have to whisper it to you, it's so bad." He got down off his chair and went around to his father. His father bent his head down and Laurie whispered joyfully. His father's eyes widened.

135 "Did Charles tell the little girl to say *that*?" he asked respectfully.

"She said it *twice*," Laurie said. "He was passing out the crayons."

Monday morning Charles abandoned the little girl and said the
140 evil word himself three or four times, getting his mouth washed out with soap each time. He also threw chalk.

Sel.
4

My husband came to the door with me that evening as I set out for the P.T.A. meeting. "Invite her over for a cup of tea after the meeting," he said. "I want to get a look at her."

145 "If only she's there," I said prayerfully.

"She'll be there," my husband said. "I don't see how they could hold a P.T.A. meeting without Charles's mother."

At the meeting I sat restlessly, scanning each comfortable matronly face, trying to determine which one hid the secret of Charles.

150 None of them looked to me haggard enough. No one stood up in the meeting and apologized for the way her son had been acting. No one mentioned Charles.

After the meeting I identified and sought out Laurie's kindergarten teacher. She had a plate with a cup of tea and a piece of

160 chocolate cake; I had a plate with a cup of tea and a piece of marshmallow cake. We moved up to one another cautiously, and smiled.

"I've been so anxious to meet you," I said. "I'm Laurie's mother."

"We're all so interested in Laurie," she said.

"Well, he certainly likes kindergarten," I said. "He talks about it

165 all the time."

"We had a little trouble adjusting, the first week or so," she said primly, "but now he's a fine helper. With occasional lapses, of course."

"Laurie usually adjusts very quickly," I said. "I suppose this time

170 it's Charles's influence."

"Charles?"

"Yes," I said, laughing, "you must have your hands full in that kindergarten, with Charles."

"Charles?" she said. "We don't have any Charles in the kinder-

175 garten."

(1,582 words)

—Shirley Jackson from *The Lottery*.

Comprehension Questions. After reading the selection, answer the following questions with *a, b, c,* or *d.*

Main Idea

_____ 1. The best statement of the main idea of this selection is
  a. Laurie was in trouble with his parents.
  b. Laurie invented Charles to discuss his own misbehavior.
  c. Laurie caused other children to misbehave in kindergarten.
  d. Laurie did not want to leave his mother and go to school.

Sel.
4

Details

_____ **2.** The person telling the story is
   a. Laurie.
   b. the mother.
   c. the father.
   d. the teacher.

_____ **3.** On Laurie's first day of kindergarten, he
   a. clung to his mother.
   b. begged not to go.
   c. forgot to wave good-bye to his mother.
   d. forgot to say good-bye to his mother.

_____ **4.** In order to get to school, Laurie
   a. was dropped off by his parents.
   b. walked with the older girl next door.
   c. rode the bus.
   d. walked with his father.

_____ **5.** According to Laurie, the other children reacted to Charles's bad behavior by
   a. not speaking to him.
   b. hitting him.
   c. yelling at him.
   d. playing with him.

_____ **6.** Laurie's parents discovered that Charles was not a classmate
   a. at the first PTA meeting.
   b. at the second PTA meeting.
   c. by calling the teacher.
   d. by talking to Laurie's classmates.

_____ **7.** When Charles told the girl to say a bad word to the teacher, Charles
   a. was blamed.
   b. was sent home.
   c. had his mouth washed out with soap.
   d. was not punished.

_____ **8.** The reaction of Laurie's parents to reports of Charles's behavior was
   a. curiosity.
   b. anger.
   c. suspicion that Laurie was lying.
   d. sympathy.

Sel.
4

_____ **9.** As Laurie continued in school, his behavior at home
   a. remained the same.
   b. became better.
   c. became more polite to his parents.
   d. became worse.

Inference

_____ **10.** The reader can infer that Laurie's school day ended at approximately
   a. 3:00.
   b. 4:00.
   c. noon.
   d. 2:00.

_____ **11.** The purpose of the story is to
   a. entertain.
   b. argue.
   c. persuade.
   d. ridicule.

_____ **12.** The overall pattern of organization is
   a. comparison and contrast.
   b. narration.
   c. cause and effect.
   d. classification.

Sel.
4

_____ **13.** As Laurie's mother leaves for the PTA meeting, the irony of her saying that she hopes Charles's mother also attends is
   a. Charles's mother will not attend.
   b. she worries too much about other people.
   c. she is Charles's mother.
   d. she should have previously talked to the teacher.

_____ **14.** The reader can infer from the teacher's response to Charles's mother that
   a. Laurie called himself Charles in class.
   b. Laurie adjusted well to the kindergarten routine.
   c. Laurie has been spanked everyday.
   d. Laurie has been engaging in some of the behaviors blamed on Charles.

_____ **15.** The story holds the reader's attention primarily because of
   a. the character development of the mother.
   b. the tone.
   c. the setting.
   d. suspense.

Vocabulary. Use sentence context clues and word parts to select the correct meaning of boldfaced words. Indicate *a, b, c,* or *d* for 1–5 and respond in your own words to items 6–10.

_____ 1. "His cap on the floor, and the voice suddenly becomes **raucous** shouting, 'Isn't anybody here?'"
   a. nervous
   b. childish
   c. rough and loud
   d. immediate

_____ 2. "Charles was **deprived** of blackboard privileges"
   a. substituted
   b. no longer allowed
   c. asked to continue
   d. forced to do

_____ 3. "My husband and I asked **simultaneously**."
   a. endlessly
   b. at the same time
   c. repeatedly
   d. eagerly

_____ 4. "'What happened?' I asked **incredulously**."
   a. knowingly
   b. angrily
   c. finally
   d. unbelievably

_____ 5. "None of them looked to me **haggard** enough."
   a. exhausted
   b. smart
   c. vicious
   d. clever

6. Why is "I didn't learn nothing" incorrect grammar? _____

_____

7. What does "He was fresh" mean? What is another meaning for **fresh?**

_____

_____

8. What are the prefix and suffix of **reformation,** as in "it looked like a

reformation in Charles"? What does *reformation* mean? _____

_____

_____

9. What is the root of **restlessly** in "At the meeting I sat restlessly"? What does the word mean? _____

_____

10. What is the root of **matronly,** and what does the word mean? _____

_____

Your instructor may choose to give you a true–false comprehension and vocabulary review.

Think and Write

1. List examples of how Laurie's behavior becomes less respectful at home as the story progresses. How does this mirror his reports of Charles?

2. What would you have said to the teacher, and what responsible preventive steps might have been taken earlier? What do you believe Laurie actually did in the classroom, and why did he lie?

3. The author, Shirley Jackson, had a very strict mother who wanted her to be perfect. However, when Shirley was away from her mother, she rebelled by drinking, smoking, and eating fattening foods. How do you see this aspect of the author's life reflected in the story?

4. What makes the story funny? How does irony contribute to the humor?

**Sel.
4**

Net Search.   Research the life of author Shirley Jackson. Discuss her relationship with her mother. How might the character of Charles have mirrored some of the frustrations and concerns that Jackson felt as a child?

Selection 5 Essay

What is a "company man"? In this parable or essay, Ellen Goodman, a Pulitzer prize-winning columnist who is syndicated in 450 newspapers, presents a character who sacrifices everything for his work. He makes choices, and we see the consequences. The essay is written as a parable, which is a short fictitious story that teaches us about morals and values. Its purpose is to make you think about your own values. The essay also uses irony where words may say one thing but mean another. The "company man" followed a dream, but was it the right dream? Although this famous essay was written in 1976, does the "company man" still exist today?

The Company Man

He worked himself to death, finally and precisely, at 3:00 a.m. Sunday morning.

The obituary didn't say that, of course. It said that he died of a coronary thrombosis—I think that was it—but everyone among his
5   friends and acquaintances knew it instantly. He was a perfect Type A, a workaholic, a classic, they said to each other and shook their heads—and thought for five or ten minutes about the way he lived.

This man who worked himself to death finally and precisely at
3:00 a.m. Sunday morning—on his day off—was fifty-one years old
10 and a vice-president. He was, however, one of six vice-presidents, and
one of three who might conceivably—if the president died or retired
soon enough—have moved to the top spot. Phil knew that.

He worked six days a week, five of them until eight or nine at
night, during a time when his own company had begun the four-day
15 week for everyone but the executives. He worked like the Important
People. He had no outside "extracurricular interests," unless, of
course, you think about a monthly golf game that way. To Phil, it
was work. He always ate egg salad sandwiches at his desk. He was, of
course, overweight, by 20 or 25 pounds. He thought it was okay,
20 though, because he didn't smoke.

On Saturdays, Phil wore a sports jacket to the office instead of a
suit, because it was the weekend.

He had a lot of people working for him, maybe sixty, and most of
them liked him most of the time. Three of them will be seriously con-
25 sidered for his job. The obituary didn't mention that.

But it did list his "survivors" quite accurately. He is survived by
his wife, Helen, forty-eight years old, a good woman of no particular
marketable skills, who worked in an office before marrying and
mothering. She had, according to her daughter, given up trying to
30 compete with his work years ago, when the children were small. A
company friend said, "I know how much you will miss him." And she
answered, "I already have."

"Missing him all these years," she must have given up part of
herself which had cared too much for the man. She would be "well
35 taken care of."

His "dearly beloved" eldest of the "dearly beloved" children is a
hard-working executive in a manufacturing firm down South. In the
day and a half before the funeral, he went around the neighborhood
researching his father, asking the neighbors what he was like. They
40 were embarrassed.

His second child is a girl, who is twenty-four and newly married.
She lives near her mother and they are close, but whenever she was
along with her father, in a car driving somewhere, they had nothing
to say to each other.

45 The youngest is twenty, a boy, a high-school graduate who has
spent the last couple of years, like a lot of his friends, doing enough
odd jobs to stay in grass and food. He was the one who tried to grab
at his father, and tried to mean enough to him to keep the man at
home. He was his father's favorite. Over the last two years, Phil
50 stayed up nights worrying about the boy.

The boy once said, "My father and I only board here."

At the funeral, the sixty-year-old company president told the forty-eight-year-old widow that the fifty-one-year-old deceased had meant much to the company and would be missed and would be hard
55 to replace. The widow didn't look him in the eye. She was afraid he would read her bitterness and, after all, she would need him to straighten out the finances—the stock options and all that.

Phil was overweight and nervous and worked too hard. If he wasn't at the office, he was worried about it. Phil was a Type A, a
60 heart-attack natural. You could have picked him out in a minute from a lineup.

So when he finally worked himself to death, at precisely 3:00 a.m. Sunday morning, no one was really surprised.

By 5:00 p.m. the afternoon of the funeral, the company presi-
65 dent had begun, discreetly of course, with care and taste, to make inquiries about his replacement. One of three men. He asked around: "Who's been working the hardest?"

(714 words)

Comprehension Questions. After reading the selection, answer the following questions with *a, b, c,* or *d.*

Main Idea

_____ **1.** The best statement of the main idea of this selection is
   a. The family and company will miss the man.
   b. The man regrettably gave up his life for work.
   c. Success requires extreme personal sacrifice.
   d. At the end the man realized his family was more important than work.

_____ **2.** The main idea of the last paragraph is
   a. The company president will find it difficult to replace Phil.
   b. The replacement was expected to be better than Phil.
   c. No one could be found who would work as hard as Phil.
   d. Phil will be easily replaced by another workaholic.

Details

_____ **3.** The author reports that the day Phil died was
   a. the day Phil went to worship.
   b. another workday for Phil.
   c. the only day of the week he did not work.
   d. early Saturday morning.

Sel.
5

_____ 4. According to the author, Phil
  a. was probably one of four being considered for the top spot.
  b. had 70 people working for him.
  c. was the president's top replacement choice.
  d. was one of six vice-presidents.

_____ 5. When working on Saturdays, Phil wore
  a. a suit.
  b. a sports jacket.
  c. jeans.
  d. a golf shirt.

_____ 6. The author describes Phil in all of the following terms except
  a. overweight by 20 or 25 pounds.
  b. always having an egg sandwich for lunch.
  c. playing golf twice a month.
  d. a nonsmoker.

_____ 7. The work schedule in Phil's company was
  a. all employees, including executives, worked six days a week.
  b. employees worked five days a week and executives worked six.
  c. most employees and executives worked a five-day week.
  d. employees, except executives, worked a four-day week.

Inference

_____ 8. The reader can infer that characteristics of a Type A personality are all of the following except
  a. trustful of others to achieve.
  b. nervous about accomplishing.
  c. overworked.
  d. worrying about details.

_____ 9. The reader can infer that Phil's eldest son spoke to neighbors about his father because
  a. he wanted to thank them for kindnesses.
  b. he wanted to learn more about the father he seldom saw and barely knew.
  c. he wanted to prepare the obituary for the newspaper report.
  d. he wanted to quote his father's close friends in a funeral speech.

_____ 10. The reader can infer that Phil's youngest son
  a. made his father proud with his accomplishments.
  b. graduated from college but had not started a career.
  c. tried to win his father's attention and affection.
  d. was also a workaholic like his father.

_____ **11.** To say that Phil's wife Helen had "no particular marketable skills" implies that
    a. she was not smart.
    b. she was lazy.
    c. she had never worked in business.
    d. she did not have relevant skills currently in workplace demand.

_____ **12.** When a company friend commented on Helen's missing her husband, Helen replied, "I already have." Helen's response suggests that
    a. he had already been gone because she lost him to his work years ago.
    b. she would no longer have a daily competition with his job.
    c. she could spend more time with her children and worry less about him.
    d. she appreciated that he had left her with plenty of money.

_____ **13.** Putting quotation marks around "dearly beloved" suggests the irony of all of the following except
    a. in funeral notices such language is used.
    b. the children were not dearly loved by their father.
    c. the children did not dearly love their father.
    d. the three children dearly loved their father, who loved them.

_____ **14.** The statement "He worked himself to death, finally and precisely, at 3:00 a.m. Sunday morning" is a statement of
    a. fact.
    b. opinion.

_____ **15.** The youngest son said, "My father and I only board here." He meant
    a. he knew his father worried about him.
    b. he was happy to be his father's favorite.
    c. they ate and slept in the same house but were not emotionally close.
    d. he was closer to his father than was his mother.

Sel.
5

Vocabulary. Use sentence context clues and word parts to select the correct meaning of boldfaced words. Indicate _a, b, c,_ or _d_ for items 1–5 and respond in your own words to items 6–10.

_____ **1.** "He worked himself to death, finally and **precisely**, at 3:00 a.m. Sunday morning."
    a. slowly
    b. easily
    c. painfully
    d. exactly

_____ 2. "The **obituary** didn't say that, of course."
a. headlines
b. radio broadcast
c. death notice
d. company newsletter

_____ 3. "It said that he died of a **coronary thrombosis**—I think that
was it—but everyone among his friends and acquaintances
knew it instantly.
a. lung cancer
b. heart attack
c. heart bypass
d. shock

_____ 4. "He was, however, one of six vice-presidents, and one of
three who might **conceivably**. . . have moved to the top
spot."
a. obviously
b. possibly
c. certainly
d. most unlikely

_____ 5. "By 5:00 p.m. the afternoon of the funeral, the company president had begun, **discreetly** of course, with care and taste, to
make inquiries about his replacement."
a. hopelessly
b. burdened with grief
c. hurriedly
d. unnoticeably

Sel.
5

6. What is the meaning and what prefix has been added as a play on
words in *workaholic* as used in "He was a perfect Type A, a

workaholic, a classic"? _____

_____

7. What is the prefix and meaning for *extracurricular* as used in "He had

no outside '**extracurricular** interests.'"? _____

_____

8. Why is *survivors* in quotes, and what two meanings could you assign
to it as used in "But it did list his '**survivors**' quite accurately."?

_____

_____

_____

9. What are the meaning here and a second meaning for *grass*, as used in "The youngest is twenty, a boy, a high-school graduate who has spent the last couple of years, like a lot of his friends, doing enough odd jobs to stay in **grass** and food."? _____

_____

10. What is the prefix and meaning of deceased as used in "the fifty-one-year-old **deceased** had meant much to the company and would be missed." _____

Your instructor may choose to give you a true–false comprehension and vocabulary review.

Think and Write

1. What is the significance of the title, "The Company Man"? Who defined the dream? What was Phil missing? Did he ever know what he was missing?

2. Since this essay is written as a parable, the author does not summarize but lets the reader draw conclusions. What does this essay make you think about your own values?

3. Why does the author repeat numbers? List those numbers that are repeated and explain their significance to the meaning of the essay. Why does the author state 5:00 p.m. in the last paragraph? What does the time make you think?

Net Search.   A parable is a story that teaches a human truth and usually has a twist. Search the net for another parable that appeals to you. Summarize the parable and state what it teaches about truth and values.

Sel.
5

Selection 6 Business

Have you heard the late-night television infomercials on how to become a millionaire? Perhaps you have seen some of the many books on the subject in the bookstore. What is the quality of this enriching advice to aspiring millionaires? Should people buy stock, own real estate, save money, or seek a secure job? Do the recommended strategies change as the economy changes? Are the people who buy the books benefiting from the advice and becoming rich? The following excerpt from an article by Damon Darlin in the *New York Times* published in November 2005 gives some insight into the world of millionaire instruction books.

Get Rich Quick:
Write a Millionaire Book

Socking away that first million used to be so simple. At least it was for people who gave rudimentary advice on how to be a millionaire. Give up that pack-a-day smoking habit, they said, and in 40 years you will have saved almost $250,000 in today's dollars, assum-
5 ing a conservative 4 percent annual return. Brown-bag your lunch, drop HBO and pay off your mortgage early and gradually, over a life-

time, you will accumulate $1 million in assets. Back then, all you had to do was live below your means and save, save, save.

These days, the money-wasting bad habit that must be broken is the daily $5 Starbucks coffee break. (Savings over 40 years: $173,422.) But giving up the small pleasures in life is no longer the advice given to would-be millionaires, whether they are sipping or puffing.

According to the spate of best-selling self-help books, it is not enough to drive used cars and squirrel money away in the company 401(k). Instead, you have to think like a millionaire. It's a popular message reflected in titles like *Secrets of the Millionaire Mind* and *Cracking the Millionaire Code.*

Robert T. Kiyosaki's *Rich Dad, Poor Dad* is the best example of the emphasis on retooling the struggling American's financial thinking. The book has sold nearly four million copies in the United States since its publication in 1998. It has spawned a dozen related titles by Mr. Kiyosaki and his co-author, Sharon L. Lechter, and another dozen titles written by Mr. Kiyosaki's financial advisers. All told, there are more than 24 million copies of Mr. Kiyosaki's books in print worldwide.

No longer is it enough to study hard at a good school and get a good job to be set for life, advice given to him by his father, the poor dad. Instead, Mr. Kiyosaki advocates the staples of late-night infomercials: investments in small stocks and distressed real estate. He argues that one has to think like a millionaire by recognizing the difference between an income-producing asset and a liability, advice given to him by a friend's father, the rich dad. The whole trick to financial success is creating passive income.

"People do respond to it," said Rick Wolf, vice president and executive editor of Warner Books, the publisher of the series. The old rules no longer apply in a world of outsourcing and pension plan collapses, he said.

"People are definitely looking for some alternative pathways to financial freedom," Mr. Wolf said. "The staying power speaks for itself."

Gaining millionaire status is still an accomplishment. It's important to note that even though the threshold for making the Forbes list of richest Americans is now $900 million, only 7 million out of 100 million American households have net assets of $1 million or more, which includes, of course, the equity built up in most people's biggest asset—their homes. That number has not changed significantly despite all the millions of books sold telling people how to join the club.

You have to ask yourself before you buy any of these books: did my neighbors get rich because they just think differently, or because

they use money more wisely? This millionaire-mind mania started in
1998 when two professors, Thomas J. Stanley, then at Georgia State
University, and William D. Danko, teaching marketing in the business
school at the State University at Albany, tried to answer that question. They described the seven characteristics of a breed of frugal and
inconspicuous millionaires, which included living below one's means,
picking smart advisers and having a spouse involved in the family finances. It was an eye-opener, and the book *The Millionaire Next Door*
sold about 2.5 million copies in hardcover and paperback while it
perched on the *New York Times* best-seller list for more than three
years. The book made the two professors millionaires.

The lesson learned here? It may have been that the way to get
rich is to write a book revealing the thinking of millionaires. Mr.
Stanley is back with a brand extension, *The Millionaire Mind*.

Why the need for inspiration? "When the stock market bubble
collapsed in 2000, ordinary Americans—who had watched their stock
portfolios effortlessly rise in value during the late 1990's—quickly
realized that the notion that they could outsmart the market was an
illusion," said Mr. David Drake, who published David Bach's, *The
Automatic Millionaire Homeowner*.

Drake continued, "They turned away from investment books that
focused narrowly on stock-picking strategies and turned instead, in
droves, to books that addressed the basics—getting out of debt, saving for the future—and promised relief from financial anxiety."

It is no accident that the authors of many of these books come
from the stage of motivational seminars and late-night infomercials.
Robert G. Allen, for example, is best known for pioneering techniques for selling people on the idea of buying distressed real estate
and flipping it. *Nothing Down: How to Buy Real Estate With Little or
No Money Down* is his 1980 classic.

T. Harv Eker, author of *Secrets of the Millionaire Mind*, is another
regular on the motivational seminar circuit. He recycles a lot of the
language and advice of seminars or hotel ballroom talkathons. Eker
says you have been conditioned to think like a poor person, but you
can remake yourself to think rich. Mr. Eker suggests a daily affirma-
tion in which you put hand over heart and say: "I am an excellent receiver. I am open and willing to receive massive amounts of money
into my life." You then touch your head and say, "I have a millionaire
mind!"

The bottom line is: save your money by not buying these books.
At about $25 a book, buying one every year probably will not deci-
mate your retirement fund. But if you don't, you'll have at least
$2,370 more in 40 years.

(977 words)

—From Damon Darlin, *New York Times*, Nov. 12, 2005. Reprinted with permission.

Comprehension Questions   After reading the selection, answer the following questions with *a, b, c,* or *d.*

Main Idea

_____ 1. The best statement of the main idea of this selection is
   a. Gaining millionaire status is an accomplishment.
   b. Making the first million is not as simple as in the past.
   c. The recent millionaire books excel in making the authors rich, rather than the readers.
   d. Invest in stocks and bonds to become a millionaire.

_____ 2. The main idea of the first paragraph (begins "Socking away that") is
   a. Making a million used to be simple.
   b. The advice of past authors made becoming a millionaire sound simple.
   c. Save on small items to become a millionaire.
   d. Become a millionaire in 40 years by saving.

_____ 3. The main idea of the fifth paragraph (begins "No longer is") is
   a. Kiyosaki advocates infomercials.
   b. Kiyosaki says to study hard and get a good job.
   c. Kiyosaki recommends income-producing assets for becoming rich.
   d. Kiyosaki supports the advice of his own father.

_____ 4. The main idea of the eighth paragraph (begins "Gaining millionaire status") is
   a. Gaining millionaire status is still an accomplishment.
   b. The Forbes list is the standard for announcing wealth.
   c. Fewer households have assets of $1 million than in years past.
   d. Homes build equity for millionaires.

_____ 5. The main idea of the next to the last paragraph (begins "T. Harv Eker") is
   a. Eker recycles language and advice.
   b. Eker says that you must remake yourself to think rich.
   c. Eker wrote *Secrets of the Millionaire Mind.*
   d. Eker is a regular on the motivational seminar circuit.

Sel.
6

Details

_____ 6. According to Forbes magazine,
   a. the richest American has $900 million.
   b. 7 million American households are worth $1 million or more.
   c. 100 million American households are worth $1 million or more.
   d. the millionaire books have significantly increased the number of millionaires over the last decade.

_____ **7.** According to the passage, the book that describes the seven characteristics of millionaires is
   a. *Rich Dad, Poor Dad.*
   b. *The Millionaire Next Door.*
   c. *The Automatic Millionaire Homeowner.*
   d. *Secrets of the Millionaire Mind.*

_____ **8.** According to David Drake, the reason people are seeking inspiration from the latest wave of millionaire books is they want
   a. stock-picking advice.
   b. increased stock portfolios.
   c. relief from financial anxiety.
   d. to outsmart the market.

_____ **9.** From the names and figures given in the selections, the author(s) who seems to have made the most money on books is
   a. Kiyosaki.
   b. Stanley and Danko.
   c. Drake.
   d. Eker.

Inference

_____ **10.** The meaning of the phrase "live below your means" is
   a. spend only the money you earn.
   b. spend less money than you have available to spend.
   c. seek investments that will increase your income.
   d. reserve money for unexpected emergencies.

_____ **11.** The author's intention is to compare the daily $5 Starbucks coffee to
   a. smoking a pack-a-day.
   b. brown bag lunches.
   c. HBO.
   d. mortgage payments.

Sel.
6

_____ **12.** By saying, in regards to becoming a millionaire, "The old rules no longer apply in a world of outsourcing and pension plan collapses," Rick Wolf means all of the following except
   a. saving is not enough because your income may fail.
   b. American companies no longer offer the financial security of the past.
   c. People want to create independent sources of income because they do not trust companies to always be supportive.
   d. a passive income can be created by avoiding outsourcing and pension plan collapse.

———— **13.** The tone of the author in describing Eker's advice on remaking yourself with a millionaire mind is
   a. unbelieving.
   b. admiring.
   c. respectful.
   d. sincere.

———— **14.** In general, the author seems to
   a. recommend the new millionaire books.
   b. not recommend the new millionaire books.
   c. think the old millionaire books created more millionaires than the new ones.
   d. prefer late-night infomercials over the new millionaire books.

———— **15.** The reader can conclude that "frugal and inconspicuous millionaires"
   a. spend a lot of money on new cars and clothes.
   b. make so much money that they do not watch what they spend.
   c. draw attention to themselves by giving large donations to charities.
   d. are careful in spending their money and not flashy.

Vocabulary   Use sentence context clues and word parts to select meaning for boldfaced words. Indicate *a, b, c,* or *d* for 1–5 and insert a written response for 6–10.

———— **1.** "Over a lifetime, you will **accumulate** $1 million in assets."
   a. earn
   b. build up
   c. spend
   d. invest in stocks

———— **2.** "According to the **spate** of best-selling self-help books . . . "
   a. quality
   b. logic
   c. opinion
   d. great amount

———— **3.** "American households have net assets of $1 million or more, which includes, of course, the **equity** built up in most people's biggest asset—their homes."
   a. debt
   b. money value
   c. mortgage
   d. commitment

Sel.
6

_____ **4.** They turned . . . in **droves** to books that addressed the
basics . . . "
a. hopes
b. large numbers
c. earnest
d. despair

_____ **5.** "At about $25 a book, buying one every year probably will
not **decimate** your retirement fund."
a. affect.
b. increase.
c. renew.
d. ruin.

6. What is the meaning of "assuming a **conservative** 4 percent annual
return"? _____

_____

_____

7. What does the author mean by "**squirrel** money away in the
company 401(k)"? _____

_____

8. The term **passive income** means _____

_____

9. Name some financial **assets** other than stocks and bonds. _____

_____

10. What is the meaning of **spawned**, which is usually applied to fish, in
"**spawned** a dozen related titles"? _____

_____

Think and Write

1. How has the message in the millionaire books changed over the
   years? Why would you expect the message to continue changing?
2. In an old Texas joke, the millionaire looks at another man and says,
   "He is all hat and no cattle." What do you think that means?
3. What are the advantages of financial independence? Do you desire
   to become a millionaire? What is your financial plan? How will you
   use what you have learned in this selection to help you?

Net Search   The authors of *The Millionaire Next Door* have conducted research on the wealthy for over twenty years. Initially, the two college business professors studied the wealthy to advise corporations on providing products and financial services. The authors were so amazed with their findings that they wrote several books. Their extensive studies of the wealthy include interviews and focus groups with over five hundred millionaires, as well as surveys of more than eleven thousand respondents.

The authors, Stanley and Danko, have inspired others to think about their lifestyles and redefine their goals. Search the Net for profiles of ordinary people who are using the research to build personal wealth. These people are practicing the characteristics of millionaires to their own advantage. What are those characteristics? Summarize one of the profiles.

Selection 7 Short Story

Short stories have interesting characters, plots that build suspense, and a message that reflects on people, events, and values. In this story, small town life is rather dull and uneventful until a stranger comes to town. The stranger charms the townspeople and leaves his mark. The author is Virginia Eiseman, and the story first appeared in *Liberty Magazine* in 1944.

The Lion Roared

If a Mr. P. Alfred Merivale ever passes your way, you'd better let me know. Just write to me, Mike Brock, assistant manager, at the Mark Twain Hotel, South Plains, Missouri. If you meet P. Alfred, it's a cinch you'll take a long look at him. He's a great big, white-
5   haired guy who wears expensive three-piece suits with silk shirts and ties.

It was a couple of months ago that this P. Alfred Merivale checks in at the Mark Twain Hotel. Minutes after he arrives, Timmy, the bell-hop, rushes in, waving a green bill.

10   "Say, Mike," Timmy yells, "This is one for the books! A big shot
from Chicago just pulled in. And guess what he asks for. A *luxury*
room! Get a load of that—a *luxury* room!"

Timmy's laughing, and I get a kick out of it, too. The Mark
Twain's a fine hotel, but it's not what you'd call a really fancy place.

15   "This dude must have us mixed up with the Waldorf Astoria,"
says Timmy. "You ought to see his leather bags—three of the
sharpest looking suitcases I've ever had my hands on. And he gave
me this ten bucks just for dumping them in his room."

Timmy sticks the bill into his pocket.

20   "Anyhow, Mike," he says, "you'll get a look at this Chicago fellow
on account of he's staying two weeks." And then our bellhop breezes
out of the lobby.

Well, I don't pay much attention to Timmy's story at first, because he gets emotional when anyone gives him more than a twenty-

25 five-cent tip, which isn't very often. But I begin wondering why a
stranger would make a point of sticking around South Plains for two
weeks. Don't get me wrong. This is a great little town, if you're born
and raised here. Still, compared to Chicago, it's a pretty tame place.

At that moment, the lobby door opens and in walks the biggest

30 and most solid-looking citizen I've ever seen. I size him up from top
to bottom—from his dark hat to his spanking white shoes. The big
guy flashes me a smile.

"For two weeks," he nods. "I'm here for a rest. Doctor's orders."

And then I notice something shiny on his suit lapel. I see it's a

35 pin—it's a gold lion pin. At first I think it's one of those pins that
colleges hand out, but it's too big for that. I can tell that it's not real
gold. And I'm about to ask him just what that gold lion pin is, when
I remember that I'm just the assistant manager, and if the customers
go in for silly jewelry—well, that's none of my business.

40   In the meantime, the man from Chicago's keeping up a steady
stream of chatter. Then he plops down on one of the chairs in the
lobby, and pretty soon the afternoon gang wanders in and I see that
my new pal has joined them.

"I'd like to introduce myself," he's saying. "I'm P. Alfred Merivale

45 from Chicago."

A great session of handshaking and backslapping follows, and in
half an hour they're making jokes a mile a minute, and Mr. Merivale's
fat pigskin wallet does the honors for sandwiches and cold drinks all
around.

50   Then all of a sudden Cy Archer, our local banker, takes some
words right out of my mouth.

"Tell us about that lion pin you're wearing, Merivale," he says.

"Yes," says Ben Woods, "I've never seen anything like it before.
Where did it come from?"

Sel.
7

55   "Well, it's a funny thing about this pin," answers Merivale. "I was down in Lima, Peru, about fifteen years ago. One afternoon I wandered into a little shop and bought a lot of trinkets. When I got back to my room and unwrapped the package, this gold pin was on top. I took it back to the man who sold the other articles to me, and he
60   said he'd never seen the pin before. So the only thing for me to do was to keep it."

"Why do you wear it?" Luke Williams asks. "Any special reason?" The big man turns on his smile full blast.

"That's another funny story. It turned out to be the luckiest little
65   pin anybody ever wore." Mr. Merivale paused for a moment. "Well, gentlemen," he continued, "I realize this is something one doesn't usually discuss, but I've been extremely successful. The reason I mention it is because of the pin. From the second I first saw the lion, the breaks have come my way in everything—oil wells, mines, real estate, the
70   stock market, just everything. And it's all due to this little pin here."

Mr. Merivale laughs. "I wouldn't part with this pin for anything in the world," he says.

Well, during the next week he and his gold lion spend a lot of time in the lobby and the hotel restaurant. You can't believe the
75   number of friends he makes. And it's all on account of the pin.

One morning, Timmy nearly collides with me in the lobby, he's in such a state. "Did you hear the news about Mr. Merivale?" he pants. "He's lost his lion pin."

Right there and then you could have knocked me over with a
80   feather. It seems that the last time Mr. Merivale remembers seeing his pin is at dinner the night before, and now he's offering a thousand dollar reward to anyone who finds it. He's buying a full-page ad in the paper, Timmy tells me.

I feel mighty sorry for Mr. Merivale. He strikes me as being the
85   most high-class customer I've ever met up with. Then I think long and hard about the thousand buck reward, which wouldn't do Mike Brock any harm at all. I can't help wondering if the pin is stolen or lost.

Mr. Merivale shows up the same as usual later in the day. "Maybe I'm carrying this thing too far," he says to the gang. "You fellows
90   must think I'm crazy to promise such a big reward, because the lion's certainly worth no more than a few dollars at most. But that pin means luck to me. I've got to go back to Chicago at the end of the week, and I'm hoping the pin will go with me."

"Don't worry, Alf, we'll find it for you," pipes up Cy Archer.

95   But we don't find it. Mr. Merivale's loss is the topic of the town all right. People wander about with their eyes glued to the ground, yet nothing happens.

Finally, the day of P. Alfred's departure rolls around. Right after Timmy brings down his bags, the big man comes over to me.

100 "I couldn't leave South Plains without telling you goodby, Mike," he says.

I make it clear how sorry I am to see him go, and then we get on the subject of his lion pin.

"That thousand dollar reward still holds," he tells me. "If you ever
105 find a clue, Mike, you can reach me at the Brownstone Hotel in Chicago."

Well, the town seems pretty dreary without Mr. Merivale. Now and then somebody mentions the gold pin, but it still doesn't show up. Everyone acts like there's been a death in the family—they're that fond of P. Alfred. They all keep saying how they wish he'd come back.

110 One afternoon—it's early and the gang hasn't dropped in yet—I notice a large stranger standing at the end of the lobby. This character hasn't had a shave or a haircut for months. He's wearing a tattered jacket and a pair of pants with patches. One toe is sticking through a hole in his shoe. I say to myself that I'm looking at the original
115 washed-up wreck.

"You'd better move along, Bud," I tell him in a polite way.

Just then my eyes almost pop out of my head. There, sitting on top of a patch in this bum's jacket is Mr. Merivale's gold lion. As fast as I can get the words out, I ask the tramp where he got it.

120 "Found it by the railroad tracks," is his answer.

I guess I'm making a whole lot of noise 'cause when I finally ask the guy how much he wants for the pin, he thinks for a minute. Then he admits the lion doesn't mean a thing to him. Still, he says, it must mean something to *me* or I wouldn't be making all this fuss, and he
125 says he won't sell it for a cent under five hundred dollars in cash.

I grab my checkbook and pen, and head for the cashier. In a minute I'm back with a wad of bills. They go straight into the bum's grimy fist, and in exchange I get Mr. Merivale's gold pin.

I'm thinking about calling Merivale right away, but I decide that it
130 can wait until after I share my good news with the gang. I'm still congratulating myself, when Cy Archer comes in later with a grin on his face.

"You'll never believe it, Mike," he says. "It's a miracle—an absolute miracle! I just met some broken-down bum outside, and you'll never guess what I bought from him!"

135 Well I can guess all right. It's Merivale's gold pin.

A few minutes later, Luke Williams comes in looking mighty happy—and afterwards, Ben Weeds, with a big smile on his face. It seems they've each paid some bum $500 for Merivale's lion.

Well, we may not exactly be geniuses, but I can tell you this. If
140 Mr. P. Alfred Merivale is as smart as I know he is, he won't ever again pick South Plains for a rest cure, or come into the Mark Twain Hotel looking for a room.

(1,624 words)

—Virginia Eiseman, *Liberty* Magazine

Sel.
7

Comprehension Questions. After reading the selection, answer the following questions with *a, b, c,* or *d.*

Main Idea

_____ 1. The best statement of the main idea of this selection is
  a. The townspeople wanted to help a man in trouble.
  b. The townspeople were cheated by a clever con man.
  c. People in a small town do not trust outsiders.
  d. Both good and bad news travels fast in a small town.

_____ 2. The main idea of the first paragraph is
  a. Let me know if you see Merivale.
  b. Merivale cheated me.
  c. Merivale will be coming to your town.
  d. Brock is the assistant hotel manager.

Details

_____ 3. All of the following are used to describe Merivale except
  a. expensive three-piece suits.
  b. white hair.
  c. shining black shoes.
  d. leather suitcases.

_____ 4. The reason Merivale gives for his stay at the hotel is
  a. business.
  b. pleasure.
  c. to visit relatives.
  d. rest on doctor's orders.

_____ 5. Merivale reports that
  a. he bought the pin in Peru.
  b. he discovered the pin in Peru.
  c. the pin was given to him by an old friend in Peru.
  d. he was awarded the pin for helping others in Peru.

_____ 6. According to the story, the tramp collected at least
  a. $1000.
  b. $1500.
  c. $2000.
  d. $2500.

Sel.
7

_____ 7. The tramp excuses his high price for the pin by saying
  a. it is real gold.
  b. the tramp wants to keep it.
  c. the buyer wants it too much.
  d. the pin will bring him good luck.

Inference

_____ **8.** The reader can infer that Brock did not ask Merivale about his pin because
   a. Brock feared his question might offend Merivale.
   b. Brock was not interested in knowing.
   c. Brock thought the pin was expensive.
   d. Brock thought the pin looked elegant on Merivale.

_____ **9.** The reader can infer that the scam works only if people act out of
   a. greed.
   b. love for mankind.
   c. honesty.
   d. fear.

_____ **10.** The reader can conclude that Merivale
   a. goes to the Brownstone Hotel.
   b. did not get the money collected by the tramp.
   c. might have been the tramp in disguise.
   d. has never previously pulled this scam.

_____ **11.** The purpose of this selection is
   a. to educate.
   b. to ridicule.
   c. to argue.
   d. to entertain.

_____ **12.** The overall pattern of organization is
   a. comparison and contrast.
   b. time order.
   c. cause and effect.
   d. definition and example.

_____ **13.** The story is told by
   a. Merivale.
   b. Timmy.
   c. Mike.
   d. Cy Archer.

_____ **14.** Merivale gave big tips and treated townspeople for all of the following reasons except
   a. he was wealthy.
   b. he wanted to make friends quickly.
   c. he wanted to build trust.
   d. he wanted to become well known in the town.

Sel.
7

_____ **15.** The reader can infer that a successful con man has to
      a. avoid victims who cannot afford loss.
      b. avoid calling attention oneself.
      c. fulfill the trust placed in you by others.
      d. be heartless in cheating others.

Vocabulary. Use sentence context clues and word parts to select the correct meaning of boldfaced words. Indicate *a, b, c,* or *d* for items 1–5 and respond in your own words to items 6–10.

_____ **1.** "It's a **cinch** you'll take a long look at him."
      a. surprise
      b. certainty
      c. guess
      d. clue

_____ **2.** "I say to him in my most **hospitable** manner, 'You must be the gentleman . . .'"
      a. welcoming
      b. irritated
      c. shy
      d. businesslike

_____ **3.** "One morning, Timmy nearly **collides** with me in the lobby"
      a. shocks
      b. runs into
      c. startles
      d. misses

_____ **4.** "Well, the town seems pretty **dreary** without Mr. Merivale."
      a. stable
      b. honest
      c. normal
      d. dull

_____ **5.** "He's wearing a **tattered** jacket"
      a. colored
      b. tweed
      c. torn
      d. plaid

Sel.
7

6. What is the meaning of the expression "it's a pretty tame place"?

_____

7. Identify and explain the meaning of the figurative language in "the man from Chicago's keeping up a steady stream of chatter."

_____

_____

8. Identify and explain the meaning of the figurative language in "Mr. Merivale's fat pigskin wallet does the honors for sandwiches and cold drinks all around." _____

   _____

9. Identify and explain the meaning of the figurative language in "Right there and then you could have knocked me over with a feather." _____

   _____

10. Identify and explain the meaning of the figurative language in "People wander about with their eyes glued to the ground, and yet nothing happens." _____

    _____

Your instructor may choose to give you a true–false comprehension and vocabulary review.

Think and Write

1. What did Merivale do to manipulate the people of South Plains so they would fall for his scam? How did he carefully set them up to trust him?
2. Explain the significance of the title of the story. Could the lion be roaring both from strength and laughter?
3. Why did the victims fall for this scam? In most scams, what human weakness must be present for people to become victims? Explain.

Net Search. Scammers prey on people who need money or want to make a fast profit. For example, did you research avenues for obtaining scholarships for college? Search the Internet to find how innocent students can lose money to scholarship scams. List five ways the scammers get money out of unsuspecting victims.

Selection 8 Essay

Who is paying your college expenses? Do you think that you should pay or that one of your parents should pay? Is it possible to make good grades if you are working your way through college? What are the disadvantages of paying your own expenses, and are there advantages? Audrey Rock-Richardson wrote this essay in 2000 after she had completed her college education. She wonders why more students don't do what she did.

Pay Your Own Way! (Then Thank Mom)

Is it me, or are students these days lazy? I'm not talking about tweens who don't want to do their homework or make their bed. I'm referring to people in legal adulthood who are in the process of making hugely consequential life decisions. And collectively, their atti-
5 tude is that they simply cannot pay for college.

Don't get me wrong. I realize that there are people out there who pay their own tuition. I know that some cannot put themselves

through school because of disabilities or extenuating circumstances. But I have to say: the notion that parents must finance their chil-
10 dren's education is ridiculous.

During college I consistently endured comments from peers with scholarships and loans, peers who had new Jeeps and expensive apartments, all who would say to me, eyes bulging, "You mean your parents didn't help you at *all*?"

15 I resented my fellow students for asking this, first because they made it sound like my parents were demons, and second because they were insinuating that I wasn't capable of paying my own way. "How did you pay tuition?" they'd ask. My response was simple: "I worked." They would look at me blankly, as though I had told them
20 I'd gone to the moon.

As an undergrad (University of Utah, 1998), I put myself through two solid years of full-tuition college by working as a day-care provider for $4.75 an hour. I then married and finished out seven more quarters by working as an interpreter for the deaf and a tutor
25 in a private school.

I didn't work during high school or save for years. I simply got a job the summer following graduation and worked 40 hours a week. I didn't eat out every weekend, shop a lot, or own a car. I sacrificed. I was striving for something bigger and longer-lasting than the next kegger.

30 Looking at the numbers now, I'm not sure how I managed to cover all the costs of my education. But I did. And I bought every single textbook and pencil myself, too.

I remember sitting in a classroom one afternoon during my senior year, listening to everyone introduce themselves. Many students men-
35 tioned their part-time jobs. There were several members of a sorority in the class. When it came to the first girl, she told us her name and that she was a sophomore. "Oh," she added, "I major in communications." After an awkward silence, the teacher asked, "Do you work?"

"Oh, no," she said emphatically, "I go to school full time." (As if
40 those of us who were employed weren't really serious about our classes.)

The girl went on to explain that her parents were paying tuition and for her to live in a sorority house (complete with a cook, I later found out). She was taking roughly 13 credit hours. And she was too
45 busy to work.

I, on the other hand, was taking 18, count 'em, 18 credit hours so I could graduate within four years. I worked 25 hours a week so my husband and I could pay tuition without future loan debt. And here's the kicker: I pulled straight A's.

50 I caught a glimpse of that same girl's report card at the end of the quarter, and she pulled C's and a few B's, which didn't surprise me. Having to juggle tasks forces you to prioritize, a skill she hadn't learned.

**Sel.
8**

I'm weary of hearing kids talk about getting financial help from their parents as though they're entitled to it. I'm equally tired of hearing stressed-out parents groaning, "How are we going to pay for his/her college?" Why do they feel obligated?

I do not feel responsible for my daughter's education. She'll find a way to put herself through if she wants to go badly enough. And (I'm risking sounding like my mom here), she'll thank me later. I can say this because I honestly, whole-heartedly thank my parents for giving me that experience.

I'm not saying that it's fun. It's not. I spent the first two years of school cleaning up after 4-year-olds for the aforementioned $4.75 an hour and taking a public bus to campus. My husband and I spent the second two struggling to pay out our tuition. We lived in a cinder-block apartment with little privacy and no dishwasher.

Lest I sound like a hypocrite, yes, I would have taken free college money had the opportunity presented itself. However, because my parents put themselves through school they expected me to do the same. And, frankly, I'm proud of myself. I feel a sense of accomplishment that I believe I couldn't have gained from 50 college degrees all paid for by someone else.

Getting through school on our own paid off in every way. My husband runs his own business, a demanding but profitable job. I write part time and work as a mother full time. I believe the fact that we are happy and financially stable is a direct result of our learning how to manage time and money in college.

So, kids, give your parents a break. Contrary to popular belief, you can pay tuition by yourself. And you might just thank your mother for it, too.

(892 words)

—Audrey Rock-Richardson, *Newsweek.*

Comprehension Questions. After reading the selection, answer the following questions with *a, b, c,* or *d.*

Main Idea

_____ 1. The best statement of the main idea of this selection is
  a. Students should accept help with college bills if help is offered.
  b. Students should pay their own way through college.
  c. Parents need their savings to build for retirement rather than college expenses.
  d. Students do not need to sacrifice grades while working to pay for college.

_____ **2.** The main idea of the first paragraph is
   a. Students today do not want to do their homework or household chores.
   b. Young adults make huge life decisions.
   c. Students who go to college are collectively lazy.
   d. Students today are lazy and think they cannot pay for college.

_____ **3.** The main idea of the next to the last paragraph (begins "Getting through school") is
   a. A college degree is essential for managing a profitable business.
   b. The author is happy to be a mother and a writer.
   c. The skills and discipline learned from paying for your own college help you become a more successful adult.
   d. Learning how to manage time and money begins in college.

Details

_____ **4.** The author's first job was
   a. fast food cashier.
   b. interpreter.
   c. in high school.
   d. day-care provider.

_____ **5.** Before finishing college, the author
   a. got married.
   b. had a baby.
   c. got divorced.
   d. borrowed money from her parents.

_____ **6.** In comparing herself with a nonworking student who was in a sorority, the author
   a. took fewer credit hours and made better grades.
   b. took more credit hours and made better grades.
   c. took more credit hours and made the same grade point average.
   d. took the same credit hours and made better grades.

_____ **7.** According to the author, she plans to
   a. pay for her daughter's education.
   b. evaluate the family finances later to decide who pays for her daughter's education.
   c. let her daughter pay for her own education.
   d. encourage her daughter to get a scholarship for college.

Sel.
8

Inference

_____ 8. The primary purpose of this essay is to
   a. narrate a story.
   b. shock the reader with a new idea.
   c. ridicule others who think differently.
   d. argue a point.

_____ 9. "I put myself through two solid years of full-tuition college by working as a day-care provider for $4.75 an hour" is a statement of
   a. fact.
   b. opinion.

_____ 10. When the author mentions questions from other students about paying her own tuition, her attitude seems
   a. sympathetic.
   b. humorous.
   c. angry.
   d. happy.

_____ 11. The author interpreted surprise responses to her parents' not helping with college expenses as
   a. a compliment to her abilities.
   b. an insult to her and her parents.
   c. a harmless comment from the responder.
   d. a sincere remark from a caring friend.

_____ 12. The author looks back on her college years as
   a. a time of fun.
   b. a time for building lasting friendships.
   c. a time to enjoy learning.
   d. a time of sacrifice.

_____ 13. The reader can infer that a hypocrite would say
   a. "I would have taken free college money had the opportunity presented itself."
   b. "I would not have taken free college money had the opportunity presented itself."

_____ 14. The reader can infer that the author
   a. applied for scholarships but did not get any.
   b. limited student loans to a small amount.
   c. is somewhat sensitive that other people look down on her parents for not helping her with college.
   d. married because she could not support herself.

_____ **15.** The reader can conclude that
    a. the author respects herself and her parents.
    b. the author's parents had poor jobs because they lacked education.
    c. the author's husband paid her tuition the last year of college.
    d. the author majored in communications.

Vocabulary.   Use sentence context clues and word parts to select the correct meaning of boldfaced words. Indicate *a, b, c,* or *d* for items 1–5 and respond in your own words to items 6–10.

_____ **1.** "During college I consistently **endured** comments from peers with scholarships."
    a. heard
    b. answered
    c. suffered
    d. ignored

_____ **2.** "All who would say to me, eyes **bulging**, 'You mean your parents didn't help you at *all*?'"
    a. bursting out
    b. half closed
    c. kindly sympathetic
    d. looking in another direction

_____ **3.** "Because they made it sound like my parents were **demons**, . . . "
    a. poor workers
    b. devils
    c. ignorant people
    d. people who did not value education

_____ **4.** "And second because they were **insinuating** that I wasn't capable of paying my own way."
    a. announcing
    b. deciding
    c. concluding
    d. slyly suggesting

_____ **5.** "I'm **weary** of hearing kids talk about getting financial help from their parents as though they're entitled to it."
    a. accustomed to
    b. always anticipating
    c. tired
    d. resistant to

Sel.
8

6. The author begins the first sentence with "Is it me," which is grammatically incorrect and should read, "Is it I." Why would an author chose to be incorrect? _____

_____

7. What is the derivation of *tween* and what does it mean? _____

_____

_____

8. The phrase *juggle tasks* is an example of figurative language. What does it mean, and what is the figurative image? _____

_____

_____

9. If you prioritize tasks, what do you do? _____

_____

10. If you feel obligated to do something, then you feel that _____

_____

Your instructor may choose to give you a true–false comprehension and vocabulary review.

Think and Write

1. What do you expect from college other than a degree? What would be or are the disadvantages of paying your own college expenses?
2. What does the author see as the advantages of paying your own college expenses? Do you agree or disagree with the author's opinion?
3. What is your opinion on the responsibility of parents to pay for college? What kind of student would reject money from parents who are willing to pay?

Net Search. The author, Audrey Rock-Richardson, is obviously both industrious and opinionated. You may or may not agree with her position on paying for college. Do you wonder what she is doing today, is she still opinionated, and is she successful? Search the Internent for the answers. You will probably have some opinions on her opinions. List two of her statements with which you agree and two with which you disagree.

Selection 9 Psychology

What do statistics say about the value of a college education? How much is it worth in terms of earning power? Are there other benefits? Since you are in college, you have decided that sacrifices made today are worth future gains. This selection is from the 2005 edition of *The World of Psychology* by Samuel Wood, Ellen Green Wood, and Denise Boyd.

The Impact of College Attendance

Have you ever wondered whether college is really worth the trouble? The answer is yes, if the measure of worth is income. As you can see in Figure 1-1, some college is better than none, but there is a

FIGURE 1-1 | Level of education and income

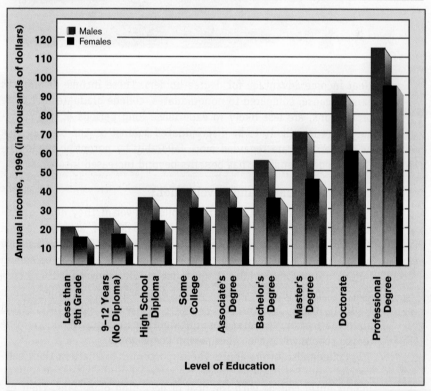

These statistics make it clear that the longer you stay in school, the more money you are likely to earn. However, note that even with equal education, men's earnings greatly exceed women's. Reasons for the differences include (1) women are more likely to be working part-time; (2) traditionally female professions (e.g., teaching) do not pay as well as traditionally male occupations (e.g., engineering), even when educational requirements are the same; and (3) most women have spent fewer years in the workforce than have their male counterparts.

clear income advantage for degree-holders. These income differences
⁵ exist because, compared to nongraduates, college graduates get more
promotions, are less likely to experience long periods of unemploy-
ment, are less likely to be discriminated against on the basis of race
or gender, and are regarded more favorably by potential employers.
But college attendance has benefits beyond increased income.

College Attendance and Development

¹⁰   The longer individuals attend college, even if they don't graduate, the more likely they are to be capable of abstract logical
thought. Years of attendance is also matched with how efficiently
people manage problems in their everyday lives, such as balancing
family and work schedules. Long-range studies show that these cog-
¹⁵ nitive gains happen between the first and later years of college. Such
findings mean that two individuals, who are of equal intellectual
ability, are likely to differ from one another in cognitive skills if one
leaves school while the other person keeps going.

College also offers adults the opportunity to sharpen their self-
²⁰ perceptions. For example, researchers have found that many biology
majors enter college with the goal of becoming physicians. Their experiences in biology classes change these goals. Some realize that becoming a science teacher is a more realistic goal. For others, the goal

of a career in medicine is reinforced when they discover that they are
more competent in science than they believed prior to taking college-
level biology classes. Mixing goals with actual academic experiences
helps college graduates achieve a better understanding of where they
can best fit into the workforce.

College attendance influences social development as well. For
many students, college is their first opportunity to meet people of
ethnicities and nationalities that are different from theirs. And students, particularly those who live on campus, learn to establish social
networks that eventually replace parents as their primary source of
emotional support. The extensive opportunities for social interaction
may explain associations that researchers have found among college
attendance, such as capacity for empathy, and moral reasoning.

Traditional and Nontraditional Students

What are the factors other than intellectual ability that predict
success in college? You may be surprised to learn that one such factor
is authoritative parenting. As is true for elementary and secondary
school students, college students whose parents display the authoritative style are more academically successful than peers whose parents exhibit other styles. More important than parenting style,
though, is a group of factors that researchers use to classify students
as *traditional* or *nontraditional*. These factors are given in Figure 1-2.

Traditional students make up roughly one-third of the college
population in the United States. The remaining two-thirds are distributed across the three nontraditional categories explained in Figure
1-2. Most students who enroll in college full-time directly after high
school do so because they have financial support from parents, have
received scholarships, or qualify for substantial financial aid awards.
But the desire to please parents is also a major reason. This may be
one area of life in which doing something to please one's parents pays
off. About two-thirds of traditional students obtain a degree within 5
years, a much higher graduation rate than that for any of the nontraditional categories. The more nontraditional students are, the less
likely they are to graduate. Among minimally nontraditional students,
just over half get degrees within 5 years of first enrolling; moderately
nontraditional students have about a 40% graduation rate; and fewer
than 30% of highly nontraditional students graduate.

One reason for the lower graduation rates of nontraditional students may be that they, in contrast to traditional students, are con-
centrated in 2-year colleges. These institutions are less likely to have
counseling centers and other support services that help students
with academic and personal problems. Two-year schools also offer
fewer opportunities for social interaction, so students don't develop

FIGURE 1-2 | Are you traditional?

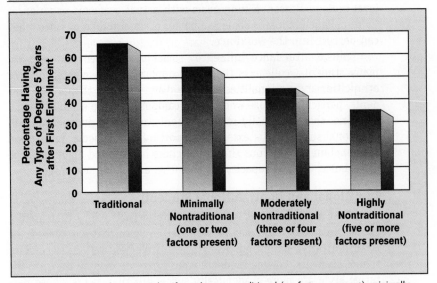

Researchers use seven factors to classify students as traditional (no factors present), minimally nontraditional (one to two factors present), moderately nontraditional (three or four factors present), or highly nontraditional (five or more factors present). The factors are (1) delaying college entry more than a year after graduating from high school, (2) living independently from parents, (3) being employed while in school, (4) enrolling part-time rather than full-time, (5) being a parent, (6) having a GED rather than a high school diploma, and (7) being a custodial parent who is single.

the kinds of social support networks that are common among students at 4-year colleges. Thus, a major goal of most community and junior colleges in recent years has been finding ways to better support students in order to decrease drop-out rates.

Gender, Race, and College Completion

70   Gender is also related to college completion. At all degree levels, women are more likely than men to graduate. Why? One reason is that female students use more effective study strategies than their male counterparts. In addition, male students are more likely to cheat and to be negatively influenced by peers in making decisions
75   about behaviors such as binge drinking.

Race is linked to graduation rates as well. White American students are more likely to drop out than are Asian American, Native American, and Hispanic American students. However, African American students have the highest drop-out rate of all these groups. About
80   44% leave college and do not return. The reason most often cited for leaving is the perception of racial hostility in the college environment.

Many African American students have their first experiences with outward racism when they go to college and often feel that they are outsiders in the college community.

85   A greater sense of belonging may explain why African American students who attend historically Black institutions show more gains in both cognitive and social competence than their peers who attend predominantly White colleges. In addition, attending historically Black colleges may help African American students achieve a stronger sense

90   of racial identify, a factor which is matched with persistence in college. Thus, when these students graduate, they may be better prepared for the demands of graduate and professional programs than are peers who graduate from colleges where African Americans are in the minority.

(964 words)

—Samuel E. Wood, Ellen Green Wood, and Denise Boyd,
The World of Psychology, 5th ed.

Comprehension Questions. After reading the selection, answer the following questions with *a, b, c,* or *d.*

Main Idea

_____ 1. The best statement of the main idea of this selection is
   a. College success can be predicted on the basis of gender, race, and a simple test.
   b. The impact of college attendance is too often measured only in the workplace.
   c. Your level of education determines your income and social status.
   d. The impact of college attendance is economic, cognitive, and social, with certain predictors of success emerging.

_____ 2. The main idea of the first paragraph is
   a. The years of college completed affect income.
   b. The benefits of college should not be measured by income.
   c. Students sacrifice for college to make money later.
   d. College graduates are discriminated against on the basis of race and gender.

_____ 3. The main idea of the fifth paragraph (begins "What are the factors") is
   a. Parenting style and a traditional/nontraditional factor scale can predict college success.
   b. Authoritative parenting style predicts academic success for elementary school students.
   c. Intellectual ability predicts success in college.
   d. Nontraditional students do less well than traditional students.

_____ 4. The main idea of the last paragraph is
   a. Most African American students do not choose to attend historically black colleges.
   b. African American students who attend black colleges show gain in graduate school achievement.
   c. African American students prefer black colleges because of the opportunity for social interaction.
   d. African American students attending historically black colleges show gains that suggest advantages.

Details

_____ 5. According to the author, female college students are more likely to graduate than male students because women
   a. are smarter.
   b. are not influenced by peers.
   c. use better study strategies.
   d. know that they need a degree to get a good job.

_____ 6. Of the following, according to the article, the most likely to drop out of college before graduation is a student who is
   a. White European.
   b. Asian American.
   c. Native American.
   d. Hispanic.

Inference

_____ 7. The author feels that community and junior colleges
   a. offer excellent support services.
   b. need to improve their counseling and support services.
   c. encourage social networks superior to 4-year colleges.
   d. should focus on traditional rather than nontraditional students.

_____ 8. The reader can infer that "to sharpen your self-perception" means
   a. to develop higher goals for yourself.
   b. to push yourself to achieve.
   c. to find a career in biology or medicine.
   d. to figure out a career that best suits your abilities.

Graphic Illustrations

_____ 9. According to Figure 1-1, the difference in the average annual income for a male with a high school diploma and a bachelor's degree is approximately $15,000 to $20,000.
   a. true.
   b. false.
   c. can't tell.

_____ **10.** According to Figure 1-1, the largest annual male and female income difference in an educational category is the doctorate degree category.
  a. true.
  b. false.
  c. can't tell.

_____ **11.** According to Figure 1-1, the average income of a male with a master's degree is three times as much as a male with a high school degree.
  a. true.
  b. false.
  c. can't tell.

_____ **12.** According to Figure 1-1, only 10% of the women with doctorate degrees make more than an average annual income of $90,000.
  a. true.
  b. false.
  c. can't tell.

_____ **13.** According to Figure 1-1, the average annual income for men is higher in every educational category than the average annual income for women.
  a. true.
  b. false.
  c. can't tell.

_____ **14.** According to Figure 1-2, a traditional student is twice as likely to graduate as a moderately nontraditional student.
  a. true.
  b. false.
  c. can't tell.

_____ **15.** According to Figure 1-2, adding a third factor reduces graduation likelihood by about 10%.
  a. true.
  b. false.
  c. can't tell.

Vocabulary. Use sentence context clues and word parts to select the correct meaning of boldfaced words. Indicate *a, b, c,* or *d* for items 1–5 and respond in your own words to items 6–10.

_____ **1.** "And are regarded more favorably by **potential** employers"
  a. unlikely
  b. possible
  c. past
  d. outstanding

_____ 2. "They are more **competent** in science than they believe prior to taking college-level biology classes."
   a. afraid
   b. absorbed
   c. detail-oriented
   d. capable

_____ 3. "Or qualify for **substantial** financial aid awards"
   a. small
   b. large
   c. difficult to get
   d. public

_____ 4. "Cited for leaving is the perception of racial **hostility** in the college environment."
   a. association
   b. group activities
   c. unfriendliness
   d. questions

_____ 5. "a factor which is matched with **persistence** in college"
   a. determination
   b. knowledge
   c. know-how
   d. talent

6. What are the prefix and suffix for **interaction** as in "social interaction," and what does it mean? _____

_____

7. What is the root of **authoritative,** and what does _authoritative parenting_ mean? _____

_____

8. What does **roughly** mean, as used in "make up roughly one-third of the college population," and what is another meaning of the root of the word? _____

_____

9. What does _net_ in **networks** suggest, and what are "social support networks"? _____

_____

10. What are "male counterparts"? _____

_____

Your instructor may choose to give you a true–false comprehension and vocabulary review.

Think and Write

1. In what ways do you think you have already benefited from being in college?

2. Evaluate the student support service at your college. Explain your opportunities and efforts in building a social support network.

3. Are you a traditional or a nontraditional student? Where do you rank on the graph in Figure 1-2? What obstacles and challenges might make it difficult for you to complete your college degree? What can you do to overcome and manage these difficulties?

Net Search.   The economic value of attending college is documented in this selection. You must agree because you are presently making sacrifices to attend college. Search the Internet for other statistics that back up this argument. List five positive economic and/or social values of a college education that are not mentioned in this selection.

Selection 10 Web Site

Many Web sites are available to help you find jobs, research salaries, and get tips on landing jobs. One very popular site is *www.monster.com*. Following are several pages from that site. Monster.com also offers advice and articles on how to be successful after you land a job. For example, the article featured here, written by Monster contributing writer Chris Lytle, gives advice on being a great salesperson. Notice the variety of links and how the Monster Web site can benefit you. To use the full resources of the site, you will need to log on and get a password.

www.monster.com

How Do You Measure Up?

Are you a member of a sales department or a sales force? There's a big difference. Members of a sales department don't make much of an impression on the prospect and, as a result, make the next person look better. Members of a sales force are tough acts to follow.

5   Consider figure skating. There are certain figure skaters—Peggy Fleming, Dorothy Hamill and Katarina Witt come to mind—who were so good that following them onto the ice was daunting for any competitor. Even competent skaters look less competent if they have to follow one of those skaters onto the ice.

10   But back to selling. We received a copy of this letter recently. It's from a satisfied client to a sales manager.

Dear Kelly,

I am writing this letter to you concerning the attention and service I have been receiving from your sales associate Kim Delwiche. She has taken my account
15   and shown me not only the benefits of WAPL, but educated our company in regards to the best approach in marketing, positioning and our media analysis. She has done an extensive amount of research, made us feel comfortable with her, and shown us the strengths and weaknesses in our media plan.

If you don't have a nickname for her, I suggest you try "The Yardstick." Why?
20   Because she is the standard of measurement by which we measure all of the other media sales associates.

If I could only instill in my own staff the tenacity and willingness to do work in the fashion she has done with our company, I would be worry-free. I believe you should know this since it is far more common to hear the negative than
25   the positive. Without Kim's attention and skills, we would have taken a less beneficial path.

[I believe] we are headed in a better direction than we were without your services and your station.

Sincerely,

30   Ray Lasee, Store Manager
Parker Coatings, Inc.

Kim is a tough act to follow into Ray's office. Clients buy the way you sell before they buy what you sell. The most interesting thing to me about Ray's letter is that, at the time Ray wrote it, Kim had only
35   been selling advertising for six months.

It's a great coup for Kim to get a letter like that. At the same time, it says a lot about the impressions the veteran salespeople and top billers are making, or not making, on the client.

Salespeople are not just competing for dollars in the market-
40   place. They are competing for precious time in front of buyers and

prospects. Until you get more face time, you'll be hard-pressed to land bigger orders.

What can you do right now to set the standard for how things are sold in your industry? Start by avoiding the top 10 things sales-
45 people do that buyers dislike. This list comes from a *Purchasing* magazine survey:

10. Failure to keep promises.

9. Lack of creativity.

8. Failure to make and keep appointments.

50 **7.** Lack of awareness of the customer's operation ("What do you guys do here anyway?").

6. Taking the customer for granted.

5. Lack of follow-through.

4. Lack of product knowledge.

55 **3.** Overaggressiveness and failure to listen.

2. Lack of interest or purpose ("Anything coming down this week?" or "Just checking in.").

1. Lack of preparation.

Being a great salesperson is more than just avoiding the 10
60 things buyers dislike. The salesperson who wants to be a member of a sales force instead of a sales department will want to make every call one that could trigger a letter like the one Ray Lasee wrote.

The goal is not to get clients to write you a letter, although that's a nice reward. The goal is to get clients to reward you with
65 larger and larger orders. Then you can write them a thank-you letter.

Your clients get better when you get better. And your clients are rooting for you to get better.

(670 words)

—Chris Lytle, www.monster.com

Comprehension Questions.   Answer the following questions with *T* (true) or *F* (false) or respond in your own words.

_____ **1.** Monster pledges to help you with interviewing and getting a promotion.

_____ **2.** It appears that you can locate jobs in a specific field in your area without getting a password.

_____ **3.** If you answer the "Give Us Your Opinion!" section, your response will probably be sent to a potential employer along with your resume.

———— 4. A personalized salary report could give you an idea of what salary you should expect for a job.

———— 5. The site indicates that Monster employees will write free resumes for you.

———— 6. The "How Do You Measure Up?" article most likely appeared from clicking the *Find Jobs* heading.

———— 7. Using monster.com, you could target your career advice to the restaurant and hotel business.

———— 8. No advice is offered for people who want to work as temporary employees.

———— 9. The article "How Do You Measure Up?" is directed to people who are looking for jobs in sales.

———— 10. "The Yardstick" is a term meant as a positive compliment for a worker.

———— 11. The site indicates that you would not be able to respond to the "How Do You Measure Up?" article.

———— 12. In the "Monster Blog" you would probably be able to make personal comments on Monster services.

Think and Write

1. How do you envision using this Web site? How could you use it now even though you may not be ready to apply for your long-range career job?

2. How do you think the Monster Web site makes money?

3. Create a resume and submit it to your instructor. In order to write an excellent resume, research the Web site for ideas.

Net Search   Go to www.monster.com and register to join. What career do you presently plan to pursue? Research salaries and job opportunities for that career. List this information and evaluate your opportunities in that career.

Appendix

A

Test-Taking Strategies

A1	How Can You Increase Your Mental Awareness Before, During, and After a Test?
A2	What Strategies Work for Standardized Reading Tests?
A3	What Strategies Work for Content-Area Exams?

A1   How Can You Increase Your Mental Awareness Before, During, and After a Test?

Receiving a passing grade on a well-constructed test should not be the result of a trick or a magic formula; your grade should be a genuine assessment of your mastery of a skill or your understanding of a body of information. High scores should depend on preparation, not gimmicks. You can, however, improve your score by understanding how tests are constructed and what you need to do for maximum performance. Study the following tips and do everything you can both physically and mentally to gain an edge.

Before Taking a Test

Get Plenty of Sleep the Night Before. How alert can you be with inadequate sleep? You could lose as many as four to six points on account of fuzzy thinking and illogical choices.

Arrive Five or Ten Minutes Early and Get Settled. If you run in flustered at the last second, you will waste the first five minutes of the test calming yourself rather than getting immediately to work.

Know What to Expect on the Test. Check beforehand whether the test will be essay questions or in multiple-choice format.

Have Confidence in Your Abilities. The best way to achieve self-confidence is to be well prepared. Be optimistic about having a positive testing experience.

Know How the Test Will Be Scored. Be clear on how many points can be earned from each section or question so that you can prioritize your time and effort. Find out if a penalty is assessed for guessing.

Plan an Attack. At least a week before the test, take an inventory of what needs to be done and make plans to achieve your goals.

During the Test

Concentrate. Tune out internal and external distractions. Visualize and integrate old and new knowledge as you work. If you become anxious or distracted, close your eyes and take a few deep breaths to relax and get yourself back on track.

Read and Follow Directions. Find out what to do, and then do it. Don't start prematurely.

Schedule Your Time. Wear a watch and use it. Size up the task and allocate your time. Periodically check whether you are meeting your goals.

Work Rapidly. Do not waste time by pondering at length an especially difficult item. Mark it to return to later if time permits.

Think. Use knowledge, logic, common sense, and the process of elimination in responding to items.

Don't Be Intimidated by Students Who Finish Early. Early departures create anxiety for those still working. Calm yourself, look at your watch, and proceed on your projected timetable.

After the Test

Analyze Your Preparation. Question yourself after the test, and learn from the experience. Did you study the right material?

Analyze the Test. Was the test what you expected? Use your memory of the test to predict the pattern of future tests.

FAST FACT

Research shows that reviewing a test after completion and making changes can improve scores.

Analyze Your Performance. For standardized tests, evaluate what the scores tell you about your strengths and weaknesses. For content-area exams that are returned and reviewed in class, ask questions and plan for the next test. Ask to see an A paper.

A2 | What Strategies Work for Standardized Reading Tests?

Read to Comprehend the Passage as a Whole

While discussing test-taking strategies a student will ask, Should I read the questions first and then read the passage? Although the answer is subject to debate, most reading experts would advise reading the passage first and then reading the questions. By examining the questions first, you tend to read with five or six purposes in mind. Not only is this method confusing, but it is detail oriented and does not prepare you for more general questions concerning the main idea and implied meanings.

Read to understand the passage as a whole. Each passage has a central theme. Find it, and the rest of the ideas will fall into place. Attempt to understand what each paragraph contributes to the central theme. If you find later that a minor detail is needed to answer a question, you can quickly use a key word to locate and reread for accuracy the sentence in which it appears.

Anticipate What Is Coming Next

Most test passages are untitled and thus offer no initial clue as to their content. Before reading, glance at the passage to find a repeated word, name, or date. Look for a quick clue to let you know whether the passage is about Queen Victoria, pit bulls, or chromosome reproduction.

Do not rush through the first sentence. Let that first sentence activate your schema or computer chip and set the stage for what is to come. Continue to anticipate and guess throughout the passage. When necessary, glance ahead to double-check your facts; this indicates your skill in monitoring your own comprehension.

Read Rapidly, But Don't Allow Yourself to Feel Rushed

Use your pen as a pacer to direct your attention both mentally and physically to the printed page. Using your pen in this manner will help you focus your attention, particularly at the times of the test when you feel more rushed. That uneasy, harried feeling tends to occur at the beginning of the test when your concentration is not yet fixed, during the middle when you discover that you are only half finished, and toward the end when the first person finishes. Check your time, keep cool, and use your pen as a pacer.

Read with Involvement to Learn and Enjoy

Reading a passage with the sole purpose of answering five or six questions is reading with an artificial purpose. Picture what you read, relate the ideas to what you already know, think, learn, and enjoy—or at least fake it.

Self-test for the Main Idea

Pull the passage together before pulling it apart. Take perhaps ten or fifteen seconds to pinpoint the focus of the passage and to tell yourself the point that the author is trying to make. Again, if you understand the main point, the rest of the passage will fall into place.

Recognize Major Question Types

Learn to recognize the types of questions asked on reading comprehension tests. Although the wording may vary slightly, most tests will include one or more of each of the following types of comprehension questions.

Main Idea. Main-idea questions test your ability to find the central theme, central focus, gist, controlling idea, main point, or thesis. The terms are largely interchangeable in asking the reader to identify the main point of the passage. Main-idea items are stated in any of the following forms:

The best statement of the main idea is . . .

The best title for this passage is . . .

The author is primarily concerned with . . .

The central theme of the passage is . . .

Incorrect responses to main-idea questions tend to fall into two categories. Some responses will be too general and express more ideas than are included in the passage. Other incorrect answers deal with details within the passage that support the main idea. The details may be attention-getting and interesting, but they do not describe the central focus of the passage. If you have difficulty finding the main idea, reread the first and last sentences of the passage. Sometimes, though not always, one of these two sentences will give you an overview or focus.

Details. Detail questions check your ability to locate and understand explicitly stated material. Such items can frequently be answered correctly without a thorough understanding of the passage. To find the answer, note a key word in the question and then scan the passage for the word or a synonym of it. When you locate the term, reread the sentence to double-check your answer. Stems for detail questions fall into the following patterns:

> The author states that . . .
>
> According to the author . . .
>
> According to the passage . . .
>
> All of the following are true except . . .
>
> A person, term, or place is . . .

Incorrect answers to detail questions tend to be false statements. Sometimes the test maker will use a pompous or catchy phrase from the passage as a distractor. The phrase may indeed appear in the passage and sound authoritative, but on close inspection it means nothing.

Implied Meaning. Questions concerning implied meaning test your ability to look beyond what is directly stated and your understanding of the suggested meaning. Questions testing implied meaning deal with attitudes and feelings, sarcastic comments, snide remarks, characters' motivation, favorable and unfavorable descriptions, and other hints, clues, and ultimate assumptions. Stems for such items include the following:

> The author believes (or feels or implies) . . .
>
> It can be inferred from the passage . . .
>
> The passage or author suggests . . .
>
> It can be concluded from the passage that . . .

To answer inference questions correctly, look for clues to help you develop logical assumptions. Base your conclusions on what is known and what is suggested. Incorrect inference answers tend to be false statements.

Purpose. The purpose of a reading passage is usually not stated but implied. In a sense, the purpose is part of the main idea; you will probably need to understand the main idea to understand the purpose. Generally, however, reading comprehension tests include three basic types of passages, and each type tends to dictate its own purpose. Study the following three types.

1. Factual

Identification: Gives the facts about science, history, or other subjects.

Strategy: If a passage is complex, do not try to understand each detail before going to the questions. Remember, you can look back.

Example: Textbook.

Purposes: To inform, to explain, to describe, or to enlighten.

2. Opinion

Identification: Puts forth a particular point of view.

Strategy: The author states opinions and then refutes them. Sort out the opinions of the author and the opinions of the opposition.

Example: Newspaper editorial.

Purposes: To argue, to persuade, to condemn, or to ridicule.

3. Fiction

Identification: Tells a story.

Strategy: Read slowly to understand the motivation and interrelationships of characters.

Example: Novel or short story.

Purposes: To entertain, to narrate, to describe, or to shock.

Vocabulary.   Vocabulary items test your general knowledge of words as well as your ability to use context to figure out word meaning. The stem of most vocabulary questions on reading comprehension tests is:

As used in the passage, the best definition of _____ is

Note that both word knowledge and context are necessary for a correct response. The question is qualified by "As used in the passage," so you must go back and reread the sentence (context) in which the word appears to be sure you are not misled by a multiple meaning. To illustrate, the word *industry* means "a manufacturing business" as well as "diligence" or "hard work." As a test taker, you would need to double-check the context to see which meaning appears in your test passage. In addition, if you knew only one definition of the word *industry*, rereading the sentence would perhaps suggest the alternative meaning to you and help you get the item correct.

Use Skill in Evaluating Multiple-Choice Responses

Consider All Alternatives Before Choosing an Answer.   Read all the options in a multiple-choice test question. Do not rush to record an answer without considering all alternatives. Be careful—not careless—in considering each option. Multiple-choice test items usually ask for the *best* choice, not just a reasonable choice.

Anticipate the Answer and Look for Something Close to It.
As you begin reading a multiple-choice question, anticipate what you would write for a correct response. Develop an answer in your mind before you read the options, then look for a response that corroborates your thinking.

Avoid Answers with 100 Percent Words.
All and *never* mean 100 percent, without exceptions. A response containing either word is seldom correct; rarely can a statement be so definitely inclusive or exclusive. Other 100 percent words to avoid are:

no	*none*	*only*
every	*always*	*must*

Consider Answers with Qualifying Words.
The words *sometimes* and *seldom* suggest frequency but do not go so far as to say *all* or *none*. Such qualifying words can mean more than *none* and less than *all*. By being indefinite, the words are difficult to dispute. Therefore, qualifiers are more likely to appear in a correct response. Other qualifiers include:

few	*much*	*often*	*may*
many	*some*	*perhaps*	*generally*

Choose the Intended Answer Without Overanalyzing.
Try to follow logically the thinking of the test writer rather than overanalyze minute points. Don't make the question harder than it is. Use your common sense and answer what you think was intended.

True Statements Must Be True Without Exception.
A statement is either totally true or it is incorrect. Adding an incorrect *and, but,* or *because* phrase to a true statement makes the statement false and thus an unacceptable answer. If a statement is half true and half false, mark it false.

If Two Options Are Synonymous, Eliminate Both.
If *both* is not a possible answer and two items say basically the same thing, then neither can be correct. Eliminate the two and spend your time on the other options.

Study Similar Options to Figure Out the Differences.
If two similar options appear, frequently one of them will be correct. Study the options to see the subtle difference intended by the test maker.

Use Logical Reasoning if Two Answers Are Correct. Some tests include the options *all of the above* and *none of the above*. If you see that two of the options are correct and you are unsure about a third choice, then *all of the above* would be a logical response.

Look Suspiciously at Directly Quoted Pompous Phrases. In searching for distractors, test makers sometimes quote a pompous phrase from the passage that doesn't make much sense. Students read the phrase and think, Yes, I saw that in the passage; it sounds good, so it must be right. Beware of such repetitions, and make sure they make sense before choosing them.

Simplify Double Negatives by Canceling Out Both. Double negatives are confusing to unravel and time-consuming to think through. Simplify a double-negative statement by first canceling out both negatives. Then reread the statement without the confusion of the two negatives, and decide on the accuracy of the statement.

Use "Can't Tell" Responses if Clues Are Insufficient. Mark an item *can't tell* only if you are not given clues on which to base an assumption. In other words, no evidence indicates whether the statement is either true or false.

Validate True Responses to "All of the Following Except" Questions. In this type of question, you must recognize several responses as correct and find the one that is incorrect. Corroborate each response and, by the process of elimination, find the one that does not fit.

Note Oversights on Hastily Constructed Tests. Reading tests developed by professional test writers are usually well constructed and do not contain obvious clues to the correct answers. However, some instructor-made tests are hastily created and contain errors in test making that can help you find the correct answer. Do not, however, rely on these flaws to make a big difference in your score because they will not occur in a well-constructed test.

Grammatical Clues. Eliminate responses that do not have subject-verb agreement. The tense of the verb as well as the modifier *a* or *an* can also give clues to the correct response.

Clues from Other Parts of the Test. If the test was hastily constructed, information in one part of the test may help you with an uncertain answer.

Length Clues. On poorly constructed tests, longer answers are more frequently correct.

Absurd Ideas and Emotional Words. Avoid distractors with absurd ideas or emotional words. The test maker probably got tired of thinking of distractors and in a moment of weakness included nonsense.

A3 | What Strategies Work for Content-Area Exams?

Almost all professors would say that the number one strategy for scoring high on content exams is to study the material. Although this advice is certainly on target, some other suggestions can help you gain an edge.

Understand the Purpose of Multiple-Choice Items

Multiple-choice, true-false, and matching items on content-area exams are written to evaluate three categories: factual knowledge, conceptual comprehension, and application skill. Factual questions tap your knowledge of names, definitions, dates, events, and theories. Conceptual comprehension questions evaluate your ability to see relationships, notice similarities and differences, and combine information from different parts of a chapter. Application questions provide the opportunity to generalize from a theory to a real-life illustration.

Stress Significance in Short-Answer Items

FAST FACT

Research shows that students who have frequent quizzes during a course tend to do better on the final exam.

Professors ask short-answer questions because they want you to use your own words to describe or identify. Usually you need to explain the *who, what, when, where,* and, most important, the significance, or the *why.* Don't waste time writing more than is needed; on the other hand, don't lose points by not writing enough. Study for short-answer items by making lists and self-testing, just as you do when studying for multiple-choice items.

Plan for Essay Questions

Essay answers demand more effort and energy from the test taker than do multiple-choice items. Rather than simply recognize correct answers, you must recall, create, and organize. On a multiple-choice test, all the correct answers are somewhere before you. On an essay exam, however, the only thing in front of you is a question and a blank sheet of paper. Your job is to recall appropriate ideas for a response and then pull them together under the central theme designated in the question.

Translate the Question.
Translate the question into your own words. Simplify it into easily understandable terms. Break it into its parts and convert the translated parts of the question into the approach that you will use in your answer.

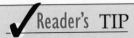 Reader's TIP

Key Words in Essay Questions

Here are key words of instruction that appear in essay questions, with hints for responding to each:

Compare: list the similarities between things
Contrast: note the differences between things
Criticize: state your opinion and stress the weaknesses
Define: state the meaning of the term and use examples
Describe: state the characteristics so that the image is vivid
Diagram: make a drawing that demonstrates relationships
Discuss: define the issue and elaborate on the advantages and disadvantages
Evaluate: state positive and negative views and make a judgment
Explain: show cause and effect and give reasons
Illustrate: provide examples
Interpret: explain your own understanding of a topic and include your
   opinions
Justify: give proof or reasons to support an opinion
List: record a series of numbered items
Outline: sketch out the main points with their significant supporting details
Prove: use facts as evidence in support of an opinion
Relate: connect items and show how one influences another
Review: overview with a summary
Summarize: retell the main points
Trace: move sequentially from one event to another

Answer the Question.   Make sure that your answer responds to the particular question that is asked rather than summarizing everything you know about the subject. Padding your answer by repeating an idea or including irrelevant information is obvious to graders and seldom appreciated.

Organize Your Response.   Do not write the first thing that pops into your head. Instead, take a few minutes to brainstorm and jot down ideas. Number the ideas in the order that you wish to present them, and use this plan as your outline for writing. In your first sentence, establish the purpose and direction of your response. Then list specific details that support, explain, prove, and develop your point. Reemphasize the points in a concluding sentence and restate your purpose. Whenever possible, use numbers or subheadings to simplify your message for the reader. If time runs short, use an outline or a diagram to express your remaining ideas.

Use an Appropriate Style. Your audience for this response is not your best friend but your learned professor who will give you a grade. Be respectful. Do not use slang. Do not use phrases like "as you know"; they may be appropriate in conversation, but they are not appropriate in formal writing.

Avoid Empty Words and Thoughts. Words like *good, interesting,* and *nice* say very little. Be more direct and descriptive in your writing.

State Your Thesis, Supply Proof, and Use Transitional Phrases to Tie Your Ideas Together. Words like *first, second,* and *finally* help to organize for levels of importance or time order. Terms like *however* and *on the other hand* show a shift in thought. Use phrases and words to help the reader see relationships.

Be Aware of Appearance. Be particular about appearance and be considerate of the reader. Proofread for correct grammar, punctuation, and spelling.

Predict and Practice Predict possible essay questions by using the table of contents, the subheadings of your text, and your lecture notes. Practice brainstorming and outlining answers.

View Your Response Objectively for Evaluation Points. Respond to earn points. (Some students feel that just filling up the page deserves a passing grade.) Although essay exams seem totally subjective, professors look for those relevant points that should be made. The student's grade reflects the quantity, quality, and clarity of those relevant points. Do not add personal experiences or extraneous examples unless they are requested; stick to the subject and the material. Demonstrate to the professor that you know the material by selectively using it in your response.

After the Test, Read an A Paper. Maybe the A paper will be yours. If so, share it with others. If not, ask to read an A paper so that you will have a model from which to learn. Ask your classmates or ask the professor. You can learn a lot from reading a good paper; you will see what you should and could have done.

Develop an Internal Locus of Control

Have you ever heard students say *I do better when I don't study* or *No matter how much I study, I still get a C*? A learning theory psychologist would interpret these comments as reflecting an external locus of control regarding test-taking. Such "externalizers" feel that fate, luck, or others control what happens to them, so they do not face matters directly and take responsibility for failure or credit for success.

People who have an internal locus of control, on the other hand, feel that they, rather than fate, control what happens to them. Such students might evaluate test performance by saying, *I didn't study enough* or *I should have spent more time organizing my essay response.* "Internalizers" feel their rewards are due to their own actions, and they take steps to ensure that they receive those rewards. When it comes to test-taking, be an internalizer, take control, and accept the credit for your success.

Appendix B

ESL Pointers: Making Sense of Figurative Language and Idioms

B1   What Is ESL?

How many languages can you speak? Are you a native English speaker who has learned Spanish, or are you a native Farsi speaker who has learned English? If you have acquired skill in a second or third language, you know that it takes many years and plenty of patience to master the intricacies of a language. Not only do you need to learn new words, you must also learn new grammatical constructions. For example, the articles that are habitually in English, *a, an,* and *the,* do not appear in Russian, Chinese, Japanese, Thai, or Farsi. In Spanish and Arabic, personal pronouns restate the subject, as in *My sister she goes to college.* In Spanish, Greek, French, Vietnamese, and Portuguese, *to* words are used where English uses *ing* words, as in *I enjoy to play soccer.* These complexities, which are innately understood by native speakers, make direct translation difficult. The English language especially has many unusual phrases and grammatical constructions that defy direct translation.

To assist students with these complexities, most colleges offer courses in ESL, or English as a Second Language. These courses are designed to teach language skills to nonnative speakers of English. If you are an ESL student, you may have been recruited through an international exchange program with another college, you may be a newly arrived immigrant, or you may be a citizen with a bilingual background. You bring a multicultural perspective to classroom discussions and campus life that will broaden the insights of others. Not only are some of your holidays different from those of others, but your sense of family life, work, and responsibility may differ as well. Share your thoughts and ideas with native English speakers as they share the irregularities of the language with you.

B2 What Is Figurative Language?

One aspect of the English language that defies direct translation and confuses nonnative speakers (and sometimes even native speakers) is **figurative language.** This manipulation of the language is used to create images, add interest, and draw comparisons by using figures of speech (see Chapter 7, Inference). The two most commonly used types are *simile* and *metaphor*.

- **Simile:** a stated comparison using *like* or *as*:
  The baby swims like a duck.
- **Metaphor:** an implied comparison:
  The baby is a duck in water.

Many figurative expressions have become commonplace in the English language. In the metaphor above the *baby* is not actually a *baby duck,* but the meaning is that *the baby swims very well.* However, neither direct translation nor a dictionary will unlock that meaning. When you encounter comparisons that seem out of the ordinary or ill chosen, ask yourself whether a figure of speech is being used, and look for clues within the sentence to help you guess the meaning.

The following practice exercises contain figurative language. Read each dialogue passage for meaning and then use the context clues to match the number of the boldfaced figure of speech with the letter of the appropriate definition. To narrow your choices, the answers to 1–5 are within a–e and the answers to 6–10 are within f–j.

Practice 1

Melanie: Jennifer is the (1) **apple of her father's eye.** He adores her and thinks she never does anything wrong. Her brother is always the one in trouble. I think Jennifer (2) **gets away with murder.**

Sue: I heard (3) **through the grapevine** that last week Jennifer (4) **got called on the carpet** for coming home at 3:00 in the morning. She blamed it on her brother Zack.

Melanie: I think Zack got (5) **the short end of the stick** on that one. Jennifer was driving her own car when I saw her at midnight.

Sue: Her father told her to drop the excuses and (6) **stand on her own two feet** and (7) **face the music.** She tried to (8) **smooth things over** with promises, but her father vowed to (9) **crack down** with new rules. She got really upset and Zack told her she was overreacting. Please (10) **keep this under your hat** because I wasn't supposed to tell anyone.

_____ 1. apple of her father's eye

_____ 2. gets away with murder

_____ 3. through the grapevine

_____ 4. got called on the carpet

_____ 5. the short end of the stick

_____ 6. stand on her own two feet

_____ 7. face the music

_____ 8. smooth things over

_____ 9. crack down

_____ 10. keep this under your hat

a. reprimanded or scolded

b. special favorite

c. is not punished for wrongdoing

d. unfair treatment

e. through gossip

f. accept the consequences

g. keep it secret

h. become more strict

i. be independent

j. make the situation more pleasant

Practice 2

George: If we go to a really expensive restaurant, I won't have enough money (1) **to pick up the tab.**

Marsha: I have some money, so let's (2) **go Dutch.** Then you won't have to be (3) **on the edge of your seat** about the bill. We'll (4) **have a ball.**

George: I've had to (5) **tighten my belt** since I paid for my books. (6) **Once in a blue moon**, I would like to have some extra cash.

Marsha: I understand. I paid (7) **an arm and a leg** for my books, too.

George: Until my parents sent me more money, I thought I would be (8) **brown bagging it** at noon. Sometimes people think I am a (9) **wet blanket** for not wanting to go out, but my finances are frequently low. You can't live (10) **high on the hog** without cash.

_____ 1. to pick up the tab

_____ 2. go Dutch

_____ 3. on the edge of your seat

_____ 4. have a ball

_____ 5. tighten my belt

_____ 6. once in a blue moon

_____ 7. an arm and a leg

_____ 8. brown bagging it

_____ 9. wet blanket

_____ 10. high on the hog

a. have a good time

b. nervous

c. spend less money

d. to pay the bill

e. each pay his or her own bill

f. person who discourages having fun

g. occasionally

h. luxuriously

i. a large amount

j. bringing a lunch

Practice 3

Michael: My parents used part of their retirement (1) **nest egg** to send me to college. I have been (2) **racking my brain** to think of some way to earn money this summer to use in the fall.

Juan: I know what you mean. Both of my parents work hard to (3) **bring home the bacon.** I already have a construction job for the summer. I will be (4) **breaking my neck** hauling lumber for new houses.

Michael: It is only February. You are an (5) **eager beaver** to already have a job lined up for the summer. Don't you think that's (6) **jumping the gun** a little?

Juan: No. My brother told me his company would be needing more workers, so I met with the supervisor and he offered me a job. I decided to (7) **strike while the iron was hot** and accepted.

Michael: I see what you mean. You certainly don't (8) **let any grass grow under your feet.** It's a (9) **feather in your cap** to plan so far ahead.

Juan: You never want to wait too long and (10) **miss the boat.**

_____ 1. nest egg

_____ 2. racking my brain

_____ 3. bring home the bacon

_____ 4. breaking my neck

a. earn money

b. ambitious hard worker

c. working very hard

d. extra saved money

_____ **5.** eager beaver   e. trying to think

_____ **6.** jumping the gun   f. take advantage of an
                                                opportunity
_____ **7.** strike while the iron was hot
                                             g. proud achievement
_____ **8.** let any grass grow under
        your feet   h. waste time

_____ **9.** feather in your cap   i. lose an opportunity

_____ **10.** miss the boat   j. starting before you should

Practice 4

Juan: Tiffany is trying out for the musical lead in the fall play. If she gets it, she will be in (1) **seventh heaven.**

Dawn: She has a beautiful voice. She'll (2) **knock them dead.** Also, she looks great. I think she's a (3) **knockout.**

Juan: She was (4) **sweating bullets** about the audition. I gave her a (5) **pep talk** on self-confidence. The theater group has lots of talented actors this year. They will choose the (6) **cream of the crop** for the lead.

Dawn: If I could (7) **put in my two cents' worth,** she would get the part.

Juan: She would appreciate that but (8) **just hold your horses.** (9) **Our hands are tied.** All we can do is hope and (10) **keep our fingers crossed** for her. We'll know the results tomorrow.

_____ **1.** seventh heaven   a. beautiful person

_____ **2.** knock them dead   b. very happy

_____ **3.** knockout   c. talk to arouse enthusiasm

_____ **4.** sweating bullets   d. nervous

_____ **5.** pep talk   e. greatly impress

_____ **6.** cream of the crop   f. wish for good luck

_____ **7.** put in my two cents' worth g. wait

_____ **8.** just hold your horses   h. give my opinion

_____ **9.** our hands are tied   i. best of the group

_____ **10.** keep our fingers crossed   j. we are unable to help

Practice 5

Kristin: Since it's spring already, it's time for us to (1) **talk turkey** about next year. Will you be my roommate?

Roberta: Yes. I am glad you asked. I have been (2) **twiddling my thumbs** on the issue. I do not want to room with Kim for another year.

Kristin: I thought we were (3) **in the same boat** and both wanted a change.

Roberta: Last week when I was (4) **under the weather** with the flu, she talked on the phone until after midnight. I couldn't sleep, and we got into a big argument. We talked for a while but did not even (5) **scratch the surface** of the problems I have with her.

Kristin: Did you make up?

Roberta: Yes. We're on better terms now. We decided to (6) **let bygones be bygones,** but I am still eager to get away from her.

Kristin: Will she think you are (7) **pulling her leg** when you tell her that you will be rooming with me next year?

Roberta: No. She'll (8) **get the picture.** I think she will know that I am serious (9) **right off the bat.** It would be (10) **playing with fire** for us to be together another year.

_____ **1.** talk turkey	a.	not doing anything
_____ **2.** twiddling my thumbs	b.	have a business discussion
_____ **3.** in the same boat	c.	sick
_____ **4.** under the weather	d.	go beyond the basics
_____ **5.** scratch the surface	e.	in a similar situation
_____ **6.** let bygones be bygones	f.	inviting danger
_____ **7.** pulling her leg	g.	understand
_____ **8.** get the picture	h.	immediately
_____ **9.** right off the bat	i.	teasing
_____ **10.** playing with fire	j.	forget past differences

B3 What Are Common English Idioms?

An **idiom** is an expression that has a special meaning that cannot be understood by directly translating each individual word in the idiom. The meaning is usually understood by native speakers because they are familiar with it, but it is confusing to those learning English as a second language.

Idioms are more common in spoken and informal language than in formal writing. In fact, most idiomatic expressions can usually be replaced by a single word. To add to the confusion, some idioms have dual meanings, and many idioms are grammatically irregular.

App.
B

| EXAMPLE | What does the idiomatic expression *go over* mean in the following sentences?

1. How did my speech *go over*?

2. I want to *go over* the exam paper with the professor.

| EXPLANATION | In both sentences the use of the idiom is informal. A more formal version of each would be:

1. How was my speech *received* by the audience?

2. I want to *review* the exam paper with the professor.

Notice the grammatical irregularity in the first sentence. *Over* is not followed by a noun (name of a person, place, or thing) as a preposition (connecting words such as *in, out,* and *at*) normally would be, according to the rules of grammar; instead, *over* becomes part of the verb phrase (words showing action). Thus the translation requires a change in wording, whereas the second use of the idiom is grammatically correct and can be directly translated by the single word *review*.

No one says that understanding idioms is easy. If you visit a bookstore, you will find that entire books have been written about categorizing, recognizing, and translating thousands of idioms. To help clear up the confusion, some books group idioms according to families based on root words; other books categorize them according to grammatical construction. Either way, understanding idiomatic expressions depends more on using context clues to deduce meaning and on familiarity with the informal, spoken language than on learning rules.

✓ Reader's TIP

Categorizing Idioms

Idioms are sometimes categorized into groups:

- Word Families: grouping around a similar individual word
  Down as in *step down, take down, pipe down, narrow down, nail down, run down, tear down, knock down, let down, die down,* and *cut down.*

(continued)

- Verb + Preposition: action word plus a connecting word
  Hammer away means "persist," *stand for* means "represent," and *roll back* means "reduce."

- Preposition + Noun: connecting word plus the name of a person, place, or thing
  On foot means "walking," *by heart* means "memorized," and *off guard* means "surprised."

- Verb + Adjective: action word plus a descriptive word
  Think twice means "consider carefully," *hang loose* means "be calm," and *play fair* means to "deal equally."

- Pairs of Nouns: two words naming a person, place, or thing
  Flesh and blood means "kin," *part and parcel* means "total," and *pins and needles* means "nervous."

- Pairs of Adjectives: two descriptive words
  Cut and dried means "obvious," *fair and square* means "honest," and *short and sweet* means "brief."

In the following practice exercises, idioms are grouped according to a common word. Use the context clues within each sentence to write the meaning of the boldfaced idiom in the blank.

Practice 6

about	across	around	away	back

1. Let's **see about** renting an apartment. _____

2. How do I **go about** getting a job? _____

3. If you **come across** my socks when you are cleaning your room, let me know. _____

4. I suspected he was trying to **put** something **across** on me.

   _____

5. Don't **fool around** with the heat controls and make it too hot again.

   _____

6. When June **rolls around,** I'll be out of school. _____

7. Can you **break away** from the office to have a quick lunch?

_____

8. The crowd got **carried away** by the music and became difficult to control. _____

9. To **cut back** pollution, more people should walk to work. _____

10. I'll **pay** him **back** for being rude to me. _____

Practice 7

by	down	for	in	into

1. We did not have tickets and were put on **standby** for the next flight.

_____

2. How do you **get by** with so little sleep? _____

3. At the end of the season, clothes are **marked down** and you can get bargains. _____

4. Professors sometimes begin class with a brief **rundown** of what will be covered during the session. _____

5. My roommate is **falling for** the soccer player down the hall.

_____

6. I **feel for** her when she discovers that her laptop computer is missing.

_____

7. The five students **piled into** Dan's car and went to the movies.

_____

8. Maggie just **blew in** an hour ago. We expected her sooner. _____

9. Do you ever **run into** my old roommate on campus? I never see her myself. _____

10. Because exams are next week, he is really **digging into** his studies.

_____

Practice 8

of	off	on	out	over

1. A winter vacation was **unheard of** in my house. We took a trip only in the summer. _____

2. We have not communicated, so I do not know what has **become of** my high school friend. _____

3. Drug dealers have a way of **knocking off** the competition.

   _____

4. The company is having to **lay off** workers because profits are down.

   _____

5. My grandmother is beginning to **get on in years** and is considering a retirement home. _____

6. Moving into a management position will mean **taking on** more responsibilities and also receiving more pay. _____

7. Take an art appreciation course to **round out** your college experience with some culture. _____

8. An aerobics class starts at five, so let's go **work out.** _____

9. You should **carry over** what you learn in an introductory course to the next course in the sequence. _____

10. Why don't you **stay over** rather than drive back late at night?

    _____

Practice 9

through	to	under	up	with

1. How can I **get through** the winter if temperatures fall below zero?

   _____

2. **Run through** the list of movies and find one we have not seen that is playing at 7:00. _____

3. Unless your brother goes to college, he will not **amount to** anything.

_____

4. After the knockout, the boxer took a few minutes to **come to.**

_____

5. No one eats dinner there during the week, so the new restaurant is about to **go under.** _____

6. Group pressure finally made him **buckle under** and accept the proposed project without references. _____

7. For New Year's celebrations, restaurants sometimes **jack up** their prices. _____

8. I'd like a **blowup** of this photo so I can put it in a larger frame.

_____

9. Since it is December, the semester will **be over with** soon.

_____

10. Sometimes you just have to **live with** your mistakes, forget them, and try not to repeat them. _____

App.
B

Practice 10

wear and tear	rank and file	ups and downs
ins and outs	odds and ends	up and about neck and neck
few and far between	short and sweet	high and dry

1. My dressy shoes do not get as much **wear and tear** as my sneakers.

_____

2. The **rank and file** of a company do not make as much money as the executives. _____

3. The Johnsons have had their **ups and downs,** but they are still married.

_____

4. Once you know the **ins and outs** of any company, you can successfully figure out how to work the system. _____

5. I am ready to move into the apartment except for a few **odds and ends** that must be resolved at the last minute. _____

6. The patient is now **up and about** after having knee surgery.

   _____

7. The marathon runners were **neck and neck** until the final half mile.

   _____

8. Lottery winners are **few and far between.** _____

9. A graduation speech should be **short and sweet** because the graduates just want to get their diplomas. _____

10. Since my wife took the car on Wednesday, I was left **high and dry** for the day. _____

Appendix

C

Writing Effectively

C1 What Should You Think About When Writing?

Electronic technology has made writing *more* important, not less important. With e-mail, your single written idea can move quickly from coast to coast. Regardless of your career choice, your writing skills can enhance your success.

Like readers, writers are not born; they are *made* through effort and persistence, and the two skills are strongly linked. Through thoughtful analysis, you can read to learn and appreciate the message, technique, and craft of a writer. As a writer yourself, you organize and mold your ideas to interest and influence your readers. You identify your purpose for writing, suggest your message in a thesis statement, and set a tone and level of formality that fits your reading audience.

Think of writing as a *process*—one that has many parts and gets easier with practice. Set your goals according to the different parts of the process, and congratulate yourself at the completion of each step.

C2 What Are the Steps in the Writing Process?

There are six basic steps in the writing process: selecting a topic, using invention techniques, outlining, drafting, revising and editing, and proofreading. For best results, keep the entire process in mind—but focus on only one step at a time.

Step 1: Select a Topic—Your Own or an Assigned Topic

To write effectively, you must clearly understand the issues. If you are selecting your own topic for a writing assignment, choose something about which you are knowledgeable, interested, or excited. If you must choose from an assigned list, first examine the topics carefully to be sure that you understand key words. Professors may list topics in the form of a statement or a question. Choose a topic about which you can be logical and resourceful.

Step 2: Use the Invention Techniques of Brainstorming and Mapping

When you have a topic, the next step is to generate ideas supporting your topic through **invention techniques.** In these *prewriting* strategies, you *invent* what you want to say before you begin to write the first draft. Depending on the complexity of the topic, you might research the subject or think about it as you fall asleep at night. Once you have selected your topic and taken a position on it, begin your prewriting with the following techniques.

Brainstorm a List.   To **brainstorm,** jot down all ideas, references, and examples that come to mind about your topic. One student, asked to write about a meaningful experience, selected an exchange trip to Argentina and brainstormed the ideas shown in Figure C-1. When satisfied with your list of words and phrases, select those that best support your position and organize them into categories.

FIGURE C-1	Brainstorming list

learn Spanish	dulce de leche	flight returned	blind landing
slept on floor	lived with families	behind friends in Spanish	summer tutoring
sí to questions	pocket translator	self-confidence	independence
ambassadors	forced speaking	Ricky Martin	discotheques	Buenos Aires

Group Your Ideas Through Mapping.   Mapping, another invention technique, uses listing with a visual twist. To map your ideas, begin by writing your topic in a central circle or box with lines radiating outward for the main ideas. Next, place the main ideas in smaller circles and put details on lines stemming off the main idea entries—as illustrated in Figure C-2.

FIGURE C-2 | Map of writing topic

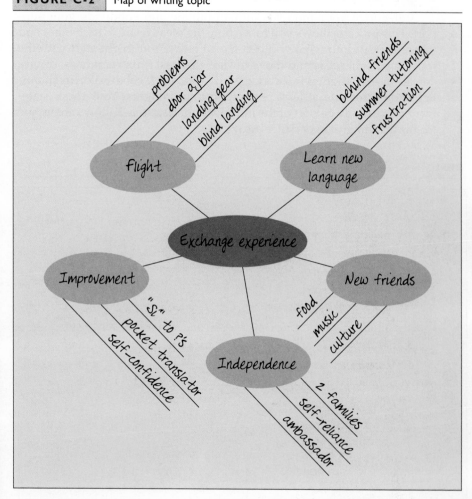

Develop Your Thesis Statement. Study your brainstorming lists to formulate your *thesis statement*—your position or focus on the topic. A thesis statement tells the reader what will be said *about* the topic and implies whether the essay is meant to persuade or to inform. This complete sentence functions as a summary or a road map for your essay. The following sentence is a thesis statement for the meaningful experience assignment:

> My month-long trip to Argentina as an exchange student was an unforgettable and extremely meaningful experience in which I grew academically, personally, and culturally.

The details of the essay should support the thesis statement.

Step 3: Create an Outline

Categorize your thoughts into an outline and subdivide your support. This process allows you to see how the ideas relate to each other and where they fit into what will become an essay. You might start with the most important ideas and move toward the least important ones, or vice versa—or you might use chronological order. Each subdivision in an outline should include at least two supporting thoughts. Your thesis statement will usually be part of the introduction. Figure C-3 shows an outline for the meaningful experience essay.

FIGURE C-3 | Outline

I. Introduction
   A. Flight problems
      1. Turned around
      2. Blind landing
   B. Slept in airport
   C. *Thesis:* My month-long trip to Argentina as an exchange student was an unforgettable and extremely meaningful experience in which I grew academically, personally, and culturally.

II. Desire to learn Spanish
   A. Behind friends
      1. Latin initially
      2. Summer tutoring
   B. Frustration

III. Self-confidence
   A. "Sí" to questions
   B. Pocket translator
   C. Self-confidence

IV. Ambassadors
   A. Independence
   B. Part of two families

V. Conclusion
   A. New friends
   B. Foods
   C. Music

Step 4: Draft the Essay

Before you begin writing a draft of your essay, you need to consider several things that will determine how you write: *purpose, audience, tone,* and *level of formality.*

Identify Your Purpose for Writing.   Are you writing to explain or explore an idea, as in the exchange trip example, or is your purpose to persuade and thus to develop a logical argument to support a position on an issue? Other examples of purpose are to *instruct* (tell how), to *inform* (tell what), to *explain* (tell why), to *entertain,* and to *summarize.* For all purposes, write convincingly, stay focused, and do not wander to other issues.

Identify Your Audience.   The word *audience* literally means "those who listen." Both the type and the amount of information you include in your essay are determined by the audience you target for your writing. As a college student, your essay writing will usually be directed toward a single person: the instructor who made the assignment. In some classes, however, the audience could also include fellow classmates. Write for your audience, and include examples that your readers will find interesting and convincing.

Set an Appropriate Tone.   A writer's *tone* relays an attitude or point of view about the subject. The tone of an essay is similar to the tone of a person's voice; it can be angry, humorous, sarcastic, or sympathetic.

✔ Reader's TIP

When to Use Formal and Informal Writing

Informal Writing	Formal Writing
Journal entries	Essays
Class notes	Research papers
Research notes	E-mail to professors
Brainstorming	Cover letters
E-mail to friends	Memo to boss

Within these levels of formality, there are variations and exceptions to the rule. An essay written in class will not usually be held to the same level of formality as a paper written out of class. A memo to your boss will usually be more formal than a letter to a friend. Know these differences and, when in doubt, be formal.

Because you cannot actually speak to the audience and use voice inflections, choose words that will communicate your negative or positive feelings on the topic.

Use an Appropriate Level of Formality.   A certain *level of formality* shows respect for the audience. You might use words in a telephone conversation with a close friend that you would not use in a classroom response to your instructor. Avoid marginally acceptable words.

Adjust the formality of your words according to how close you are to your audience. If in doubt, be formal. If you were writing a formal essay about *The Jerry Springer Show* and its effects, you might use adjectives such as *unconventional* and *outrageous*. In an e-mail to a friend, however, you might use stronger descriptive words—*depraved, sexual lunacy, disgusting*. Although all the terms may describe your feelings, *unconventional* and *outrageous* are more formal and less emotionally offensive.

Write an Introduction.   Your introduction, which will usually consist of one paragraph, should introduce the subject, state your position, and set the tone for your essay. You can open your essay with an anecdote, brief description, recent news story, question, quotation, or historical fact. You want to catch the reader's attention and arouse curiosity. Most typically your thesis sentence will come at the end of your introductory paragraph, as shown in Figure C-4.

FIGURE C-4   Draft of introductory paragraph

¿Como se dice . . . ?

by Julie Wakefield Smith

I remember it all vividly. I was on a 747 at one a.m. when the pilot announced that one of the doors was ajar and that he would keep us posted. About three minutes later, he announced that the landing gear was faulty. Then he said that we were turning around. This is how my trip to Argentina began. Luckily, we did survive, persevering against the forces of a blind landing, a burnt-down communication center, and a city of fully booked hotels. Even though I cringe when I remember the chaperone from Dubuque pointing a video camera at my face at five a.m. on our second night of sleeping in the airport, my month-long trip to Argentina as an exchange student was an unforgettable and extremely meaningful experience in which I grew academically, personally, and culturally.

If you cannot think of an effective introduction, insert the words "Introduction Here" as a placeholder and proceed with the rest of your paper. Often a clever introductory idea will come to mind as you write or when you finish the rest of the essay.

Support Your Thesis with Paragraph Development. Your completed essay will contain a group of interconnected paragraphs, each covering one of the supporting ideas from your thesis. Let your thesis and your outline act as a controlling guide to keep you on track, but don't be afraid to add ideas or expand ideas as long as they support your thesis. The support suggested in the thesis and in your outline should always be reflected in the body of the essay. For example, if your thesis statement mentions three points, you must either write about all three in three separate paragraphs or alter your thesis to match the completed essay. Note how each paragraph in Figure C-5 relates to a Roman numeral in the outline in Figure C-3.

App.
C

Develop Coherent Paragraphs: Topic Sentences and Transitions. Within an essay, paragraphs can vary in style, but each paragraph must have a **topic sentence** that tells the reader what will be discussed in that paragraph. Stick to the topic so that your paragraphs will have coherence. All the supporting sentences should be directly related to the topic sentence of the paragraph. If you are unfocused, adding many small bits of information without tying them to the topic sentence, the result will be a lack of unity—an essay that doesn't "hold together." Your topic sentence may appear at the beginning, middle, or end of the paragraph. Your related sentences should use vivid examples and details to support your topic sentence. These examples and details will bring your paper alive for the reader. Avoid empty and vague statements, and avoid repeating the same thought over and over in new words. The level of specificity and the quality of the examples and details differentiate an A paper from a C paper.

Connect the ideas in your paragraphs and throughout the essay in a cohesive manner. Logically link the content, and technically link the sentences and paragraphs with transitions. Use *transitional words or phrases* within and between your paragraphs to act as pointers for easy reading. You can repeat key words to link paragraphs, and use pronouns to link sentences. Transitions are usually needed anywhere in your essay that an abrupt change occurs. Refer to Chapter 6 for more on transitional words.

Select the Organizational Patterns for Your Paragraphs. Your writing instructor will probably have given you assignments to develop your skills in using all of the familiar patterns: narration, description, cause and effect, comparison/contrast, and argument or persuasion.

FIGURE C-5   Essay

> One of the most meaningful parts of my trip was learning to communicate in a different language. I had always wanted to learn Spanish. However, in my first year at school, I was required to take Latin. When I switched over to Spanish the following year, I found myself a year behind my friends, so I spent the summer in seemingly endless tutoring sessions to catch up. I was then placed in a class in which I felt lost. However, the frustration that I had felt in my Spanish class increased tenfold when I was put in a country and a house where the inhabitants had known Spanish from birth.
>
> Initially, I struggled through, painfully responding with a smile and a "Sí" regardless of the question. But I slowly improved, carrying my pocket translator with me under the table at dinner, writing in a journal every night in my new language, and forcing myself to speak at all costs. I soon developed a passion for learning the language, attacking nearly every available person with "Como se dice . . . ?" ("How do you say . . . ?"). After four weeks of spongelike learning in Argentina, I found myself a different student, possessing a newfound confidence to speak up in class and to share my opinions.
>
> The trip also taught me about independence. We were told over and over again by our chaperone that we were ambassadors for our school and our country. To me, this was a huge responsibility. I had to become part of two new families, one in Salta and one in Buenos Aires. From making my own breakfast to handling my own money, I was forced to be self-reliant. When I returned, I knew myself better than I ever had before.

Narration. *Narration* is considered one of the easiest patterns of essay writing. The writer tells a story and follows a time order. Transitional expressions help the reader keep events in the proper sequence.

Description. The successful use of *description* depends on your making careful observations and having a distinct purpose for the description. You want the reader to see, smell, hear, taste, and feel what is described. Description is rarely used alone in an essay, but this technique combines well with other patterns to add interest to an essay.

Cause and Effect. You can set up the *cause-and-effect* essay by asking a *why* question. The *cause* refers to actions or circumstances, and the *effects* refer to results. For instance, your topic may be reflected by the question *Why do my friends continue smoking even though they know its risks and consequences?* To develop an essay on this topic, you would examine the motivation for smoking and the results.

Comparison/Contrast.   The purpose of *comparing and contrasting* is to examine the ways two things are similar *and* different, and to make a judgment about the two. This technique is often used for an entire essay. Suppose you are answering the question *Would you rather shop in a big city shopping mall or at a neighborhood store?* You have two options for developing an essay about the similarities and differences. All the characteristics or attributes of the mall—parking, selection of goods, service—can be discussed, followed by a discussion of the same attributes of the neighborhood store. Alternatively, you can discuss one characteristic at a time, first for the mall and then for the neighborhood store. This pattern would continue until all characteristics have been discussed. Adverbs that specify *how, when, what, where, how often,* and *to what extent* are often used effectively in writing that compares and contrasts.

Argumentation or Persuasion.   In *argumentative* or *persuasive* writing, you define an issue, make a claim, and usually counter opposing claims in an effort to persuade the reader to accept your point of view. Argumentation is sometimes considered to be an attitude rather than a true pattern because it is a position that the writer takes toward a subject that can be defended with evidence.

A logical argument is based on sound reasoning. Your reasoning will be sound only if you have enough evidence to support your claim and if you avoid common fallacies, or errors in logic or reasoning (see Chapter 10 on critical thinking).

Write Your Conclusion.   Signal the end of your essay by summarizing the main points from the body or including one of the following:

- Make a call for action concerning the central problem.
- Suggest a possible solution to the problem.
- End with a famous quotation that supports the stated position.

A conclusion is generally brief. As a rule, no information should appear in the conclusion that was not discussed or implied in the body of the essay. Figure C-6 shows the conclusion to the meaningful activity topic.

Step 5: Revise and Edit

In **revising** you improve the content of your essay by paying attention to major issues such as organization, purpose, and audience; you sharpen your focus, develop ideas, add specific examples or supporting

FIGURE C-6 | Draft of conclusion

> Another extremely meaningful part of the trip was the new friends that I made. I now have countless "amigos" south of the equator. They showed me the rich culture of their country, taking me dancing at the discotheques until sunrise and introducing me to the tea-time treat of *dulce de leche*. Luckily, I have a support group for Argentina-withdrawal, the group of nine students from my school who also went. We get together frequently; we are unable to resist the temptation to execute a group rendition of the words and dance steps to Ricky Martin's "La Copa de la Vida" ("The Cup of Life"), the theme song of the 1998 World Cup. What could be more meaningful?

details that you had overlooked, and delete unnecessary repetitions. You look at your work critically (through the eyes of your readers) to analyze what works and what doesn't work.

✓ Reader's TIP

Ask Revision Questions

Ask yourself these questions as you revise your essay:

- Does the thesis express one main idea?
- Does the thesis express your position?
- Do the paragraphs support the thesis?
- Is the information accurate, to the best of your knowledge?
- Do transitions make the appropriate connections?
- Do sentences flow smoothly from one to another? Is the writing concise?
- Have you used evidence and examples in your support?
- Do the tone and level of formality of the essay work for the intended audience?
- Is your purpose clear by the end of the first couple of paragraphs?
- Does your conclusion agree with your introduction?
- Can readers recognize your pattern of organization?
- Have you found any gaps and filled them in?

After you are satisfied that the content has been revised to convey your meaning, the next step is **editing.** Editing changes not the content, but the form of the writing; it involves correcting mechanical errors. When you edit, you pay attention to the details of grammar and usage, style, and punctuation. Pay special attention to the common errors.

✔ **Reader's TIP**

Common Mechanical Errors

- Incomplete sentences (sentence fragments)
- Incorrect subject–verb agreement
- Inconsistent verb tenses
- Faulty pronoun and antecedent agreement
- Incorrect placement of modifiers
- Inappropriate or incorrect punctuation
- Incorrect spelling
- Improper word choice
- Clichés

App.
C

Step 6: Proofread Your Final Copy

Your essay is now complete. After all your revisions and editing sessions, you have reached the last step in the writing process: **proofreading.** This time you read not for meaning, but for errors only. Always proofread on a printed (hard) copy. Again you are checking punctuation, spelling, grammar, usage, and conventional form, as well as watching for typographical errors (*typos*) such as strikeovers, omissions, repetitions, or transposed letters. When you think your paper is perfect, ask a friend to proof it for you. Your final copy should be free from all errors.

✔ **Reader's TIP**

How to Write an A+ Paper

- Use brainstorming and mapping to organize before writing.
- Do not be too general, predictable, or boring.
- Always use complete sentences.

(continued)

- If you are using a word processor, use the spell check function.
- Proofread your paper for technical and typographical errors.
- Do not use slang language.
- Use specific details for excitement and interest.
- Improve on empty words such as *nice, good, awesome*.
- Use an active rather than a passive voice; use vivid and specific verbs.
- Fix run-on sentences. Create more than one sentence when a sentence is overly long.
- Be formal. Never begin a sentence with "Well,"
- Ask a friend, parent, or enemy to proofread your work.

Follow directions. Always write two pages if the assignment says two pages. If you are asked to double-space, then double-space. Unless instructed otherwise, use a 12-point business font. For more help, consult *The Longman Handbook for Writers and Readers* by Chris M. Anson and Robert A. Schwegler. (New York: Longman, 2005)

C2   Brief Punctuation and Grammar Guide

The following concise punctuation and grammar review is merely a quick reference. For more details, consult a college-level grammar handbook such as *The Little, Brown Handbook* or *The Scott, Foresman Handbook for Writers*.

Commas

1. Use a comma after an introductory word, phrase, or clause that comes before the main clause. Even though in some cases a comma can be omitted, it is never wrong to use one after an introductory element.

   As a matter of fact, I am already late.

2. Use a comma before a linking word (called a *conjunction*) such as *and, or, nor, for, but, yet,* or *so* when there is a complete sentence both before and after the conjunction.

   He will not practice writing, nor will he study spelling.

3. Use a comma to set off an element that can be left out without changing the meaning of the sentence.

   My second husband, Bill, is my favorite.

4. Use a comma to separate items in a series. The final comma is optional in many cases, but it is always correct in a list.

> The four ribbons were red, yellow, green, and white.

Semicolons.   Semicolons create a stronger pause than a comma. A complete sentence must precede and follow a semicolon. Be cautious in your use of semicolons; they are often misused.

> John said he went to the movie; however, the theater was closed on Monday.

Colons.   A colon precedes a list or an explanation. A complete sentence always precedes a colon.

> Tom purchased four items: a blue book, a pen, a ruler, and a pencil.

Sentence Fragments.   A fragment is only a part of a sentence. To identify a fragment, check for a missing subject or verb.

> *Fragment:*   For example, a large tree covered with moss.
>
> *Corrected:*   For example, my grandmother's backyard has a large tree covered with moss.

If the fragment is a subordinate clause beginning with a word such as *although, if, unless,* or *while* (subordinating conjunctions), attach the clause to a complete sentence.

> *Fragment:*   Melanie suspected that Sarah was angry. *Because* of the way Sarah was behaving.
>
> *Corrected:*   Melanie suspected that Sarah was angry because of the way Sarah was behaving.
>
> *Or:*   Because of the way Sarah was behaving, Melanie suspected that Sarah was angry.

The most common subordinating conjunctions include:

- although
- because
- even though
- since
- for example
- until
- unless
- while
- which
- if

Comma Splices. A comma splice occurs when two or more independent clauses (or sentences) are joined by a comma alone.

Comma Splice: The wind was cold, they decided not to walk.

Corrected: The wind was cold; they decided not to walk.

Or: The wind was cold. They decided not to walk.

Or: They decided not to walk because the wind was cold.

As you can see, there is usually more than one way to correct a sentence structure problem.

Relative Pronouns

Use *who, whom,* and *whose* to refer to *people.*

Use *which* to refer to *things.*

Use *that* to refer to either *people* or *things.*

✓ Reader's TIP
Avoiding Common Errors

■ Write out the numbers one through ten, and use numerals for numbers larger than ten. The two forms can be mixed for large round numbers: *13 billion.*

■ Avoid trite expressions such as "in this day and age," "in today's society," "stubborn as a mule," "sly like a fox," and "sleep like a baby."

■ Use: *since*   Not: *being as, being that*
   many   *a lot*
   themselves   *theirselves*
   himself   *hisself*

■ *Its* is the possessive form of *it; it's* is a contraction of *it is.*

■ Avoid sexist language by avoiding sexist pronouns.

Sexist Language: After each NASA training mission has been completed, there is a party for the astronauts and their wives.

Corrected: After each NASA training mission has been completed, there is a party for the astronauts and their spouses.

Sexist Language: The policeman was selling tickets to the Policeman's Ball.

Corrected: The police officer was selling tickets to the Police Officer's Ball.

(continued)

■ Use apostrophes correctly.

Use *'s* after singular nouns (Keats*'s* house).

Use *'* only for plural nouns (her two sons*'* room).

To show joint ownership, add *'s* only to the last word (Mac and Flo*'s* house).

To show individual ownership, add *'s* to each word (Jane*'s* and Brian*'s* apartments).

Quotation Guidelines. Whenever you use someone else's words or ideas in an essay, you must give credit by naming the source.

■ Direct Quotation: Someone else's exact words are set off by quotation marks.

■ Indirect Quotation: The *rewording* of someone else's words is not set off by quotation marks, but be sure that you have paraphrased the words.

EXAMPLE

Direct Quotation: My father said, "Baseball is not the same as it was in the old days."

Indirect Quotation: My father said that baseball was different decades ago.

✔ Reader's TIP

Knowing the Rules for Technicalities

■ Use quotation marks for titles of short pieces of poetry and literature, and for magazine articles.

■ Underline titles of books and magazines in handwritten text and use italics for typed text.

■ Capitalize the first word of directly quoted speech even though it may appear in the middle of your sentence. The exception is if you are quoting only a few words.

■ Set off a direct quotation within a sentence by commas.

■ Place periods and commas within the closing quotation marks; place colons and semicolons outside.

Glossary

Note: The numbers in parentheses are the page numbers on which the glossary terms first appear.

A

abstract A short paragraph that summarizes an article, stating the author's premise, the subject or location of the project, and the conclusions. (317)

accounting The study of recording, classifying, summarizing, and reporting financial data to measure business performance. (301)

allied health sciences The application of science to promote the mental and physical well-being of the population. (280–281)

almanac A compilation of millions of current facts about countries, cities, census data, astronomy tables, foreign exchange rates, election and sports results of the previous year, and much more. Popular almanacs include *The World Almanac, The New York Times Almanac, The Wall Street Journal Almanac,* and *The Time Almanac.* (321)

analogies Comparisons that measure not only your word knowledge, but also your ability to see relationships. (67–68)

annotating Method of highlighting main ideas, significant supporting details, and key terms using a system of symbols and notations so that the markings indicate pertinent points to review for an exam. (222)

applied level A level of reading comprehension that calls for reaction, reflection, and critical thinking and involves analyzing, synthesizing, and evaluating. You integrate what is said with what is meant and apply it to new situations and experiences, thereby making wider use of what you have just learned. (13)

argument An assertion or set of assertions that supports a conclusion and is intended to persuade. (195)

automotive technology Application of automotive electronics and mechanics. (307)

B

bar graph A graph comprising a series of horizontal or vertical bars in which the length of each bar represents a particular amount. Often, time is represented by the vertical scale and quantity is measured by the horizontal scale. (183)

bias The author's attitude, opinion, or position on a subject, suggesting that the facts have been slanted toward the author's personal beliefs. As commonly used, *bias* has a negative connotation suggesting narrowmindedness and prejudice. (159)

bibliography A list of the sources consulted by the author of a scholarly article. When you write a paper, you will also include a bibliography of the sources you used in researching your topic. (319)

biography The story of a person's life or a portion of it as told by another person. (260)

biology The study of living organisms and life processes. (276)

body A group of interconnected paragraphs in an essay, each covering one of the supporting ideas of a thesis. (C-7)

bookmarking A save-the-site technique that lets you automatically return to the designated Web site with just one or two mouse clicks. (344)

brainstorming Quickly jotting down all ideas, references, and examples that come to mind when given a topic. (C-2)

browser The software that searches to find the URL. (342)

build meaning Good readers develop an understanding of what they read by using five thinking strategies: predict, picture, relate, monitor, and correct. (15)

C

characters In a story, the main people; they should be consistent in behavior and should grow and change according to their experiences. (249)

citation In an index entry, a reference to an article that includes the title, author(s), name of the periodical, volume and page numbers, issue date, and descriptive notes or key search terms. (316)

cliché An overworked phrase that should be avoided in formal writing, such as "working like a dog." (144)

climax In literature, the turning point near the end of a story, in which conflict intensifies to a peak. (249)

communications The study of speech, journalism, film, and video. (242)

computer science Courses that focus on the use of the computer, as well as on the principles and processes that enable computer communication. (295)

concentration The process of paying attention. (3)

conclusion A logical deduction from both stated and unstated ideas, using the hints as well as the facts to interpret motives, actions, and outcomes. Conclusions are drawn on the basis of perceived evidence, and because perceptions differ, conclusions can vary from reader to reader. (150)

conflict The clash of ideas, desires, or actions as incidents in a plot build progressively. (249)

connotation The feeling or emotion associated with a word that goes beyond its dictionary definition. (141)

context clues Hints within a sentence that help unlock the meaning of an unknown word. (32–33)

Cornell Method A system of notetaking in which you put questions on one side of a vertical line and notes that answer the questions on the other side. (226)

critical thinking Deliberating in a purposeful, organized manner so as to assess the value of old and new information. (191)

D

databases Computer-based indexes to assist research. A single article may be listed under several topics and may appear in several different indexes. (316)

demographic map A modern map that highlights nongeographic characteristics or population distributions of a particular area. For example, a map of the United States might highlight all states with gun control laws in red and all states without gun control laws in blue. (179)

denotation The dictionary definition of a word. (141)

denouement After the climax of a story, the outcome of the main dramatic complication. (249)

details Specifics in a passage that develop, explain, and support the main idea. Details can include reasons, incidents, facts, examples, steps, and definitions. (98)

diagram An outlined drawing or illustration of an object or a process. (175)

directory path A particular location within a Web site's host computer. (341)

domain name A name registered by a Web site owner. (341)

domain type The category to which a Web site owner belongs. (341)

E

ecology The study of the interrelationship of organisms and their environment. Ecologists seek to prevent the balance in our ecosystem from being upset by industrial pollution, deforestation, and toxic waste dumping. (285)

economics The study of the use of formulas to predict supply and demand, plot trends, and monitor inflation. (301)

editing Correcting your paper for mechanical errors rather than content errors. (C-11)

editorials Subjective articles that express the opinion of a person or organization. A newspaper's editorial pages feature the views of its management and editors. (331)

electronic mail (e-mail) A message sent from one person or organization to another person or group of people using the World Wide Web. These messages can be read, printed, saved, forwarded to someone else, and/or discarded. (348)

electronics A branch of science that applies electrical principles to the behavior of electrons. (305)

emoticons In e-mail communication, symbols used to represent emotions in a lighthearted way. They are not appropriate for formal correspondence. (351)

encyclopedias Reference books that give comprehensive coverage of a subject. Many different encyclopedias are available for specific topics, such as the *Encyclopedia of African American Religions, Encyclopedia of Earth Sciences,* and *The Cambridge Encyclopedia of Astronomy.* (314)

environmental scientists Experts who study issues such as pollution, overpopulation, the agricultural revolution, global warming, and alternative energy sources in an effort to protect the Earth's natural resources. (285)

essay A short work of nonfiction that discusses a specific topic. An essay does not develop as a story does; it lacks both characters and a plot. (251)

etymology The study of word origins, involving the tracing of words back to their earliest recorded appearance. (60)

F

fact A statement based on evidence or personal observation. It can be checked objectively with empirical data and proved to be either true or false. (164)

fallacy An inference that appears to be reasonable at first glance, but on closer inspection proves to be unrelated, unreliable, or illogical. It is a tool used in constructing a weak argument. (197)

feature stories In journalism, human-interest stories that differ from typical news stories in their timeliness, style, and length. (330)

fiction Writing that is invented from the author's imagination. (253)

figurative language Words used intentionally out of a literal context so that they take on new meaning. (141–142)

file name A specific file within the host's directory. (341)

finance The study of planning and controlling the inflow and outflow of an organization's monetary resources. (301)

fixations Stops lasting a fraction of a second that your eyes make to read. On the average, 5 to 10 percent of reading time is spent on fixations. (213–214)

flaming Personal attacks via e-mail. (352)

flexibility In mathematics, the possibility of *several* correct ways to solve a problem. (294)

flowchart A diagram showing relationships and sequences of elements or events. Key ideas are stated in boxes, along with supporting ideas linked by arrows that show the movement between boxes. (187)

G

generalizability In mathematics, the ability to see repeated patterns so that you do not have to start from scratch on each new problem you attempt to solve. (294)

H

health sciences (see **allied health sciences**) (280–281)

home page The main terminal of a Web site through which other areas of the site can be reached. (341)

humanities The studies of literature, composition, languages, history, philosophy, fine arts, and communication. The connecting link among these disciplines is a focus on human culture, including ideas, art, and societal history. (237)

hyperbole Exaggeration using figurative language to describe something as being more than it actually is. (143)

Gloss.

hypertext links In Web technology, phrases that appear as bold blue, underlined text. Clicking on them will not only move you from one page to another within the Web site, it can also send you to other related Web sites. The words chosen and underlined as the link will describe the information you are likely to find at that destination. (341)

I

idioms Expressions that have taken on a generally accepted meaning over many years of use but do not make sense on a literal level. Idioms can be similes and metaphors. For example, "sleeping like a log" is both a simile and an idiom because it is an accepted and often used expression that is not literally true. (144)

index A research tool that contains listings of articles organized by the topics within the articles. Most libraries have periodical indexes in electronic format. (345)

inference A meaning that is not directly stated but suggested through clues that lead you to make assumptions and draw conclusions. (132)

intent Your reason or purpose for writing, which is usually to inform, persuade, or entertain. (166)

Internet An electronic system of more than 25,000 computer networks using a common language that connects millions of users around the world. The Internet is the networked system that allows the World Wide Web to function. (318)

interpersonal communication A two-person exchange of ideas, such as a conversation with a friend or an interview. (242)

interpretive level At this level of reading comprehension you make assumptions and draw conclusions by considering the stated message, the implied meaning, the facts, and the author's attitude toward the subject. You combine the stated and unstated clues to answer *why* questions so as to figure out relationships, connections between ideas and events, character development, figurative language, and complex sequences of events. (131)

introduction A beginning paragraph that introduces the subject, states the position of the author, and sets the tone for an essay. (C-6–C-7)

invention techniques Prewriting strategies where you *discover* what you want to say *before* you write the first draft. (C-2)

inverted pyramid The format of newswriting that begins with a summary paragraph and continues with paragraphs that explain details in descending order of importance. (328)

issue An assertion or position statement in an argument. It is what the author is trying to convince you to form an opinion on. (194)

J

journalism Writing designed for publication in newspapers or magazines and characterized by a direct presentation of the facts or a description of events. (327)

L

lead In a news story, the first paragraph that catches the reader's attention, establishes a focus, and summarizes the essential points of the story. (328)

letter Formal communication appropriate for outside the company. (356)

line graph A graph incorporating a continuous curve or *frequency distribution*. The horizontal scale (or *axis*) measures one aspect of the data (or *variable*), and the vertical scale measures another aspect, making it easy to see the relationship between the variables at a glance. As the data fluctuate, the line will change direction and, with extreme differences, can become very jagged. (186)

links See **hypertext links.** (341)

literal level A level of reading comprehension at which you might be able to answer *who, what, when,* and *where* questions but not understand the overall purpose of the passage. (13)

literature The art form of language. Its purpose is to entertain an audience, to explore the human condition, and to reveal universal truths through shared experiences. (248)

M

main idea The central message that the author is trying to convey about the material. (70)

management The study of planning, organizing, leading, and controlling activities using available resources to accomplish company objectives. (301)

map A visual representation of a geographic area. (179)

mapping A visual system of condensing ideas or cognitive material through diagramming of major points and significant subpoints to show relationships and importance. (230)

marketing The study of pricing and promoting products. (301)

memo A short, informal business note usually for internal business purposes. (355)

metacognition Knowledge of the processes involved in reading and the ability to regulate and direct them. (22)

metaphor A direct comparison of two unlike things that does not use the word *like* or *as.* A metaphor and a simile can communicate the same idea and are differentiated only by the presence or absence of *like* or *as.* (142–143)

mnemonics Techniques to help your brain organize and recall information by incorporating your senses through pictures, sounds, rhythms, and other mental tricks to create extrasensory "handles" or hooks. (231)

multiple meanings Some words are confusing because they have several different meanings. For example, the dictionary lists more than 30 meanings for the word *run.* (61–62)

N

newsletter Mini-newspaper published within an organization to build group spirit. (358)

news stories Articles that report the facts of news events in descending order of importance. (328)

notetaking A method of jotting down important ideas for future study from a lecture or text. (226)

novel An extended fictional work that has all the elements of a short story. Because of its length, a novel usually has more character development and more conflicts than a short story. (254)

O

opinion A statement of personal feeling or a judgment. It reflects a belief or an interpretation rather than an accumulation of evidence, and it cannot be proved true or false. (164)

outline A method of organizing major points and subordinating items using Roman numerals, letters, numbers, and indentations to show clearly how one idea relates to another and how all aspects relate to the whole. (227)

P

paragraph A group of sentences about a single topic that express a single main idea. (73)

pattern of organization The organizational structure of a passage, which can be simple listing, time order, definition with examples, comparison-contrast, or cause and effect. (115)

periodicals Publications that come out on a regular schedule. They include newspapers, popular magazines, and scholarly journals. (315)

Gloss.

personification Attributing human characteristics to nonhuman things. (143)

pie graph A circle that is divided into wedge-shaped slices, with each slice representing a percentage of the whole. The complete pie or circle represents 100 percent. (182)

plot The action in a story or a play. It is a sequence of incidents or events that are linked in a manner that suggests causes for the events. (249)

point of view The author's attitude, opinion, or position on a subject. In literature, point of view describes who tells the story and is indicated most commonly by the third person (in which the author is the all-knowing observer). Alternatively, first person (in which the main character tells the story, using the word *I*) or second person (in which the story is told using the word *you*) may be used. (156)

political science The study of politics and government. (269)

prefix A group of letters with a special meaning that is added to the beginning of a word. (47)

previewing The first stage of reading; a method of looking over the material to guess what it is about, assess what you already know about the topic, decide what you will probably want to know after you read, and plan your reading. (14)

prior knowledge What you already know about a subject, which is the single best predictor of your reading comprehension. (20)

proofreading Rereading your paper to correct surface errors. (C-11)

protocol The type of language computers that are networked via the Internet use to communicate with each other. (340)

psychology The study of the behavior and mental processing of humans and animals, focusing on observable actions as well as thoughts and feelings. (264)

public speaking Making a presentation in front of a large audience with the intent to inform or persuade the group. (243)

purpose Your reason or intent for writing, usually to inform, persuade, or entertain. (166)

R

recalling Telling yourself what you have learned when you finish reading, relating it to what you already know, and reacting to it to form your own opinion. (26)

regression Rereading sentences or paragraphs because one's mind was wandering during the initial reading of the material. (213)

resolution After the denouement in a narrative, the answering of any remaining questions and the explanation of the outcome. (249)

reversibility In mathematics, the ability to work forward to a solution or backward to the original problem when you are given any part of a problem. You can use reversibility to check your work, too. (295)

revising Improving the content of a piece of writing by reorganizing, rewriting, sharpening your focus, developing ideas, and omitting repetitions. (C-9)

root The stem or basic part of a word, derived primarily from Latin and Greek. (45)

S

scanning The process of searching for a single bit of information. During scanning, you merely need to pinpoint a specific detail, rather than comprehend the general meaning of the material. (219)

schema The compartment similar to a computer chip in your brain that holds all you know on a subject. Each time you learn something new, you pull out the computer chip on that subject, add the new information, and return the chip to storage. (20)

scholarly journals Publications that come out on a regular schedule that are aimed at scholars, specialists, and students. They contain detailed research results written by specialists in the academic field of study and are frequently theoretical in nature. (318–319)

search engine A program that looks throughout the Internet for information. Search engines can be found at such Web sites as Yahoo!, AltaVista, Excite, Infoseek, and Lycos. (343)

server name Indicates the computer network over which you will "travel" to reach the desired location. In most cases, it will be the World Wide Web. (341)

setting The backdrop for a story and the playground for the characters. It may include the place, the time, and the culture. (250)

short story A brief work of narrative fiction with a beginning, a middle, and an end that ranges from 500 to 15,000 words. (253)

simile A comparison of two unlike things using the word *like* or *as*. Exmaple: "His words were like knives to my heart," where the simile describes the words as cutting and hurtful. (142)

situational irony When events occur contrary to what is expected, as if in a cruel twist of fate. For example, Juliet awakens and finds that Romeo has killed himself because he thought she was dead. (144–145)

skimming The technique of selectively reading for the main idea and quickly overviewing material. Skimming involves skipping words, sentences, paragraphs, and even pages. (218)

small-group communication Communication among a number of people with a common purpose operating under a common set of rules. (243)

social sciences Disciplines that include psychology, sociology, anthropology, and political science. (263)

sociology The use of logic and the scientific method to observe and explain interpersonal interaction, group membership, and social institutions. (267)

subvocalization The little voice in your head that reads for you. (214)

suffix A group of letters with a special meaning that is added to the end of a word. A suffix can alter the meaning of a word as well as the way the word can be used in the sentence. (49)

summary A brief, concise statement of the main idea of a piece of writing and its significant supporting details. The first sentence should state the main idea or thesis, and subsequent sentences should incorporate only the significant details. (224–225)

suspense As conflict builds in a plot, the reader's anxious concern about the characters' well-being. (249)

T

table An organized listing of facts and figures in columns and rows to compare and classify information for quick and easy reference. (178)

tabloids Half-size newspapers, often available at the checkout counter in retail stores, that sensationalize the news. (334)

theme The heart, soul, or central insight of—or universal truth expressed by—a work. This message is never preached but is revealed to your emotions, senses, and imagination through powerful shared experiences. (334)

tone The writer's attitude toward the subject or the audience. For example, an author's word choice may suggest humor, cutting remarks may suggest sarcasm, and ironic remarks can show the gap between the actual and the expected. (168)

topic A general (rather than specific) term that forms an umbrella under which the specific ideas or details in a passage can be grouped. (70–71)

topic sentence A sentence that condenses the thoughts and details of a passage into a general, all-inclusive statement of the author's message. (C-7)

transitions Signal words that connect parts of sentences and lead readers to anticipate a continuation or a change in the writer's thoughts. (117)

Gloss.

U

Uniform Resource Locator (URL) On the World Wide Web, specific directions for finding your way to a specific site, just as an address and zip code are required to mail a letter. A URL is similar to an e-mail address, except that it routes you to a source of information called a *Web page* or *Web site* rather than to the mailbox of an individual person. (340)

V

verbal irony The use of words to express a meaning that is the opposite of what is literally said; in other words, saying one thing and suggesting another. If the intent is to ridicule, the irony can also be called *sarcasm*. (144)

W

Web pages The locations or "sites" of information provided by individual people, businesses, educational institutions, or other organizations on the Internet. (340)

World Wide Web (WWW) Electronic information network that is similar to an enormous library, with Web sites being like books and Web pages being like the pages in the books. (340)

Credits

Illustrations

Pages 1, 3, 12, 30, 70, 98, 115, 132, 156, 173, 189, 191, 208, 221, 235, 237, 248, 263, 275, 289, 300, 314, 325, 327, 354, 375, 377, A-1, B-1, C-1: ©Harry Seipling/HMS Images/Getty Images

Page 18: ©Susan Leavines/Photo Researchers, Inc.

Page 31: ©Bryan Burchers/New Monic Books

Page 35: ©Petr David Josek/AP-Wide World Photo

Page 39: ©Bryan Burchers/New Monic Books

Page 42: ©Bryan Burchers/New Monic Books

Page 58: ©Mark Parisi/www.offthemark.com, printed with permission

Page 58: ©Hilary B. Price/King Features Syndicate

Page 72: ©Lowe Worldwide

Page 87: ©Horsey/Seattle Post Intelligencer/Tribune Media Services

Page 133: ©The Advertising Archives

Page 136: ©United Feature Syndicate, Inc.

Page 137: The Far Side © by Gary Larson © 1981 FarWorks, Inc. All Rights Reserved. The Far Side © and Larson © signature are registered trademarks of FarWorks, Inc. Used with permission.

Page157: ©Wasserman/The Boston Globe/Tribune Media Services

Page 194: ©Jeff Cadge/Getty Images

Page 211: ©Mike Baldwin/www.Cartoonstock.com

Page 293: ©The New Yorker Collection 1989 Henry Martin from Cartoonbank.com. All rights reserved.

Page 371: ©David M. Grossman/Photo Researchers, Inc.

Page 378: ©Marc Romanelli/Getty Images

Page 388: ©The Granger Collection

Page 396: ©Burazin/Masterfile

Page 404: ©Frank Conlon/Star Ledger/Corbis

Page 413: ©Bruce Ayres/Getty Images

Page 420: ©Tobbe/zefa/Corbis

Page 428: ©H. Armstrong Roberts/Corbis

Page 436: ©Peter Turnley/Corbis

Page 444: ©Andrew Douglas/Masterfile

Text

Chapter 3

From *Vocabulary Cartoons* by Sam, Max and Bryan Burchers. Copyright © 1998 Sam Burchers; Cartoon Copyright © 1998 Sam Burchers. Reprinted by permission of Sam Burchers, New Monic Books.

Glossary entries from *Psychology: An Introduction*, 8th ed., by Josh Gerow and Kenneth Bordens, p. 592. Copyright © 2005. Reprinted by permission of Harrison Press.

Entries from *Roget's 21st Century Thesaurus in Dictionary Form*, 2nd ed., Princeton Language Institute, Barbara Ann Kipfer, ed. Copyright © 1999. Reprinted by permission of The Philip Lief Group.

Chapter 4

James Henslin, *Essentials of Sociology*, 5th ed., p. 127. Boston: Allyn and Bacon, 2004.

James Fagin, *Criminal Justice*, p. 371. Boston: Allyn and Bacon, 2003.

Roy Cook et al., *Guide to Business Etiquette*. Upper Saddle River, NJ: Pearson Prentice Hall, 2005.

Mark Carnes and John Garraty, *The American Nation*, 11th ed., pp. 8–9. New York: Longman, 2003.

National Highway Traffic Safety Administration (NHTSA) Web site, http://www.nhtsa.dot.gov/cars/testing/ncap/Rollover.

Department of Navy, Navy Historical Web site, www.history.navy.mil/faqs/faq61-1.htm.

Chapter 5

From Samuel Wood et al., *The World of Psychology*, 5th ed., pp. 256, 557, 561. Published by Allyn and Bacon, Boston, MA. Copyright © 2005 by Pearson Education. Reprinted by permission of the publisher.

David Goldfield, et al., *The American Journey: A History of the United States*, Brief Third Edition, pp. 23–24. Upper Saddle River, NJ: Pearson Prentice Hall, 2005.

Adapted from "Lipids" in Campbell, Reece, and Simon, *Essential Biology*, 2nd ed., pp. 42–43. Copyright © 2004 Pearson Education, Inc., publishing as Benjamin Cummings. Reprinted by permission.

Chapter 7

Reader's Digest, *Laughter: The Best Medicine*. Pleasantville, NY: 1997.

Department of Navy, Navy Historical Web site, http://www.history.navy.mil/photos/sh-usn/usnsh-i/ca35.htm

Sarah N. Cleghorn, "The Golf Links," 1915.

Lester A. Lefton and Linda Brannon, *Psychology*, 8th ed., p. 447. Boston: Allyn and Bacon, 2002.

Chapter 9

From Neil A. Campbell et al., *Biology: Concepts and Connections* 2nd ed., p. 580. Copyright © 1997. Reprinted by permission of Pearson Education, Inc., publishing as Benjamin Cummings.

From John W. Hill, *Chemistry for Changing Times*, 8th ed., Fig. 14.15. Copyright © 1995. Reprinted by permission of Prentice Hall, Inc., Upper Saddle River, NJ.

Nutritional Guide graphic from "Game for Something Good? Try Low-Fat Meats" by Marcia Langhenry, *Atlanta-Journal Constitution*, June 17, 1999. Reprinted by permission of Stacks Information Service for The Atlanta Journal-Constitution

From James Henslin, *Sociology: A Down-to-Earth Approach*, 7th ed., pp. 221, 356, 452, 596. Published by Allyn and Bacon, Boston, MA, a division of Pearson Education, Inc. Copyright © 2005 by James Henslin. Reprinted by permission of the publisher.

From Wynn Kapit, *The Geography Coloring Book*, 2nd ed. Copyright © 1999. Reprinted by permission of Prentice Hall, Inc., Upper Saddle River, NJ.

From Ronald Ebert and Ricky Griffin, *Business*, 4th ed., p. 258. Copyright © 1996. Reprinted by permission of Prentice Hall, Inc., Upper Saddle River, NJ.

Chapter 10

Figure "Four-Step Procedure to Guide Critical Thinking" by Professor Helen R. Carr, San Antonio College. Reprinted by permission of the author.

Chapter 11

Pages 64−67 from *Panati's Extraordinary Origins of Everyday Things* by Charles Panati. Copyright © 1987 by Charles Panati, Reprinted by permission of HarperCollins Publishers.

Chapter 13

James Kirby Martin et al., *America and Its Peoples: A Mosaic in the Making, Volume 2, From 1865*, pp. 456, 497−498, 690, 703, 718. New York: Longman, 2004.

From John Garraty, *The American Nation*, 8th ed., p. 534. Copyright © 1995. Reprinted by permission of Pearson Education, Inc.

Joseph A. DeVito, *The Interpersonal Communication Book*, 8th ed., p. 268. New York: Longman, 1998.

Larry Barker and Deborah Roach Gaut, *Communication*, 8th ed., p. 164. Boston: Allyn and Bacon, 2002.

Dennis Wilcox et al. *Public Relations*, 5th ed., p. 594. New York: Longman, 1998.

Ann Raimes, *Keys for Writers*, 2nd ed., p. 229. Boston: Houghton Mifflin, 1999.

Maxine Hairston et al., *The Scott, Foresman Handbook for Writers*, 5th ed., pp. xii, 428, 513, 925. New York: Longman, 1998.

Chapter 14

Julie Wakefield Smith, "Two Reflections of Helen of Troy." Reprinted by permission.

John Savage, "The Getaway." Reprinted from *The Saturday Evening Post* magazine. © 1966. By permission of The Saturday Evening Post Society.

Chapter 15

From Uba/Huang, *Psychology*, pp. 180, 487. Copyright © 1999. Reprinted by permission of Prentice Hall, Inc., Upper Saddle River, NJ.

From Josh Gerow, *Psychology: An Introduction*, 5th ed., pp. 129–131, 286. Copyright © 1997. Reprinted by permission of Prentice Hall, Upper Saddle River, NJ.

From Uba/Huang, *Psychology*, p. 500. Copyright © 1999. Reprinted by permission of Prentice Hall, Inc., Upper Saddle River, NJ.

Alex Thio, *Sociology*, 5th ed., p. 173, 256–257, 357–358. New York: Longman, 1998.

Edward Greenberg and Benjamin Page, *The Struggle for Democracy*, 4th ed., pp. 40, 411. New York: Longman, 1999.

Chapter 16

From Audesirk/Audesirk, *Biology: Life on Earth*, 6th ed., Fig. E1-1 and p. 10. Copyright © 2001. Reprinted by permission of Pearson Education, Inc., Upper Saddle River, NJ.

Robert A. Wallace, *Biology: The World of Life*, 7th ed., p. 201. New York: Longman, 1997.

From Barbara Kozier et al., *Fundamentals of Nursing: Concepts, Process, and Practice*, 7th ed., pp. 1352, 646, 601. Copyright © 2004. Adapted by permission of Pearson Education, Inc., Upper Saddle River, NJ.

From Nebel/Wright, *Environmental Science: The Way the World Works*, 6th ed., p. 353 and Fig. 14-6. Copyright © 1986. Reprinted by permission of Prentice Hall, Inc., Upper Saddle River, NJ.

From Neil A. Campbell et al., *Biology: Concepts and Connections*, 3rd ed., pp. 70–71. Copyright © 2000. Reprinted by permission of Pearson Education, Inc., publishing as Benjamin Cummings.

Chapter 17

From J. Glenn Brookshear, *Computer Science: An Overview*, 6th ed., pp. 2–4. © 2005, 2003, 2000 Pearson Education, Inc. Reprinted by permission of Pearson Education, Inc., publishing as Pearson Addison Wesley. All rights reserved.

Chapter 18

From Ronald Ebert and Ricky Griffin, *Business*, 4th ed., pp. 115–116, 656. Copyright © 1996. Reprinted by permission of Prentice Hall, Inc., Upper Saddle River, NJ.

From Ronald Ebert and Ricky Griffin, *Business Essentials* 2/e, pp. 149, 225, 226. Copyright © 1998. Reprinted by permission of Prentice Hall, Inc., Upper Saddle River, NJ.

From Timothy L. Alton, *Electricity for Heating, Ventilation, Air Conditioning, and Related Areas*, pp. 13–14. Copyright © 1998. Reprinted by permission of Prentice Hall, Inc., Upper Saddle River, NJ.

Figure, "The Four Strokes in the 4-Stroke Cycle, Gasoline Engine." Reprinted by permission of National Learning Corporation.

"The Four Stroke Cycle" from Gary Lewis, *Engine Service*, 2nd ed., pp. 1–2. Copyright © 1986. Reprinted by permission of Prentice Hall, Inc., Upper Saddle River, NJ.

Chapter 19

"Most Expensive Dress," *The Guinness Book of World Records 2002*, p. 66.

Bartlett's Familiar Quotations, p. 654.

The Great Thoughts, George Seldes, ed., p. 190.

Famous Last Words, Jonathon Green, ed., p. 95.

The Speaker's Sourcebook II by Glenn Van Ekeren, p. 283.

Chapter 20

From Mark Sherman, "Authorities Shut Down Web Site in Crackdown on Internet Piracy," Associated Press, May 25, 2006. Used with permission of The Associated Press. Copyright © 2005. All rights reserved.

From Rosie Mestel, "Gloves or Bare Hands? It's a Wash," *Los Angeles Times*, February 14, 2005. Copyright 2005, Los Angeles Times. Reprinted with permission.

Adapted from Susan Pongratz, "Tune Out TV—And Turn On Life," *Daily Press*, April 24, 2005. Reprinted by permission of the author.

Home Page for Get Caught Reading. http://www.getcaughtreading.com/ getcaughtreading/index.html. Reprinted by permission of the Association of American Publishers. Spider-Man Get Caught Reading image, SPIDER-MAN: ™ & © 2003 Marvel Characters, Inc. Used with permission.

Part 5

From Rebecca J. Donatelle, *Access to Health*, 7th ed. Copyright © 2002 Pearson Education, Inc., publishing as Benjamin Cummings. Reprinted by permission.

Figure, "Stretching Exercises to Improve Flexibility." Drawings excerpted/adapted from *Stretching, 20th Anniversary Edition* by Bob Anderson, illustrated by Jean Anderson. © 2000 Shelter Publications. Reprinted by permission of Shelter Publications.

Figure, "The Overload Principle" from *One Rep Max: A Guide to Beginning Weight Training* by Phillip A. Sienna, Fig. 2.1, 8. © 1989. Reprinted by permission of Phillip Sienna.

Index

Reader's TIPS